Turkish Economy

Ahmet Faruk Aysan • Mehmet Babacan
Nurullah Gur • Hatice Karahan
Editors

Turkish Economy

Between Middle Income Trap and High Income Status

palgrave
macmillan

Editors
Ahmet Faruk Aysan
Department of Economics
School of Management and
Administrative Sciences
Istanbul Sehir University
Istanbul, Turkey

Mehmet Babacan
Department of Economics and Finance
School of Business
Istanbul Medipol University
Istanbul, Turkey

Nurullah Gur
Department of Economics and Finance
School of Business
Istanbul Medipol University
Istanbul, Turkey

Hatice Karahan
Department of Economics and Finance
School of Business
Istanbul Medipol University
Istanbul, Turkey

ISBN 978-3-030-09953-4 ISBN 978-3-319-70380-0 (eBook)
https://doi.org/10.1007/978-3-319-70380-0

Softcover re-print of the Hardcover 1st edition 2018

Cover illustration: Clearview / Alamy Stock Photo

Printed on acid-free paper

This Palgrave Macmillan imprint is published by the registered company Springer International Publishing AG part of Springer Nature
The registered company address is: Gewerbestrasse 11, 6330 Cham, Switzerland

To the memory of my sister
Ahmet Faruk Aysan

To my dearest loves in life
Mehmet Babacan

To my grandfathers (Abdülkadir and Murat) and grandmothers (Munise and Sabiha) for their strong and sincere support
Nurullah Gur

To the memory of my father
Hatice Karahan

Contents

Notes on Contributors

Ali T. Akarca Department of Economics, University of Illinois at Chicago, Chicago, IL, USA

Nihat Alayoglu School of Business, Istanbul Medipol University, Istanbul, Turkey

Ali Ari Department of Political Science and Public Administration, Marmara University, Istanbul, Turkey

Halil Kürşad Aslan Istabul Medipol University, Istanbul, Turkey

Murat Aslan Yıldırım Beyazıt University, Ankara, Turkey

Hakan Aslan Islamic Economics and Finance, Sakarya University, Adapazari, Turkey

Resul Aydemir Department of Economics, Istanbul Technical University, Istanbul, Turkey

Ahmet Faruk Aysan Department of Economics, Istanbul Sehir University, Istanbul, Turkey

Mehmet Fatih Aysan Department of Sociology, Istanbul Sehir University, Istanbul, Turkey

Mehmet Babacan Department of Economics and Finance, Istanbul Medipol University, Istanbul, Turkey

Abdurrahman Babacan School of Humanities and Social Sciences, İstanbul Medipol University, Istanbul, Turkey

Mehmet Huseyin Bilgin Istanbul Medeniyet University, Istanbul, Turkey

Huseyin Cirpan School of Business, Istanbul Medipol University, Istanbul, Turkey

Hakan Danis MUFG Union Bank, San Francisco, CA, USA

Muhammed Habib Dolgun CBRT, Ankara, Turkey

Lokman Gündüz TCMB, Ankara, Turkey

Nurullah Gur Department of Economics and Finance, Istanbul Medipol University, Istanbul, Turkey

Hatice Karahan Department of Economics and Finance, School of Business, Istanbul Medipol University, Istanbul, Turkey

Gozde Nur Kazazoglu-Sahin Istanbul Technical University, Istanbul, Turkey

Gokhan Ovenc Department of Economics, Istanbul University, Istanbul, Turkey

Mucahit Ozdemir Islamic Economics and Finance, Sakarya University, Adapazari, Turkey

Emine Nur Ozkan-Gunay Grand National Assembly of Turkey, Istanbul, Turkey

Mevlüt Tatlıyer Department of Economics and Finance, Istanbul Medipol University, Istanbul, Turkey

Murat Yas Islamic Finance, INCEIF, Kuala Lumpur, Malaysia

Murat A. Yülek Center for Industrial Policy and Development, Istanbul Commerce University, Istanbul, Turkey

List of Figures

expenditures because the Turkish Statistical Institute has been publishing social expenditures series only since that year. The tax-structure-adjusted private saving rate was calculated as 1 minus the tax-structure-adjusted private consumption rate (the ratio of private expenditures plus extra collected indirect taxes in excess of 1.3 times collected direct taxes in a given year to private disposable income plus the extra collected indirect taxes in the same year). The social-expenditure-adjusted private saving rate was calculated as 1 minus social-expenditure-adjusted private consumption rate (the ratio of private expenditures plus extra social expenditures in excess of the 2000 level to private disposable income plus extra collected social contributions in excess of the 2000 level). Lastly, the inflation-adjusted private saving rate was calculated as 1 minus the inflation-adjusted private consumption rate (which was calculated by subtracting the realized inflation part of the interest payments made by the government from private disposable income). We are subtracting interest payments from income. The wedge between the original and adjusted private saving rates expands as the inflation effect strengthens in the second half of the 1990s; however, in the 2000s this effect dwindles substantially. While all three of these factors affect the *calculated* private saving rate, only the effect of inflation has an impact on the public saving rate. Therefore, the aggregate saving rate is also affected owing to the other two effects. However, these two effects cancel each other out almost completely, thereby exerting a negligible effect on the aggregate saving rate. Source: Ministry of Development of Turkey, Turkish Statistical Institute, and the author's own calculations) 249

Fig. 3 Narrowly and broadly defined saving ratios (1990–2013) (Note: While NDASR denotes narrowly defined aggregate saving rate, BDASR designates broadly defined aggregate saving rate with education, health, and R&D effects. Lastly, BDASR+D denotes BDASR plus durable goods effect. While BDASR+D has returned roughly to the levels seen in the 1990s in recent years, BDASR declined in the late 1990s and in the early 2000s, as did NDASR, though much less pronouncedly. In the end, while NDASR was below 15 per cent, BDASR stood at 22.5 per cent, and BDASR+D was nearly 40 per cent

Chapter 15

Chapter 16

List of Tables

On the Path to High-Income Status or to Middle-Income Trap: The Turkish Economy in Search of Its Future

Ahmet Faruk Aysan, Mehmet Babacan, Nurullah Gur, and Hatice Karahan

1 Introduction

The growth episode of the Turkish economy in the 2000s was written based on two integrated fundamentals: fixing the deteriorating dynamics and implementing further reforms to stimulate economic activity. This basic formula led to attractive rates of economic growth, fueled particularly by domestic private investments along with revived consumption and exports. Integrated with the political stability established by single-party governments in the post-2002 period, the improving economic outlook also helped Turkey enjoy record levels of foreign investment, adding momentum to the growth story.

A. F. Aysan (✉)
Department of Economics, School of Management and Administrative Sciences, Istanbul Sehir University, Istanbul, Turkey

M. Babacan • N. Gur • H. Karahan
Department of Economics and Finance, School of Business, Istanbul Medipol University, Istanbul, Turkey

A. F. Aysan et al. (eds.), *Turkish Economy*,
https://doi.org/10.1007/978-3-319-70380-0_1

In that sense, the 2008–2009 Global Financial Crisis (GFC) serves as a milestone against which to test the strength of the Turkish economy. While having contracted in 2009, the economy weathered the storm quite well and exhibited conspicuous growth rates following the crisis. On the other hand, gearing up the economy at high speed started to show side effects, with a concomitant risk of overheating. In this context, the rising ratio of current account deficit with regard to GDP appeared as a leading concern that contributed to the vulnerabilities of the economy. At that point, policies to cool down the economy were successfully implemented, which soon brought the growth rates to the required but not-so-desired lower levels.

What the Turkish experience in the postcrisis period implies is that for an ideally fast and – more importantly – sustainable growth rate, the economy needs a new generation of structural reforms that simultaneously heal fragilities and vitalize economic activity. In this framework, this edited volume scrutinizes the last 15 years of the Turkish economy, while also attempting to do something more that was absent in many earlier studies covering Turkey. Each chapter in this volume aims to provide professional assessments and assistance to the relevant parties, particularly policymakers, on the new directions to take the Turkish economy.

For this purpose, the book is composed of three broad sections covering the key dimensions of the Turkish economy in search of its future: (1) state, institutions, and political economy; (2) the financial system; and (3) the real economy.

2 State, Institutions, and Political Economy

The quality of institutions is crucial for a strong fiscal capacity and a sustainable welfare state. Although there have been noteworthy improvements in governance in Turkey since 2002, it is undeniable that Turkey could and should improve its quality of institutions even more to escape from the middle-income trap. In addition, business–government relations need to be more effective. It is known that governance and institutions, could have sizeable effects on economic development. Social trust, which is observed to be weak in Turkey, is crucial to improving the quality of institutions. This is because, in all countries, a lack of trust could lead to heavy-handed regulations, inefficient bureaucracy, and a cumbersome legal system. Hence, given the vital importance of the issue, this section analyses business–government relationships, the transformation of elites, the role of the military in the formation of coalitions, social trust, and bureaucratic performance in Turkey to show paths to improving the quality of institutions. In addition, it also examines the political economy of policy formation in social policy and strategic industrial policies.

The section starts with a chapter that focuses on the role of the state in the Turkish economy over the last 15 years. In this chapter (The Role of the State in the Turkish Economy), Gur evaluates the effect of government policies on the Turkish economy and advances some policy proposals to make state mechanisms more growth- and development-friendly. There is no doubt that Turkey needs new investments and reforms to raise its income level and extract itself from the middle-income trap. To make this happen, the author suggests that the state should undertake a number of important tasks in various areas, from industrial policies to institutional reforms.

In the next chapter (Political Economy of Transformation of Capital Structure in Turkey: A Historical and Comparative View), A. Babacan provides a historical and comparative view of the way the capital structure has evolved in Turkey. The political economy approach employed here offers novel and comprehensive insight into the transformation of Turkish capital structure. In this context, Babacan positions the two main business groups of industrial and businessmen's associations in the country, namely, MUSIAD and TUSIAD, within the framework of this transformation. The roles of these groups appear more clearly in this historical process as representatives of the two different political-economic bases in terms of magnitude, volume, geography, mental and cultural codes/roots, and, hence, differentiated visions and structural realities.

Akarca, on the other hand, examines another important political-economy phenomenon in Turkey – the military coups in the nation's history. In his chapter (Single-Party Governments as a Cause and Coalitions as a Consequence of Coups in Turkey), Akarca asserts that single-party governments and coalitions in the country are a cause and a consequence of coups, respectively. In this connection, he documents that economic performance under coalition governments, especially those involving both right- and left-wing parties, was not as good as under single-party governments. Akarca investigates the 1950–2015 period historically and empirically through descriptive statistics and regression analysis. The results reveal that the postcoup governments in Turkey were created artificially by the military, using a coup as a tool to fashion Turkish politics. While the causes and consequences of such interventions are also discussed in the chapter, it is shown that the adverse impacts of coups in Turkey were not only restricted to the periods of military rule but also continued through the chain of the coalition governments that emerged. Akarca's chapter (Single-Party Governments as a Cause and Coalitions as a Consequence of Coups in Turkey) is especially interesting in terms of seeing the historical and institutional causes of political economy formations in Turkey.

Aysan (Between Risks and Opportunities: Social Policies in Contemporary Turkey) touches upon another important and rapidly changing institutional and political economy issue in Turkey: social policies in contemporary Turkey. This chapter deals with recent social policies in the country, which typically characterize the Turkish political-economy story, especially in the last 15 years. In this study, Aysan analyses Turkish social policies in the 2000s in relation to welfare regime discussions in the literature. He demonstrates that Turkey has experienced significant improvements both in social expenditures and the quality of social provisions in the relevant time period, while revealing that the family and the state have been the most important welfare players in Turkey. On the other hand, considering the challenges ahead, the author concludes that a new social policy strategy is needed to establish a sustainable welfare regime in Turkey, and to this end he provides some policy recommendations.

In the last chapter of the section (Turkey's Struggle to Achieve High-Income Status Through Adaptation to the Knowledge Economy), Aslan and Aslan follow a political-economy approach to analyse Turkey's developmental policies in the recent decade with a special focus on its higher-education institutions and national innovation system. Authors evaluate the performance of Turkey in different areas of the knowledge economy and put forth policy proposals to improve the education system in Turkey in order for the country to escape the middle-income trap.

3 Financial System

The 2000/2001 crisis opened up a new avenue for a structural reform route in Turkey, where efforts mainly focused on the banking sector as the major cause of the crunch. The comprehensive banking sector reform initiative turned out to be so successful that the effects of the GFC on the Turkish economy remained limited. On the other hand, new financial system reforms are now needed to make the financial system more stable and development-friendly. Hence, this section addresses the globally accepted need for "good finance" in the context of Turkey for potential improvements. Moreover, a particular emphasis is placed on banking given that the country's financial sector is still dominated by banks. For one thing, strategies of the banks have changed quite radically in the past 15 years, and it is very likely that they will change again in the years ahead. Hence, an assessment of the experience will provide valuable insight into how the banking sector should proceed in the coming decades. The same is true of subsectors like Islamic financial institutions in Turkey. That is why various subsectors in the Turkish financial system are also investigated in this section.

The section starts out with an overall outlook drawn by Ari on financial openness, financial stability, and macroeconomic performance in Turkey. Although economic theory argues that financial openness and development promote economic growth, several experiences in different developing countries do not provide firm support of this theoretical reality. The Turkish liberalization experience is one of the best examples of this disparity. Turkey suffered three full-fledged financial crises in 1994, 1998–1999, and 2000–2001, following the liberalization policies implemented through the 1980s, but managed to remarkably improve economic outcomes such as growth and inflation in the post-2001 crisis period. This result is mainly due to more effective fiscal and monetary management, strengthened banking regulation and supervision, and conservative banking practices pursued over the last decade and a half. Ari (Financial Openness, Financial Stability, and Macroeconomic Performance in Turkey: A Comparative Perspective) argues that in order to increase the possible benefits of financial openness and development for economic growth, particularly in emerging countries such as Turkey, financial liberalization needs to be implemented in a well-designed, effective supervisory and regulatory framework and in a sequenced manner.

The next chapter (Capital Inflows and Banking in the Turkish Economy), written by Aydemir and Ovenc, focuses on the capital inflows and banking in the Turkish economy. It evaluates the developments in the Turkish banking industry in the context of capital and financial inflows, with a specific focus on cross-border banking liabilities. The authors first analyse how the Turkish economy, as an emerging market, has been affected by inflows at various points in global markets. Then they describe the transformation of the Turkish banking sector by paying special attention to the post-2001 period. In particular, they investigate the association between cross-border liability and banking performance. The analysis concludes with some policy recommendations based on the current outlook of the Turkish banking sector.

Dolgun and Gunduz (Turkish Banking Industry: A CAMELS Analysis) approach the Turkish banking system from another angle and assess it using the CAMELS method, with a focus on recent financial developments. Their analysis reveals that the return on assets and return on equity of the Turkish banking industry are at relatively acceptable levels and have been following an upward trend lately. An increase in profitability strengthens capital while a slowdown in loan growth rate limits risk-weighted asset growth. The Turkish banking system continues to remain resilient to interest-rate shocks and maintains its strength against exchange rate risks. The authors show that foreign resources of the banking sector remain stable and the liquidity buffers are sufficient to weather any shock that could arise as a result of global liquidity conditions. The article also discusses current and future opportunities and challenges facing the Turkish financial industry. With respect to opportunities, there is ample room for the development and diversification of financial markets, institutions, and instruments. However, relying mostly on the banking sector, having an increasing loan-to-deposit ratio, facing tightening global liquidity conditions, and depending on foreign capital inflows are highlighted as important challenges for the Turkish financial sector. Readers interested in the financial growth strategy of Turkey in the last 15 years will find this chapter especially useful in terms of acquiring a thorough understanding of the associated dynamics.

In another piece, Yas, Aslan, and Ozdemir (Modern History of Islamic Finance and a Strategic Roadmap for Its Development in Turkey) analyse another growing segment of the financial markets in Turkey, namely, Islamic finance. Turkey has been providing Islamic financial services for more than 30 years now. On the other hand, while it is ranked second in terms of GDP among Muslim-majority countries, its share of total Islamic assets is just around 3 percent. However, Turkey has placed special emphasis on promoting Islamic financial markets in recent years. The government has declared that the share of Islamic banks should reach 15 percent of the industry by 2023. In this sense, this chapter discusses the challenges that the Islamic finance industry has encountered and provides a general framework for designing the initiatives needed and integrating them in the financial sector policies. To this end, the modern history of Islamic finance of Turkey, Islamic capital markets, the Sukuk market, Islamic indices and funds, Takaful (Islamic insurance), and Islamic pension funds are all briefly discussed in the chapter.

In a similar framework, recent financial and real sector reforms have sought to raise savings rates in Turkey. In this context, the chapter (Saving Behaviour in Turkey: Where Are We? And What Can We Do About It?) written by Tatliyer provides a critical assessment of the measurement of savings in the country and raises some doubts on the presumed consensus that the nation's savings rates are low. Analysing the course of saving behaviour in Turkey since the 1990s, the author argues that roughly half of the decrease in the aggregate savings rate can be attributed to the rapid increase in education and health expenditures, which can simply be regarded as investments under a broader savings definition. He further suggests that limiting credit expansion and improving credit composition, which can be fulfilled by developing Islamic financial instruments as well as wealth and pension funds, for example, could induce households to save more and boost the productivity level of the whole economy.

4 Real Economy

In 2005, Turkey graduated to the status of upper-middle-income country and tripled its GDP per capita within a decade following the rise of the single-party government to power. In that regard, the ongoing target is to climb up the income ladder within a reasonable timespan so that the economy does not become stuck in the so-called middle-income trap. On the other hand, completing the transition to a high-income economy can only be achieved on a more solid basis, in which competitiveness is strengthened and weaknesses are fixed. In this connection, data clearly reveal that Turkey deals with the deficits it runs on energy and technology, further indicating that it must adopt reforms that would reduce its level of dependence on foreign inputs. That is why some chapters in this section focus on gaining national competence in related areas. While inhibiting imports is a big necessity for Turkey, efforts also need to be directed at exports, with the aim of boosting the value and the penetration of products and services.

Empirical results in the literature indicate that technological change and innovation are significant drivers of economic development, but inclusive growth is also essential for a sustainable story. In this regard, Gunay and Kazazoglu (Towards Inclusive Growth and Sustainable Development: Science, Technology, and Innovation Strategies and Policy Implications) focus on the recent status of national science, technology, and innovation (STI) policies in Turkey and their relevant impacts. Based on a detailed analysis, they conclude that Turkey has made significant progress in building up its STI capacities since 2007, though it still underperforms in many key performance indicators compared to the OECD median and the EU average. In this context, the authors offer specific policy recommendations for Turkey around the second-generation STI reforms underlined.

In this context, Yulek (Thinking About a New Industrial Policy Framework for Turkey) emphasizes that Turkey can be considered a medium-level industrialized economy that faces difficulties in progressing to Stages II and Stage III in the industrialization process. On the other hand, it is well recognized that furthering the level of industrialization in Turkey is likely to help boost overall economic growth rates, increase export earnings, and get the country out of the current middle-income trap. In this connection, the chapter suggests that in order to continue its progress in the industrialization process, Turkey's industrial policy framework, its administrative structure, and its state formation with respect to facilitating better strategic industrial policy need to be reviewed. For this purpose, key policy proposals developed by the author are outlined in the chapter.

In another chapter (Turkish Labour Market: Outlook, Key Challenges, and Policy Recommendations), Bilgin and Danis focus on the persistently high unemployment rate in the country. They argue that the problem is the result of several rigidities and structural issues in the economy. In this context, they examine the Turkish labor market in detail in terms of supply and demand and develop some recommendations that would ensure long-lasting improvement. The authors conclude that the inability of the Turkish economy to generate sufficient employment makes structural reforms related to the labor market inevitable.

The following chapter (Developing National Competence in Nuclear Energy: The Case of Turkey) by Karahan focuses on the energy policy of Turkey. As is well known, Turkey has long dealt with the problem of a current account deficit, which largely stems from its energy dependence on foreign countries. The insufficiency of national energy resources poses challenges for Turkey not only economically but also in terms of energy supply security. In this regard, Karahan touches upon the recent attempts of the country regarding the adoption of nuclear power plants (NPPs). She claims that while Turkey has understandably launched its nuclear adventure based on international collaboration, countries relying on external expertise in NPPs must do their best to be intelligent customers. Based on this argument, she draws a basic framework for Turkey to adopt a national energy strategy.

Furthermore, M. Babacan (Beyond Planning and Liberalization: Foreign Trade and Industrial Development in Turkey) investigates the Turkish foreign trade strategy that is considered to be one of the main contributors to Turkey's growth story in the last 15 years. After a brief open-economy experience during the 1920s, the Turkish economy could be regarded as state-controlled, planned, and partially closed for the following half century, where trade meanwhile played a limited role. In this period, industry developed to a limited extent under an import-substitution strategy adopted in the 1960s and 1970s. In the 1980s, on the other hand, Turkey witnessed a period of commercial and financial openness, with an export-oriented industrial production and growth model that led to high growth rates along with increasing indebtedness as well as budget and current account deficits. Political and macroeconomic instability for the entire 1990s caused unsteady growth cycles under the unfinished industrialization and non-regulated liberalization processes. In this context, the author asserts that the AK Party period (2002–2017) represents a threshold for Turkish industrial, commercial, and financial expansion within a relatively stable environment, which then faced several challenges. New challenges due to the changing nature of world politics, regional and internal dynamics, and global economic developments are now forcing Turkey to revisit its export-led growth strategy based on reindustrialization by producing more capital-intensive goods with a greater technology component. In this connection, the chapter asserts that Turkey's rising global trade could support strong reindustrialization in strategic sectors.

The last chapter of the section focuses on the challenges of Turkish family businesses related to effective management strategies. This chapter stresses the importance of effective management for the sustainability of family businesses in Turkey. Family firms dominate business life and make a large contribution to job creation and exports in Turkey. The authors of the chapter (Developing National Competence in Nuclear Energy: The Case of Turkey), Cirpan and Alayoglu, argue that family dynamics tend to affect business dynamics, and vice versa. Thus, managing family relationships is an important characteristic of a family business. When they are managed effectively, success on many fronts is achieved; if they are not, however, the business, not to mention the family, may face many problems, leading to bankruptcy. Therefore, it is important to determine the predictors of family business sustainability for the benefit of both the economy and the families owning the firms.

Cirpan and Alayoglu explain how to resolve the problems and conflicts in Turkish family businesses and suggest some systems and strategies for effective management.

To conclude, avoiding the so-called middle-income trap and reaching a higher level of income require more thought and policy experimentation in a rapidly changing global environment. Hence, to this end, the chapters in this volume focus on different economic aspects of Turkey's economy and provide an overview of their subject matters while also putting forth policy recommendations. Such an approach is indeed well needed. Therefore, we wish to see more academic work that would go beyond analysing the past to offer policy advice. In this edited book, we have done our best to follow that approach. We hope the book will prove useful in that regard.

Part I

Political Economy

The Role of the State in the Turkish Economy

Nurullah Gur

1 Introduction

There is no successful development story without the state (Chang 2002). A well-functioning bureaucracy, strong public finance, smart industrial policies, and welfare state institutions have been seen as key state-related factors that promote economic growth and development (Musgrave 1959; Amsten 1989; Wade 1990; Evans 1995; Weiss and Hobson 1995; Chang 2002; Rodrik 2008; Mazzucato 2013). The state should also secure property rights, protect patents, enforce contracts, control corruption, and ease red tape to further spur development and prosperity (North 1990; Acemoglu and Robinson 2012). Considering the crucial role of the state in economic growth and development, it is important to analyse the effect of the state on the Turkish economy.

Before the 1980s in Turkey, except for a few years of quasi-liberal policies, the state played a significant role in the economy by implementing

N. Gur (✉)
Department of Economics and Finance, School of Business Istanbul Medipol University, Istanbul, Turkey

A. F. Aysan et al. (eds.), *Turkish Economy*,
https://doi.org/10.1007/978-3-319-70380-0_2

development planning and import substitution industrialization. Because of military coups, the limited competence of entrepreneurs, and low bureaucratic capacity, state-led development strategy did not work well. In the 1980s, Turkey, along with most of the major developing countries, began to implement neo-liberal economic policies. The so-called Washington Consensus reduced the state's economic interventions to a certain extent in the 1980s. These policies initially gave the Turkish economy some momentum, but the rapid and unplanned liberalization process paved the way for the economic crisis of 1994. The coalition governments of the 1990s led to an increase in the desire for state intervention in the economy, but these interventions were typically not smart, but corrupt and populist (Öniş 2003). Short-lived coalition governments, a high level of corruption, and the duty losses of the state-owned banks ruined public finances. A crisis was inevitable. The 2000/2001 crisis was one of the most catastrophic economic events that Turkey has ever experienced. High inflation and a current account deficit, an excessive public sector borrowing requirement (PSBR), and a fragile banking system were the main economic culprits of this devastating crisis (Akin et al. 2009).

According to old Turkish proverb, one misfortune is better than a thousand pieces of advice. This underlines the notion that one learns better from one's own misfortunes than from the advice of others. Following this proverb, it could be said that there was at least one good side to the 2000/2001 crisis: the intense governance reform process that followed. In addition to the restructuring of the banking system, public sector reforms ensured macroeconomic stability in Turkey. Although this was a standard IMF-led stabilization policy, Turkey increased its health and education expenditures, invested in mega infrastructure projects, and encouraged firms to produce and export more. Thanks to this reform process, gross domestic product (GDP) per capita increased from USD 3,058 in 2001 to USD 10,382 in 2008.[1]

Turkey was one of the countries least affected by the global financial crisis (GFC).[2] While many European countries such as United Kingdom, Greece, Italy, Spain, and Portugal have imposed austerity measures since 2008, Turkey's low public deficit and debt enabled it to use expansionary fiscal policies during the GFC. Turkey has also engaged in research and development (R&D) and export incentives to boost economic growth and has used social welfare programmes to relieve the economic and social conditions of low-income individuals.

Squeezed global liquidity, economic slowdowns affecting trading partners (especially European Union countries), escalating geopolitical risks in the Middle East, terrorist attacks, and a failed coup attempt have caused the Turkish economy to grow below its potential since 2012, and GDP per capita has been stuck at around $10,000. To overcome this trend and reach developed-country status, Turkey needs to do more. In this sense, the state must do its own part to support economic growth and development; from enforcing contracts to easing red tape, the state should improve the quality of institutions, and to reduce income inequality, the tax system—which is very reliant on indirect taxes—should be reformed. The state should review its industrial and technology policies, and instead of giving incentives to all firms and industries, the state should pick the winners and support promising firms and industries.

This chapter aims to analyse the role of the state in the Turkish economy over the last 15 years. After evaluating the effectiveness of the state in the Turkish economy, the chapter puts forth policy proposals to make the state mechanisms more growth- and development-friendly.

2 Public Finance and Fiscal Policies

One of the most important actions involved in the restructuring of the Turkish economy after the 2000/2001 crisis was establishing sound macroeconomic governance; without a doubt, reforming the public finance system was necessary for sound macroeconomic governance. Turkey targeted the maintenance of high primary surplus and to reduce Turkey's public debt burden to well below the Maastricht criterion of 60 per cent. To achieve this, Turkey privatized some public companies and reduced the level of corruption and redundant expenditures in public institutions and the duty losses of state banks.[3] These policies worked; the central government's budget-deficit-to-GDP ratio fell from 11.5 per cent in 2002 to 1.2 per cent in 2015. This is a remarkable achievement in terms of public finance, and public debt decreased significantly after the

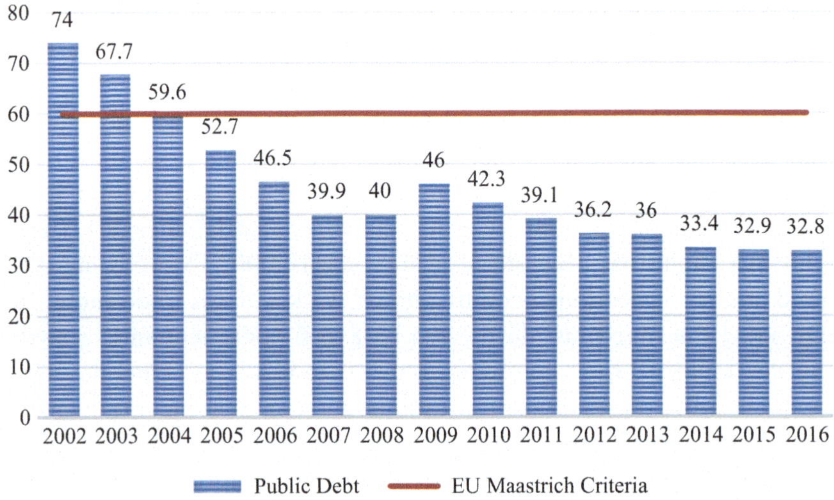

Graph 1 Public debt as a share of GDP in Turkey (Source: Undersecretariat of Treasury; Note: *Red line* denotes the Maastricht Criterion of 60 per cent. The ratio in 2016 is the expected value)

2000/2001 crisis. As Graph 1 shows, the EU-defined debt-stock-to-GDP ratio was 74 per cent in 2002, and the ratio had dropped to 59.2 per cent by the end of 2004. Turkey has met the Maastricht criterion in terms of public debt since then. Although public debt rose in 2009 due to the expansionary fiscal policies following the GFC, the public debt ratio has been steadily declining since 2010; it is currently around only 32 per cent, which is one of the lowest among developed and developing countries.[4]

The real interest rate was more than 30 per cent in the 1990s, and the high interest rate represented a huge burden on the public treasury and the Turkish economy. Strong public finance and macroeconomic stability helped to reduce the real interest rate to single-digit levels after the 2000/2001 crisis, decreasing the borrowing costs for the Turkish treasury. The ratio of external public-debt-interest payments to GDP ratio reduced from 2.8 per cent in 2002 to 1.3 per cent in 2015.

While the AK Party was trying to carry out the IMF's reform packages from one side in order to attract international investors and lenders, it also wanted to make room for social expenditures and infrastructure investments from the budget in order to improve the conditions of low-income citizens and fulfil its election promises.[5] The government achieved this to a significant extent by reducing inflation and the public deficit while at the same time improving economic conditions.

The IMF was unhappy with the increase in public investment in the health system and infrastructure, concerned that it would harm the budget; many people claimed that these investments would not be possible owing to the tight budget. For example, in an interview on a divided road project, Muharrem Kayhan, a member of the executive board of Turkish Industry and Business Association (TUSIAD), which represents the interests of big business in Turkey, criticized public investment on the paved road project as follows: "*The economic programme has limits. The thesis that public investments will enliven the economy is an old thesis…if you say 10,000 workers will make 100 kilometres of road, it means that you are creating 10,000 minimum wage jobs that will only cover their food costs. The road will not pay for itself in 20 years. Moreover, you will be financing this at 20–25 per cent real interest rates. With what money will these roads be made? Where will you find the money? There is no money for this in the budget—the roads cannot be made.*"[6]

However, governments have made infrastructure investments through financing from the public budget. To make room in the budget, for example, the government raised taxes on alcoholic beverages, cigarettes, and luxury goods (Patton 2006). Turkey has also extensively used the public-private-partnership (PPP) model to finance infrastructure projects in the country and has become one of the top PPP-implementing countries in the world (Sönmez 2014; Invest in Turkey 2015).

In the end, Turkey succeeded in making these infrastructure investments. The divided road network in Turkey has rapidly expanded over the past 12 years, from a total of 6,101 kilometres of divided roads in 2003 to 24,280 kilometres in 2015.[7] Improving the quality and capacity of the country's roads increased the connectivity of underdeveloped and ignored regions to international trade routes, bringing them into the pathways of global trade. In an empirical paper, Cosar and Demir (2016) found that road infrastructure increased regional exports and imports by substantially reducing transportation costs. The results showed that the present value of a 10-year stream of trade flows generated by a one-dollar investment in road infrastructure ranges between USD 0.7 and 2. Big infrastructure projects financed via the PPP model both increased people's quality of life and decreased costs for companies.

Public expenditures since 2002 have allowed many socio-economic factors in Turkey to improve. There has been a substantial expansion of the middle class in Turkey, which seems to be the backbone of development and democracy; Azevedo and Atamanov (2014) show that the middle class increased from 21 per cent to 41 per cent between 2002 and 2011. Since 2002, there has been a significant increase in the minimum wage in Turkey compared with other European countries.[8] As discussed in what follows, public social expenditures have skyrocketed since the AK Party came to power. As a result of these developments, poverty rates have declined substantially. According to estimates by the Turkish Statistical Institute, the proportion of individuals whose income is below USD 4.3 per day fell from 30.3 per cent in 2002 to 1.62 per cent in 2014. Şeker and Jenkins (2015) show that absolute poverty declined rapidly, especially between 2003 and 2008 but fell only slightly after the GFC.

Governments in Turkey have increased expenditures on public education since 2002. The number of universities rose from 76 to 183 between 2002 and 2016, many of them public universities. Thanks to an increase in the number of schools and classrooms, the average class size in primary education classrooms throughout all of Turkey's territories has decreased; according to OECD figures, the number of students per classroom decreased from 31 in 2001 to 23 in 2014.[9] The number of students who go abroad for post-graduate studies on government scholarships has also skyrocketed. Although it is good to see that quantities in education (the number of universities, classrooms, and scholarships) are increasing, the government should focus more on the quality of education. Modernizing the education system in vocational schools to meet the needs of the real workforce, promoting university–industry collaboration, and increasing the quality of teachers and academics should be among Turkey's top priorities in education.

After 2002, an almost universal health care system was introduced. Life expectancy at birth increased from 71 to 75 years between 2002 and 2015, and satisfaction with the health care system has improved substantially. According to figures from a population life satisfaction survey undertaken by the Turkish Statistical Institute, the proportion of the population that is satisfied with health services increased from 39.5 per cent in 2003 to 75.9 per cent in 2011 (Atun et al. 2013).

It is certain that significant improvements have taken place in socio-economic conditions in Turkey compared to the past. The World Bank (2014: 5) underlines the improvements in the standards of living of the poor and gives credit to the role of the state: '*The improvements in the income of the poor…reflect rising labour market earnings across the distribution, and public investment in the expansion of health, education and municipal infrastructure, as well as the strengthening of Turkey's social security arrangements. These investments were made possible by the fiscal consolidation in the early 2000s which allowed spending to be reallocated from debt service to public services.*'

In 2000, Turkey devoted around 8 per cent of its GDP to public social spending, excluding education and since then, there has been an increasing trend in such spending. In 2016, public social spending as a share of GDP stood at 13.5 per cent—below the OECD average of 21 per cent.[10] Turkey is using around 75 per cent of its public social spending on health care and pension payments. The social assistance programmes that have been implemented since 2002 vary in terms of quality, coverage, and target group (Karagöl and Dama 2015). The government has been increasing its expenditures on disadvantaged population such as unemployed and disabled individuals, but income support for disadvantaged population is still under the OECD average (Üçkardeşler 2015).

Although these developments and figures indicate that economic growth is relatively inclusive in Turkey, not all the socio-economic conditions are at the desired level. Income inequality and unemployment are two of most important issues for which Turkey has not yet made much progress. Income inequality is one of the key topics that have been debated hotly since the GFC. One of the common approaches to monitoring the distribution of income is to calculate the Gini coefficient. After the 2000/2001 crisis, high economic growth and development-friendly government expenditures ameliorated income inequality, and the Gini coefficient was reduced from 0.44 in 2002 to 0.38 in 2005. However, the figure fluctuated around 0.4 between 2006 and 2013 and according to the latest data released, in 2015, the Gini coefficient stands at 0.397. Income inequality is not particularly high in Turkey, compared to other developing countries[11]; however, the problem is that there has been no significant improvement in income inequality since 2007, and each quintile's household disposable income has increased at similar rates for the last couple of years. In other words, the share of each quintile of the total household disposable income has remained almost the same, showing that the Gini coefficient has followed a stable path in recent years. Rising unemployment following the GFC has also prevented the income distribution from showing further improvement.

Another common way to evaluate the income distribution is to calculate the share of total national income that each of the factors of production receives—what is known as the functional or factor share distribution of income (Todaro and Smith 2011). The share of labour income has increased since 2002, while thanks to the falling levels of interest rates, inflation, and public debt, the share of interest income has fallen. However, due to the unequal distribution within its own factor group, interest income is the major source of disparity in income inequality (Selim et al. 2014). This underlines that policies to reduce interest rates are crucial to combat income inequality in Turkey.

Growth—and development-promoting government expenditures—requires high tax revenues, and therefore collecting taxes efficiently and reducing the size of the informal economy play a key role in equipping the state with stronger tools. According to estimates by Schneider (2015), the share of the informal economy in Turkey's GDP fell from 32.2 per cent in 2003 to 27.8 per cent in 2015. Not only should the Ministry of Finance use the latest technology available to audit economic transactions and uncover tax evasion, the government should help informal economy entrepreneurs move their economic activities into the formal economy.[12]

Tax revenues as a share of GDP increased from 17.58 per cent to 21.52 per cent between 2002 and 2016, mostly via increases in indirect tax channels. The share of direct taxes in GDP has been hovering around 6 per cent, while the share of indirect taxes has risen from 11.08 per cent to 14.40 per cent. The share of indirect taxes as a part of total tax revenues stands at around 67 per cent, which is high compared to low-inequality countries. In countries where income distribution is more fair (especially Scandinavian countries), the share of indirect taxes is around 40–50 per cent. Direct taxes are collected on income and profits, and in this respect, they are counted as progressive, while indirect taxes are regressive since they are taken from individuals regardless of their income. Though direct taxes seem to be harmful for stimulating entrepreneurship and investment (Alesina and Rodrik 1994; Djankov et al. 2010), they are more beneficial in terms of reducing inequality (Piketty 2014). In Turkey, the tax system has been heavily dependent on indirect taxes, distorting income distribution. The main reason the government puts so much emphasis on indirect taxation is because it is much easier to collect indirect taxes than direct taxes. The government should make the tax composition more balanced, and to do that, it needs to make tax administration more efficient by increasing the number of qualified excisemen and using state-of-the-art technological systems.

3 Quality of Institutions

Creating a well-functioning institutional infrastructure is another crucial task for the state to promote economic growth and development. Securing property rights, enforcing contracts, controlling corruption, and reducing red tape, for example, increase productive investments and galvanize innovation and entrepreneurship (Baumol 1990; Djankov et al. 2002; Acemoglu and Johnson 2005; Tebaldi and Elmslie 2013).

Thanks to first-generation reforms that were made in the environment of political stability brought about by the single-party government, Turkey has improved its institutional structure in some respects since 2002. Bribery, which previously had been a feature of the police force and customs agencies, has been significantly reduced, and some red tape has been cut; for example, the average time required to start a business has been reduced from 39 days in 2004 to 7 days in 2017. A similar improvement has been seen in taxpaying; the time it takes to prepare, file, and pay taxes has fallen to 216.5 hours per year in 2017 from 254 hours in 2006. Turkey has also made progress in some other dimensions of institutional quality. According to Worldwide Governance Indicators, the Turkish government's effectiveness index rose from 0.04 in 2002 to 0.23 in 2015. The cost of enforcing a contract, which is measured as the total cost in court and attorney fees as a percentage of the debt value, fell from 27.3 per cent in 2004 to 24.9 per cent in 2017.

Although Turkey has experienced a partial improvement in the quality of its public institutions since 2002, there is still ample room for improvement. The government should create necessary institutions and reform existing ones on each rung of the economic development ladder (Acemoglu et al. 2006). Turkey has done a good job implementing first-generation reforms since the 2000/2001, crisis but to escape the middle-income trap, second-generation reforms are needed. So far, Turkey has not succeeded in implementing the latter, mostly owing to the negative fallout from the GFC, escalating geopolitical risks in the Middle East region, fabricated political instabilities, terrorist attacks, and the 15 July failed coup attempt.

As Table 1 shows, although Turkey is performing better in many aspects of institutional quality than developing countries such as China, India, Mexico, Brazil, and Russia, it is lagging behind other major players in the global economy. In terms of corruption, Turkey shows a worse performance than other European countries but has a better record than almost all developing countries. According to data from the Enterprise Surveys conducted by the World Bank on developing and transitioning countries, 5.4 per cent of firms in Turkey experience at least one bribe payment request during six transactions dealing with utilities access, permits, licences, and taxes (Graph 2). This rate is lower than that of many developing countries with which Turkey competes in the global economy.[13]

To promote private-sector investments in R&D and innovation, revive the spirit of 'creative-destruction'-type entrepreneurship, and attract technology-intensive foreign direct investment, Turkey needs to lift its institutional quality higher and become more inclusive. The government should take measures to ensure that the legal system operates more effectively and fairly; it is crucial to ensure that the courts work properly, from enforcing contracts to easing the resolution of insolvency and obtaining external financing. More specialized courts should be established in areas of interest to the economy. The bureaucratic system in the

Table 1 Indicators of institutional quality for selected countries

Country	Time to pay taxes (hours per year)	Cost of enforcing contracts (percentage of claim)	Strength of minority investor protection index	Time for starting a business (days)	Cost of starting a business (percentage of income per capita)	Cost of resolving insolvency (percentage of estate)	Time to resolve insolvency (years)	Government effectiveness	Rule of law
United States	175	30.5	6.5	5.6	1.1	1.5	10.0	1.46	1.60
United Kingdom	110	43.9	7.8	4.5	0.1	1.0	6.0	1.74	1.81
Turkey	216	24.9	7.0	6.5	16.4	4.5	14.5	0.23	−0.06
Russia	168	16.5	6.0	9.8	1.0	2.0	9.0	−0.18	−0.72
Mexico	286	33.5	6.0	8.5	19.1	18.0	1.8	0.21	−0.47
South Korea	188	12.7	7.3	4.0	14.6	1.5	3.5	1.03	0.95
Japan	175	23.4	6.0	11.2	7.5	0.6	4.2	1.79	1.51
India	241	39.6	7.3	26.0	13.8	4.3	9.0	0.1	−0.06
Germany	218	14.4	6.0	10.5	1.9	1.2	8.0	1.74	1.78
France	139	17.4	6.5	3.5	0.7	1.9	9.0	1.44	1.41
Czech Republic	234	33.0	6.0	9.0	5.7	2.1	17.0	1.05	1.01

(*continued*)

Table 1 (continued)

Country	Time to pay taxes (hours per year)	Cost of enforcing contracts (percentage of claim)	Strength of minority investor protection index	Time for starting a business (days)	Cost of starting a business (percentage of income per capita)	Cost of resolving insolvency (percentage of estate)	Time to resolve insolvency (years)	Government effectiveness	Rule of law
China	259	16.2	4.5	28.9	0.7	1.7	22.0	0.42	−0.34
Brazil	2038	20.7	6.5	79.5	5.2	4.0	12.0	−0.19	−0.19

Source: Doing Business 2016 and Worldwide Governance Indicator 2015

Note: Definitions of the variables, taken from the Doing Business (http://www.doingbusiness.org/methodology) and Worldwide Governance Indicators (http://info.worldbank.org/governance/wgi/#faq-2) websites, are provided in what follows

Time to Pay Taxes: The time it takes to prepare, file, and pay (or withhold) corporate income taxes, value-added or sales taxes, and labour taxes, including payroll taxes and social security contributions (in hours per year)

Costs of Enforcing Contracts: The costs in court fees and attorney fees, where the use of attorneys is mandatory or common, expressed as a percentage of the debt value

Time for Starting a Business: The total number of days required to register a firm

Cost of Starting a Business: Costs are recorded as a percentage of the economy's income per capita. They include all official fees and fees for legal or professional services if such services are required by law

Time to Resolve Insolvency: Time for creditors to recover their credit, recorded in calendar years

Cost of Resolving Insolvency: The cost of the proceedings is recorded as a percentage of the value of the debtor's estate

Rule of Law: Reflects perceptions of the extent to which agents have confidence in and abide by the rules of society, and in particular the quality of contract enforcement, property rights, the police, and the courts, as well as the likelihood of crime and violence

Government Effectiveness: Reflects perceptions of the quality of public services, the quality of the civil service, and the degree of its independence from political pressures, the quality of policy formulation and implementation, and the credibility of the government's commitment to such policies

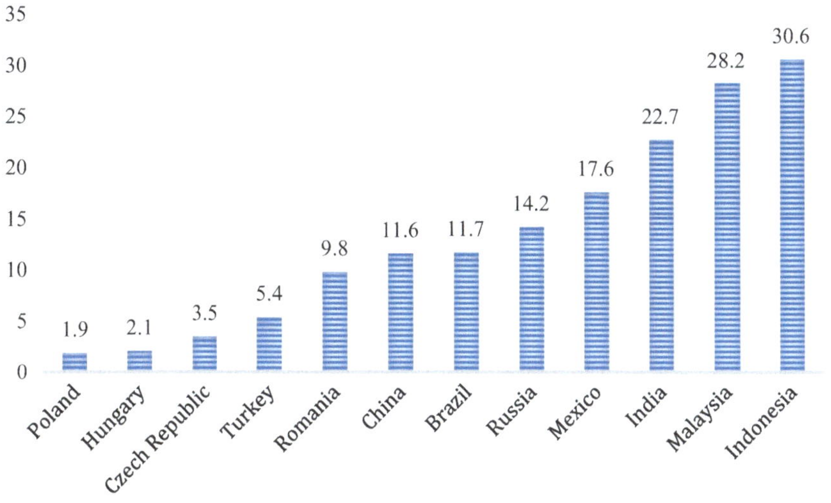

Graph 2 Bribe incidence (Source: Enterprise Surveys)

country usually makes life difficult for individuals and firms and hampers the implementation of reforms. The bureaucracy in general is in favour of the preservation of the status quo, rather than development and reforms, and therefore must be reformed to increase government effectiveness and reduce red tape. All these institutional reforms will help Turkey to stand out compared to its global competitors and break out of the middle-income trap.

4 Smart Industrial Policies

Turkey has put in a solid performance in the real economy over the last decade. An important breakthrough in exports and R&D took place in this era; Turkish exports increased to USD 142.5 billion in 2016 from USD 36 billion in 2002. After the AK Party took power, Turkey improved its political relations with neighbouring countries, which has boosted its export performance (Babacan 2010). The adoption of a multidimensional and proactive foreign policy also increased economic cooperation with the Middle East, the Balkans, the South Caucasus, Asia, and Africa

(Ünay 2010). These developments have not only expanded Turkey's export volume; they have also reduced the country's dependence on exports to EU countries. However, although there has been a noticeable increase in Turkey's export performance, the amount of high-tech exports is low and the current account deficit is high compared to rival developing countries.

According to estimates by the Turkish Statistical Institute, R&D expenditures relative to GDP—a proxy of R&D intensity—increased from 0.53 per cent in 2002 to 1.06 per cent in 2015. Thanks to generous incentives offered by the state for R&D activities, the share of private investment in R&D increased from 33 per cent to 50 per cent; however, Turkey has not yet succeeded in transforming R&D investments into innovation to the desired extent.

Turkish manufacturing has been the locomotive of the significant jump in exports and R&D since 2002, expanding its product range in industrial production in this period. The country has made important progress in the domestic production of many products, such as unmanned air vehicles, helicopters, cars, and tanks (Tiryakioğlu 2016). Despite these developments, Turkey is facing a problem when in terms of becoming a service economy without fully completing the industrialization process. Rodrik (2016) calls this problem 'premature deindustrialization'. Manufacturing value added relative to GDP fell to 18 per cent, with a two-percentage-point decrease from 2002.[14] Profit opportunities in the construction and services sectors have caused some Turkish manufacturers to divert their resources from manufacturing to these industries, and certain difficulties in doing business in the manufacturing industry are also playing a role in this shift.

All the aforementioned developments regarding the real economy make it clear that Turkey should boost the performance of its manufacturing industry to increase prosperity and reach high-income status. To do this, smart industrial policies are needed; instead of giving incentives to all firms and industries, the government should identify the most promising firms and industries and support them. Smart industrial policies use not only incentives but also disciplinary measures. Rodrik (2009) argues that the carrot-and-stick approach was one of the most important reasons that made East Asian countries more successful than

Latin American countries: 'While tax incentives (Taiwan) and credit subsidies (South Korea) were generous, they were conditioned on performance, and especially on export performance. Non-abiding firms were penalized by withdrawal of subsidies and in other ways.' This experience indicates that just providing incentives would not be effective; when giving support, the government should set targets for firms and industries and monitor them.

The government should consider upstream and downstream industries when designing industrial policies. In the past, the government has made serious mistakes on this issue by overlooking the interactions between upstream and downstream industries. For example, during the import substitution period in Turkey, while governments provided huge incentives to the textile industry, they did not give importance to the manufacture of textile machines (Yülek 2016). Owing to similar mistakes in strategic sectors, Turkey suffered from years of low productivity and high current account deficit problems. Therefore, having emerged from this stage, the government should approach industrial policies with a more comprehensive focus and prioritize industries with the strongest backward and forward linkages, as Hirschman (1958) argues.

Because industrial policies have many different dimensions, ministries and government agencies should work in a coordinated fashion to ensure that policies are successful. The government should bring its infrastructure investments and institutional reforms in line with its industrial strategy; coordination between institutions and harmony between the policies pertaining to different economic areas are key to ensuring that policies are implemented quickly and effectively.

At a time when protectionist rhetoric is increasing on the global stage, all possible measures that support and protect domestic firms should be taken by pushing the boundaries of international rules, such as those of the World Trade Organization, to increase domestic industrial production. This does not mean reducing the global economic integration of the Turkish economy; Turkey should advance economic integration in a planned manner, as Japan and South Korea did in the past and China has been doing since the late 1970s. Turkey, of course, needs foreign direct investment (FDI), but rather than welcoming all types of investments, the government should roll out the red carpet to FDI that provides technological spillovers and creates new jobs.

The state should also use smart industrial policies not only to avoid the middle-income trap but also to prepare itself for the new techno-economic paradigm. Worldwide, industry is entering a new phase; some scholars call this new techno-economic paradigm the *fourth industrial revolution* (Schwab 2017), while others have termed it the *second machine age* (Brynjolfsson and McAfee 2014). From the 'Internet of things' to cyber-physical systems, 3D printers, and robotics, global giants are continuously integrating intelligent technologies with industrial production. Of course, technology has been a part of industry from the beginning, but considering the scale, scope, and complexity of new technologies, the world is entering a special paradigm (Schwab 2017). Using these technologies, developed countries have been trying to regain the competitive advantage they lost to developing countries in many industrial sectors over the last 20–30 years. This might represent a threat to countries that have increased their global economic strength in recent years, such as China, India, South Africa, Brazil, and Turkey.

If Turkey fails to take the necessary precautions and impose the right policies, it will lose its power even in many sectors such as textiles, food, domestic appliances, auto spare parts, and automotive production, where it has a comparative advantage. To prepare for this new paradigm, which has the potential to affect economic, social, and political life, the Turkish government should shape its institutions and policies according to the new paradigm. Mazzucato and Pena (2016: 15) show this need in the following way: 'When a new technological revolution emerges, the socio-economic system remains stuck within the bounds of the previous (socio) techno-economic paradigm, which means that market forces are incapable of directing the system towards a new one; consequently, the modernising and rejuvenating potential of the new revolution is stifled. In other words, there are mismatches between elements of the social-, techno and economic systems (for example, social expectations, R&D routines, tax regimes, labour regulations, etc.). In order to overcome these mismatches, it is necessary to build new institutions that favour the diffusion of the new paradigm. In all previous technological revolutions, governments have led the process of institution-building that allowed new techno-economic paradigms to replace the old ones.'

Integrating into the new techno-economic paradigm means being able to produce robots and 3D printers, write algorithms to enable communication between computers and machines, innovate new management practices compatible with technological developments, and so on. Relying heavily on foreign investment and technology transfers will not help Turkey to enter the new phase in industry. If the government manages to implement smart industrial policies, as discussed earlier, Turkey will turn this paradigm shift into an opportunity to accelerate its economic development process by transforming its manufacturing industry.

5 Conclusion

Like it or not, the critical role that the government plays in economic performance is a fact that cannot be ignored. Free enterprise and the market economy are, of course, important for economic prosperity, but there are always some missing pieces left when trying to complete the puzzle of economic development. The government can make up for the missing pieces by sometimes regulating markets, creating the right institutions, making investments that no one else dares to do, leading industries, and incentivizing firms.

A well-functioning state is also crucial for Turkey to be prosperous and have a larger say in the global economy and for its citizens to raise their standards of living. Turkey needs new investments and reforms to avoid the middle-income trap. To make this happen, the state should undertake a number of important tasks.

To raise income levels and avoid the middle-income trap, Turkey should work intently on second-generation reforms. The country did a great job implementing first-generation reforms; following the referendum on the presidential system, which defused political tensions and reduced political uncertainties, there is no reason for the government not to implement new reforms. In terms of both the legal system and the tax system, the government needs to make the institutional infrastructure more 'inclusive'; in addition, Turkey should also put reforms into practice that will make it easier for firms to do business so that they gain a competitive advantage over their global peers.

Turkey needs to increase the quality of its economic growth. Economic growth between 2002 and 2007 was driven by physical and infrastructure investments and productivity. The growth performance after this period, on the other hand, has been fuelled mainly by consumption and government expenditure. As in the first years of the AK Party government, to ensure stable and high economic growth figures, investment and productivity should be increased.

To do this, the state should attach more importance to industry, especially manufacturing, in the economic structure and use well-designed, selective, and coordinated industrial policies—so-called smart industrial policies. The state has been offering generous incentives for export and R&D activities for more than a decade, and it should become more selective and use a so-called carrot-and-stick approach to increase the effectiveness of these incentives. Picking winners and monitoring firms and industries are not easy tasks; to do this, ministries and government agencies should work in a coordinated way.

Increasing GDP per capita should not be the main aim of economic development; reducing poverty and income inequality and facilitating access to high-quality health and education services are as important as raising per-capita GDP. The steps the country has made towards inclusive social policies in recent years are undeniable, but the state still has much to do to institutionalize the welfare system. The state should also use micro-based social policies that target the relative losers of the structural transformation that has taken place in Turkey over the course of the last decade.

Notes

1. To look at the data, see the World Development Indicators (accessed 1 May 2017): http://data.worldbank.org/indicator/NY.GDP.PCAP.CD?end=2008&start=2001.
2. Economic growth declined by 4.7 per cent in 2009. However, in the two following years, the Turkish economy bounced back spectacularly, with an average growth rate of around 9 per cent. See Tatliyer and Gur (2016).

3. To reduce redundant public expenditures, the government reduced, for example, the number of ministries and sold government-owned properties for members of parliament. See Patton (2006) for further discussion.
4. Thanks to budget discipline and low public debt, the government used expansionary fiscal policies to galvanize economic activity when it was necessary; for example, after the GFC and the failed coup attempt.
5. The state has started using public finance more freely since the compulsory relationship with the IMF finished. The 19th stand-by agreement with the IMF ended in 2008. Turkey paid the last debt instalment of USD 421 million in 2013 and wiped out all debt owed to the IMF. This move brought an end to the 52-year debt history with the IMF.
6. Düzel (2003), quoted from Patton (2006: 523).
7. "Istanbul's Yavuz Sultan Selim Bridge Toll Set to Be $3 Plus VAT" Daily Sabah, 15 August 2016. Accessed 12 April 2017. https://www.dailysabah.com/business/2016/08/15/istanbuls-yavuz-sultan-selim-bridge-toll-set-to-be-3-plus-vat.
8. For example, the minimum wage was increased by 30 per cent in a single year (2016).
9. To look at the data, see the OECD https://stats.oecd.org/Index.aspx?DataSetCode=EDU_CLASS (Accessed on 17.04.2017) and http://www.oecd.org/edu/skills-beyond-school/educationataglance2008oecdindicators.htm (Accessed on 17.04.2017).
10. To look at the data, see the OECD http://www.oecd.org/social/expenditure.htm (Accessed on 18.04.2017).
11. For example, the Gini coefficient is 0.42, 0.47, 0.54, and 0.63 in China, Mexico, Brazil, and South Africa, respectively. See http://hdr.undp.org/en/content/income-gini-coefficient (Accessed on 12.04. 2017).
12. "Turkey's Shadow Economy Decreasing in Size", Daily Sabah, 15 January 105. Accessed 15 April 2017. 15 January 2015, https://www.dailysabah.com/economy/2015/01/15/turkeys-shadow-economy-decreasing-in-size.
13. It is important to note that Turkey performs better in terms of the quality of institutions when the indicators of institutional quality are based on objective data, not perceptions.
14. To look at the data, see the World Development Indicators http://data.worldbank.org/indicator/NV.IND.MANF.ZS?end=2015&start=1999 (accessed 20 April 2017).

References

Acemoglu, Daron, and Simon Johnson. 2005. Unbundling Institutions. *Journal of Political Economy* 113 (5): 949–995.

Acemoglu, Daron, and James A. Robinson. 2012. *Why Nations Fail: The Origins of Power, Prosperity and Poverty*. London: Profile Books.

Acemoglu, Daron, Philippe Aghion, and Fabrizio Zilibotti. 2006. Distance to Frontier, Selection, and Economic Growth. *Journal of the European Economic Association* 4 (1): 37–74.

Akin, Guzin G., Ahmet F. Aysan, and Yildiran Levent. 2009. Transfomation of the Turkish Financial Sector in the Aftermath of the 2001 Crisis. In *Turkey and the Global Economy: Neo-Liberal Restructuring and Integration in the Post-Crisis Era*, ed. Ziya Öniş and Fikret Şenses, 73–100. New York: Routledge.

Alesina, Alberto, and Dani Rodrik. 1994. Distributive Politics and Economic Growth. *Quarterly Journal of Economics* 109 (2): 465–490.

Amsden, Alice. 1989. *Asia's Next Giant: South Korea and Late Industrialization*. New York: Oxford University Press.

Atun, Rıfat, Sabahattin Aydın, Ssarbani Chakraborty, Safir Sümer, Meltem Aran, Ipek Gürol, Serpil Nazlıoğlu, Şenay Özgülcü, Banu Ayar, Uğur Dilmen, and Recep Akdağ. 2013. Universal Health Coverage in Turkey: Enhancement of Equity. *The Lancet* 382 (9886): 65–99.

Azevedo, Joao Pedro, and Aziz Atamanov. 2014. *Pathways to the Middle Class in Turkey: How Have Reducing Poverty and Boosting Shared Prosperity Helped?* World Bank Policy Research Working Paper No. 6834.

Babacan, Mehmet. 2010. *Whither Axis Shift: A Perspective from Turkey's Foreign Trade*, SETA Policy Report No. 4. Ankara: SETA.

Baumol, William J. 1990. Entrepreneurship: Productive, Unproductive, and Destructive. *Journal of Political Economy* 98 (5): 893–921.

Brynjolfsson, Erik, and Andrew McAfee. 2014. The Second Machine Age. In *Work, Progress, and Prosperity in a Time of Brilliant Technologies*. New York: WW Norton & Company.

Chang, Ha-Joon. 2002. *Kicking Away the Ladder: Development Strategy in Historical Perspective*. London: Anthem Press.

Coşar, Kerem A., and Banu Demir. 2016. Domestic Road Infrastructure and International Trade: Evidence from Turkey. *Journal of Development Economics* 118: 232–244.

Djankov, Simeon, Rafael La Porta, Florencio Lopez-de-Silanes, and Andrei Shleifer. 2002. The Regulation of Entry. *Quarterly Journal of Economics* 117 (1): 1–37.

Djankov, Simeon, Tim Ganser, McLiesh Caralee, Ramalho Rita, and Andrei Shleifer. 2010. The Effect of Corporate Taxes on Investment and Entrepreneurship. *American Economic Journal-Microeconomics* 2: 31–64.

Düzel, Neşe. 2003. *Hükümet Duble Yollari Yapamaz* [The Government Cannot Build Divided Highways]. *Radikal*, January 27. http://www.radikal.com.tr/turkiye/hukumet-duble-yollari-yapamaz-658973/. Accessed 12 June 2017.

Evans, Peter. 1995. *Embedded Autonomy: States and Industrial Transformation*. Princeton: Princeton University Press.

Hirschman, Albert O. 1958. *The Strategy of Economic Growth*. New Haven: Yale University Press.

Invest in Turkey. 2015. *Turkey Ranks Second in PPP Investment Projects—World Bank*. http://www.invest.gov.tr/en-US/infocenter/news/Pages/100615-turkey-ranks-second-in-ppp-infrastructure-projects.aspx. Accessed 10 April 2017.

Istanbul's Yavuz Sultan Selim Bridge Toll Set to Be $3 Plus VAT. *Daily Sabah*, August 15, 2016. https://www.dailysabah.com/business/2016/08/15/istanbuls-yavuz-sultan-selim-bridge-toll-set-to-be-3-plus-vat. Accessed 12 Apr 2017.

Karagöl, Erdal, and Nergis Dama. 2015. *Geçmişten Günümüze Sosyal Yardımlar* [Social Benefits From Past to Present], SETA Analiz No: 139. İstanbul: SETA.

Mazzucato, Mariana. 2013. *The Entrepreneurial State: Debunking Public vs. Private Sector Myths*. London: Anthem Press.

Mazzucato, Mariana, and Caetano C. Penna. 2016. Beyond Market Failures: The Market Creating and Shaping Roles of State Investment Banks. *Journal of Economic Policy Reform* 19 (4): 305–326.

Musgrave, Richard A. 1959. *The Theory of Public Finance*. New York: McGraw-Hill Book Company, Inc.

North, Douglas. 1990. *Institutions, Institutional Change and Economic Performance*. Cambridge: Cambridge University Press.

Öniş, Ziya. 2003. Domestic Politics Versus Global Dynamics: Towards a Political Economy of the 2000 and 2001 Financial Crises in Turkey. *Turkish Studies* 4 (2): 1–30.

Patton, Marcie J. 2006. The Economic Policies of Turkey's AKP Government: Rabbits from a Hat? *The Middle East Journal* 60 (3): 513–536.

Piketty, Thomas. 2014. *Capital in the Twenty-First Century*. Cambridge, MA: Harvard University Press.

Rodrik, Dani. 2008. *One Economics, Many Recipes: Globalization, Institutions, and Economic Growth*. Princeton: Princeton University Press.

———. 2009. Industrial Policy: Don't Ask Why, Ask How. *Middle East Development Journal* 1 (1): 1–29.
———. 2016. Premature Deindustrialization. *Journal of Economic Growth* 21 (1): 1–33.
Schneider, Friedrich. 2015. *Size and Development of the Shadow Economy of 31 European and 5 Other OECD Countries from 2003 to 2015: Different Developments*. Mimeo. Linz: Department of Economics, Johannes Kepler University.
Schwab, Klaus. 2017. *The Fourth Industrial Revolution*. New York: Crown.
Şeker, Sırma Demir, and Stephen P. Jenkins. 2015. Poverty Trends in Turkey. *Journal of Economic Inequality* 13 (3): 401–424.
Selim, Raziye, Günçavdı Ömer, and Ayşe A. Bayar. 2014. *Türkiye'de Bireysel Gelir Dağılımı Eşitsizlikleri: Fonksiyonel Gelir Kaynakları ve Bölgesel Eşitsizlikler*. TÜSİAD-T/2014-06/554.
Sönmez, Mustafa. 2014. Private-Public Partnership Projects Reach $88 Billion. *Hürriyet Daily News*, April 28. http://www.hurriyetdailynews.com/private-public-partnership-projects-reach-88-billion.aspx?pageID=238&nID=65626&NewsCatID=344. Accessed 4 Apr 2017.
Tatliyer, Mevlüt, and Nurullah Gur. 2016. *The Resilience of the Turkish Economy After the Failed Coup Attempt*, SETA Analysis, No: 20. İstanbul: SETA.
Tebaldi, Edinaldo, and Bruce Elmslie. 2013. Does Institutional Quality Impact Innovation? Evidence from Cross-Country Patent Grant Data. *Applied Economics* 45 (7): 887–900.
Tiryakioğlu, Murat. 2016. *Türkiye Ekonomisinde Geç Kalkınmanın ve Yerli Üretimin Ekonomi Politiği* [The Political Economy of Late Development and Domestic Production in Turkish Economy]. *Ege Academic Review* 16 (2): 177–195.
Todaro, Michael P., and Stephen Smith. 2011. *Economic Development*. Essex: Pearson Addison Wesley.
Turkey's Shadow Economy Decreasing in Size. *Daily Sabah*, 105, January 15, 2015. https://www.dailysabah.com/economy/2015/01/15/turkeys-shadow-economy-decreasing-in-size. Accessed 15 Apr 2017.
Üçkardeşler, Emre. 2015. Turkey's Changing Social Policy Landscape. *Turkish Policy Quarterly* 13 (4): 149–161.
Ünay, Sadık. 2010. Economic Diplomacy for Competitiveness: Globalization and Turkey's New Foreign Policy. *Perceptions* 15 (3–4): 21–47.
Wade, Robert. 1990. *Governing the Market: Economic Theory and the Role of Government in East Asian Industrialization*. Princeton: Princeton University Press.

Weiss, Linda, and John M. Hobson. 1995. *States and Economic Development: A Comparative Historical Analysis*. Cambridge: Polity Press.
World Bank. 2014. *Turkey's Transition: Integration, Inclusion and Institutions*, Main Report No. 90509. Washington, DC: World Bank Group.
Yulek, Murat A. 2016. Industrial Policies and Outcomes: A Comparison of Pre-liberalized Korean and Turkish Economies. *Journal of Comparative Asian Development* 15 (1): 179–200.

Political Economy of Transformation of Capital Structure in Turkey: A Historical and Comparative View

Abdurrahman Babacan

1 Introduction

The political-economic transformation of Turkey, particularly in the last 40 years, requires a deep reading in terms of the historical background, as well as current facets, including the policy implications bringing about the transformation process as reflected in todays' capital structure. Thus, the historical basis of the issue should include center-periphery relations,[1] mainly evidenced as tension between the two blocs of the Turkish political-economic juncture. Historically, state-led capitalism in Turkey and its privileges given to the political-economic elite constituted the very basis of the capital structure in the country. A comprehensive look at the breakthrough period initiated by the Özal era in the early 1980s should focus on the main policies aimed at transforming society based on political and economic liberalism and its direct/indirect reflections in a newly emerging capital group mainly based in Anatolia, along with the statistical rise of some new local cities/regions/corporations, and its political-economic content.

A. Babacan (✉)
School of Humanities and Social Sciences, İstanbul Medipol University, Istanbul, Turkey

A. F. Aysan et al. (eds.), *Turkish Economy*,
https://doi.org/10.1007/978-3-319-70380-0_3

In this framework, the two main interest groups of industrial and business associations, Turkish Industry and Business Association (TUSIAD) and Independent Industrialists' and Businessmen's Association (MUSIAD), appear more clearly in this historical process as representatives of the two different political-economic bases in terms of magnitude, volume, regional/geographic distribution of the members, institutional codes/roots, and, hence, differentiated vision and structural realities. It has been widely accepted that TUSIAD stands more on the conventional status quo, largely relying historically on a state-led capitalism model, while MUSIAD relies on a civil and private sector–led model. Yet the Özal era had partially switched relations between economic actors and the state and changed the characteristics and direction of this relation while creating newly emerging economic actors favored by the transformed political-economic sphere in Turkey.

In this regard, MUSIAD, by its development process and revealed vision since its foundation in 1990, represents a new economic sense and strategy in Turkish politics as well. Surely, this has been related to the liberalization of Turkey's political-economic base since the 1980s, followed by the Europeanization and globalization of Turkish politics during the 1990s and 2000s, which resulted in MUSIAD's sphere of influence becoming more institutionalized and deepened in the AK Party era.

On the other hand, TUSIAD, despite some dramatic and hard-fought internal battles on the path toward a smooth in line with the newly emerging structure, generally has coped with the fluctuations regarding problematic issues such as the content, form, momentum, and direction of the reaction to be given to the challenging transformation of Turkey's political economy. The most prominent example of this was the group's reaction to and political stance regarding the 28th of February process,[2] which led to the collapse of the Erbakan government by a postmodern military coup in 1997. This process and its aftermath, which paved the way for the 1999 and 2001 financial crises as the biggest economic events in modern Turkish economic history, were altogether a resistance against democratization, and had a substantive and significant economic base that provided the "rationality" of this political stance.

2 A Historical View: Two Different Perspectives and Political-Economic Bases

As an expression of political positions within the political spectrum, the terminology used within the right-left spectrum has been meaningful to some extent. However, this context has been subject to major changes through complex political-economic developments on a global scale since the 1980s. Therefore, because the term *center* has gained more importance in determining the political-economic positions in transition countries like Turkey, terminology around the center implies a deeper consideration of the political, economic, and sociological aspects. Sartori (1976: 186–214), in a two-pole-based political analysis, stressed that the space between two poles regarding political stances would determine and shape the scope and role of the *center* and thereby cause one to rethink political relations. While associating the term *center* with its urban, upper-middle-class components, Wilson (1980: 25–49) also notes that the conventional understanding of the characteristic of this political-economic classification has also undergone qualitative transformations and has begun to lose its former influence with the emergence of new conceptualizations and rapid developments.

In this sense, to understand the term *center* in Turkish politics and Turkish political-economic history, one should go beyond right-left contradictions or party politics, which requires a deeper interrogation and a new look that basically relies on the contradiction between political-statist center and societal center. There has been a dualistic structural composition of political culture in Turkey since the foundation of the modern republic, which created a bipolar political-economic pattern. We can regard this controversy as a differentiation and even dispute in the political and economic spheres between statist and state-centric identity values, conventionally represented as the *center*; and liberal or conservative ideology–based identity values, again conventionally represented as the *periphery*. For some, this expresses some kind of "oligarchy-democracy tension" which immediately spurs a political cultural debate in our discussion. Inspired by Edward Shils' (1982) center-periphery model, Mardin (1973) has proposed applying the model to political artifacts in

Turkey. Whether we use the classification of the two sides as statist elites and traditionalist liberals (Kongar 2012), also characterized as cultural dualism in Timur (1968), or the categorization of state bureaucracy and producer groups (Karpat 2009), all these attributions draw a picture of a bipolar structure in the Turkish political-economic mold.

The differentiation between early republican elites and emerging potential power groups becomes evident with respect to their attitudes toward the modernization of the state, law, culture, and lifestyle, as well as economic and social development, free markets, civil and democratic rights, and religious, national, and traditionalist values, which are undergoing partial and gradual changes in perspective. Mannheim (2013), in this regard, conceptualizes *bureaucratic conservatism* to argue that conventional republican political elites are defenders of the Kemalist construction with its all components, compressing the political-economic sphere and restricting the horizon of new sorts of comprehension and initiatives. In contrast, the newly emerging groups from rural Anatolia have been motivated in taking a dynamic position toward widening the scope of politics and economics for various societal groups. Küçükömer (2009), in this connection, has labeled the core contradiction as, on the one hand, pro-Western seculars, which denotes the continuation of the bureaucratic character of centrist statism and the creation of a new capitalist class involving state-led capitalism, and, on the other hand, Eastern Islamists who defend decentralization and the exclusion of the state from the field of societal, civil, and economic rights and activities.

While the political-economic dimension of the break is as described above, the interpretation of this struggle among political actors refers to a confrontation of two streams, namely the Committee of Union and Progress (İTC) to the Republican People's Party (CHP) versus the Freedom and Accord Party (HİF) to the Democrat Party (DP), Motherland Party (ANAP), and AK Party. The transition to a multiparty system by the late 1940s eroded the absolute domination of the *old* center. The early republican period was shaped in accordance with the demands of the mostly upper-class civil-military bureaucracy and big agrarian elites and gentry, which shows an elitist political-economic base formed and governed by the CHP for years. The political stream began with the Progressive Republican Party (TCF) to the Free Republican Party (SCF) and continued with the DP, ANAP, and AK Party, on the other hand, reflected by demands for reform in social, economic, and political concerns to be practiced through a more liberal and individual-based structure.

Many scholars have highlighted the tension between Republican elitist secularism, which is authoritarian in nature, and the broad masses, which are closer to traditional and religious values and have been excluded from the mainstream political-economic and social realm for years. Thus, the Republican experience since the early years of the new state has shown a sharp divide regarding the mode of modernization. Economic and societal relations shape politics and political relations such as state-society and state-economy in many ways; but it has been more significant in the Turkish experience than in any institutionalized Western or Eastern country owing to its unique characteristics and historical vulnerabilities. Thus, the Turkish experience, in the construction of a new mode of the modernization project, involved coping with challenges regarding the anachronistic nature of the project, which stemmed both from its mindset and methodology. That is to say, by changing the parameters of economic activity and societal relations in the contemporary world, the political and institutional mindset was subject to a critical test, and the question was whether traditional Republican state practices would be able to handle or even change the crux of the problem. As Buğra (2002: 191) points out, "While the state has extensively intervened in economic life, it has not done so, first, in a rule-based manner via formal institutional arrangements, but through particularist relations between political authorities and individual businessmen. Second, extensive state intervention in economic and social life was not successful in assuring social integration. Large segments of the population have remained excluded from economic benefits of modernization and no significant uniformization of life styles could materialize. Many of the problems today stem from this double failure of the Kemalist modernization process in Turkey."

The direct and positive relation between state-led capitalism and the dominance of secularism in the Turkish experience would give insight into the rationale of demands for restructuring Turkish politics, economics, culture, and society, in line with contemporary schemes and frameworks. In this context, when the critical stance of *periphery* against state-led modernization initiatives has been attributed to political-economic concerns, there is an underlying rationale. In terms of their class origins, these societal groups predominantly come from small shopkeepers, merchants, artisans, peasantry, and even working classes. For a long time they lacked the necessary physical and social capital to compete with bigger firms in the market and largely relied on favors from the state, such as cheap credit, subsidies, and public contracts.

3 Breakthrough Period: Özal Era, Policy Implications, and Formation of a New Capital Structure

After the DP carried the *periphery* to power with a social base composed of peasants, urbanite liberals, conservatives, local middle class, and mainly small industrialists and businessmen and disturbed the monopolistic and partisan role of the state in economic life, the second major breakthrough took place during the ANAP governments in the 1980s.

The global environment Turkey went through by the 1980s has opened a new age with rapid changes in the economic, political, and ideological spheres, spurred a reformulation of global political economy by globalization and capital mobilization, and brought about the replacement of the welfare state by neoliberal and new right politics. This has brought new formations of governance and various sorts of sovereignty for world politics. Integrated with globalization, and its emphasis on individualism, a market economy, restricted/minimal state, and liberal rationalism, neoliberal policies have opened new vistas and a new form of politics referred to as the new right or liberal conservatism, composed of neoconservative politics. Giddens (1994: 22–45) states that such a paradigmatic change in neoconservatism has a sociological content rather than philosophical and in this regard has no reservation with being integrated with liberal democracy. Such a convergence of liberalism and conservatism is a sign of new political-economic measures for Turkish political culture in the age of globalization. Structural transformation in economics associated with politics mainly relied on a change of mindset in the Özal era. The prolonged political, legal, and bureaucratic modernization process since the time of Tanzimat began to give way to a new modernization paradigm, highlighting an economic rationalism via commercial, fiscal, and technical modernization.

The 1980s brought paradigmatic changes in cultural and mental codes alongside the political and economic developments. Cultural impulses, with changing structures, generated a new tendency toward cultural relativism in most societies. This has led to an acceptance of new conceptions of diversity, the recognition of local and traditional values, and the path to multiple perspectives opposing the unilinear conception of modernization associated with the West. Cultural pluralism, in this regard, associated with postmodernism, brings with it a structural transformation in political mindsets, implying a radical shift from a simplistic right-left division to the acknowledgment of new and complex identity issues. In addition, in the economic field we have witnessed new forms of production, referred to by some as flexible production in post-Fordist conditions. This allows some sectors of the production and wholesale supply-chain processes to take place in different countries or different districts within a country with relatively low costs thanks to technological developments and new economic rationalities. Within this new form, small cities and small-sized firms in these cities, including the wider metropolitan areas, took on new functions and roles. As a result, Turkey has been one of the core actors embodying the implications of the aforementioned global framework.

The transformation of Turkish capitalism from the 1950s to the late 1990s has been instructive in comprehending the political-economic stances of several governments vis-a-vis the compatibility of a developing country's changing economic mindset with global developments. Öniş (2010: 48) classifies the developmental process of the Turkish economy in the last 50 years starting with a multiparty system as a gradual process and also a sort of cyclical pattern with a break, continuity, and overlap.

> The 1950s correspond to the liberal turn in the Turkish economy involving an attempt to reverse the statist and protectionist policies of the inter-war era. The second phase, under successive five-year plans implemented during the 1960s and 1970s, represents a shift to national developmentalism and ISI (import substitutive industrialization)-based strong protectionism of the domestic market. This phase resulted in the institutionalization of the domestic market. The third phase, the 1980s and the 1990s, corresponds to

Turkey's encounter with neoliberal policies and the logic of the Washington consensus which is based on the liberalization of key sectors of the economy. The fourth and final phase constitutes the regulatory phase of neoliberalism with policy-makers emphasizing strong regulatory institutions and paying more attention to social protection. This phase reflects Turkey's encounter with the emerging post-Washington consensus.

The policy phases of this development path imply and correspond to qualitative changes within the nature and form of domestic capital structure in Turkish business community considering the reality that essential determinant of this process is the relation, even the alliance, between state and domestic capital primarily. As mentioned in an earlier section concerning the historical basis, the Turkish domestic capital structure, which was substantially survived under protectionist policies, had begun its transformation by the 1950s and continuing into the 1970s' new political-economy. The industrialization and urbanization of societal and economic relations were effective in the transitional process of large firms from agrarian or commercial form to a domestic-capital-based industrial structure, followed by a shift toward export orientation in the next phase by the 1980s and early 1990s. Depoliticization of the market occurred in this period, following the considerable political and economic instability of the 1970s' domestic and global political-economic environment. One important consequence inherently attached to this path has been the development of small and medium-sized enterprises (SMEs), within the last phase of globalization of industrial relations by the 2000s, under a setting conducive to local enterprises to mobilize their economic capacity. Diffferent industrialization and growth waves would be defined in the sliding scale for Anatolia in this period starting with channeling the savings of Turkish immigrants in Europe to their homelands, which in turn were being invested in newly established SMEs. That was followed by the involvement of the state in the form of the State Planning Organization's medium and long-term development strategies with the inclusion of SMEs as the key actor in this state-led development projection by the 1980s (Özcan and Çokgezen 2003). Yet the debate over the expansion of SMEs, mainly in Anatolia, is one of the most contentious within the last 30 years in the academic and political literature in the Turkish case and is associated with arguments on modern ideological patterns and new forms, actual political processes such as voting behavior theories, discussions on democracy, Islamism and its main objections to the establishment, responses by secular elites, and new horizons within political-economic contexts.

The appeal of the new horizons mentioned previously has to do with moral and actual concerns regarding poverty, income distribution, social justice, and the improvement of the material conditions of disadvantaged groups. This vision, placing developmental goals on a moral basis, has opened up a wide scope for an alternative pattern to the entrenched *center* or establishment and enabled the birth of a cross-class alliance through an awareness of the common ground of being a part of the *excluded.* This sociopsychological and socioeconomic basis, with all its rationalities, has formed and provided a transformational vision, under the favor of global and domestic events, essentially implemented and realized in the Özal era by the 1980s.

In this context, the main determinants of the economic approach in the Özal era were empowerment and securing economic development of the middle class, deep trust in market mechanisms, a transition from import-substitution development to an export-oriented economic perspective, opening up to international competition, a shift from state-led capitalism to free markets, and from patron-client relationships to economic interest-based policies of the DP and AP governments. The institutional and legal regulations of those policies were realized via fiscal, monetary structural adjustment decisions taken on January 24, 1980. Three main stages of the new policy, also indicating a shift toward a free-market economy, were the adjustment of fiscal and monetary regulations, an export-oriented development strategy, and the liberalization of commercial and financial markets. Privatization, flexible exchange rates, new central bank credits, tax incentives, removal of quotas and restrictions on imports, reductions in government expenditures, promotion of supply-side economics and exports, and an overhaul of the bureaucracy were the main policy goals of the new era. The late 1970s' great economic crisis, while causing all to rethink state-economy relations, in the meantime was causing an essential breakup of the Turkish political-economic structure. A comprehensive approach to a new political-economic mindset was being accepted and expanded, with an inclusion of social and cultural aspects alongside the political and economic ones. A set of discussions was held concerning the role of the state in economic life and societal relations such as social service mechanisms, the creation of trust and justice, interpersonal and social relations, and finally the question of whether the state or society has ontological priority. This has created a new form of combination of economic liberalism with political liberalism, appearing in political and social processes as a function of the economic mindset and activities. Such a conception of economic-based modernization also represents a paradigmatic break from Kemalism's state-centric and culturally based modernization perspective. Kadıoğlu (1999) argues that Özal transformed the modernization perspective of the Republican epistemology in two senses: first, by transforming the Kemalism-based modernization mindset and practice by replacing ideology with economic thinking; and second, by attempting to impose an individualism-oriented development and growth strategy rather than the state-centric model.

The critical point here concerns the historical pattern of Turkish public administrative thinking, which mainly relies on the general consent of a transcendent, sacred state, which implies an ontological priority of the state over citizens, which has the power to settle almost in all spheres of life (Habermas 1991). One of the basic changes realized by Özal here is the transformation of this state-dominated sphere, which resulted in the recognition henceforth of the individual as a *political subject*.

In addition, the principle of *populism* as one of the central tenets of Republican epistemology that pictures the societal envisagement and shapes relations between state and citizens started to be questioned and challenged. As Parla (2006) stated, the Republic, with its generality perspective, has tried to merge all citizens in a corporatist manner and to generate a uniform society via populist and solidarist relations, whereas, because the corporatist philosophy repudiates liberal individualism, the presence of social classes, and, hence, the reality of class conflicts, this would open the way to Özal's reforms, which advocate an individual-based society with an entrepreneurial and civil mindset on a more reasonable and rational base, and convince the society for their necessitation. He, in such a framework, by avoiding the generation of a common solidarity among occupational clusters, rather backed up the

Anatolian capital against the major political-economic actors in İstanbul. In this respect, the political-economic factors that create the present dynamism in Anatolia have been very important in explaining the transformational process. Yet the capital structure in the Anatolian business community represents a new growing power, independent of state support, at least at the initial stage.

The Özal era has to be understood as a shift from a slow, bulky, bureaucratic, ineffective, and state-centric structure of big capital to a new one that has spurred a political-economic transformation achieved with improvements in the infrastructure of the Turkish economy and huge leaps in communication, transportation, and energy investments. The Anatolian capital and newly rising middle classes, thus, found their economic and social demands being met in the new political model with ANAP. In other words, the rationalities of internal dynamics to realize the transformation for Anatolia coincided with Özal's perspective and policies. If the two facades of Turkish modernization were to be discussed, the societal facade benefited from serious improvements both in mentalities and practices in the Özal era (Kasaba and Bozdoğan 2010). The societal transformation, connected with urbanization, new waves in cultural production, and gradual establishment of global perspective signifies, on the one hand, an expansion of the periphery, while the establishment of the new middle-class structure points to an immanence and embeddedness[3] of an economic mindset in the political and societal relations on the other. Özal, at this juncture, as a leading actor carrying correspondence of the mentioned transformation to historical processes and realities, once again is worth mentioning. He, in particular, represents a break from Republican epistemology by his transformational vision with its emphasis on individual-based political-economic configuration and an expansion of liberties and democratic and civil rights. In this way, he embodies different political and social tendencies in a synthetist approach that works toward the harmonization of conflicting components of conventional ideologies and class struggle processes. The new societal center includes agricultural producers, workers, officials at all ranks, artists, artisans, and businessmen, and in this sense comes to the focus of the debate for its meaning as a new construction of the center in Turkish political-economic life.

The historical episode of the break from Republican epistemology, which led to the transformation horizon in Özal era, created its own path by the 1990s in a more institutional framework. Specifically relying on the criticism of Justice Party (AP) management for its dependency on big and foreign capital, one distinctive type of social mobilization, sociopolitically called National Outlook (Milli Görüş), was led by Erbakan, starting in the 1960s, with its small and medium-sized businessman, artisan, and merchant components in Anatolia. Since then, the central focus of the National Outlook movement has been income distribution and poverty reduction, foreign aid and capital dependency, poor financial statements, and the necessity of industrialization and heavy industry. In the cultural sphere, a Western-oriented social structure and education mode and a value-free pro-Western political-economic perspective and practices of other political parties were termed by Erbakan as counterfeiting and rentier capitalism.

The economic sphere opened up by Özal's liberal policies in the 1980s and early 1990s eased the institutionalization of the aforementioned social mobility, which was critical of the past and thereby has been promoted to set a new political-economic mold in Anatolia since the 1960s. Thus, there have been social, political and economic rationalities and growth dynamics for the new capital. Small businessmen and shopkeepers in the small or medium-sized Anatolian cities were important actors in binding political demands to economic ones during the 1970s. From the National Salvation Party (MSP) to the Welfare Party (RP), this ground had gradually been nourished in accordance with the development process of Turkish capitalism. After the 1960s and 1970s industrialization wave, a second but more essential and dramatic was established and was strongly connected with the deregulatory and liberal policies of the 1980s.

In the classification of the dynamics that led to the transformation, three main issues should be handled in depth. One is about the new policy phase incorporating an export-orientated growth strategy, part of general trade liberalization. The export-orientation strategy, in this framework, while providing benefits for large conglomerates, also created great opportunities for SMEs operating in rising sectors such as textiles, construction, and services, mainly located in new industrial growth centers in inner Anatolian towns. As statistics show, the share of exported manufactured goods of firms having wholesale and retail chains both in Turkey and abroad increased from 31% in 1980 to 48% in 1994 (Adaş 2003: 42, cited by Hoşgör 2011). As part of trade liberalization in a broader sense, this process was directly enhanced by other components of the free-trade regime where liberalized trade policy provides opportunities to import required production inputs at low cost and to export final goods to a wide and diversified range of districts without any local, national, or transnational obstacles. This eased and opened ways for firms to expand their scope with an eye toward reaching a transnational level through investments in the USA, Europe, the Middle East, and Central Asia by the post-2001 era. Yet firms, mostly SMEs operating especially in the three favored sectors of textiles, construction, and services, took advantage of the growth strategy, such that more than 500,000 firms were established between 1983 and 2000, and by 1990, the SMEs constituted almost 90% of all manufacturing firms in Turkey and employed more than one-third of all workers in the manufacturing sector (Adaş 2003: 71–72, cited by Hoşgör 2011).

This situation was not only related to compatibility with the external environment but also very closely related to government policies, including cheap credit opportunities from public banks, direct/indirect investment incentives, preferential public contractual regulations, legislation conducive to growth, and the formation of industrial districts in various cities and towns. In addition, public expenditures were more concentrated in infrastructure investments such as transportation, communication, energy, and urban renewal projects. Hence, the neoliberal period led by Özal did not simply signify a shift from a state-led development model to a purely free market economy with minimal state intervention. Along with significant liberalization in key areas of economic activity such as financial markets, trade regime, and capital movements, the state has continued to play a role in facilitating the growth of real sectors within the economy. However, this presents another problem in the form of discriminatory use of state facilities in the private sector. This assigned an economic rent allocator role for the state, followed by unfair distributional processes, abuse of state subsidies and incentives, and high-interest-rate loans from the private sector to the state, resulting in two major financial crises in 1999 and 2001. That is, if the transformation process has not been enhanced and empowered by a strong institutional foundation, in the long run the path will be subject to structural failures that affect all the components including even the beneficiaries.

A third issue to consider in depth is investment fund mechanisms, including attracting foreign capital, particularly from European and Gulf countries, capital financing instruments, and institutions especially required by SMEs and newly emerging capital owners in Anatolia.

Financial liberalization and capital mobility have brought new opportunities for capital inflow, particularly from the Gulf region in the form of interest-free banking (IFB). The introduction of IFB facilitated the financing of investments by aggregating the small amounts of capital to into large amounts as required for new investments, particularly for SMEs, which also mostly consider some moral and religious sensitivities in their economic activities. The first interest-free banks were Turkish–Saudi joint ventures; the Al Baraka Finance House and the Faisal Finance were established in 1985, followed by another Arab–Turkish investment, the Kuwait Turkish Finance House, in 1989; and Anadolu Finance, Ihlas Finance House, and Asya Finance House were formed by Turkish shareholders in 1991, 1995, and 1996, respectively. The interest-free banks functioned in the capital supply process by attracting the savings from the conventional banking system owing to various factors, such as value-based sensitivities, lack of trust owing to political and financial instability, or the presence of some structural/bureaucratic barriers in getting credits from public or private commercial banks. The significance and impact are so huge that when interest-free banks were introduced, an estimated $50 billion of savings was kept out of the system (Hoşgör 2011).

In addition, as another capital source, the remittances saved by Turkish migrant workers in Europe have been a matter of debate since 1960s on how to save this accumulation within Turkish financial circles. In this framework, deregulation and export-oriented policies have led these deposits to be functionalized in the creation of new investment opportunities in the homeland. As some statistics show, in the 1990s, capital inflows to Turkey from over three million migrant workers amounted to about $5 billion (Yeşilada 2002: 78).

4 Positioning the Two Main Business Groups MUSIAD and TUSIAD Within the Junction of Transformation

A comprehensive insight into the depth of the breaking points requires an evaluation of the two differentiated positions represented by the two major industrial and businessmen's associations MUSIAD and TUSIAD. The composition and development processes of the two groups may explain some of the mentality codes, future projections, and socio-economic foundations as well. That is to say, the majority of the members of MUSIAD joined after the 1980s, while the history of most of TUSIAD's members is based on the earlier period of the development story of Turkish capitalism. When looking at the dates of incorporation, we can observe that the 1980–1989 period saw a surge in MUSIAD memberships, with the creation of 744 newly established companies in comparison with only 98 TUSIAD members in the same period. Again, while the records indicate that there were no newly established members of TUSIAD after 1990, the same period shows that there were 589 newly established companies enrolled in MUSIAD membership (MÜSİAD 1995; TÜSİAD 1989).

Likewise, in a perspective based on geographical distribution along with size in terms of number of employees, while TUSIAD members come from large firms, geographically concentrated in Istanbul and adjacent industrial districts of the Marmara region, MUSIAD is mainly comprised of various Anatolian SMEs employing fewer than 50 workers (Öniş and Türem 2001). According to records from the late 1980s and early 1990s, out of 473 TUSIAD member companies, 323 of them were located in İstanbul and the rest were mostly in İzmir and Ankara. MUSIAD has a comparatively different story: even if some Anatolian districts like Konya, Kayseri, Kahramanmaraş, Malatya, and Adana have a considerable proportion of the whole picture, the largest number, with 488 members out of 1717, also belongs to İstanbul, followed by Ankara, Konya, İzmir, Kayseri, Bursa, Kocaeli, and others scattered in various cities (MÜSİAD 1995; TÜSİAD 1989).

Contrary to general perceptions, this picture tells us that no representative group can be totally squeezed into a tight geographical and unidimensional cultural framework, as demonstrated by MUSIAD's diverse membership. This reality of diversity and multiculturalism also gives them the opportunity to operate their business according to a global vision. Another important conclusion to be drawn from the picture is the issue concerning the date of incorporation of the enterprises represented by MUSIAD and TUSIAD. The difference between these organizations is that one group has historically been granted many privileges by the state and the other has not. Despite the disadvantageous position that has lasted almost 30 years until the transition to a multi-party system, these companies and MUSIAD, as the association represents them, have enjoyed the benefits of liberal turn by 1980s, which equates the conditions for all parties in economic activity. This historical period has brought significant changes in domestic and global patterns, also creating positive impacts for MUSIAD's socio-economic base. Yet, the promotion of SMEs in a liberal scope has implied the removal of the state's destructive partisan policies on the path to industrialization and business operations.

The AK Party era, in this sense, institutionalized and deepened the existing process, which has largely focused on the expansion of investment opportunities via improvement of the economy's capacity to grow. And when the economy continues on a high-growth path, SMEs also share in the benefits of the growing economy. In this regard, MUSIAD's support for the AK Party's political position is clear since the political-economic perspective and stance of the AK Party towards SMEs coincide with the political-economic interests represented by MUSIAD. Hence, protection and enhancement of the rights and interests of shareholders of these SMEs was declared to be one of the most important tasks of the party's Urgent Action Plan, prepared before the 2002 elections (AK Party 2002).

A dynamic economic environment, therefore, attracted different economic actors under a stable political circle, figured by the AK Party since its victory in 2002 elections. That has allowed the AK Party to set itself on a broad base of support. The very success of the AK Party in its earlier periods particularly was based on the ability to forge a broad social base composed of different segments of society. The main strategy was designed not only on the articulation of economic demands of the newly arisen

SMEs in Anatolia, but also by persuading large companies to adopt a selective strategy including strategic colloborations with others to foster an effective dynamism on the basis of economic commonalities. This project bore fruits in the form of various compromises and even cooperation, including strategies for labor relations, socioeconomic policies, economic prosperity, social inclusiveness, democratic consolidation, and international relations (Hoşgör 2011).

The contradiction between the two associations' perspectives over (1) cultural references (secular, pro-Western perspective versus religious, value-based perspective), (2) preferred modes of development (Western capitalism versus East Asian development model), (3) policy orientations (more EU-focused versus more Eastern oriented), (4) societal and economic grounds (individualism-based model versus communitarian model), and (5) stress on strategic priorities (rights and freedom of the individual versus social justice, social rights, and income distribution) gives a parallel framework to the historical evolution of the Turkish political-economic structure. Thus, it would be important to answer the question of whether this framework would bring major changes toward a convergence of the poles, in a process whereby the *center* would have play a more important role in the democratization of Turkish politics and rising economic interdependence. The consolidation of positions in societal status and obtaining greater share from public and private sources imply a new form of thinking regarding democratic politics by learning from the past. While the SMEs' role and that of their biggest representative association, MUSIAD, by its dynamic, rapid, and energetic character, in this regard, are manifesting as a catalyst for transformation, TUSIAD, with its protectionist, cumbersome, and anemic structure, has mainly been directed to preserve and improve the social and economic status of a largely state-created bourgeoisie. That is, this is a situation that can be explained by both historical conditions and the structural characteristics of both institutions.

Yet in the 1980s, the global and domestic environment brought one of the most serious challenges for TUSIAD, forcing it to review its engagements including various issues such as the unequal structure of the relationship between the state and the economy, the deep gap between the statist center and societal center, the problematic historical legacy regarding the issue of democracy, and the subordination of individual and social values to etatist ones throughout the history of the republic. But consequently it is clear that it has been difficult for TUSIAD's perspective to stand against the secular statist forces, as explicitly seen in the historic ruptures like in February 1997 and recently the Taksim Gezi Park incidents. Yet, despite its own studies, such as *Perspectives on Democratization* report published in 1997, which was widely and harshly criticized even internally immediately after publication, a strong and decisive stance could not be exposed, partially and surely due to its intellectual legacy.

Even if there are some obstacles from internal and external dynamics, Turkey desperately needs to follow the path it embarked upon after 2001, which opened a virtuous cycle whereby political and economic democratization reforms moved in tandem. The principal actors of the economic sphere supporting economic reforms also fully support political reforms such as the EU admission process and expansion of the scope of civil, individual, political, and cultural freedoms. In such a framework, the market has become an important tool of leverage for the political reform process, where politics in turn helps to generate an appropriate climate conducive to both domestic and foreign investments. Hence, such a mutually reinforcing cycle will ultimately bring the structural transformation in favor of institutionalization, unattached to any personal, informal, arbitrary, or subjective concerns.

Notes

1. As a political sociological conception, "center-periphery" refers to a distinct context in the Turkish experience alongside its conventional meaning, as explained in the first and second sections.
2. The overthrow of Erbakan's government through illegitimate ways using different parameters. Since the most prominent breakthroughs in the process have been made by the military on February 28, 1997 at the National Security Council, the whole process is called the 28th of February process.
3. In his influential book *The Great Transformation* (2001), Polanyi argues that the most striking feature of the new economic mindset and practice

has been penetration to all the social, political, and cultural matters by shaping the mentality codes and life practices as a function of economics. He uses the term "embeddedness" in referring to this sort of qualitative relationship.

References

Adaş, Emin Baki. 2003. *Profit and the Prophet: Culture and Politics of Islamic Entrepreneurs in Turkey*. PhD Dissertation, University of Illinois, Urbana-Champaign.

AK Party. 2002. Urgent Action Plan.

Buğra, Ayşe. 2002. Labour, Capital, and Religion: Harmony and Conflict Among the Constituency of Political Islam in Turkey. *Middle Eastern Studies* 38 (2): 187–204.

Giddens, Anthony. 1994. *Beyond Left and Right*. Stanford: Stanford University Press.

Habermas, Jürgen. 1991. *The Structural Transformation of the Public Sphere: An Inquiry into a Category of Bourgeois Society*. Cambridge, MA: MIT Press.

Hoşgör, Evren. 2011. Islamic Capital/Anatolian Tigers: Past and Present. *Middle Eastern Studies* 47 (2): 343–360.

Kadıoğlu, Ayşe. 1999. *Cumhuriyet İradesi Demokrasi Muhakemesi*. İstanbul: Metis Yayınları.

Karpat, Kemal. 2009. *Osmanlı'dan Günümüze Kimlik ve İdeoloji*. İstanbul: Timaş Yayınları.

Kasaba, Reşat, and Sibel Bozdoğan. 2010. *Türkiye'de Modernleşme ve Ulusal Kimlik*. İstanbul: Tarih Vakfı Yurt Yayınları.

Kongar, Emre. 2012. *21. Yüzyılda Türkiye*. İstanbul: Remzi Kitabevi.

Küçükömer, İdris. 2009. *Batılılaşma ve Düzenin Yabancılaşması*. İstanbul: Profil Yayıncılık.

Mannheim, Karl. 2013. *Ideology and Utopia*. London: Routledge

Mardin, Şerif. 1973. Center-Periphery Relations: A Key to Turkish Politics? *Journal of the American Academy of Arts and Sciences* 102 (1): 169–190.

MUSIAD Members' Company Profiles. 1995. Istanbul: MUSIAD.

Öniş, Ziya. 2010. Crises and Transformations in Turkish Political Economy. *Turkish Policy Quarterly* 9 (3): 45–61.

Öniş, Ziya, and Umut Türem. 2001. Business, Globalization and Democracy: A Comparative Analysis of Turkish Business Associations. *Turkish Studies* 2 (2): 94–120.

Özcan, Gül Berna, and Murat Çokgezen. 2003. Limits to Alternative Forms of Capitalization: The Case of Anatolian Holding Companies. *World Development* 31 (12): 261–284.
Parla, Taha. 2006. *Ziya Gökalp, Kemalizm ve Türkiye'de Korporatizm*. İstanbul: İletişim Yayınları.
Polanyi, Karl. 2001. *The Great Transformation*. Boston: Beacon Press.
Sartori, Giovanni. 1976. *Parties and Party Systems: A Framework for Analysis*. Cambridge: Cambridge University Press.
Shils, Edward. 1982. *The Constitution of Society*. Chicago: The University of Chicago Press.
Timur, Taner. 1968. *Türk Devrimi: Tarihi Anlamı ve Felsefi Temeli*. Ankara: Ankara Üniversitesi Siyasal Bilgiler Fakültesi Yayınları.
TUSIAD Members' Company Profiles. 1989. Istanbul: TUSIAD.
Wilson, Francis G. 1980. *The Case for Conservatism*. London: Penguin Books.
Yeşilada, Birol A. 2002. The Virtue Party. *Turkish Studies* 3 (1): 62–81.

Single-Party Governments as a Cause and Coalitions as a Consequence of Coups in Turkey

Ali T. Akarca

1 Introduction

Sixty-seven years have passed since the first fairly contested direct election took place in Turkey. The country was ruled by single-party governments during 38 of these years, by the military during 5, and by coalition and minority governments (henceforth both referred to as coalitions) during 24.[1] As can be seen from Table 1, the average growth rate under the latter two types of government was 2.3 and 1.5 percentage points lower than

Earlier versions of this paper were presented at the 15th International Conference of the Middle East Economic Association held in Doha, Qatar, 22–25 March 2016; at the seminars organized by the Foundation for Political, Economic and Social Research (SETA) in Ankara, Turkey, 7 April 2016, and in Istanbul, Turkey, 25 March 2017; at the International Social Sciences Congress – Turkistan Forum III held at the Hoca Ahmet Yesevi International Turk-Kazak University in Turkistan, Kazakhstan, 26–28 April 2017; at the 5th International Conference in Economics held at the Anadolu University in Eskişehir, Turkey, 11–13 May 2017. I have benefited greatly from the comments made by the audiences at these meetings.

A. T. Akarca (✉)
Department of Economics, University of Illinois at Chicago,
Chicago, IL, USA

A. F. Aysan et al. (eds.), *Turkish Economy*,
https://doi.org/10.1007/978-3-319-70380-0_4

Table 1 Turkish economic performance under different types of government (1950–2015)

Type of government	Average growth rate Real GDP	Per capita real GDP	Average inflation rate GDP deflator
Single-party *(37 years)*	5.6	3.4	18.6
Military *(4.75 years)*	3.4	0.8	26.7
Coalition or minority *(24.25 years)*	4.1	2.1	45.3
Overall average *(66 years)*	4.9	2.7	29.0

Sources: The growth and inflation rates are computed using the data provided by TurkStat for all years except 1948 and 1968. For the latter two years, growth and inflation rates for the GNP, provided by the State Planning Organization, are substituted for the missing GDP-related figures. The GDP series, from which growth and inflation rates are obtained, is 1968-based for years prior to 1968, 1987-based for years between 1969 and 1998, and 1998-based for years after 1999. The new 2009-based GDP series released by TurkStat on December 12, 2016, is not used because it goes back only as far as 1998, and for the period after 2010 it differs from the old series substantially, in not only level but growth as well.

Notes: Figures reported are in percentage points and are obtained from annual data, as quarterly data are available only for the recent years. In computing the averages, years in which more than one type of government prevailed are given a weight of 0.25, 0.50, or 0.75 depending on whether the regime in question ruled one, two, or three quarters. A quarter is assumed to be under the type of government that prevailed during the majority of that period.

If the first and later terms of single-party governments were considered separately, the three entries in their rows would be 7.7, 5.5, and 16.3 for the former and 3.9, 1.9, and 20.4 for the latter, respectively. If the coalition governments ruling during 1965, 1975–1977, the second half of 1996 and the first half of 1997, which essentially included only right-wing parties, were left out, the coalition row would read 3.5, 1.6, and 47.7.

under single-party governments, and the average inflation rate was 8.1 and 26.7 percentage points higher, respectively.[2] The notes to the table indicate that the poor economic performance under coalition governments was even worse when they involved parties from opposite ends of the political spectrum. The growth rate gap between single-party and coalition governments then rises to 2.1 points and the inflation rate gap to 29.1 points. Had the average growth rate of per capita real GDP during the 1950–2015 period been the same as the rate achieved under single-party governments, Turkey's per capita real income today would be

Table 2 Economic performance in Turkey during various periods (1950–2015)

Period	Average growth rate		Average inflation rate
	Real GDP	Per capita real GDP	GDP deflator
1950.Q3 – 1960.Q2	6.8	3.9	10.0
1960.Q3 – 1965.Q3	4.1	1.8	4.5
1965.Q4 – 1971.Q1	5.9	3.2	7.0
1971.Q2 – 1983.Q4	4.1	1.7	34.1
1984.Q1 – 1991.Q4	5.0	2.7	54.1
1992.Q1 – 2002.Q4	3.4	1.9	68.5
2003.Q1 – 2015.Q4	4.7	3.4	9.1
Overall Average	4.9		29.0

Sources: Same as in Table 1
Notes: Periods under a single-party rule are shaded darker. Notes to Table 1 apply here as well

1.6 times higher.[3] Table 2 shows that the picture emerging from Table 1 is not restricted to particular periods but was consistently the case throughout. Each era under military and coalition governments was preceded and succeeded by periods of single-party rule, which had far better economic outcomes.

If the coalitions had merely reflected genuine diversity in the public opinion and been negotiated accordingly, their economic performance would probably not have been as bad, or their poorness could be justified as a price paid for democracy. However, as will be argued in this paper, such governments, in particular those involving ideologically incompatible parties, were created artificially by military interventions, often with the participation of the judiciary, to prevent conservative parties from gaining full power. All of the successful *coups d'état* (or coups) were conducted against such parties, as they are viewed by the military and the bureaucratic establishment in general as a threat to the secular and Western orientation of the country.[4] The religious-right and economic-right voters in Turkey show a tendency to unite under one roof and most of the time have more than sufficient public support to form a single-party government. After each time they came to power alone, however, their government was toppled and their party was split up by military coups. What moved the armed forces and the bureaucracy in that direction was also the fear of losing their influence and guardianship roles. As Acemoğlu and Robinson (2006) point out, the driving force behind transitions from democracy to non-democracy is the realization by the elites that their *de facto* power is temporary. Before it slips away, they intervene to change political institutions towards those that give them more *de jure* power. Political fragmentations created by coups were the main cause of coalition governments, and single-party governments formed by united conservatives were the main reason behind the coups.

Although economic crises, social unrest, political instability, and, ironically, threats to democracy are often cited in the literature as causes of coups, numerous memoirs written and interviews given by Turkish junta leaders reveal that the planning for coups began years before they took place, when the economy was performing well and there were no signs of social strife, political instability, or authoritarianism. It is true that coups often overlapped with the aforementioned events, but only because juntas timed them that way to make them more justifiable to the public and international community. Acemoğlu and Robinson (2006) show that opponents of democracy are more likely to attempt coups at times of political or economic crises, when the balance of *de facto* power temporarily tilts in their favor. In fact, in several instances street demonstrations were organized by the coup plotters themselves. Again, through the interviews and memoirs of junta leaders, we know that on some occasions the dates of the coups were moved back for fear of snap elections being called. At least in one instance, a planned coup was postponed because the conditions were not ripe yet. We also know that economic crises far worse than those experienced prior to the coups and the crises while non-conservative parties were in power have failed to trigger military interventions. In fact, if poor economic performance was really the cause of coups, they would occur more frequently while a coalition government was ruling, but that was not the case, as pointed out earlier. Thus, a bad economy facilitates a coup but does not cause it.

The purpose of this paper is to provide evidence to support the foregoing assertions. In the next section this will be done through a study of the historical record, and in the section following that through statistical analyses of the 1950–2015 period. Then in the last section, the conclusions reached will be summarized. However, three things should be set straight right from the beginning. First, the paper's claim is not that coups are the only way coalition governments occur, but that that was the way they occurred in Turkey and that without coups coalition governments would be less frequent. The economic voting literature indicates that losses typically suffered by ruling parties as a result of strategic voting to create checks and balances against them and due to depreciation in their political capital over their tenure usually cannot be offset by incumbency advantage unless economic performance is exceptionally good or a political realignment takes place in their favor.[5] As indicated in the notes to Table 1, the economic performance of single-party governments in Turkey deteriorates after the first term. Thus, it would not be unreasonable to expect the vote share of the ruling party to decline eventually to a level forcing it either to lose power or to form a coalition government. However, the coup plotters in Turkey either did not realize this or did not have the patience to wait for it. Second, nor is it claimed that economic conditions cannot cause coups. They very well may have in other countries, but in the Turkish case they only affected the timing of coups.[6] Third, it is not argued that all coups in Turkey were motivated by a desire to keep the power of the conservative bloc under control. Effective use of coups as a tool to control the power of conservative incumbents encouraged other types of coups. The

1960 takeover, organized by a small number of low-ranking officers and carried out quite easily, was particularly inspiring in this regard. The leaders of that coup prepared the ground for prospective coups also by implicitly "legitimizing" coups as a tool for removing "bad" governments, in the preamble of the 1961 constitution.[7] Also, military and judicial interventions undermined the parliament and shifted the goal of political competition from gaining seats in the parliament to controlling the state institutions at the center directly. Marginal groups, with no hopes of achieving power through elections, tried to obtain it with the help of armed forces or the courts.[8] Some of these groups went so far as to infiltrate the military, the police, the judiciary, and other state institutions clandestinely, with the intention of gradually taking them over and controlling the state through them, bypassing the parliament.[9] Furthermore, because after each coup officers who were part of the junta that effected it got promoted while the remaining officers were either left behind or forced into retirement, the coups encouraged the formation of competing juntas in the armed forces, which eventually led to more coups.[10] Although the latter kind of coups caused a lot of damage through the disruptions and instability they created, they were not a cause of coalitions because their goal was not to dilute the power of the main conservative party but to take power themselves permanently and replace the old order with a totally undemocratic one. They were not successful in the first place. We will refer to the coups aimed at checking the power of the conservative bloc as Type 1 and to coups carried out by marginal groups, motivated by the early successes of Type 1 coups, aimed at grabbing power permanently as Type 2.[11] The former believes in democracy but a guided one, whereas the latter rejects any type of democracy.

2 Historical Background

The Turkish electorate exhibits a tendency to gather in four camps: left-statist, right-conservative, Turkish-nationalist, and Kurdish-nationalist parties. At present, the Republican People's Party (CHP), the Justice and Development Party (AK Party or AKP), the Nationalist Action Party (MHP), and the People's Democracy Party (HDP) represent these groups, respectively.[12] Before 1946, only the first group was allowed to organize formally, except in the period 1924–1925 and 1930 when the Progressive Republican Party (TCF) and the Liberal Republican Party (SCF), representing the second group, were permitted for about six and three months, respectively. After 1946, the second and third and after 1995 the fourth entered the picture formally.

The CHP is the party that founded the republic in 1923 and shaped many of its institutions, most of which were inherited from the Ottoman Empire. The party itself has its roots in the Union and Progress Party (Ittihat ve Terakki Fırkası), which ruled the empire during its final years. Consequently, the CHP can be thought of as the establishment or the center, representing the elites. The party accelerated the modernizing and westernizing reforms, many of which began in earnest at the end of the eighteenth century in Ottoman times to stem constant defeats against Western powers. Most significant of these was the secularization of the state. These reforms were instituted in a heavy-handed, top-down, and revolutionary fashion and aimed at redesigning not only the political system but also society at large. Consequently, they generated strong resistance.[13] To counter that, it was felt necessary to establish rigid centralization in both the political and economic spheres and equip the bureaucracy with increasingly more authoritarian powers and immunity. In particular, the military and the judiciary were appointed the enforcers and guardians of the reforms and the new regime. Members of these institutions were granted even greater powers and privileges.[14] This led to sharp divisions not only between the center and the periphery but also between different segments of the center. Consequently, for more than two decades all opposition parties were banned, including those supporting modernization but through evolutionary and democratic means and a free market economy. The center not only alienated the periphery, but it also began to treat it as suspect. For that reason and because modernity was not fully understood and its definition not revised with the changing times, when modernity began to be achieved, it was viewed by the ruling elites as counterrevolutionary. Any attempt to modernize the modernizing methods was considered reactionary. Ironically, the one-time reformers became the greatest obstacle to carrying out the changes that were needed for further political and economic progress. Of course, the reluctance of the bureaucratic elites to give up their power and privileges was also a factor motivating them to view the old reforms as not needing any fine-tuning and needing unending protection. With the military and the judiciary on their side, these elites continued to wield enormous power, even after opposition parties were permitted once again and gained power in 1950.[15] Until recently, such governments had to restrict themselves to managing the economy and public order and defer consequential decisions to the military, even those not involving defense and security. Many of their decisions were nullified by the courts or not implemented by the bureaucracy. Politics was viewed by the elites as an obstacle to efficient administration. Election outcomes were belittled as choices of an ignorant and gullible public. Full democracy was considered a threat to the republic, and pluralism a road leading to the partition of the country. Successful businessmen in general were viewed as looters of the state and exploiters of the uneducated public and thus needed to be restrained by the bureaucracy or balanced by state enterprises. Any attempt by conservative governments to push the boundaries placed on them, even the possibility of its occurring, faced a coup or the threat of a coup. This in essence was the military/judiciary tutelage or guardianship (*vesayet*) system, as it started to be called in Turkey.[16] Acemoğlu and Robinson (2008) refer to such regimes, in which elites respond to attempts to reduce their *de jure* power in some political institutions by offsetting increases in their *de facto* power and by raising their *de jure* powers in other institutions, as captured democracies.

The right-conservative movement, which essentially represents the grievances and worldview of those looked down upon and ostracized by the center for many years, is the largest of the four political tendencies. Under normal circumstances, it is unified and enjoys more than sufficient support from the public to form a single-party government. However, each time it took office, or got close to doing so, it was fragmented by interventions from outside the political system such as coups by the military and party closures by the judiciary. Between 1950 and 2016, five such (Type 1) coups took place (Table 3).[17] Four of these succeeded. In the 1960 and 1980 coups, the military took over, but briefly. In the former, the incumbent party and in the latter all of the parties, including the CHP, were banned. In the one in 1971, the military forced the parliament

Table 3 Turkish governments before and after Type 1 coups

	Government			
Coup	Immediately before coup	Immediately after coup	Elections	Following postcoup general elections
May 27, 1960	**DP**	Military	1961	CHP + **AP**
				CHP + **YTP** + CKMP
				CHP (minority)
				AP + **YTP** + CKMP + MP
			1965	**AP**
			1969	**AP**
March 12, 1971	**AP**	CHP + **AP** + MGP	1973	CHP + **MSP**
		AP + CGP		**AP** + **MSP** + CGP + MHP
			1977	**AP** + **MSP** + MHP
				CHP +CGP + **DP2** + Ind.
				AP (minority)
September 12, 1980	**AP**	Military	1983	**ANAP**
			1987	**ANAP**
			1991	**DYP** + SHP/CHP
			1995	**ANAP** + **DYP**
				RP + **DYP**
February 28, 1997	**RP** + **DYP**	**ANAP** + DSP + **DTP**	1999	DSP + MHP + **ANAP**
		DSP (minority)	2002	**AKP**
April 27, 2007	**AKP**	**AKP**	2007	**AKP**
			2011	**AKP**
			2015 (JUN)	**AKP**
			2015 (NOV)	**AKP**

Sources: Tuncer (2002, 2007, 2011b, 2012b), Tuncer et al. (2003, 2015), and Tuncer and Tuncer (2016)

Notes: For party names represented by the acronyms see the appendix. The right-conservative parties are in bold and underlined. The largest coalition partner is listed first. The governments are listed in chronological order. Governments that failed to receive a vote of confidence are ignored

under threat of takeover to change the composition of the government. In the 1997 case known as the postmodern coup, using a similar threat, they forced the prime minister to resign. To avoid the formation of a new government under the same incumbent parties, one of them was split up with the help of the president, who was the former leader of that party. The other incumbent party and its leader were banned by the Constitutional

Court for violating the secularism clause of the constitution. Although an attempt was made by the military also in 2007 to bring down the conservative government, the incumbent party thwarted it by cleverly calling a snap election and winning it handily.

Certain patterns can be observed from Table 3. All of the five coups mentioned took place when right-conservative parties were in power. Only one party ruled in all of them, except the one in 1997, when two parties were in a coalition but both were from the right-conservative side. A chain of coalition governments followed each successful coup immediately, except the one in 1980, when coalitions appeared after a delay for reasons that will be explained below. In each instance, however, the conservative parties eventually got together again, which in turn led to another coup and then another period of coalitions.

The postcoup coalitions always included a statist party. The pieces of the fragmented conservative parties were not allowed to form a government by themselves but were forced to partner with a statist party so that they could be controlled more easily than through the bureaucracy alone.[18] Even though in 1961 the right-wing Justice Party (AP), the New Turkey Party (YTP), and the Republican Peasant's Nation Party (CKMP), which captured the votes of the Democrat Party (DP) ousted by the 1960 coup, were willing and able to form a government, the military junta forced a CHP-AP coalition instead. Nevertheless, the planned coalition was formed later, shortly before the next general election in 1965, which brought the AP to power alone. When the 12 March 1971 coup toppled the AP government, leaders of the junta demanded a cabinet composed of AP, CHP, and National Reliance Party (MGP) deputies and a number of unelected technocrats, headed by a prime minister from the CHP.[19] The latter two parties were from the leftist-statist camp. To avoid the AP from coming to power again, the leader of an Islamist party that had been banned only a year earlier, shortly after its establishment, was invited by the generals to return from self-exile abroad to establish a similar party with the aim of splitting the AP votes. That party, named the National Salvation Party (MSP), was encouraged to form and did form a coalition government with the CHP after the 1973 election, the first one following the coup. However, as will be discussed in what follows, when the Welfare Party (RP), which succeeded the MSP and shared with it the very same leadership, formed a coalition government in 1996 but this time with the conservative True Path Party (DYP), it was toppled by the military within a year. To erect yet another barrier in the AP's path to power, the 1971 junta engineered also the separation of a faction from the party by forcing the party leadership, under threat of another coup, to table a proposal granting amnesty to the banned leaders of the DP. Those opposed to the move formed the short-lived Democratic Party (DP2). This time it took two legislative terms for the AP to acquire the power alone, but it was toppled once more in less than a year by the 1980 coup.

By 1980, the military came to the realization that fragmenting conservative parties was futile and had harmful side effects, and it changed tactics. They decided to control the right-conservative bloc directly by establishing their own conservative party headed by a retired general they trusted. To make the party attractive also to voters from the Turkish-nationalist segment, they gave it a nationalistic slant by naming it the Nationalistic Democracy Party (MDP). Because the leader of the CHP had taken strong stands against both the 1971 and 1980 coups, it was felt necessary to establish a new left-statist party as well.[20] That party was named the Populist Party (HP2).[21] To give the MDP and HP2 a head start, the junta excluded from the 1983 election all parties that were continuations of the previous parties. However, the outcome of the election was a total shock for the military. The winner turned out to be not the MDP as planned but the conservative Motherland Party (ANAP), the only party among the three permitted to participate in the election that was not formed by the junta. The ANAP was allowed to enter the election to give it the appearance of a true contest and to avoid the MDP from dominating Turkish politics. The party was not supposed to win the 1983 election, just as the DP was not supposed to win the 1950 election. The MDP could not last even until the next parliamentary election. Although the ANAP was able to form a single-party government in 1983, its support dropped significantly by the entry of other parties that had been excluded from the 1983 election. The party was barely able to hold on to power for another term by calling the 1987 election before other parties could organize, by capturing some of those who had left the MDP, and by benefiting from its incumbency advantage and the success of its market-oriented reforms. In the 1989 local elections, the party's vote share dropped below that of the True Path Party (DYP), a conservative party formed by the leadership of the defunct AP. After the 1991 parliamentary election the third wave of coalition governments began.

One of those governments, formed by two conservative parties, the DYP and the Welfare Party (RP), was forced by the military to give up power in 1997. It was replaced by another coalition government formed by the conservative ANAP and the Democrat Turkey Party (DTP), and the left-statist Democratic Left Party (DSP). As mentioned earlier, the DTP was the party that was splintered from the DYP in 1997. It took not the next election but the one after that in 2002 for a right-conservative party (AK Party) to form a single-party government again. The AK Party has managed to hold on to power ever since. A coup was attempted in 2007 to change that but, as mentioned earlier, it failed. Ironically, the 2007 coup, rather than fragmenting, actually facilitated the consolidation of right-conservative votes under the AK Party. That happened because the military inadvertently discredited the ANAP and the DYP in the eyes of their supporters by making them complicit in that coup. To stop the AK Party from electing its candidate as president, the military organized a series of mass protest rallies against the party, and on April 27, 2007 posted on the armed forces web page a thinly veiled threat to take over if they did. A highly controversial decision was announced by the Constitutional Court two days later requiring participation of two-thirds of the deputies in the first round of the presidential balloting in the parliament, a rule not practiced in any of the earlier presidential elections. This took away the AK Party's ability to elect its candidate without the aid of other parties. When the ANAP and DYP decided not to participate in the presidential balloting so that the quorum required by the Constitutional Court could not be reached, they alienated their supporters, who switched their allegiances to the AK Party, which stood firm against the military and later took measures to dismantle the military tutelage system. The AK Party's disavowal of political Islam no doubt facilitated this consolidation.

The failures of the 2007 coup attempt and a later attempt by the Constitutional Court to close the AK Party, the constitutional changes instituted in their aftermath, and more importantly the changes over time in the attitudes of various segments of society (including the members of the military and the judiciary) toward coups, as a result of globalization, urbanization, the advent of the Internet, the ending of the state monopoly on television and radio, major improvements in the transportation and telecommunication systems, and the market-oriented reforms instituted since early eighties brought the guardianship system to an end. Although a coup was attempted on July 15, 2016 by a religious order to fill the void created, the way it was suppressed with the involvement of the political parties (including the opposition), media, police, majority of the armed forces, and especially the public reinforces this view. In fact, this attempt, which nearly succeeded, made even those who supported the guardianship come to the realization that such a system could easily change hands and be turned against them. Furthermore, this incident created an opportunity for politicians to initiate a number of legal measures to establish supremacy of the elected officials over those appointed and establish effective civilian control over the military. However, at this point it is not absolutely certain that the vacuum created by dismantling of the military guardianship system is going to be filled by institutions of a liberal democracy and not by another guardianship.

3 Empirical Evidence

Vote shares of the four political tendencies in 31 parliamentary and local administration elections (National Assembly general and by-elections, Senate elections, and Provincial Council elections) held between 1950 and 2015 are presented in Table 4. Also given in the table are the shares of the largest parties in each group. The aggregate vote share of the latter is shown in Fig. 1. There, one can see at a glance the political fragmentation and reconsolidation process described in the previous section. The aggregate vote share in question is almost 100 per cent in the 1950s but begins to decline after the first coup. The downward trend continues in a stepwise fashion until the mid-1990s. Noticeable drops occur after the 1960, 1971, and 1980 coups. Each time, the series recovers somewhat but gets pulled down to an even lower level by the next coup. Then a reconsolidation process begins in 1994, which continues until 2011.

Table 4 Major political tendencies in Turkey and their vote shares

Election date	Election type	Provinces covered by the election	Right-conservative		Left-statist		Turkish-nationalist		Kurdish-nationalist	
			Largest party	All parties	Largest party	All parties	Largest party	All parties	Largest party	All parties
May 14, 1950	A	63 of 63	55.22	55.22	39.59	39.59	4.63	4.63	0.00	0.00
Sep. 16, 1951	B	17 of 63	52.73	52.73	38.68	38.68	8.01	8.01	0.00	0.00
May 2, 1954	A	64 of 64	58.42	58.49	35.11	35.11	5.28	5.28	0.00	0.00
Oct. 27, 1957	A	67 of 67	48.62	52.10	41.35	41.35	6.53	6.53	0.00	0.00
Oct. 15, 1961	A	67 of 67	34.79	48.52	36.74	36.74	13.96	13.96	0.00	0.00
Nov. 17, 1963	L	67 of 67	45.46	51.97	36.20	36.60	3.10	6.19	0.00	0.00
Jun. 7, 1964	S	26 of 67	50.28	53.78	40.85	40.85	3.03	3.03	0.00	0.00
Oct. 10, 1965	A	67 of 67	52.87	56.60	28.75	31.72	6.26	8.50	0.00	0.00
Jun. 7, 1966	S + B	24 of 67	56.48	58.76	29.77	33.72	5.17	7.07	0.00	0.00
Jun. 2, 1968	L	67 of 67	49.06	49.78	27.90	38.88	3.50	4.50	0.00	0.00
Oct. 12, 1969	A	67 of 67	46.53	48.71	27.36	39.42	3.22	6.25	0.00	0.00

(continued)

Table 4 (continued)

Election date	Election type	Provinces covered by the election	Right-conservative Largest party	Right-conservative All parties	Left-statist Largest party	Left-statist All parties	Turkish-nationalist Largest party	Turkish-nationalist All parties	Kurdish-nationalist Largest party	Kurdish-nationalist All parties
Oct. 14, 1973	A	67 of 67	29.82	53.51	33.30	39.70	3.38	3.96	0.00	0.00
Oct. 12, 1975	S + B	27 of 67	41.34	52.94	43.32	43.85	3.12	3.12	0.00	0.00
Jun. 5, 1977	A	67 of 67	36.88	47.29	41.38	43.78	6.45	6.45	0.00	0.00
Oct. 14, 1979	S + B	29 of 67	47.84	57.27	29.22	35.21	6.44	6.44	0.00	0.00
Nov. 6, 1983	A	67 of 67	45.14	68.41	30.46	30.46	0.00	0.00	0.00	0.00
Sep. 28, 1986	B	10 of 67	32.12	63.53	22.74	32.53	2.20	2.20	0.00	0.00
Nov. 29, 1987	A	67 of 67	36.31	62.61	24.74	33.27	2.93	2.93	0.00	0.00
Mar. 26, 1989	L	71 of 71	25.13	56.73	28.69	37.72	4.14	4.14	0.00	0.00
Oct. 20, 1991	A	74 of 74	27.03	67.92	20.75	31.50	0.00	0.00	0.00	0.00
Mar. 27, 1994	L	76 of 76	21.44	61.53	13.57	26.97	7.97	9.23	0.00	0.00
Dec. 24, 1995	A	79 of 79	21.38	60.21	14.64	25.35	8.19	8.19	4.17	4.17
Apr. 18, 1999	A	80 of 80	15.41	41.22	22.19	30.90	17.98	19.45	4.75	4.75

(continued)

Table 4 (continued)

Election date	Election type	Provinces covered by the election	Right-conservative		Left-statist		Turkish-nationalist		Kurdish-nationalist	
			Largest party	All parties	Largest party	All parties	Largest party	All parties	Largest party	All parties
Nov. 3, 2002	A	81 of 81	34.28	51.44	19.39	29.01	8.36	9.38	6.22	6.22
Mar. 28, 2004	L	81 of 81	41.67	58.16	18.23	23.20	10.45	11.61	5.15	5.15
Jul. 22, 2007	A	81 of 81	46.58	54.34	20.88	23.92	14.27	14.27	3.84	3.84
Mar. 29, 2009	L	81 of 81	38.39	48.19	23.08	25.93	15.97	18.33	5.70	5.70
Jun. 12, 2011	A	81 of 81	49.83	52.52	25.98	26.23	13.01	13.76	5.67	5.67
Mar. 30, 2014	L	81 of 81	43.40	46.90	25.62	25.95	17.62	19.19	6.53	6.53
Jun. 7, 2015	A	81 of 81	40.87	43.09	24.95	25.14	16.29	16.29	13.12	13.12
Nov. 1, 2015	A	81 of 81	49.50	50.32	25.32	25.39	11.90	12.43	10.76	10.76

Sources: The dates, types, and coverage of elections are taken from Tuncer (2002, 2007, 2009, 2010, 2011a, b, 2012a, b), Tuncer and Kasapbaş (2004), Tuncer et al. (2003, 2014, 2015), and Tuncer and Tuncer (2016)

Vote shares in parliamentary elections were computed by the author using the data provided by Tuncer (2010) for the 1950 election, by Tuncer (2011a) for the 1954 election, by Tuncer (2012a) for the 1957 election, by Tuncer (2012b) for the 1961 election, by Tuncer (2002) for elections between 1965 and 1999 (including by elections), by Tuncer et al. (2003) for the 2002 election, by Tuncer (2007) for the 2007 election, by Tuncer (2011b) for the 2011 election, by Tuncer et al.

(*continued*)

Table 4 (continued)

(2015) for the June 2015 election, and by Tuncer and Tuncer (2016) for the November 2015 election. In aggregating the Grand National Assembly by-elections and Senate elections held in 1975 and 1979, the province-level vote data provided by the Turkish Institute of Statistics (TurkStat) are also utilized. It should be noted that for 1950, 1954, 1957, and 1961 the election data in Tuncer (2002) differ slightly from those given in Tuncer (2010, 2011a, 2012a, b). Here the latter are used as they are based on more detailed and more recent studies

Vote shares in local administration elections are obtained from Tuncer and Kasapbaş (2004) for the 2004 election, from Tuncer (2009) for the 2009 election, and Tuncer et al. (2014) for the 2014 election. The source of data for all other local administrations elections is TurkStat. The figures given for all elections, except the one in 2014, are for provincial general councils. For the 2014 election, the sum of the votes cast for district municipal councils in 30 provinces officially classified as metropolises and for provincial general councils in the remaining 51 provinces is used

Notes: Only parties that received more than one per cent of the vote in at least one election and parties that split from them are considered. For parties included in each category, and the largest party in each category, see the appendix

The following symbols are used to indicate the type of election:

A: National Assembly general election

B: National Assembly by-election

S: Senate election

L: Local administration election (election for provincial councils until 2014 and election for district municipal councils in 30 provinces officially classified as metropolises and for provincial general councils in the remaining 51 provinces in 2014)

S+B: Senate election plus National Assembly by-election (in provinces where no Senate election was held simultaneously)

In instances where different types of elections are held simultaneously, the priority for inclusion in the sample was given first to National Assembly general elections, then to local elections, then to Senate elections, and last to by-elections. The Senate and by-elections were given lower priorities because, unlike the National Assembly general elections and local elections, they did not cover the whole country. The Senate elections involved only a third of the provinces and only a third of the seats in the Senate that were subject to election. The coverage of by-elections was even lower, about 15–27 per cent of the provinces when they did not coincide with a Senate election. When the Senate and by-elections were held simultaneously, their results were aggregated to increase the coverage of the country. In such aggregations, for provinces where the two elections overlapped, the outcome of the Senate election is considered. Local administration elections held in 1977 and 1984 only a few months after the 1977 and 1983 parliamentary elections, respectively, are ignored

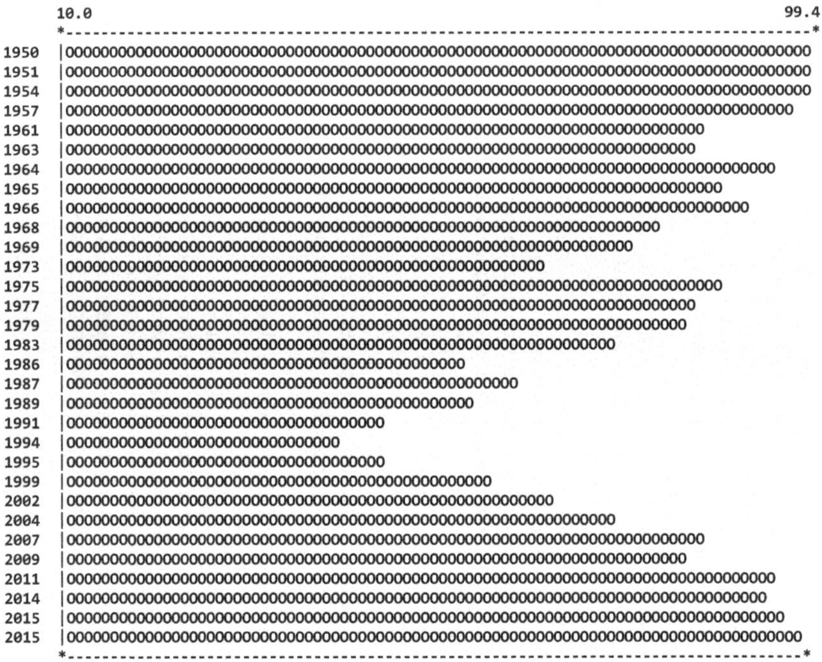

Fig. 1 Aggregate vote share of largest parties in each of the four political tendencies (Source: Table 4)

In Fig. 2, the vote share of the largest right-conservative party is plotted separately. The similarity of the patterns in Figs. 1 and 2 shows that the fragmentation in the right-conservative segment was the main source of the overall fragmentation. The greater prominence of the postcoup vote drops in Fig. 2 makes this even clearer. However, the two figures differ slightly. In the latter, the reconsolidation is delayed by 5 years and the vote share level reached after 2011 is still slightly less than the peaks reached in the 1950s and the 1960s. The first is due to the 1997 coup and the second to vote shifts towards the Turkish-nationalist MHP as a reaction to the entry of a Kurdish-nationalist party into the political scene in 1995.[22] Most of the increase in the MHP's vote share after 1995 came from the CHP, but a portion was from the right-conservative parties.

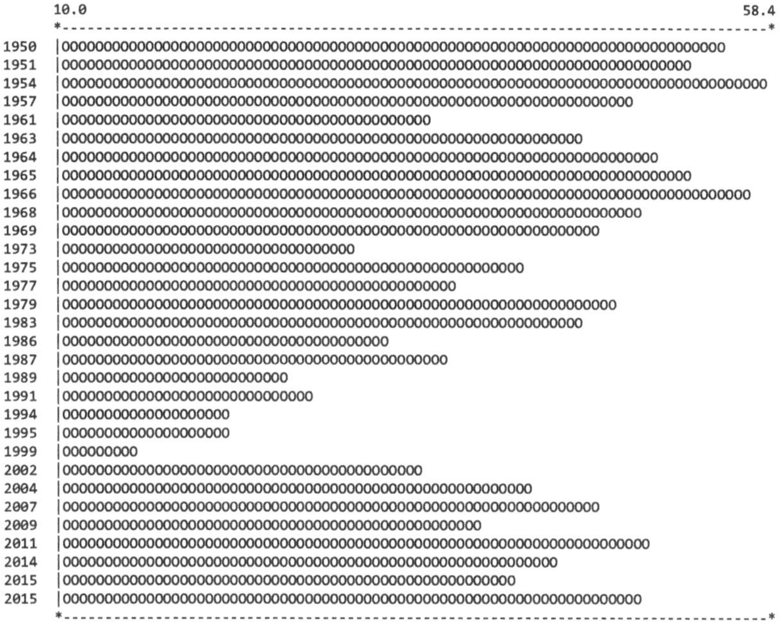

Fig. 2 Vote share of largest right-conservative party (Source: Table 4)

Another thing one can gather from Fig. 2 and Table 4 is the tendency of right-conservative voters to make up about half of the electorate. Only in the 1999 and June 2015 elections did that segment's aggregate vote share not exceed 47 per cent, a level probably sufficient to capture the majority of seats in the parliament. In the same table and the figure, one can observe also the tendency of right-conservative voters to unite under one roof. The DP surpassed the 50 per cent vote share in 1950 and 1954 and came very close to it in 1957. After it was toppled by the military in 1960, its leader executed, members of parliament imprisoned, and the party banned, its votes got scattered in 1961. However, in the Senate election held in 1964 and in the parliamentary general election held in 1965, the vote share of the AP which emerged as the successor to the DP exceeded 50 per cent. The party's share was only slightly less than that in 1969, but following the military intervention in 1971, the right-wing vote was split again. This time it took until the 1979 Senate election for the AP to come close to the 50 per cent vote share. Then another military coup in 1980 fragmented the conservative segment once more. Although the right-wing ANAP received 45 per cent of the vote in 1983, after the ban on other parties and political leaders was lifted in a referendum in 1987, the fragmentation that resulted was even greater than the ones experienced previously. As mentioned earlier, the 1997 intervention prolonged the fragmentation but, unlike the previous interventions, did not increase it significantly. It took until 2011 for right-conservative voters to gather in a single party, the AK Party. From a short-run perspective the AK Party may appear as an anomaly, but it is really a reincarnation of the broad coalition represented by the DP in the 1950s and the AP in the second half of the 1960s and late 1970s. However, the realignments that began immediately and took 3 and 6 years respectively after the 1960 and 1971 coups, was delayed by almost two decades after the 1980 coup and took 9 years to complete. In addition to the greater magnitude of the fragmentation, the closeness of the vote shares of the conservative parties that emerged after the latter coup was a factor in delaying the consolidation process. The address at which conservative voters can viably gather began to clarify only after 2002, when the AK Party outdistanced other conservative parties. Even after that date, the realignment occurred at a much slower pace than the previous episodes. Just as the AP did in 1961, the AK Party received slightly less than 35 per cent of the vote in 2002, in the first election in which it was on the ballot. However, unlike the AP, which reached 50 per cent before the end of its first term in office, it took the AK Party not the next general election but the one after that held in 2011 to achieve that level.

To measure political fragmentation more precisely, political scientists often use an index devised by Laakso and Taagepera (1979) that aims to measure the effective number of political parties. This index is really the reciprocal of the well-known Herfindahl index of industrial concentration used by economists but applied to the vote shares of parties rather than the market shares of companies. Herfindahl's index sums the squared shares and varies between zero and one. Its reciprocal, on the other hand, can vary between one and infinity and makes a more suitable dependent variable for regression analysis. It is also easier to interpret. The effective number of parties in each political segment and in the country as a whole is reported in Table 5. The one

Table 5 Political fragmentation and preelection economic conditions

		Effective number of parties					Economy	
Election date	Type of election	Right-conservative	Left-statist	Turkish-nationalist	Kurdish-nationalist	All	Growth rate	Inflation rate
May. 14, 1950	A	1.00	1.00	1.00	0.00	2.13	3.5	−0.2
Sep. 16, 1951	B	1.00	1.00	1.00	0.00	2.28	9.2	4.3
May 2, 1954	A	1.00	1.00	1.00	0.00	2.11	4.8	4.9
Oct. 27, 1957	A	1.14	1.00	1.00	0.00	2.42	3.6	20.3
Oct. 15, 1961	A	1.68	1.00	1.00	0.00	3.34	−0.7	4.2
Nov. 17, 1963	L	1.28	1.02	2.00	0.00	2.61	6.8	5.7
Jun. 7, 1964	S	1.14	1.00	1.00	0.00	2.26	4.2	4.1
Oct. 10, 1965	A	1.14	1.20	1.63	0.00	2.54	0.1	4.2
Jun. 7, 1966	S + B	1.08	1.26	1.65	0.00	2.40	4.6	5.2
Jun. 2, 1968	L	1.03	1.82	1.53	0.00	2.67	3.0	5.3
Oct. 12, 1969	A	1.09	1.93	2.00	0.00	2.97	2.1	6.5
Oct. 14, 1973	A	2.45	1.39	1.33	0.00	4.07	1.7	19.2

(continued)

Table 5 (continued)

Election date	Type of election	Effective number of parties					Economy	
		Right-conservative	Left-statist	Turkish-nationalist	Kurdish-nationalist	All	Growth rate	Inflation rate
Oct. 12, 1975	S + B	1.56	1.02	1.00	0.00	2.71	4.4	21.0
Jun. 5, 1977	A	1.56	1.12	1.00	0.00	2.98	4.7	19.4
Oct. 14, 1979	S + B	1.38	1.44	1.00	0.00	2.98	−2.2	68.4
Nov. 6, 1983	A	1.81	1.00	0.00	0.00	2.79	2.0	26.8
Sep. 28, 1986	B	2.49	1.79	1.00	0.00	4.36	3.9	40.3
Nov. 29, 1987	A	2.26	1.62	1.00	0.00	4.02	7.1	33.6
Mar. 26, 1989	L	2.68	1.57	1.00	0.00	4.57	−2.5	69.2
Oct. 20, 1991	A	2.90	1.82	0.00	0.00	4.62	1.5	55.2
Mar. 27, 1994	L	2.99	2.57	1.31	0.00	5.92	6.4	66.1
Dec. 24, 1995	A	2.99	1.95	1.00	1.00	5.90	5.6	87.2
Apr. 18, 1999	A	3.05	1.68	1.16	1.00	6.30	−1.8	68.4
Nov. 3, 2002	A	2.04	1.95	1.24	1.00	5.02	−0.6	46.4

(*continued*)

Table 5 (continued)

		Effective number of parties					Economy	
Election date	Type of election	Right-conservative	Left-statist	Turkish-nationalist	Kurdish-nationalist	All	Growth rate	Inflation rate
Mar. 28, 2004	L	1.82	1.57	1.22	1.00	4.12	4.5	18.8
July 22, 2007	A	1.34	1.29	1.00	1.00	3.24	4.6	9.0
Mar. 29, 2009	L	1.53	1.24	1.29	1.00	4.10	-5.6	13.3
June 12, 2011	A	1.11	1.02	1.11	1.00	2.87	7.3	7.6
Mar. 30, 2014	L	1.16	1.03	1.18	1.00	3.35	3.5	7.1
June 7, 2015	A	1.11	1.02	1.00	1.00	3.49	1.6	7.4
Nov. 1, 2015	A	1.03	1.01	1.09	1.00	2.92	2.2	7.2

Sources: Effective number of parties was computed by the author using the formula given in earlier notes and the data from the sources given in Table 4. The growth and inflation rates were computed by the author, as explained in earlier notes, using the data provided by TurkStat for all years except 1948 and 1968. For the latter two years, the rates of change in real GNP and the GNP price deflator, provided by the State Planning Organization of Turkey, are substituted for the missing growth rate figures on real GDP and the GDP price deflator. Population growth rates, provided by TurkStat, are utilized to transform real GNP growth into growth in per capita real GNP. The Turkstat GDP series, from which the growth rates are obtained, is 1987-based for the years prior to 1998 and 1998-based for the years after 1999. The new 2009-based GDP series released by TurkStat on December 12, 2016, is not used because it goes back only as far as 1998, and for the period after 2010 it differs from the old series substantially, in not only level but growth as well

Notes: See the Table 4 notes for the symbols used to indicate the type of election and the appendix table for the parties included in each political branch

(continued)

Table 5 (continued)

Effective number of parties in political branch j in year t (Y_{jt}) is computed according to the definition suggested by Laakso and Taagepera (1979):

$$Y_{jt} = 1 / \sum_{k=1}^{I_t} {s_{kjt}}^2$$

where s_{kjt} stands for the proportion of votes the kth party received within political branch j in the election held in year t, and I_t is the number of parties in that branch at that time.

The growth rate (g_t) is taken as the growth rate of per capita real GDP during the four-quarter period preceding the election. The latter is obtained by adjusting the growth rate of real GDP during the four-quarter period before the election with the annual growth rate of the population during the year of the election if the election was held in the second half of the year and during the year before if the election was held in the first half of the year. The quarter of the election is included in the four-quarter period if the election was held in the second half of the quarter, and not if otherwise

For the period prior to 1989 when quarterly data were not available, g_t is computed as follows:

$$g_t = m\,G_t + (1 - m)\,G_{t-1}$$

where G_t and G_{t-1} are the annual growth rates for the year in which the election was held and the one prior to that

$m = 0.00$ if the election was held between January 1 and February 14

$m = 0.25$ if the election was held between February 15 and May 15

$m = 0.50$ if the election was held between May 16 and August 15

$m = 0.75$ if the election was held between August 16 and November 15

$m = 1.00$ if the election was held between November 16 and December 31

except for elections in 1965, 1975, and 1984, where m is taken as unity because the governments then were either not in power during the year preceding the election or were in power for less than half a quarter.

For the year 1968, the growth rate of per capita real GNP is substituted for the missing growth rate for per capita real GDP

The inflation rate (p_t) is taken as the rate of change in the GDP implicit price deflator during the four-quarter period preceding the election. The quarter of the election is included in the four-quarter period if the election was held in the second half of the quarter, and not if otherwise. For the period prior to 1989, when quarterly data were not available, p_t is computed as the weighted average of the annual inflation rates during the election year and the one before it, in a similar way the g_t was computed as explained previously

For the year 1968, the rate of change in the GNP deflator is substituted for the missing rate of change in the GDP deflator

```
       1.0                                                                                 3.1
       *-------------------------------------------------------------------------------------*
1950   |0
1951   |0
1954   |0
1957   |0000000
1961   |00000000000000000000000000000
1963   |0000000000000
1964   |0000000
1965   |0000000
1966   |0000
1968   |00
1969   |00000
1973   |0000000000000000000000000000000000000000000000000000000000000
1975   |000000000000000000000000
1977   |000000000000000000000000
1979   |00000000000000000
1983   |00000000000000000000000000000000000
1986   |000000000000000000000000000000000000000000000000000000000000000
1987   |00000000000000000000000000000000000000000000000000000
1989   |0000000000000000000000000000000000000000000000000000000000000000000000
1991   |00000000000000000000000000000000000000000000000000000000000000000000000000000000
1994   |000000000000000000000000000000000000000000000000000000000000000000000000000000000000
1995   |000000000000000000000000000000000000000000000000000000000000000000000000000000000000
1999   |0000000000000000000000000000000000000000000000000000000000000000000000000000000000000
2002   |00000000000000000000000000000000000000000000
2004   |00000000000000000000000000000000000
2007   |000000000000000
2009   |00000000000000000000000
2011   |000000
2014   |00000000
2015   |000000
2015   |00
       *-------------------------------------------------------------------------------------*
```

Fig. 3 Effective number of conservative parties (Source: same as Table 5)

obtained for the right-conservative group is plotted in Fig. 3. The effective number of conservative parties shows a tendency to move towards a level of unity but spikes after each military intervention. Although the impacts of such interventions increase in magnitude and duration until 1995, they become much smaller and even self-defeating after that date.

To measure the impact of coups on the number of conservative parties more accurately and more credibly, one needs to control for other factors that contribute to fragmentation. According to the economic voting literature, voters tend to reward incumbent parties for a good economic performance and punish them for a poor one. Consequently, we can expect some vote traffic between conservative parties owing to economic conditions when one of them is in the government and others are not. This probably will not be noticeable when the incumbent party is a small one but can cause fragmentation to rise when the economy is performing poorly and to fall when the economy is doing well if the major incumbent party is a conservative one.

Incumbent parties lose votes also due to strategic voting. Some supporters of the party shift their votes to the party's ideological cousins to check its power and to signal their displeasure with those of its decisions with which they disagree. This urge is magnified in local elections and parliamentary by-elections because then the incumbent party can be given a message without toppling it. The existence of threshold regulations in parliamentary general elections, such as the minimum 10 per cent nationwide vote share requirement to gain representation in the Turkish Grand National Assembly, contributes to this effect as well. In parliamentary elections, many small party supporters vote strategically for one of the major parties so as not to waste their vote. Then they return to their first choices in elections where no such handicaps apply, such as parliamentary by-elections and local administration elections in Turkey. Therefore, we should expect the effective number of parties to rise in local and by-elections that follow a parliamentary election and decrease in parliamentary elections that follow a local or by-election if the main conservative party is in power and other conservative parties are in the opposition.

An equation that measures the impact of coups on the effective number of right-conservative parties, controlling for the other influences discussed earlier, is

$$\begin{aligned} Y_t = a + bY_{t-1} + c_0 D61_t + d_0 D73_t + d_1 D73_{t-1} + h_0 D83_t \\ + h_1 D83_{t-1} + h_2 D83_{t-2} + h_4 D83_{t-4} + h_5 D83_{t-5} \\ + m\, g_t \times I_t + n\, p_t \times I_t + w\Delta(L_t + B_t) \times I_t + e_t \end{aligned} \quad (1)$$

where

Y_t: effective number of right-conservative parties at time t;

$D61_t$: a dummy variable that takes a value of one in 1961 (the year the first election after the1960 coup was held), and zero otherwise;

$D73_t$: a dummy variable that takes a value of one in 1973 (the year the first election after the 1971coup was held), and zero otherwise;

$D83_t$: a dummy variable that takes a value of one in 1983 (the year the first election after the 1980 coup was held), and zero otherwise;

I_t: a dummy variable that takes a value of one if the major incumbent party is a right-conservative party at time t, and zero otherwise[23];

g_t: growth rate of per capita real GDP during the four quarters preceding the election held at time t (henceforth referred to as the growth rate);

p_t: inflation rate in GDP implicit price deflator during the four quarters preceding the election held at time t (henceforth referred to as the inflation rate);

L_t: a dummy variable that takes a value of one if the election at time t is for local administrations, and zero otherwise;

B_t: a dummy variable that takes a value of one if the election at time t is a National Assembly by-election only (that is, not held simultaneously with a Senate election), and zero otherwise;

e_t: error term.

It should be noted that $\Delta(L_t + B_t)$ equals -1 in a parliamentary general election that follows a local or parliamentary by-election and equals $+1$ in local and parliamentary by-elections that follow a parliamentary general election. It takes a value of zero when elections of the same type follow each other. The lagged dependent variable is included in the model to allow shocks, including those created by coups, to have persistent effects. Lagged values of the coup dummies are included as well to allow for sophisticated response patterns. Initially, six lags of the dummy variables were considered. Then the lags for which the coefficient turned out to be insignificant in the preliminary estimation are dropped. I_t was treated as a separate independent variable as well, besides appearing in the interaction terms, but its coefficient estimate was very small and statistically insignificant. Dummy variables for the 1997 and 2007 coups were considered, too, but proved unnecessary, as one would expect from our discussion in the previous section.

The model implies that the effective number of conservative parties fluctuates around a mean given by $a/(1-b)$. The coup-related and random shocks and changes in the growth and inflation rates cause deviations from this mean, but the series return to it eventually. The magnitude of parameter *b* determines how slow or fast the mean reversions occur. Inclusion of growth and inflation rates in the model permits us not only to take into account the temporary fragmentations due to the economy but to check whether Turkish coups were caused by economic conditions. If bad economic conditions are the cause of coups and coups in turn cause political fragmentation, then the coup-related dummy variables should have no effect on the number of parties once the factors describing the economy are introduced as independent variables.

Table 6 presents the ordinary least-squares estimates of the parameters in Equation 1. Also included in the table are the t-statistics for the parameter

Table 6 Regression results

Variables	Coefficient estimates
Constant	0.502 (10.80)
Y_{t-1}	0.508 (16.83)
$D61_t$	0.601 (8.43)
$D73_t$	1.163 (16.30)
$D73_{t-1}$	−0.379 (5.09)
$D83_t$	0.612 (8.62)
$D83_{t-1}$	0.539 (7.22)
$D83_{t-2}$	0.233 (3.00)
$D83_{t-4}$	0.378 (4.96)
$D83_{t-5}$	0.186 (2.19)
$\Delta(L_t + B_t) * I_t$	0.060 (2.96)
$g_t * I_t$	−0.020 (4.20)
$p_t * I_t$	0.014 (16.79)
F	257.10
Prob > F	(0.00)
Durbin-h	−0.830
Prob > h	(0.20)
White Chi-square	17.53
Prob > Chi-square	(0.89)
R-square	0.994
Adj. R-square	0.991

Sources: Author's computations using the data given in Table 5 and appendix

Notes: The dependent variable in the regression is Y_t, the effective number of right-conservative parties. For the definitions of variables, see Sect. 3, and for the data, Table 5 and the appendix. The equation is estimated using the ordinary least-squares method. The numbers in parentheses, next to the parameter estimates, are the absolute values of their t-statistics. All parameters, except the one for D94, are significant at the 1 per cent level. The latter is significant at the 4 per cent level estimates, R-square, adjusted R-square, and F values, for judging the fit of the equation, and Durbin's (1970) h and White's (1980) chi-square statistics and their probability values, for checking autocorrelation and heteroscedasticity in the residuals and any misspecification in the model. The equation fits the data very well in all respects. Table 5 presents the data used, gives their sources, and explains in detail how the variables are defined and measured. As noted earlier, the data pools different types of elections: National Assembly general and by-elections, Senate elections, and Provincial Council elections. Furthermore, the elections examined are not equidistant. Thus, the series at hand is not a typical time series. The lags $t - 1$, $t - 2$, and so forth refer to the previous election and the election before that and not to the number of years that have passed. The results should be viewed with that caveat.

According to the estimates obtained, the effective number of right-conservative parties fluctuates around an equilibrium of 1.02 [= 0.502/(1 − 0.508)], which is not significantly different than one. The deviations from this equilibrium are related negatively to the growth rate and positively to the inflation rate under conservative ruling parties. The effect of growth is much greater in magnitude than that of inflation, consistent with the findings of Akarca and Tansel (2006) and Akarca (2009, 2010, 2011a, b, 2015a, b) on Turkish voter behaviour. Fragmentation increases in local and by-elections relative to parliamentary elections when the major right-conservative party is one of the incumbents. However, while the effects of these three factors are highly significant, they are quite small in magnitude. The fragmentations observed are due mainly to the coups. The fact that coup effects are large and statistically significant, even after controlling for the economy, implies that the coups transmit far more than the effects of economic factors.

Owing to the presence of a lagged dependent variable in the model, the dynamics of the coup effects cannot be deciphered easily from Table 6. For that reason Table 7 is constructed to present them more comprehensively.[24] The figures in that table suggest that the political fragmentations created by the 1960 and 1971 coups were short-lived. However, the immediate impact of the latter coup on the effective number of right-conservative parties was twice that of the former one (increase of 0.6 vs. 1.2 parties). While the effect of the 1980 coup was initially the same as the one in 1960, its impact in later periods was much greater and lasted

Table 7 Estimated coup-induced changes in effective number of conservative parties

	Coups		
Elections after coup	May 27, 1960	March 12, 1971	September 12, 1980
1st	0.601	1.163	0.612
2nd	0.305	0.212	0.850
3rd	0.155	0.108	0.665
4th	0.079	0.055	0.338
5th	0.040	0.028	0.550
6th	0.020	0.014	0.465
7th	0.010	0.007	0.236
8th	0.005	0.004	0.120

Sources: Author's computations using results presented in Table 6
Notes: The figures in each column are obtained as a ratio of the following polynomials, respectively:
$(0.601) / (1 - 0.508\ B)$
$(0.612 + 0.539\ B + 0.233\ B^2 + 0.378\ B^4 + 0.186\ B^5) / (1 - 0.508\ B)$
$(1.163 - 0.379\ B) / (1 - 0.508\ B)$
where B is the backshift operator

for a much longer time. Even after more than a decade and five elections, its impact was almost as large as the 1960 coup's immediate impact.[25] Nevertheless, in each case there was a consolidation towards a single right-conservative party.

4 Summary and Conclusions

Often electoral and governmental systems are seen as the culprits behind governmental fragmentations in Turkey. Although multiparty governments can emerge owing to these and other factors, in the Turkish case they were a consequence of political engineering by the military. The only time the country came close to having a coalition naturally was on June 7, 2015, when the AK Party temporarily lost its parliamentary majority. Had the opposition parties in the parliament joined forces, or at least one of them agreed to partner with the AK Party, the November 1, 2015, snap election would not have been called and the first Turkish coalition government not created by a coup would have happened.[26]

In the absence of military interventions, single-party governments would be far more common in Turkey because conservative voters, in an economic or cultural sense, make up the majority of the Turkish electorate and exhibit a tendency to gather in a single-party. Whenever their party came to power, however, it was viewed by the military as a threat to the secular, modern state and the supremacy of the military in the established order, and was toppled. Even though the conservative bloc was fragmented after each of these incidents and faced additional obstacles placed in their way to keep them from regaining full power, eventually they managed to come together anyway, first in a right-wing coalition and then in a single-party government. For that reason, Turkish political history consists of single-party government => coup => military rule => coalition governments (first incompatible, then compatible) => single-party government => coup cycles. Since economic growth appears to be highest during the first terms of single-party governments, followed by compatible coalitions, later terms of single-party governments, incompatible coalitions, and then military governments, these cycles in turn generate parallel cycles on the economic front, with economic performance going from good to not as good then to bad to slightly better to good again.

Many reasons are given in the literature to explain why economic performance is not good under coalitions. In the Turkish case, in addition to these factors, the fact that such governments were fruits of coups played an important role as well. First of all, coalitions in Turkey often were not voluntary but forced marriages between left- and right-wing parties laden with frictions and conflicts of interest. Economic performance was especially bad under coalitions of ideologically incompatible parties. Second, frequent party closures and bans on political leaders hindered political parties from institutionalizing, developing democratic traditions (inter- and intraparty), and accumulating valuable experience on good governance. Worse, it caused politicians to develop a reflex of avoiding making decisions on critical issues, passing them on to the guardianship institutions. These adversely affected the performance of single-party governments as well.

It appears that after experiencing the disastrous effects of coup cycles and integrating with the rest of the world, Turkish society (ordinary citizens as well as the elites) transformed in a fundamental way, which in turn brought the military guardianship system at the root of these cycles to an end. Ironically, the vacuum created by this led to a coup attempt on July 15, 2016, by a small "religious" order aiming to impose their own regime and perhaps another guardianship system. However, the way this takeover attempt, the bloodiest of all, was quashed, with immediate resistance from all political parties (including those that sided with some of the previous coups), mainstream media, business associations, and most members of the armed forces, police, judiciary, and other state institutions, and most importantly the active involvement of ordinary people from all ethnic, regional, cultural, and political backgrounds, a first in Turkish history, suggests that the democratic maturity of the society had reached such a level that coups will no longer be tolerated. Acemoğlu and Robinson (2006) explain how democracies become consolidated as civil society and middle class develops, and the economy becomes more urbanized, industrialized, and globalized. Indeed, all of these have occurred in Turkey over the last three decades, largely as a result of the introduction of the Internet, the ending of the state monopoly on television and radio, major improvements in the transportation and telecommunication systems, and the market-oriented reforms instituted in the 1980s by Turgut Özal, the prime minister at the time.

If coups are indeed out of the picture now, that will be good news for the economy. Then coalitions will be rarer in the future, and when they occur they will not be very harmful since they will be formed voluntarily and will be less likely to involve parties from the opposite ends of the political spectrum. However, as long as a sizable number of people remain who believe that some types of coups are good and who would not object to coups that are compatible with their ideology, and as long as the public looks to charismatic leaders rather than democratic institutions to solve their problems, the possibility of undemocratic interventions cannot be ruled out entirely. To move from a semiconsolidated to a fully consolidated democracy, and to avoid the possibility of another guardianship system altogether, it is necessary to fill the vacuum mentioned earlier with new political institutions that have strong checks and balances. Some of the legal measures initiated in the aftermath of the July 15 coup attempt, such as those putting the military under civilian control and eliminating the military judiciary are promising in that regard but not sufficient.[27] Further efforts are needed to reform the civilian judiciary too, to establish intraparty democracy, and to empower members of parliament, especially in the face of executive powers being increased and concentrated.[28] Perhaps these will aid in closing the performance gap between first and later terms of single-party governments as well.

Appendix: Classification of Turkish Political Parties

Election date	Right-conservative	Left-statist	Turkish-nationalist	Kurdish-nationalist
May.14, 1950	DP	<u>**CHP**</u>	MP	–
Sep. 16, 1951	<u>**DP**</u>	CHP	MP	–
May 2, 1954	<u>**DP**</u>, TKP	CHP	CMP	–
Oct. 27, 1957	<u>**DP**</u>, HP	CHP	CMP	–
Oct. 15, 1961	AP, YTP	CHP	CKMP	–
Nov. 17, 1963	AP, **YTP**	<u>**CHP**</u>, TIP	**CKMP**, MP2	–
Jun. 7, 1964	AP, YTP	<u>**CHP**</u>	CKMP	–
Oct. 10, 1965	<u>**AP**</u>, **YTP**	CHP, TIP	**MP2, CKMP**	–
Jun. 7, 1966	<u>**AP**</u>, YTP	CHP, TIP	MP2, CKMP	–
Jun. 2, 1968	<u>**AP**</u>, YTP	CHP, TIP, CGP, TBP	MP2, CKMP	–
Oct. 12, 1969	<u>**AP**</u>, YTP	CHP, TIP, GP, TBP	MP2, MHP	–
Oct. 14, 1973	<u>**AP**</u>, DP2, MSP	CHP, **CGP**, TBP	MHP, MP2	–
Oct. 12, 1975	<u>**AP**</u>, DP2, **MSP**	CHP, TBP	**MHP**	–
Jun. 5, 1977	<u>**AP**</u>, DP2, **MSP**	CHP, **CGP**, TBP, TIP2	**MHP**	–

(continued)

(continued)

Election date	Right-conservative	Left-statist	Turkish-nationalist	Kurdish-nationalist
Oct. 14, 1979	AP, MSP	**CHP**, **CGP**, TBP, TIP2, TSIP, SDP	MHP	–
Nov. 6, 1983	ANAP, MDP	HP2	–	–
Sep. 28, 1986	**ANAP**, DYP, RP, HDP, VAP	SHP, DSP, BVP	MÇP	–
Nov. 29, 1987	**ANAP**, DYP, RP	SHP, DSP	MÇP	–
Mar. 26, 1989	DYP, **ANAP**, RP	SHP, DSP	MÇP	–
Oct. 20, 1991	DYP, **ANAP**, RP	SHP, DSP	–	–
Mar. 27, 1994	**DYP**, ANAP, RP	**SHP**, DSP, CHP	MHP, BBP	–
Dec. 24, 1995	RP, ANAP, **DYP**,	DSP, **CHP**	MHP	HADEP
Apr. 18, 1999	FP, **ANAP**, DYP, **DTP**	**DSP**, CHP	MHP, BBP	HADEP
Nov. 3, 2002	AKP, DYP, **ANAP**, SP	CHP, **DSP**, GP, YTP2	**MHP**, BBP	DEHAP
Mar. 28, 2004	ANAP, DYP, **AKP**, SP	CHP, DSP, GP, YTP2	MHP, BBP	SHP
July 22, 2007	**AKP**, DP3, SP	CHP, GP	MHP	DTP
Mar. 29, 2009	**AKP**, ANAP, DP3, SP	CHP, DSP,	MHP, BBP	DTP
June 12, 2011	**AKP**, DP3, SP, HAS	CHP, DSP	MHP, BBP	BDP
Mar. 30, 2014	**AKP**, DP3, SP	CHP, DSP	MHP, BBP	BDP+HDP
June 7, 2015	**AKP**, DP3, SP	CHP, DSP	MHP	HDP
Nov. 1, 2015	**AKP**, DP3, SP	CHP, DSP	MHP, BBP	HDP

Sources: Same as Table 4

Notes: Only parties that received more than 1 per cent of the vote in at least one election and parties that split from them are considered. Incumbent parties are in bold. Major incumbent parties are also underlined. In each category, the party that received the highest number of votes is listed first. The Turkish acronyms used in the table and the parties they represent are as follows:

AKP: Justice and Development Party

ANAP: Motherland Party
AP: Justice Party
BBP: Grand Unity Party
BDP: Peace and Democracy Party
BVP: Grand Nation Party
CGP: Republican Reliance Party
CHP: Republican People's Party
CKMP: Republican Peasant's Nation Party
CMP: Republican Nation Party
DEHAP: Democratic People's Party
DP: Democrat Party (1946–1960)
DP2: Democratic Party
DP3: Democrat Party (1975–1981)
DSP: Democratic Left Party
DTP: Democrat Turkey Party
DTP2: Democratic Society Party
DYP: True Path Party
FP: Virtue Party
GP: Young Party
HADEP: People's Democracy Party
HAS: People's Voice Party
HDP: Free Democrat Party
HDP2: People's Democracy Party
HP: Freedom Party
HP2: Populist Party
MÇP: Nationalist Work Party
MDP: Nationalist Democracy Party
MHP: Nationalist Action Party
MP: Nation Party (1948–1954)
MP2: Natıon Party (1962–1981)
MSP: National Salvation Party
RP: Welfare Party
SDP: Socialist Revolution Party
SHP: Social Democratic People's Party
SP: Felicity Party
TBP: Turkish Unity Party
TIP: Turkish Labor Party (1961–1971)
TIP2: Turkish Labor Party (1975–1981)
TKP: Turkish Peasant's Party
TSIP: Turkish Socialist Labor Party
VAP: Citizen Party
YTP: New Turkey Party (1961–1971)
YTP2: New Turkey Party (2002–2004)

Notes

1. Minority governments ruled for 3 and coalition governments for 21 years. Here the two types of government are lumped together because minority governments in essence are coalitions, as they require the consent and support of another party or parties to survive.
2. Economic conditions under coalition and minority governments are reported separately in the notes to the table.
3. The reason why economic performance is poorer under coalition governments compared to single-party governments is beyond the scope of the present study. However, we can mention here some of the key reasons given for this in the literature. Reaching decisions in a timely fashion is more difficult when the number of partners involved is large. Because the probability of government's dissolution at any given moment is higher in the case of coalitions than single-party governments, the former are more prone to postponing painful adjustments that are needed for the long-run health of the economy. The shorter time horizons of coalition governments also causes fiscal discipline to be weaker under them. Furthermore, incentives to indulge in populist policies and transfer activities is greater for coalition governments because under such governments it is more difficult for voters to apportion blame among partners for the adverse effects of these, and as long as one partner indulges in them, there is little benefit for the other partners of not indulging.
4. In this paper, coups are defined as in Powell and Thyne (2011): "illegal and overt attempts by the military or other elites within the state apparatus to unseat the sitting executive." Note that this definition allows for the possibility of coups not being led by the military and considers overthrowing governments through threats of military intervention but without use of force as coups as well. According to O'Kane (1987), a coup is considered to be to be successful if it leads to the "installation in power of a government of the conspirators' own choosing." Thus we can say that coups were attempted in Turkey in 1960, 1962, 1963, 1971, 1980, 1997, 2007, and 2016. Of these, the ones in 1960, 1971, 1980, and 1997 were successful.
5. For surveys of the economic voting literature, see Lewis-Beck and Paldam (2000), Lewis-Beck and Stegmaier (2000, 2008, 2009, 2015), and Stegmaier and Lewis-Beck (2013). Akarca and Tansel (2006, 2007) and

Akarca (2009, 2010, 2011a, b, 2015a, b) show that Turkish voters behave very similarly to the patterns described in that literature.

6. Kim (2016), Bell (2016), Gassebner et al. (2016), Hiroi and Omori (2013), and Bouzid (2011) survey studies on coups in other countries. The first one investigates in particular whether the economy is a determinant of coups.
7. Londregan and Poole (1990) dub such dynamics of one coup leading to another coup a "coup trap."
8. For example, the 9 March 1971 coup plot, which was prevented by the March 12 1971 coup, was planned by some socialist intellectuals and leftist officers. The political parties that espoused the views represented by the organizers of that coup plot received no more than 3 per cent of the vote in various elections they contested democratically.
9. The Gülen movement, which masterminded the 15 July 2016 takeover attempt, is a prime example of this. Can (2014) explains how and why this religious organization "that probably has 2–3 per cent support at most came to control nearly the entire judiciary and became an asymmetrical power center." In recent years, it has become apparent that prosecutors and judges belonging to this group had tried to eliminate rivals from the military and civilian bureaucracy and embarrass and destabilize the government through various rigged investigations. To help their members in the military schools succeed, they provided them the questions to various tests in advance and arranged the dismissal of cadets competing with them through trumped-up charges and manipulated health and performance evaluations.
10. For example, the failed coup attempt on 22 February 1962 was organized by officers who were about to be removed from their positions by another junta. The 21 May 1963 coup attempt, on the other hand, was a come-back effort by those removed after the unsuccessful 1962 attempt. The 12 March 1971 coup was implemented to some extent to counter the leftist junta that planned the 9 March 1971 coup. Similarly, the 15 July 2016 coup was timed by the Gülenists to preempt the dismissal of their members from the armed forces; it was suspected that it would take place in about a month.
11. The 1960, 1971, 1980, 1997, and 2007 coups were of Type 1. The coups in 1962, 1963, and 2016 were of Type 2.
12. For classification of parties into the four categories, see the Appendix. The left-statist group is labeled as such, even though its leading parties

cannot be considered left, because they label themselves as such at least since late sixties and occasionally small leftist parties have emerged from them. Also left-leaning people vote for them. In many studies, the Turkish nationalist and conservative parties are grouped together, and analyzed as the Turkish right wing. However, since a distinct Turkish nationalist party existed constantly since 1950, except for brief periods when it was banned by military juntas, it is more appropriate to treat it as a separate movement. Although the rest of the right wing occasionally fragmented into several parties, they always regrouped, as will be explained below.

13. It was the French version of secularism (laïcité) that was adopted, which keeps religion from interfering in state affairs but allows the state to control religious institutions, rather than its Anglo-Saxon version, which keeps the state from interfering in religious affairs and vice versa. Also, unlike Ottoman reform efforts, which allowed many of the old institutions and traditions to coexist with the new modern ones, republican administrations aimed to eradicate the *ancien régime* altogether. These exacerbated the resistance.
14. This was not new. The military was the first institution to be westernized and modernized in the Ottoman Empire, and it was given the duty and powers to guard the reform efforts. Interestingly, over time the military leaders took this duty to heart and increased their powers so much that they gained the ability to replace the emperors who had entrusted them with this task for not westernizing and modernizing fast enough and for trying to curtail their guardianship role.
15. Actually, the right-conservative Democrat Party (DP), which came to power in 1950, was expected to serve as a small opposition party, facilitating the emergence of democracy without rocking the boat. The party's success was a total surprise both for the party itself and for the CHP. This is evident from the fact that the DP demanded a proportional election system before the 1950 election, while the CHP insisted on retaining the majoritarian system, and then the two parties reversed their positions after the election.
16. For excellent discussions on how the guardianship system evolved, the cleavages it created in society, and the distortions it generated in the political system, see Mardin (1973), Can (2014), and Koçak (2014, 219–77). Aydınlı (2012) discusses how it transformed over time, and Ünay and Dilek (2016, 211–15) show how it extended into the economic sphere.

17. All of the Type 1 coups except one were successful (those in 1960, 1971, 1980, and 1997, but not the one in 2007). None of the Type 2 coups (in 1962, 1963, 1971, and 2016), on the other hand, were successful. For that reason and because their goal was not just the fragmentation of the conservative bloc but a permanent or long-term takeover, Type 2 coups are not included in Table 3.
18. As stated earlier, economic performance under such coalition governments was particularly poor.
19. The prime minister resigned from his party before taking office, though, to appear as an independent.
20. It should be noted, however, that the leader of the CHP in 1980 was not the leader of the party in 1971 but its secretary general, and also that he supported the 1960 coup, and his party cooperated with the juntas in 1960 and 1971 and nominated one of the 1971 junta leaders as their presidential candidate in 1980.
21. All of the parties banned after the 1980 coup were legalized in 1994, but of those only the CHP regained prominence and eventually reunited the fragmented left-statist segment. The Turkish-nationalist and right-conservative groups continued under the banners of their new parties.
22. The MHP's vote share, which was at most 8 per cent until 1995 (except right after the banning of the DP in 1960), rose to double digits after that date, except in 2002 when the party was one of the incumbents.
23. I_t is taken as zero in 1975 and 1977, even though the major incumbent was a right-conservative party because almost all of the other right-wing parties were in power as well.
24. In Table 7, the elections are treated as if they are equidistant from each other. Therefore, the table should interpreted with this caveat in mind.
25. It should be noted that part of the slight jump in the impact between the fourth (1989) and fifth (1991) elections and the small drop between the fifth (1991) and sixth (1994) elections are due to the Turkish- nationalist MHP entering the 1991 election under the banner of the right-conservative RP. Raising the vote share of the third largest conservative party gave the appearance of greater fragmentation in that camp. A desire to circumvent the 10 per cent election threshold was the motivation behind the RP-MHP partnership in 1991.
26. However, had that coalition materialized, it could still be tied to a coup. Most AK Party supporters who deserted the party on June 7, 2015, especially the ethnic Kurdish ones, did so strategically to help

the HDP gain representation in the parliament. Rather than fielding independent candidates, as it and its predecessors had done in the past to circumvent the 10 per cent election threshold, the HDP decided to participate in the June 2015 election officially. The unusually high threshold was established by the leaders of the 1980 coup. After observing that the HDP surpassed the threshold handily and regretting the instability they created, many of the same voters returned to the AK Party on November 1, enabling it to form a single-party government. For a more detailed analysis of the election outcomes mentioned, see Akarca (2015b).

27. Ünay and Dilek (2016, 227–28) list these measures.
28. For example, it would be desirable to couple the presidential system that will take effect in 2019, with single-member parliamentary districts for which party candidates are chosen through primaries rather than picked by the party leaders, and winning candidates chosen through two-round elections as will be the case with the president.

References

Acemoğlu, Daron, and James A. Robinson. 2006. *Economic Origins of Dictatorship and Democracy*. New York: Cambridge University Press.

———. 2008. Persistence of Power, Elites, and Institutions. *American Economic Review* 98: 267–293.

Akarca, Ali T. 2009. A Prediction for AK PARTY's Nationwide Vote Share in the 29 March 2009 Turkish Local Elections. *İktisat İşletme ve Finans* 24 (276): 7–22.

———. 2010. Analysis of the 2009 Turkish Election Results from an Economic Voting Perspective. *European Research Studies Journal* 13: 3–38.

———. 2011a. A Prediction for AKP's Nationwide Vote Share in the 12 June 2011 Turkish Parliamentary Election. *İktisat İşletme ve Finans* 26 (302): 53–74.

———. 2011b. Inter-election Vote Swings for the Turkish Ruling Party: The Impact of Economic Performance and Other Factors. *Equilibrium* 6: 7–25.

———. 2015a. Modeling Political Performance of Islamist and Islamist-Rooted Parties in Turkey. *Middle East Development Journal* 7: 49–69.

———. 2015b. Putting Turkey's June and November 2015 Election Outcomes in Perspective. *Insight Turkey* 17: 81–104.

Akarca, Ali T., and Aysit Tansel. 2006. Economic Performance and Political Outcomes: An Analysis of the Turkish Parliamentary and Local Election Results Between 1950 and 2004. *Public Choice* 129: 77–105.

———. 2007. Social and Economic Determinants of Turkish Voter Choice in the 1995 Parliamentary Election. *Electoral Studies* 26: 633–647.

Aydınlı, Ersel. 2012. Turkey Under the AKP: Civil-Military Relations Transformed. *Journal of Democracy* 23: 100–108.

Bell, Curtis. 2016. Coup d'état and Democracy. *Comparative Political Studies* 49: 1167–1200.

Bouzid, Bechir. 2011. Using a Semi-parametric Analysis to Understand the Occurrence of Coups D'état in Developing Countries. *International Journal of Peace Studies* 16: 53–79.

Can, Osman. 2014. The Structural Causes of Political Crisis in Turkey. *Insight Turkey* 16: 33–41.

Durbin, James. 1970. Testing for Serial Correlation in Least Squares Regression When Some of the Regressors Are Lagged Dependent Variables. *Econometrica* 38: 410–421.

Gassebner, Martin, Jerg Gutmann, and Stefan Voigt. 2016. When to Expect a Coup d'état? An Extreme Bounds Analysis of Coup Determinants. *Public Choice* 169: 293–313.

Hiroi, Taeko, and Sawa Omori. 2013. Causes and Triggers of Coups d'état: An Event History Analysis. *Politics and Policy* 41: 39–64.

Kim, Nam Kyu. 2016. Revisiting Economic Shocks and Coups. *Journal of Conflict Resolution* 60: 3–31.

Koçak, Cemil. 2014. *Resmi Tarihe Meydan Okuyorum*. Istanbul: Timaş Yayınları.

Laakso, Markku, and Rein Taagepera. 1979. "Effective" Number of Parties: A Measure with Application to West Europe. *Comparative Political Studies* 12: 3–27.

Lewis-Beck, Michael S., and Martin Paldam. 2000. Economic Voting: An Introduction. *Electoral Studies* 19: 113–121.

Lewis-Beck, Maichael S., and Mary Stegmaier. 2000. Economic Determinants of Electoral Outcomes. *Annual Review of Political Science* 3: 183–219.

———. 2008. The Economic Vote in Transitional Democracies. *Journal of Elections, Public Opinion and Parties* 18: 303–323.

———. 2009. American Voter to Economic Voter: Evolution of an Idea. *Electoral Studies* 28: 625–631.

———. 2015. Economic Evaluations and Electoral Consequences. In *International Encyclopedia of the Social and Behavioral Sciences*, ed. James D. Wright, vol. 7, 2nd ed., 26–32. Oxford: Elsevier.

Londregan, John B., and Keith T. Poole. 1990. Poverty, the Coup Trap, and the Seizure of Executive Power. *World Politics* 42: 151–183.
Mardin, Şerif. 1973. Center-Periphery Relations: A Key to Turkish Politics. *Daedalus* 102: 169–190.
O'Kane, Rosemary. 1987. *The Likelihood of Coups*. Avebury: Aldeshot.
Powell, Jonathan M., and Clayton L. Thyne. 2011. Global Instances of Coups from 1950 to 2010: A New Dataset. *Journal of Peace Research* 48: 249–259.
Stegmaier, Mary, and Michael S. Lewis-Beck. 2013. Economic Voting. In *Oxford Bibliographies in Political Science*, ed. R. Valelly. New York: Oxford University Press. http://www.oxfordbibliographies.com/view/document/obo-9780199756223/obo-9780199756223-0057.xml.
Tuncer, Erol. 2002. *Osmanlıdan Günümüze Seçimler: 1877–1999*. Ankara: TESAV.
———. 2007. *22 Temmuz 2007 Milletvekili Genel Seçimleri: Sayısal ve Siyasal Değerlendirme*. Ankara: TESAV.
———. 2009. *29 Mart 2009 İl Genel Meclisi ve Belediye Seçimleri: Sayısal ve Siyasal Değerlendirme*. Ankara: TESAV.
———. 2010. *1950 Seçimleri*. Ankara: TESAV.
———. 2011a. *1954 Seçimleri*. Ankara: TESAV.
———. 2011b. *12 Haziran 2011 Milletvekili Genel Seçimleri: Sayısal ve Siyasal Değerlendirme*. Ankara: TESAV.
———. 2012a. *1957 Seçimleri*. Ankara: TESAV.
———. 2012b. *1961 Seçimleri*. Ankara: TESAV.
Tuncer, Erol, and Bülent Tuncer. 2016. *1 Kasım 2015 Milletvekili Genel Seçimleri: Sayısal ve Siyasal Değerlendirme*. Ankara: TESAV.
Tuncer, Erol, and Coşkun Kasapbaş. 2004. *28 Mart 2004 İl Genel Meclisi ve Belediye Seçimleri: Sayısal ve Siyasal Değerlendirme*. Ankara: TESAV.
Tuncer, Erol, Coşkun Kasapbaş, and Bülent Tuncer. 2003. *2002 Milletvekili Genel Seçimleri: Sayısal ve Siyasal Değerlendirme*. Ankara: TESAV.
Tuncer, Erol, Hanife Yurtseven, and Bülent Tuncer. 2014. *30 Mart 2014 İl Genel Meclisi ve Belediye Seçimleri: Sayısal ve Siyasal Değerlendirme*. Ankara: TESAV.
———. 2015. *7 Haziran 2015 Milletvekili Genel Seçimleri: Sayısal ve Siyasal Değerlendirme*. Ankara: TESAV.
Ünay, Sadık, and Şerif Dilek. 2016. July 15: Political Economy of a Foiled Coup. *Insight Turkey* 18: 205–231.
White, Halbert. 1980. A Heteroskedasticity-Consistent Covariance Matrix Estimator and a Direct Test for Heteroskedasticity. *Econometrica* 48: 817–838.

Between Risks and Opportunities: Social Policies in Contemporary Turkey

Mehmet Fatih Aysan

1 Introduction

Studies on social policy and social expenditures are increasingly attracting researchers across the world. In Turkey, such studies have increased pronouncedly since the early 2000s. These studies have generally taken the form of case studies on specific policy areas – such as poverty, retirement, or health (Agartan 2012; Aysan 2013; Ceylan 2016) – rather than that of broader studies addressing the social policy system as a whole, though there have also been more extensive studies with conceptual and often ideological motives (Bugra and Adar 2008). Both sorts of studies have their flaws. While case studies are inadequate for researchers to situate macro social changes and social policy transformations correctly, more

This research is supported by the Scientific and Technological Research Council of Turkey-TUBITAK (Project no: 114K117). The author thanks to the editors, referees, and Hugh J. Turner for their valuable comments and contributions.

M. F. Aysan (✉)
Department of Sociology, Istanbul Sehir University, Istanbul, Turkey

A. F. Aysan et al. (eds.), *Turkish Economy*,
https://doi.org/10.1007/978-3-319-70380-0_5

conceptual but non-empirical studies have generally been limited to generic criticisms of neo-liberalism.

In fact, no systematic study on the main roles of the welfare regime in Turkey has ever been published. This short chapter offers a modest step in this direction, focusing on the social policies of Turkey since the 2000s. It is based on a nation-wide empirical study (N: 1630) entitled "Understanding the Welfare Regime of Turkey: Institutions and Individuals" (Aysan 2016a). This study aimed to understand the effects of various welfare players, particularly social policy institutions, on welfare distribution and citizens' welfare perceptions and satisfaction levels. In addition to the quantitative data obtained during the study, interviews with citizens and experts working in public and private institutions contributed a qualitative element to the research.

When social policies in Turkey are examined over the 2000s, two dominant trends stand out. First, it is possible to talk about a path dependency in the social policy regulations of the contemporary period. Populism and a family-centred social policy perspective constitute the foundation of this continuity. Hence, due to this path dependency, there has been confusion about the types of reforms and the logic of social provisions preventing the institutionalisation of social policies in Turkey. Secondly, there has been a remarkable increase in public social spending since the 2000s, which cannot simply be explained by the populism of the Justice and Development Party (AK Party) or by the transition of the Turkish welfare regime to a Social Democratic one. The main causes of this rapid increase in public social spending include Turkey's status as a latecomer welfare state, its increasing levels of prosperity, and structural factors such as an ageing population and new social risks leading to the rapid increase in public social spending in the 2000s. Hence, recent developments in Turkey's social policies and social spending must be explained not only through global developments but also through the country's own endogenous characteristics.

This paper consists of three main parts. The first part will detail the basic characteristics of the Turkish welfare regime and contemporary social policies. The second part will focus on the five basic pillars of social policy –education, social security, health, social services, and housing – to show how the basic arguments highlighted in the previous paragraph have dominated Turkey's policy implementations since the 2000s. The third part will offer a brief discussion of some of the challenges facing sustainable social policies in Turkey and offer recommendations for addressing them.

2 The Main Characteristics of the Turkish Welfare Regime and Social Policies in Turkey

The welfare state classification has occupied much of the welfare state research focusing on social expenditures, inequality, and the commodification of public services since the 1990s (Esping-Andersen 1990; Ferrera 1996; Korpi and Palme 1998; Trifiletti 1999; Scruggs and Allan 2006). In light of these studies, Organisation for Economic Co-operation and Development (OECD) countries can be examined in four welfare regime clusters: the social democratic, liberal, continental European, and southern European. Researchers have also studied and conducted comparative research on other parts of the world, especially post-Soviet countries or eastern Europe (Deacon 2000), East Asia (Gough 2001; Walker and Wong 2005), and the Middle East (Jawad 2009; Aybars and Tsarouhas 2010), which often have diverse historical and institutional characteristics that affect welfare distribution.

In welfare regime classifications, some comparative studies analyse Turkey under the southern European or Mediterranean welfare regime (Gough 1996; Bugra and Keyder 2006; Gal 2010; Aysan 2013), while others consider it to be part of the Middle Eastern group (Aybars and Tsarouhas 2010). Whether it is considered a member of these groups or not, the Turkish welfare regime has undergone substantial transformations since 2000. These changes stem both from global socio-economic determinants and from other factors that are peculiar to the social structure and demographic characteristics of Turkey.

One of the essential characteristics of the Turkish welfare regime is the role of families in the management of social risks, which has parallels with southern European and Middle Eastern countries. The Turkish welfare regime can be characterised by a preference for family solutions to welfare problems. In this regime, people rely primarily on their families, some extended forms of kinship, or other social networks. In addition to the family, another important player in the Turkish welfare regime is local actors. These can take the form of a particular religious group or a network of people who migrated from the same rural region. The influence of religious values and regional ties is especially significant in the provision of social welfare in Turkey.

During the Ottoman period, *vakıfs* (foundations) undertook social responsibilities that the state did not or could not fulfil. Their services extended into the areas of education, health, shelter, infrastructure, and religion. Even though most of them have since disappeared, their functions continue to be carried out by non-profit organisations and non-governmental organisations heavily influenced by religious and traditional values. Such organisations provide social services both for Turkish citizens and for people in need outside of the country.

Another important feature of the Turkish welfare regime is the role of populism and patronage in welfare distribution. According to Ferrera (1996) and Gal (2010), populism and patronage in southern European countries are linked to historical commonalities, particularly those related to the process of political mobilisation and the establishment of state institutions in these countries. In countries like Turkey that experienced a rapid urbanisation process and high rural–urban domestic migration, populism and patronage are considered to be a general welfare distribution mechanism, where welfare benefits are offered in return for political support in elections. These cliental relations have been strengthened by ongoing political tensions among political parties and ideologies as well as by weak political institutions, especially in the 1980s and 1990s. For example, the decision to lower Turkey's official retirement age in 1992 was a populist move that negatively affected the long-term sustainability of the pension system and public budget (Aysan 2013). In cases like these, despite financial risk in the long term, politicians use populist policies to gain a majority of electors' votes for upcoming elections. Such populist policies are not peculiar to right-wing parties; on the contrary, they have been championed by all political parties in the 2010s. In the 2016 general-election campaigns, for example, one of the opposition parties promised a tremendous increase in the minimum wage and pension benefits without any economic explanation of how it would happen.

In Turkey, due to the historical strength of statist economic policies, the market did not have a significant role in any aspect of social life, especially in welfare distribution, until the 1980s. With the implementation of export-oriented industrialisation and neo-liberal policies, the private sector started to flourish after the 1980s. Parallel to neo-liberal trends in the world, new economic policies led to the privatisation of state-owned enterprises, the rise of subcontracting, and increasing flexibility in labour markets. These new policies affected welfare distribution in Turkey in two important ways. First, the state gradually withdrew from its important welfare role as an employer through the privatisation of state-owned enterprises. Second, neo-liberalism led private entrepreneurs to invest in various sectors that had traditionally been dominated by the state, such as healthcare and education. These trends brought new challenges to workers in relatively secure and well-paid jobs in the public as well as private sector.

Four main pillars determine the distribution of the welfare: the state, the family, the market, and local actors such as non-profit organisations, associations, and foundations. Figure 1 shows the role of these

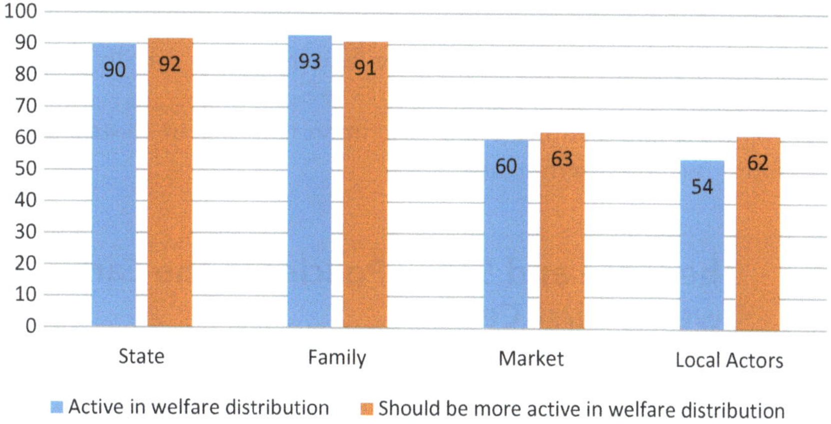

Fig. 1 The role of welfare actors in welfare distribution in Turkey (%), 2016 (Source: Aysan 2016a)

four welfare actors in Turkey. Family (93%) and the state (90%) are the most important welfare actors in Turkey, while market (60%) and local actors (54%) are less significant players in welfare distribution. When asked their view on the role these actors should play in future, 92% of respondents said that the state should play a more active role in welfare distribution; 91% said the same of the family, while 63% and 62% said the same of the market and local actors, respectively.

Although some researchers have described Turkey as a residual and weak welfare state (Bugra and Keyder 2006; Bugra and Adar 2008), the Turkish state has a significant role in welfare distribution, particularly in the areas of health, social security, and social services. The family is another important player in welfare distribution in Turkey, and people want these two players to continue their welfare roles. Even though market and local actors do not contribute to the welfare system in Turkey to the degree that the state and family do, they still serve some welfare distribution functions. In light of these four players, the main characteristics of the Turkish welfare regime can be summarised as follows:

(1) Welfare is distributed through state- and family-centred institutional mechanisms.
(2) Local actors based on traditional and religious values, such as non-profit organisations or religious or ethnic groups, have welfare functions.
(3) The market has a relatively minor but increasing role in welfare distribution.
(4) Populism and patronage are two important welfare distribution forms used by governments.

3 The State and Social Policies in the Early Twenty-First Century

According to Ferrera and Rhodes (2000), the erosion of ideological consensus and economic crises have led to a recasting of European welfare states. Economic globalisation has generated a debate on neo-liberal convergence, as states increasingly make cuts to their social expenditures and people come increasingly to rely on the market for social services. The privatisation of social services and the individualisation of social risks are the main markers of the neo-liberalisation process. The convergence approach asserts that European welfare states' adoption of policies of retrenchment and neo-liberalisation has led to a process of neo-liberal convergence. Hence, the extent to which welfare regimes are stable and path dependent is under debate as a result of the neo-liberalisation process in various welfare regimes.

An analysis of public social expenditure is one way to assess these neo-liberalisation arguments. According to the OECD (2008, 499), public social expenditure is the provision of benefits and financial contributions by public institutions to households and individuals to provide support during circumstances that adversely affect their well-being, provided that the provision of these benefits and financial contributions constitutes neither a direct payment for a particular good or service nor an individual contract or transfer. Table 1 shows public social expenditure as a percentage of GDP in the OECD region and Turkey between 1980 and 2013. Turkey devoted only 4% of its GDP to public social expenditure in 1980, in contrast to the OECD average of 14.9%. Old-age and survivor spending, which covers pensions and other types of cash and in-kind benefits, was one of the biggest spending areas among these expenditures. The weight of this expenditure area increased, particularly in Turkey, from 2.3% in 1990 to 8.2% in 2013. Another important expanding policy

Table 1 Public social expenditure and selected branches as percentage of GDP, 1980–2013

	Turkey					OECD				
	Health	Old Age	Family	Other	Total	Health	Old Age	Family	Other	Total
1980	1.4	1.3	0.6	0.7	**4.0**	4.2	5.7	1.5	3.5	**14.9**
1985	0.8	1.4	0.5	0.5	**3.2**	4.2	6.2	1.5	4.6	**16.5**
1990	1.5	2.3	0.9	0.8	**5.5**	4.4	6.4	1.6	4.5	**16.9**
1995	1.8	2.7	0.2	0.9	**5.6**	4.7	7.0	1.8	5.3	**18.8**
2000	2.9	4.0	0.2	0.6	**7.7**	4.9	6.8	1.8	4.5	**18.0**
2005	3.5	6.0	0.3	0.5	**10.3**	5.4	6.8	1.9	4.7	**18.8**
2010	4.2	7.7	0.4	0.5	**12.8**	6.0	7.8	2.3	5.0	**21.1**
2013	4.0	8.2	0.4	0.8	**13.4**	6.0	8.2	2.1	4.8	**21.1**

Source: OECD (2017)

area is health services. In 2013, 4% of GDP in Turkey and 6% of GDP in the OECD was spent on public health services. Hence, contrary to some researchers who argue that there has been a retrenchment of the welfare state (O'Connor 1973; Offe 1984; Mishra 1999), the social expenditures of the welfare state have not decreased. In the Turkish case, public social spending increased from 4 to 13.4%, the highest increase in the OECD region, between 1980 and 2013.

According to Spicker, social policy focuses on the provision of social services, and the welfare state provides social services through the big five social policy areas: education, social security, health, social services, and housing (1995, 3). Important social policy reforms occurred in these areas during the 2000s. In Turkey, social security and health reforms in 2006 and the establishment of the Ministry of Family and Social Policies in 2011 were particularly important in helping to cope with long-term demographic and economic problems. The following section will analyse these five social policy areas to provide a better understanding of the social policies being implemented in them and any changes that have taken place to these policies over the past decades.

3.1 Education

Education is principally considered in terms of schooling, though in actuality it extends far beyond this to various sorts of training aimed at social development and employment. While the main emphasis within this is on children, there is scope for education for all age groups through the lifelong learning approach (Spicker 2014, 152). The Turkish National Education System consists of formal education and non-formal education. While formal education refers to the regular education conducted within a school for individuals in a certain age group, informal education provides all people regardless of their education level and age with the opportunity for education to help them adjust to scientific, economic, technological, and cultural developments.

According to statistics from the Ministry of National Education (2017), the formal education system has improved significantly since 2002. The percentage of primary-school-age children enrolled in school increased from

91% in 2002–2003 to 95% in 2015–2016. The number of students going on to higher education increased from 15% in the 2002–2003 academic year to 41% in 2015–2016. During this period, a number of important new laws and administrative reforms were implemented. Compulsory education was expanded to 12 years as of the 2012–2013 school year. The number of teachers also increased significantly, and the infrastructure of schools was improved. For example, the student–teacher ratio in primary education improved from 28:1 in 2002–2003 to 18:1 in 2016–2017. Similarly, the student–teacher ratio in secondary education improved from 16:1 in 2002–2003 to 13:1 in 2016–2017. The number of students per class was also lowered through the creation of new schools. Even though the total number of secondary-school students increased from 2.4 million to 5.2 million between 2002 and 2017, the number of students per class declined from 30 to 20 during the same period.

During the 1990s and 2000s, the market started to play a more active role in welfare distribution in the educational sector in Turkey. The number of students in private schools increased nearly eightfold from 51,000 to 390,000 over the period between 2002 and 2017. In the 2016–2017 academic year, 15% of all types of schools from kindergarten to high schools were private schools, which covers about 8% of all students (TURKSTAT 2017). In 2017, there were 112 public universities, 65 private universities, and 6 private vocational schools in Turkey.

3.2 Social Security

Despite efforts to address the fragmented structure of the Turkish social security system in 2006, the system maintains a threefold structure, with the Sosyal Sigortalar Kurumu (Social Insurance Institution, henceforth SSK) for blue-collar workers, Emekli Sandigi (Retirement Fund, henceforth ES) for white-collar employees working in public institutions, and Esnaf ve Sanatkarlar ve Diger Bagimsiz Calisanlar Sosyal Sigortalar Kurumu (Social Security Institution for Craftspeople, Tradespeople, and Other Self-Employed People, henceforth Bag-Kur) for craftspeople, merchants, agricultural workers, and other self-employed people.

In 1950, active insured people who contributed to the social security system and their dependents constituted only 4% of the total population. The institutionalisation of social security services led to an increase in the insured population over the following decades. By 2015, the percentage of insured people (active insured, dependents, and pensioners) increased to 86% of the total population (Social Security Institution 2017). Nevertheless, the total number of active insured people contributing to the system has not increased considerably over the past 70 years. The significant increase in the total insured population has been due mainly to an increase in pensioners and dependents. In 2015, the active–passive (insured–pensioner) ratio was only 1.92 to 1.0 (Social Security Institution 2017).

Pension income is provided by the state for those who have paid old-age pension premiums. Pension benefits are central instruments that help the state distribute welfare (Aysan 2013). The Turkish state plays a more active role in the welfare of older people than of other age cohorts. In spite of Turkey's relatively young population, the share of public pension spending in total government expenditure is relatively higher in Turkey compared to more aged populations such as Canada and Denmark.

Owing to various systemic changes based on populist measures, the retirement system for the young Turkish population has faced many problems since the late 1960s. A 1992 law replaced the minimum age requirement for retirement with a minimum period of attachment to the social security system. The 1992 legislation effectively brought down the pension eligibility age to 38 for women and 43 for men for those who started to work at the age of 18. Therefore, owing to the option for early retirement, Turkey has the longest average period of pension eligibility among OECD countries (OECD 2011, 29). Numerous changes in pension laws show how populism has played an important role in pension polices. Most of these pension laws were passed before elections in order to get political support. These early retirement policies also highlight the populist characteristics of the welfare regime. These populist regulations were promoted by the governments not only as a gift for current employees who retired at very young ages but also as an employment opportunity for unemployed youth. Considering the present high unemployment rates for the 15–24 age group in Turkey, which stood at 21.9% in April

2017 (TURKSTAT 2017), increasing conflicts in domestic politics, and global economic fluctuations, it seems likely that similar populist regulations will once again be implemented in the near future. Hence, as Esping-Andersen (1999) and Myles (2002) have shown for the continental and southern European welfare regimes, early retirement options have been used by governments to reduce persistent high unemployment rates.

3.3 Health

Healthcare is another significant service that influences the well-being of citizens through social security. Basic healthcare is provided by the state for those who pay social security premiums. Spouses and dependent children of the insurant also enjoy healthcare benefits through three different social security institutions (ES, SSK, and Bag-Kur). The AK Party government first introduced a 10-year health system reform called the health transformation programme, which aimed to develop a public universal healthcare system for all citizens. Various reforms during the 2000s increased the number of social services provided by the market. For example, the healthcare reform, Law 5502 on Universal Health Insurance, was enacted in 2006. This law, which accompanied Law 5510 on Social Security and Universal Health Insurance, aimed to unify the health services of different occupation-based social security institutions (ES, SSK, and Bag-Kur). These new reforms led to a rapid expansion of health insurance coverage and access to healthcare services for all citizens, especially for the poor in Turkey (Atun et al. 2013). In addition to dependents of insured people, the poor and children under 18 years are entitled to benefit from the same healthcare services without paying social security premiums. When dependents and people who have general health insurance are included, the healthcare system covered 98% of the total population as of 2015 (Social Security Institution 2017).

The proportion of government and compulsory health insurance schemes as a percentage of current expenditures on health increased from 70% in 2002 to 77% in 2015, while the OECD average increased only from 72 to 73% during the same period (OECD 2017). The total number of medical institutions rose from 9,685 to 30,449 between 2002 and 2015.

During the same period, owing to the increase in the number of medical institutions, the number of hospital beds per 1,000 people increased from 2.48 to 2.66. Healthcare improvements such as the introduction of family-medicine-centred primary care, the expansion of hospital capacity, and health-insurance coverage for the poorest citizens increased the quality of healthcare services and helped lower mortality rates. Life expectancy at birth for both sexes increased from 72 to 78 between 2002 and 2015, while infant mortality (deaths per 1,000 live births) declined from 29.6 to 10.7 in the same period (OECD 2017).

3.4 Social Services

Social services are a range of public services provided by the state, market, and voluntary organisations to deal with the social risks individuals, families, and communities may face in their life course. The main objective of social services is to increase the individual and collective well-being of citizens. Care that necessitates a variety of types of personal and medical assistance and counselling is a key part of social services. In Turkey, the Ministry of Family and Social Policies provides three principal groups with care services: people with disabilities, children, and older people.

Long-term care service is the institutional care provided by state or private organisations. With the new incentives provided by the state for private nursing homes, the number of private nursing centres increased gradually from 10 in 2007 to 156 in 2015. The number of clients at such centres also increased rapidly from 351 to 10,823 during the same period. In contrast, the number of official nursing centres run by the ministry tripled from 64 to 203, and the total number of clients who received services rose from 4,000 to almost 7,000 during the same period. Hence, the increase in state-based nursing centres is relatively lower compared to the significant increase in private nursing centres and home-based nursing.

In spite of the significant increase in institutional formal care, there is considerable evidence that informal care substitutes for formal care. Long-term care at home has been mostly carried out by mothers and daughters who have limited or no education (Aysan and Aysan 2016).

Nevertheless, the number of applicants for long-term, care at home options have increased since such an option was first established in 2007. While there were about 30,000 people with disabilities who received homecare support in 2007, this increased to 508,000 in 2015. Since new people are receiving information about homecare support in increasing numbers, the number of homecare beneficiaries is projected to increase in the near future. The total amount paid by the state for homecare nursing increased from 35 million Turkish lira (TL) to 3.8 billion TL between 2007 and 2015.

The gendered division of labour also affects the labour force participation rates of women in Turkey. This is mainly due to a lack of childcare support for families and the traditional role of women in childcare. In Turkey, early childhood education and care are centralised under the authority of the Ministry of National Education and the Ministry of Family and Social Policies. Despite an emphasis on increasing the availability of services and programmes for young children and families since the early 1990s, preschool remains non-compulsory and the preschool enrolment rate among children aged 3–5 is very low, at 31% in 2015 (OECD 2015). For children aged 0–35 months, there is no public provision of childcare services mandated by law. For children aged 36–47 months, public provision of childcare services is very limited. Moreover, full-day childcare options are mainly provided by the market, while public preschools generally operate either in two half-day shifts or only on a half-day basis (World Bank 2015, 22). The high cost of institutional childcare is another problem for Turkish mothers. Public care services are very limited in terms of age (for all mothers) and hours of operation (for working mothers in particular).

3.5 Housing

According to Spicker (2014), the root of many problems in Europe is a shortage of adequate housing. This shortage means that households have to fit into a limited number of available dwellings, which are often expensive for middle-income citizens. Many of the key issues in deprivation and inequality are related to housing and neighbourhood characteristics.

In Turkey, the Toplu Konut Idaresi Baskanligi (Housing Development Administration, henceforth TOKI), established in 1984, is the key public institution responsible for providing affordable housing for citizens. New regulations in the early 2000s helped TOKI to broaden its scope. Today, TOKI operates in various fields, such as social housing, urban renewal projects, disaster housing applications, migrant dwellings, and income-sharing projects, based on a revenue-sharing model.

This new scope and new development strategy led to a significant increase in the number of houses constructed by TOKI. While approximately 44,000 residential buildings were produced by TOKI between 1984 and 2002, it constructed over 500,000 residential units between 2003 and 2011. TOKI aims to construct an additional 700,000 housing units by 2023 (TOKI 2017).

A detailed analysis of TOKI projects shows that it is mostly upper-middle-class citizens who benefit from TOKI projects. About 41% of the social housing projects benefited the targeted middle-income groups, while only 23% were for the low-income group. Urban transformation projects have recently become increasingly significant, with 15% of housing projects done by TOKI. Resource-development projects developed in partnership with big construction companies are also an important part of TOKI's activities. About 17% of its housing projects are produced through such collaborations, yet these houses are generally very expensive even for middle-income citizens.

4 Policy Recommendations for the New Challenges Ahead

According to Pierson (2007), there are three main challenges –globalisation, demographic changes, and new social risks – for the welfare regimes of the twenty-first century. These problems are also valid for Turkey. First, globalisation has given rise to various economic challenges to the post-Second World War economic system. The production system has evolved from a Fordist one based on large stocks (just-in-case), standardised products, and mass production to a post-Fordist production system based on flexible machinery, lean production, minimal stocks (just-in-time), and differentiated products (Krahn et al. 2007). In addition, the characteristics of the labour market have changed since the 1980s. Rifkin (2004) interpreted technological developments and deskilling as the main characteristics of a new era in which fewer workers are needed to produce goods and services. Competitive global trade and profit maximisation goals have led multinational companies to move their production to newly industrialising countries that have less regulation and job security. The impact of outsourcing and the increase in precarious jobs also have a significant impact on unskilled workers and their social security in Turkey.

Second, the continuing change in the demographic structure of the Turkish population poses noteworthy challenges in terms of meeting the needs of the ageing population. Population ageing has a negative effect on economic growth owing to the old-age dependency ratio – the ratio of the population aged 65 and older to the population aged 15–64. In the contemporary world, it is difficult for ageing populations to sustain generous retirement benefits and increasing health costs due to slow economic growth. The Turkish welfare regime faces a double burden. First, despite its younger population, its pension system suffers from budget deficits (Aysan 2013, 158). Second, according to projections, Turkey will have lost its demographic opportunity by the 2050s, meaning that the financial constraints on the pension system will become more intense. Despite the significant progress of a 2006 reform in achieving a sustainable and fair social security system, more needs to be done to encourage standard employment opportunities and intergenerational justice.

Third, new social risks, particularly changes in family formation and gender roles, pose important challenges to welfare regimes (Pierson 2007, 222–223). Welfare in Turkey has traditionally been distributed on the basis of the gendered division of labour in the family, reproducing the well-known male-breadwinner model (Aysan 2013). Men have been responsible for meeting the economic needs of the household, while women have been responsible for unpaid domestic labour and caring for children and older people (Aysan and Aysan 2016, 43). However, this situation is changing. The rise in women's educational level and rates of participation in the labour force has challenged traditional gender roles in society as well as within families. Especially in the early twenty-first century, Turkish families underwent rapid changes, such as increased flexibility in modes of entry into and exit from the labour force, increased variability in work-force participation across families, changes in the social meaning of fatherhood and motherhood, and new associations between gender and family earnings (Koc et al. 2015; Aysan 2016b). Changes in family structure and increases in labour force participation among young and educated women challenged the family's dominant role in traditional welfare distribution in Turkey. Another important social challenge has been the huge migration flows from Syria and other neighbouring countries into Turkey. As of 2017, there are over 3 million immigrants in Turkey. In addition to the security issues these migrants pose, their social and economic adaptation to Turkey will pose some of the greatest challenges for the Turkish welfare regime in the years ahead.

Alongside these three global trends, two other challenges peculiar to the Turkish welfare regime limit the success of social policy reforms: populism and patronage. As highlighted earlier, populism and patronage have been two indirect welfare distribution mechanisms since the beginning of Turkey. Governments use them not only to secure citizens' electoral support but also to distribute welfare in a developing and rapidly urbanizing country. These welfare mechanisms now pose a significant threat to the sustainability of social policies and recent gains in social citizenship. Both politicians and citizens must work hard to get rid of these traditional and archaic welfare mechanisms.

In light of these challenges and the global and local dynamics with which they are intertwined, some regulations can be proposed for the Turkish case. While some of the regulations are relevant to the challenges pointed out in this article, some of them are key to improving social policies and associated institutions. Their successful implementation will be crucial for the future of the Turkish welfare regime:

1. The Ministry of Family and Social Policies must be the central actor in social policies, and its institutional infrastructure must be developed.
2. Longitudinal and cross-sectional data on social assistance, social policies, and the needs of citizens must be collected regularly.
3. Comprehensive and detailed social policies must be designed to meet the overlapping needs of various groups.

4. Equity and justice must be the key determinants of social policies for all types of groups, whether based on gender, ethnicity, age, class, or religion.
5. There must be sustainable social policies that will not threaten intergenerational equity and younger generations' welfare.
6. New policies and regulations that address the needs of different types of families must be developed to strengthen families.

5 Conclusion

This study has argued that the Turkish welfare regime is undergoing significant transformations through the impact of internal and external dynamics. Contrary to what has been documented in other countries, it is difficult to argue that the Turkish welfare regime has transformed either into a liberal welfare regime dominated by market actors or into a social democratic welfare regime based on a universalist and rights-based system. While Turkey's EU accession process, ageing population, and increasing living standards have led the state to play a more active role in the welfare of citizens, its increasing social expenditures have forced the state to collaborate with other actors, particularly the market. Populist policies and family-centred regulations – used in the 1990s by various parties – remain valid welfare distribution mechanisms in the 2010s.

In light of the particular challenges Turkey faces in the twenty-first century, further empirical research is needed to elaborate the Turkish welfare regime. Given the multiple challenges facing the Turkish welfare regime, any research contributing to the literature must have a broad and analytical perspective. Comparative studies focusing on Turkey and other welfare states are especially needed to understand how and in what ways the Turkish case differs from that of other welfare regimes. Such comparisons can also help Turkey to draw lessons from ageing welfare states where welfare institutions are already well established and their responses to similar socio-economic challenges in the twenty-first century.

References

Agartan, Tuba I. 2012. Marketization and Universalism: Crafting the Right Balance in the Turkish Health Care System. *Current Sociology* 60 (4): 456–471.

Atun, Rifat, Sabahattin Aydin, Sarbani Chakraborty, Safir Sumer, Meltem Aran, Ipek Gurol, Serpil Nazlioglu, Senay Ozgulcu, Ulger Aydogan, Banu Ayar, Ugur Dilmen, and Recep Akdag. 2013. Universal Health Coverage in Turkey: Enhancement of Equity. *The Lancet* 382 (9886): 65–99.

Aybars, Ayse I., and Dimitris Tsarouhas. 2010. Straddling Two Continents: Social Policy and Welfare Politics in Turkey. *Social Policy & Administration* 44 (6): 746–763.

Aysan, Mehmet F. 2013. Reforms and Challenges: The Turkish Pension Regime Revisited. *Emerging Markets Finance and Trade* 49 (Suppl. 5): 148–162.

———. 2016a. *Understanding the Welfare Regime of Turkey: Institutions and Individuals*, TUBITAK 3501 Final Report.

———. 2016b. Social and Cultural Reasons of the Fertility Decline: Turkey in the 2010s, In *Proceeding of the 4th Turkish Demography Conference*, 155–168. Ankara: HUNEE.

Aysan, Mehmet F., and Ummugulsum Aysan. 2016. Who Cares?: Elderly Care in Turkey. *Economia & Lavoro* 50 (3): 33–46.

Bugra, Ayse, and Sinem Adar. 2008. Social Policy Change in Countries without Mature Welfare States: The Case of Turkey. *New Perspectives on Turkey* 38: 83–106.

Bugra, Ayse, and Caglar Keyder. 2006. The Turkish Welfare Regime in Transformation. *Journal of European Social Policy* 16 (3): 211–228.

Ceylan, Harun. 2016. *Yaslilik ve Refah Devleti*. Istanbul: Acilim.

Deacon, Bob. 2000. Eastern European Welfare States: The Impact of the Politics of Globalization. *Journal of European Social Policy* 10 (2): 146–161.

Esping-Andersen, Gosta. 1990. *The Three Worlds of Welfare Capitalism*. Cambridge: Polity Press.

———. 1999. *Social Foundations of Post-Industrial Economies*. Oxford: Oxford University Press.

Ferrera, Maurizio. 1996. The Southern Model of Welfare in social Europe. *Journal of European Social Policy* 6 (1): 17–37.

Ferrera, Maurizio, and Martin Rhodes. 2000. *Recasting European Welfare States*. London: Frank Cass.

Gal, John. 2010. Is There an Extended Family of Mediterranean Welfare States? *Journal of European Social Policy* 20 (4): 283–300.
Gough, Ian. 1996. Social Assistance in Southern Europe. *South European Society and Politics* 1 (1): 1–23.
———. 2001. Globalization and Regional Welfare Regimes: The East Asian Case. *Global Social Policy* 1 (2): 166–180.
Jawad, Rana. 2009. *Social Welfare and Religion in the Middle East: A Lebanese Perspective*. Bristol: Policy Press.
Koc, Ismet, Tugba Adali, Serdar Polat, and Hande D. Turk. 2015. Changes in Family Structure in Turkey: 1968–2013. In *Hacettepe University Institute of Population Studies, Turkey Demographic and Health Survey: Study of Advanced Analysis*, Hacettepe University Institute of Population Studies, 1–47. Ankara: T. R. Ministry of Development and TUBITAK.
Korpi, Walter, and Joakim Palme. 1998. The Paradox of Redistribution and Strategies of Equality: Welfare State Institutions, Inequality, and Poverty in the Western Countries. *American Sociological Review* 63: 661–687.
Krahn, Harvey, Graham S. Lowe, and Karen Hughes. 2007. *Work, Industry and Canadian Society*. Toronto: Thompson-Nelson.
Mishra, Ramesh. 1999. *Globalization and the Welfare State*. Cheltenham/Northampton: E. Elgar.
Myles, John. 2002. A New Social Contract for the Elderly. In *Why We Need a New Welfare State*, ed. Gosta Esping-Andersen, 130–172. Oxford: Oxford University Press.
O'Connor, James. 1973. *The Fiscal Crisis of the State*. London: St Martins Press.
OECD. 2008. *OECD Glossary of Statistical Terms*. Paris: OECD.
———. 2011. *Pensions at a Glance: Retirement-Income Systems in OECD Countries*. Paris: OECD.
———. 2015. *Education at a Glance 2015: OECD Indicators*. Paris: OECD.
———. 2017. *OECD Health Statistics 2016*. http://www.oecd.org/els/health-systems/health-statistics.htm. Accessed 10 April.
Offe, Claus. 1984. *Contradictions of the Welfare State*. London: Hutchinson Education.
Pierson, Christopher. 2007. *Beyond the Welfare State? The New Political Economy of Welfare*. Pennsylvania: The Pennsylvania State University Press.
Rifkin, Jeremy. 2004. *The End of Work*. Rev. ed. New York: Tarcher/Penguin.
Scruggs, Lyle, and James Allan. 2006. Welfare-State De-Commodification in 18 OECD Countries: A Replication and Revision. *Journal of European Social Policy* 16 (1): 55–72.

Social Security Institution. 2017. *Work Place and Insured Person Statistics 2015*. http://www.sgk.gov.tr/wps/portal/sgk/tr/kurumsal/istatistik/sgk_istatistik_yilliklari. Accessed 25 May.
Spicker, Paul. 1995. *Social Policy: Themes and Approaches*. London: Prentice Hall.
———. 2014. *Social Policy: Theory and Practice*. Bristol: Policy Press.
The Ministry of National Education. 2017. *National Education Statistics Formal Education 2016–2017 (1st Semester)*. Ankara: Ministry of National Education.
TOKI. 2017. *TOKI Housing Programs*. https://www.toki.gov.tr/en/housing-programs.html. Accessed 15 April.
Trifiletti, Rossana. 1999. Southern European Welfare Regimes and the Worsening Position of Women. *Journal of European Social Policy* 9 (1): 49–64.
TURKSTAT. 2017. *Main Statistics*. http://www.turkstat.gov.tr. Accessed 20 June.
Walker, Alan, and Chack Kie Wong. 2005. Conclusion: From Confucianism to Globalisation. In *East Asian Welfare Regimes in Transition*, ed. Alan Walker and Chack Kie Wong, 213–224. Bristol: Policy Press.
World Bank. 2015. *Supply and Demand for Child Care Services in Turkey*, Report No. 98884TR. Washington, DC: World Bank.

Turkey's Struggle to Achieve High-Income Status Through Adaptation to the Knowledge Economy

Halil Kürşad Aslan and Murat Aslan

1 Introduction

In the international relations discipline, the realist argument emphasizes that states brutally compete with each other to ensure that their own share in the global distribution of power outweighs that of others. In the global economy of the twenty-first century, the most important factor is knowledge; thus, the primary goal of all state leaders would be to gain advantage in terms of the knowledge economy against all other competitors. The balance and distribution of power among states in the global political system could change if one state accumulates ever more knowledge than others. Thus, the possession of knowledge and its commercialization is the most important indicator of power in the global political system. During the Cold War era in the international relations literature

H. K. Aslan (✉)
Istabul Medipol University, Istanbul, Turkey

M. Aslan
Yıldırım Beyazıt University, Ankara, Turkey

A. F. Aysan et al. (eds.), *Turkish Economy*,
https://doi.org/10.1007/978-3-319-70380-0_6

among the most widely used terms were "arms race," "mutually assured destruction," and "deterrence;" in the new era the global power competition is more about technological development, high-tech exports, innovation ecosystem, and the management of knowledge.

Accordingly, this chapter employs a political economy approach to analyzing Turkey's development policies in the most recent decade with a special focus on the knowledge economy, higher education, technology, and innovation policies. Taking into consideration the macroeconomic performance of Turkey in the 2000s, this study tries to determine whether Turkey has been successful regarding joining the knowledge economy in its national production processes. In this connection, the literature on the middle-income trap will be beneficial since before Turkey achieves high-income status, it needs to mature from its middle-income position. In light of the macroeconomic performance of Turkey in the past decade, this study tries to determine whether there are indications of a middle-income trap or not. Additionally, technology and human capital investments, along with education policies, are emphasized as the most important reform areas through which to escape the middle-income trap and move to high-income levels. It is important to note that particular concentration is placed on the reform needs of Turkey's national innovation and higher education systems.

Turkey's General Directorate of Productivity, which remains under the Science Ministry of Industry and Technology, issued a report titled Productivity Strategy and Action Plan covering the years 2014–2017: the conclusion of the report emphasizes that a large part of the limitations in Turkey's productivity is based on the structural problems of the education system (Çağlar and Acar 2013). Another report, the Global Competitiveness Report published by the World Economic Forum (WEF), carried out a similar extrapolation. According to the Global Competitiveness Report (2015–2016), two indicators, inadequate training of workforce and low innovation capacity, were identified as among the most important deficiencies in Turkey's productivity and competitiveness. In another global report by the OECD (2016b), Education at a Glance, many deep structural problems along with quality deficiencies in Turkey's education system are highlighted. Taking all those together,

Turkey's education system, especially its higher education system, remains a serious obstacle to entering the knowledge economy.

Consequently, this study aims to combine middle-income-trap literature with comparative development studies with an eye towards the evolution of global political economy structures. At the center of the paper are Turkey's development policies, innovation ecosystem, human capital, and higher education system. In this context, several parameters are collected from official sites regarding enrollment rates, faculty and student profiles, academic outputs such as publication records, university rankings, public expenditures, research and development (R&D) activities. Comparisons with successful developing and other countries, OECD members, and their macroeconomic and development figures are provided to depict the relative position of Turkey. Several official and private data sources are used from national institutions such as the Turkish Statistical Institute (TÜİK), Turkish Higher Education Council (YOK), Scientific and Technological Research Council of Turkey (TÜBİTAK), Turkish Academic Network and Information Center (ULAKBIM), and Turkey's Informatics Industry Association (TÜBİSAD). Additionally, data are also obtained from major international organizations such as the World Economic Forum, OECD, United Nations Education, Scientific and Cultural Organization, United Nations Development Programme (UNDP), International Telecommunications Union (ITU), and the World Bank.

2 Middle-Income-Trap Literature

After World War II an extensive literature emerged about economic growth and development. The most notable model was designed by Robert Solow, which was extremely simplified. The Solow model, which attempted to explain the determinants of long-run economic growth by means of capital accumulation and labor growth, has become very popular in this body of literature. The main assumption of the model was that there are constant returns to scale with regard to capital and effective labor. In the following decades new studies were introduced. The goal of these new studies was to explain productivity increases that were not revealed by the Solow model.

Scholars compared country cases in terms of their growth differentials. For example, Robert Lucas (1993) asked why South Korea had achieved tremendous numbers in its growth of national income while the Philippines could not attain such success. However, in 1960 both countries had about the same standard of living, as measured by their per-capita gross domestic products (GDPs) of about $600, population numbers, urbanization levels, and so forth. From 1960 to 1988, in the Philippines average annual per-capita GDP growth was about 1.8%; in South Korea, over the same period, this number was 6.2%. So the critical question is why in recent decades have Korea, Singapore, and Taiwan achieved sustainable development records and higher living standards, but the Philippines, Mexico, Turkey, and Brazil have not.

In the economic growth studies, "middle-income trap" is a relatively new phenomenon that relates to countries where rapidly growing economies stagnate at some point in their economic growth trajectory. More specifically, a middle-income trap refers to growth slowdowns that are identified as large, sudden, and sustained deviations from the growth path predicted by a basic conditional convergence framework (Aiyar et al. 2013).

The increase in the frequency and popularity of this concept is evident in the daily programs of economic bureaucracy, international institutions, and politicians, as well as in academic circles. On the other hand, despite extensive use of this concept, it still lacks a commonly accepted definition and sound theoretical framework (Im and Rosenblatt 2015; Gill and Kharas 2015); however, this phenomenon is generally described in terms of relative "catch-up" with the United States' per-capita income levels or alternatively in terms of the number of years a country takes to move one step forward regarding income levels and thresholds (Felipe et al. 2012).

The World Bank data indicate that middle-income countries make up almost two-thirds of the global population (5 out of 7.5 billion) and earns almost one-third of global income (Gill and Kharas 2015). As of 2016, Turkey sits in the upper middle-income group with approximately US$9,500 per-capita income. Based on 2016 metrics, upper middle-income economies are those with a GNI per capita between

US$4,036 and US$12,475; high-income economies are those with a GNI per capita of US$12,476 or more.

Middle-income countries face many common issues. Characteristically, these countries have remained stuck in a middle-income growth trap either because they are unable to attract sufficient funds from domestic or outside sources or because of political instabilities, poor educational and health standards, low levels of human capital, inadequate physical and institutional infrastructures, lack of diversification in manufacturing and exports, and, most importantly, total factor productivity.

In the early 1960s, 101 countries were in the middle- or low-income group, whereas by the early 2000s only 13 of those countries had succeeded in crossing over into the high-income category without getting stuck in the middle-income trap (Gill and Kharas 2015; Wilson 2014). In addition to these countries, in recent years it has been observed that some countries in the European Union (EU) integration process, such as the Czech Republic and Slovakia, have reached high-level income status.

In this chapter, the Turkish economy and its structural problems are analyzed with an eye toward the concept of middle-income trap. Looking at economic conditions and the position Turkey occupies in the global context in terms of the knowledge economy, one might ask whether Turkey will remain stuck in the middle-income trap. Employing several parameters and indicators such as competitiveness, productivity, innovation capacity, and others, this study tries to gain a better understanding of Turkey's propensities to fall into the middle-income trap or, alternatively, attain high-income levels with an innovation-driven knowledge economy. Special attention is paid to the innovation system, human capital, and Turkey's higher education system as a potential policy area with which Ankara might reach the high-income category. Thus, experiences of country cases are essential for Turkey to design a suitable development program in which higher education and national innovation systems are crucial.

Table 1 shows human development indicators for selected countries. All the countries in the table (except Turkey) have managed to escape the middle-income trap in recent decades. Figures for Turkey can be seen in the last row for comparison purposes. It is clear that socioeconomic indi-

Table 1 Human development indicators of selected countries, 2016

Country	HDI rank	Population (millions)	Per capita income in US dollars (PPP)[a]	Life expectancy	Average schooling
Singapore	5	5.5	85.382	82.6	10.2
Ireland	8	4.6	68.513	81.1	11.7
Hong Kong	12	7.3	56.923	83.9	10.1
Japan	17	126.9	40.763	83.6	11.6
S. Korea	18	50.6	34.647	82.1	11.9
Slovenia	25	2.1	28.664	80.6	12.1
Spain	27	46.4	34.906	83.0	9.8
Czech Rep.	28	10.5	28.144	78.8	12.3
Greece	29	10.8	26.379	81.3	10.3
Chile	38	17.9	21.665	82.0	9.9
Slovakia	40	5.4	26.764	76.4	12.2
Turkey	71	78.6	20.008	75.3	7.9

Source: Human Development Report 2016; for population figures, world development indicators 2016 (World Bank 2017)

[a]Figures show gross national product (GNP) calculated according to Purchasing Power Parity (PPP)

cators of the other countries are significantly better than they are for Turkey. Common characteristics of these achievers might help countries trapped in the middle-income category. All countries in the table remained in the "very high human development" group in the given year. Economic and social indicators are balanced. All have excellent education and life expectancy figures, and average schooling generally exceeds 10 years for their populations.

The middle-income-growth trap is related to the transformative difficulties of national economies. As a country becomes richer, the structure of the national economy evolves from economic activities with low productivity into relatively high-productivity sectors. In the early stages of their development efforts these countries experience input-driven production where the achievement of a moment of growth is not difficult since labor is cheap and abundant. These countries experience large productivity gains at first through a reallocation of rural labor from the agricultural sector to relatively high-productivity light industrial manufacturing activities. After a certain amount of time has elapsed, these new urban classes reach middle-income levels, the pool of low-wage workers diminishes, and wage levels gradually rise. Wages increase as the economy evolves from low-skilled, labor-intensive activities into relatively advanced and complex ones. As discussed in the literature, the progression from middle to high income is not an easy and guaranteed destination on a linear growth path (Felipe et al. 2012; Berg et al. 2012). The types of goods and services produced and exported would not have the same impact for further growth and development in this economy. At some point it becomes harder to increase per-capita income (Gill and Kharas 2015).

In the development literature it is well documented that hardships for countries in their middle-income stages are essentially due to productivity issues. According to a World Bank study, 85% of the slowdown in the rate of output growth in middle-income economies is explained by the total factor productivity growth (Agenor et al. 2012). In other words, the growth of the economy should be coupled to improvements in the total factor productivity. To be able to compete successfully in the global market, a middle-income country must be equipped with a sound national innovation framework, high-quality human capital, a skilled labor pool, and technological advancements.

For the Turkish economy we could look at the experiences of countries that have recently achieved high-income status such as South Korea, Spain, Ireland, Portugal, and Singapore. These countries managed to overcome the middle-income trap. A simple keyword for their success is total factor productivity, which accounted for the national economy's transformative dynamism. Gains in efficiency may come from all economic factors or inputs into the production processes. Thus, improvements in labor (human capital and education), technological advancements (innovation), and efficiency gains in capital (saving and investment) are all important for capturing total factor productivity. For instance, to avoid the middle-income trap, South Korea strengthened its education system in order to ensure for the essential standard required for building human capital. It also prioritized R&D activities along with a national innovation infrastructure. By 2015, the proportion of the population with university degrees in Turkey and South Korea was at about the same levels for the age group 55–65; however, for the age group 25–34 this figure was 65% for Korea and 18% for Turkey (Gür et al. 2017). This was the performance differential due to South Korea's sound and timely education reforms in the 1990s.

3 Findings and Discussion

According to a World Bank (2007) study regarding knowledge economies and economic development, countries need to make deep structural reforms, particularly in their education and innovation systems, along with domestic ICT infrastructure. For these economic transformation policies to be successful, national governments must have an attainable strategic vision that is shared by all domestic stakeholders. Then the government should put together necessary reform packages that contain systematic, gradual, and simultaneous policy aspects. The World Bank's (2007) knowledge economy framework is based on four pillars:

(1) the country's education and training base,
(2) its information and telecommunications infrastructure,
(3) the innovation system,
(4) the overall business and governance framework.

Accordingly, in the following subsections each pillar is analyzed in order to evaluate institutional and organizational setbacks in the Turkish framework.

3.1 First Pillar: Turkey's Education and Training Base

Since the industrial revolution, the capitalist world system has brought about deep inequalities among social groups and nations as well. In the twenty-first century this trend has gained momentum. Saving, investment, capital accumulation, and technological advancements, all of which are strongly associated and interconnected, further deepen these inequalities. It is interesting to note that R&D expenditures made by only one giant global corporation exceeds the total R&D expenditures made by Turkey. For example, companies such as Volkswagen, Samsung, Microsoft, Roche, and Intel allocated more than US$10 billion for R&D in 2014; Samsung has about 320,000 employees around the world, and one out of four (around 80,000) works in R&D. In contrast, Turkey was able to allocate almost US$7 billion (1% of its GDP) and the total number of R&D personnel in Turkey is reportedly 111,000 as of 2016.

As can be seen in the following table, the largest corporations with the highest market value have also concentrated in a few countries, regions, and selected sectors only. According to market research institutions such as Forbes, Interbrand, and Brand Finance, the most valuable brands are generally technology and telecom companies. Transnational corporations account for almost half of world trade volume, yet over half the world's 500 largest corporations are in only four countries: the United States, Japan, France, and Germany. In 2016, Interbrand found that Apple, the American technology corporation, was the most valuable firm in the world. Its reported revenue was US$50 billion and its brand value was US$179 billion; second was Google, worth US$133 billion. Additionally, based on May 2017 data from the New York Stock Exchange, the market value of Apple Corp. reached US$776 billion, nearly equal to Turkey's annual GDP. In the following table, company brands are ranked by Brand Finance for the year 2017. Another important note is that the overwhelming majority of the world's patents belong to this handful of giant companies (Table 2).

Given these numbers and the realities of scale economy, it would appear that small and medium-sized economies have very little if any chance of competing on global production structures. South Korea owes its development success to its strategic decision in the aftermath of the East Asian Crisis to concentrate on a few sectors and allocating its scarce investment funds to these sectors. Today, South Korea makes up 50% of world ship production, and it is the world's sixth largest automotive manufacturer and third largest steel producer.

According to 2015 figures, the economy of South Korea, with a population of around 51 million, is worth US$1.2 trillion, while Turkey, with a population of 80 million, has a an economy worth US$800 billion. South Korea exports about US$550 billion worth of goods and services, yielding a US$120 billion foreign trade surplus, making it the world's

Table 2 World's most valuable brands (2017)

No.	Company	Brand value (in billion $)	Sector	Country
1	Google	109.4	IT	USA
2	Apple	107.1	Telecom	USA
3	Amazon	106.4	Retail	USA
4	AT&T	87	Telecom	USA
5	Microsoft	76.2	IT	USA
6	Samsung	66.2	Telecom information	South Korea
7	Verizon	65.8	Telecom	USA
8	Walmart	62.2	Retail	USA
9	Facebook	62	IT	USA
10	ICBC	47.8	Finance	China
11	China Mobile	46.7	Telecom	China
12	Toyota	46.2	Automotive	Japan
13	Wells Fargo	41.6	Finance	USA
14	China Construction Bank	41.3	Finance	China
15	NTT Group	40.5	Telecom	Japan
16	Mc Donald's	38.9	Food	USA
17	BMW	37.1	Automotive	Germany
18	Shell	36.7	Energy	Netherlands
19	Deutsche Telekom	36.4	Telecom	Germany
20	IBM	36.1	IT	USA

Source: Brand Finance Global 500 (2017)

sixth largest exporter; Turkey exports $152 billion in goods and services, has a US$48 billion foreign trade deficit, and ranks 30th in world exports. More importantly, 27% of South Korea's exports are high-technology products, while that number is 2% for Turkey.

As of 1990, South Korea was ranked 30th in world automobile exports and Turkey followed right behind in the 31st spot. Fast forward 25 years later to 2015, and South Korea's rank rose to 5th place in world automotive production and exports, whereas Turkey was ranked 19th. South Korea had more than 30 multinational corporations before the 1996 crisis; because of restructuring and the elimination of inefficient players, this number dropped to 11. Out of seven automotive companies, only two survived. After the East Asian Crisis, South Korea focused on a couple of select sectors: electronics and automotive industries. As giant corporations of South Korea went bankrupt, the remaining *chaebols* (industrial conglomerates run and controlled by an owner or family in South Korea) carried out serious restructuring procedures. The East Asian Crisis was seen as an opportunity to transition to high-efficiency sectors. It is doubtless that as specialization in certain sectors increases, factor shifts occur rom less efficient sectors toward more efficient ones.

In Turkey, officials and especially bureaucrats in planning bodies have enough awareness of this fact. The Supreme Council for Science and Technology (SCST) specified a small number of priority areas for R&D activities and it designed Turkey's National Innovation System. Automotive, machine manufacturing, information and communication technologies, defense, space, health, energy, water, and food sectors are specified as priority areas. A number of selective measures and incentives have been included, especially in the 9th and 10th Development Plans prepared by the Ministry of Development to reach development targets in Turkey in certain industries. Furthermore, a National Science, Technology, and Innovation Strategy Document (2011–2016) was also issued by TÜBİTAK. One of the most important preconditions for Turkey to increase its share of high-tech products in its overall exports is delivering high-quality human capital to be trained in these priority sectors; thus, national universities and technology centers have important roles in this matter.

As countries become mature enough to export higher proportions of high-tech products thanks to their well-educated workforce, it is easier to get out of the middle-income trap. For example, in 2015, Turkey imported goods in the electronics sector in the amount of US$24.6 billion and exported goods worth US$13.4 billion. If Turkey were good enough in terms of quality, innovation, and technology in the electronics sector, it would reduce its dependence on these goods and bring down its current account deficit significantly.

The proportion of R&D expenditures in terms of national income and number of people employed in R&D services, the proportion of high-tech commodities in the overall export figures are some of the major indicators of the strength of knowledge economies. There is a positive correlation between the magnitude of R&D expenditures and the level of high-tech exports in national income. According to World Development Indicators (2015) data, the percentage of high-tech exports is approximately 11% for Indonesia, 16% for Germany and Japan, and at or above 20% for South Korea, the USA, and China (People's Republic of China, or PRC).

It is obvious that Turkey needs to concentrate on a few industrial sectors and allocate its scarce human and financial capital so as to develop those sectors and gain a competitive advantage in global markets. However, it seems that Turkish authorities have not paid enough attention to education, particularly higher education, to complement national innovation efforts in those sectors. There are a couple of points to elaborate on weaknesses in the development and use of human capital. The first point is that inputs to the Turkish higher education system are weak and misallocated. The second point is that human capital output from the higher education system does not match well with the industrial needs of those sectors to make Turkey competitive in the world markets. In sum, the structure of the higher education system and Turkey's selected priority sectors do not match well.

The most important input of the higher education system is incoming students. Trends in International Mathematics and Science Study (TIMSS) statistics on the international field of mathematics and science provide insight into comparative student performance. It is a test applied to fourth- and eighth-grade students, and since 1995 it has been conducted every 4 years. The following table shows the country rankings. The successful countries and Turkey's position are closely aligned with the results of the Program for International Student Assessment (PISA) test conducted by the OECD. These international tests give an idea about the state of education in those countries Table 3.

In the PISA program, proficiency levels are divided into seven clusters for each part: reading, science, and math. Among them the most critical proficiency groups are Level 5 (607–669) and Level 6 (669) students. In PISA tests, students in Levels 5 and 6, particularly in mathematics and science, are important in terms of developing the necessary human capital for innovation and production of intellectual property. Students in these two top performing groups must systematically be placed in university departments that Turkey sees as priority development areas. The proportion of these top-ranked students within the national system is a very important indicator. In 2012, Levels 5 and 6 top performers made up

Table 3 TIMSS student performance indicators

2011 Indicators			2015 Indicators		
No.	Country	Score	No.	Country	Score
1	Singapore	606	1	Singapore	618
2	South Korea	605	2	Hong Kong	615
3	Hong Kong	602	3	South Korea	608
4	Taiwan (PRC)	591	4	Taiwan (PRC)	597
5	Japan	585	5	Japan	593
6	North Ireland	562	6	North Ireland	570
7	Belgium	549	7	Russia	564
35	Turkey	469	39	Turkey	483

Source: National Center for Education Statistics (NCES 2015)

13% of students in mathematics on average among all OECD members, and the OECD average for science and reading was approximately 8%. For Turkey, these figures were 5.9% in mathematics, 4.3% in science, and 1.8% in reading (MEB 2013). There are two critical inferences to make from these data. First, in Turkey, input to the higher education system is weak at the beginning. Second, these top performers are not systematically channeled into Turkey's higher education institutions in compliance with Ankara's selected priority sectors such as biotechnology or pharmaceutical manufacturing.

Turkey also has deep quality problems regarding outputs from the higher education system. There are also quality assurance issues, misallocation problems, and mismatch between graduates and industrial demand. A couple of examples might be sufficient to highlight these points. According to 2014 figures, 1 out of every 10 students enrolled in graduate programs and only 1 out of 20 doctoral students were able to graduate from their programs. This means that graduate programs could not produce efficient turn out rates. Moreover, compared to the OECD figures, Turkey's higher education programs were relatively more concentrated on agriculture and social sciences and relatively less concentrated on necessary fields for innovation such as science, humanities, and engineering (Tekneci 2016).

Another important indicator in the higher education system is academic staff and their work. Employment of qualified faculty members has critical importance in enhancing the effectiveness of a higher education system and research activities. In Turkey, with the rapid expansion of universities in the last decade, the number of full-time faculty members was doubled. It was about 82,000 in 2004 and reached almost 150,000 by 2014. However, it is useful to note that the student/faculty ratio was 25 in 2004, and this figure worsened to 41 in 2014 (Tekneci 2016). In other words, the amount of time that academics can devote to R&D has diminished.

Regarding the shortage of qualified faculty, especially in science and engineering fields, there are some programs for training prospective faculty members such as the Faculty Member Training Program (ÖYP), which is being implemented by YOK, and scholarships that are given by TÜBİTAK and the Ministry of Education. However, these programs are conducted without coordination and there are rumors about their over-politicization. Additionally, the total number of doctorate graduates is comparatively low in Turkey. According to OECD (2016a) data, the USA is the leading country in terms of PhD output, with 67,449 graduates from all fields, Germany has 28,147 graduates, the UK has 25,020 graduates, and Turkey has 4,516 graduates. Unfortunately, most new PhDs in Turkey are in the social sciences and agricultural studies.

There are also important problems regarding the promotion of faculty members and tenure issues (Açıkgöz 2012). In this phase, in addition to quantitative inadequacies, it is useful to underline two important problems: overpoliticization of universities and a very limited incentive system. In sum, a high-quality education system, especially higher education, should be restructured in a rational incentive-based system. Rewards and punishment must be put in place in the institutional mechanisms.

According to a study conducted by TÜBİTAK (2015), the number of total articles published during the 2004–2014 period by higher education or research institutions based in Turkey was 228,856 and the number of citations was 1,517,691 in the same period. In terms of the number of publications, Turkey ranks 26th in the world; however, in terms of citations, the rank is much lower at the 42nd spot in the world according to data by the TÜBİTAK (2015) during the 2004–2014 period. The Web of Science database has shown that Turkish universities produced publications above the world average in only 17 subfields out of 250. Among these subfields the most important for Turkey's development in priority areas are integrative and complementary medicine, medical laboratory technology, nuclear physics, applied chemistry, thermodynamic, mechanics, instrumentation, water resources, energy and fuels, construction engineering, and chemical engineering (Tekneci 2016).

Although the deficiencies in Turkey's education system and in particular the higher education system are partly related to inadequate resources, the most important problem is the lack of an all-inclusive system. More precisely, there is no well-established system in which the input, output, and process dimensions of the system are determined in light of reward and punishment parameters. In Turkey, both the number of universities and the number of students have experienced huge increases in the last decade; the number of universities, which was 73 in 2004, reached 180 by 2016. The total number of university students, including those enrolled in open education, almost quadrupled, reaching 7.2 million students in 2016 from approximately 1.8 million students in 2000 (Gür et al. 2017). However, this rapid expansion has not been accompanied by quality increases and institutional adaptation to new conditions.

The turmoil brought on by Turkey's rapid increase in the number of universities began to be felt after 2006. New universities have many administrative, financial-infrastructural, academic, and social problems (Özoğlu et al. 2016). To restructure the national economy in accordance with the requirements of the knowledge economy and innovation, it is possible to carry out quality control processes at three points in the education system: input control, process control, and output control. In Turkey's higher education system, the most rigorous control is made in the input phase, while there is no systematic and meaningful control mechanism in the process and output phases (Açıkgöz 2012).

Another parameter regarding educational quality is government expenditures. Public expenditures in higher education are on average 1.63% of GDP in OECD countries. In Turkey, this number is 1.32% in 2011 (OECD 2016a). It is striking that Turkey remains among the lowest ranked among OECD countries in terms of education expenditures per student. The share of the education budget in Turkey has increased in recent years; however, per-pupil expenditure has improved slightly due to a huge expansion in enrollment. The largest share of Turkey's 2014 budget appropriations was allocated to national education. It is striking to observe that approximately 80% of the public funds allocated to the education system in Turkey go to personnel wages. The funds received by the top ten universities of Turkey from the national budget are around US$2.4 billion. For comparison, recall that in the USA, the public budget allocation for Harvard University in 2016 was around US$4.5 billion, and according to a study by the Council for Aid to Education, Harvard raised US$1.19 billion in gifts and donations in fiscal year 2016. This study revealed that all colleges and universities in the USA collectively raised nearly US$41 billion in fiscal year 2016 (Dixon and Yared 2017).

Another problem area regarding the input structure of the Turkish higher education system is the low level of internationalization. In terms of the percentage of foreign students enrolled in universities, Turkey ranked second from the last row among 35 OECD countries in 2013 (Tekneci 2016). Moreover, while there are approximately 150,000 academic personnel in Turkey, the number of foreign academics is 1,703, representing about 2% of the total (Şeremet 2015). Moreover, the majority of foreign faculty members have been clustered around a few universities, such as Bilkent and Koç Universities. In a comparative study of global higher education systems by the British Council (2016), the major deficiencies of Turkey's higher education system are identified as the lack of internationalization and institutionalization and, more importantly, weaknesses in quality assurance and international recognition.

BRICS countries attach special importance to modernization and internationalization of their national education systems. The PRC hosted about 250,000 foreign students by 2012 and aims to increase this number of international students to half a million by 2020 (Hu et al. 2015). With the same purpose, South Korea has reached its target of hosting 100,000 foreign students in 2012 (Byun et al. 2013). On the other hand, Turkey's legal system and regulations are not flexible enough to enhance internationalization demands. Phil Baty, editor of the *Times Higher Education* magazine comments that Turkey's universities are pretty good in research; however, in terms of reputation and recognition, much remains to be done compared to the top universities in the world. Dr. Ahmet Acar, Middle East Technical University (METU) president, touched upon crucial problems of higher education institutions in an interview:

> One of my colleagues, who was an assistant professor at electronics department, waited 8 months for tenure position, and out of hope he had to leave for Stanford Univeristy. He told me that "I left METU with brokenheartedly, but I cannot stand it anymore" ... In the last 8 years, the number of undergraduate students at METU increased 15%, the number of graduate students increased 25%, and the number of doctoral students increased 35%. Nonetheless, the number of faculty members decreased by 5%. We are not allowed to fill vacant positions... Per student budgets for worldwide universities at the top ranks are 10 times more than our institutions. (Yüzak 2014)

It is generally acknowledged that higher education institutions, and especially elite research institutions, play a very important role in terms of productivity and innovation. Countries with strong innovation records such as PRC, South Korea, Japan, Russia, and Singapore have developed elite university policies to increase the quality of research in higher education institutions. Recently the Russian government started a new project at elite universities. Russia aims to have at least 5 Russian universities in the rankings of the top 100 world-class universities. Moscow will prioritize 15 universities with extra support so as to get 5 of them into the top 100 list (Milliyet, 27 September 2014).

In these countries, certain universities or specific programs have been selected and financial resources have been transferred to these universities or programs. It seems that successful East Asian developing countries and the PRC have been coordinating their industrial structure, employment projections, and education policies and planning. In these countries, governments specify where, when, and how much educated human capital is needed in their industrial establishments.

The PRC issued the 13th Development Plan (2016–2020), in which the second section is about the "Innovation-Driven Economic Development." In the most recent plan, the goal is developing world-class universities, enabling PRC to become the world leader in certain disciplines. The PRC government has identified a specific number of universities in the elite university category.

Since the late 1990s, the South Korea government has been actively engaged in selective incentive policies aimed at raising universities to world-class status. Seoul officials selected the top 10 universities planning to be in the top 500 world-class universities by providing serious incentives. The Brain Korea 21 (BK21) project and World-Class-University-WCU projects were influential (Moon and Kim 2001; Byun et al. 2013). Another project, Work in South Korea, aimed to attract talented students and researchers. The South Korean Advanced Institute of Science and Technology (KAIST) was established to attract Korean scientists from developed countries to the homeland (Michalski et al. 2013). In the period between 2003 and 2011, 10 South Korean universities entered the rankings of the top 500 universities in the world (Michalski et al. 2013).

After the introduction of the BK21 project, it was observed that the total number of articles published in the Science Citation Index (SCI) journals has increased significantly. The number of publications, which was 10,700 in 1998, reached 40,000 in 2010. It is important to underline that the most significant contribution to this increase came from the elite universities discussed earlier. Note that the number of foreign students coming to the country under the Study in South Korea project has increased significantly (Jon and Chung 2014). The number of foreign students, which was 16,000 in 2004, approached 100,000 in 2010, which indicates an almost sevenfold increase. Also, the number of foreign faculty members working in South Korea during the period from 2000 to 2009 increased threefold (Byun et al. 2013).

3.2 Second Pillar: Turkey's Information and Telecommunications Infrastructure

A strong information and communication technology (ICT) infrastructure enables countries to conduct a rapid and efficient exchange of information. ICT variables measure the penetration of telephones (fixed and mobile), computers, and the Internet. To create and sustain a strong overarching ICT infrastructure, it is imperative to mobilize the many stakeholders involved in its deployment and use: government, businesses, universities, telecommunications and information service providers, rural representatives, and so on.

The World Economic Forum has suggested that we are on the brink of a technological revolution that will fundamentally alter the way we live, work, and relate to one another. The Third Industrial Revolution was about electronics and information technology, which led to automation in production. The Fourth Industrial Revolution, a continuation of the Third, will bring about the digital revolution, and it is characterized by a fusion of technologies that is blurring the lines between the physical, digital, and biological spheres.

For a country to register a strong development record in the ICT sector, human capital is one of the most important factors. Based on 2015 World Bank data, Turkey ranks 19th in terms of telephone lines, with almost 11.5 million subscriptions and 14 subscriptions per 100 inhabitants; in terms of cell phones, Turkey's world rank is 21st with 73.5 million users and 93% penetration; in terms of Internet access, Turkey has 42.5 million users, 54% of the population has access to the Internet, and the country rank is 19.

According to TÜBİSAD data (Turkey's Informatics Industry Association) from 2015, 113,000 people are employed in the ICT sector, and market volume is at around US$30 billion. A survey conducted by TÜBİSAD (2017) revealed that the number one complaint among ICT firms has to do with the lack of qualified talent (61% of respondents), the second major problem area is public procurement policies (51% of respondents), and the third problem area was reported to be high taxes and the complex tax system (39% of respondents).

3.3 Third Pillar: Turkey's Innovation Base

There exists a social geography of innovation: Silicon Valley-like technology clusters have emerged around the world, and the vast majority of them are concentrated in a few regions or countries. It is becoming increasingly difficult to enter the league of worldwide tech giants. As of 2008, almost half of the 4,000 innovation centers around the world are in the USA. The vast majority of worldwide patents are concentrated in five centers: the USA, Japan, South Korea, the PRC, and Europe, whose patent offices signed about 77% of the 727,000 patents registered in 2006.

Table 4 R&D as a share of national revenue in OECD and other countries

Year	South Korea	PRC	Germany	Japan	Czech Republic	Israel	OECD	Turkey
1995	2.20	0.57	2.13	2.66	0.88	2.44	1.68	0.28
2000	2.18	0.89	2.39	3.00	1.12	3.93	1.77	0.48
2005	2.63	1.31	2.42	3.31	1.17	4.05	1.78	0.59
2010	3.47	1.71	2.71	3.25	1.34	3.94	1.99	0.84
2011	3.74	1.78	2.8	3.38	1.56	4.02	2.03	0.86
2012	4.03	1.91	2.87	3.34	1.78	4.16	2.06	0.92
2013	4.15	1.99	2.82	3.48	1.90	4.15	2.07	0.94
2014	4.29	2.02	2.89	3.59	1.97	4.27	2.10	1.01
2015	4.23	2.07	2.87	3.49	1.95	4.25	2.08	1.02

Source: OECD (2016a) "International Comparisons," Main Science and Technology Indicators http://www.oecd.org/sti/msti.htm

It is obvious that in order to transform the Turkish economy into a more innovative and competitive one, government must increase R&D activities both quantitatively and qualitatively. In advanced countries, the share of R&D expenditures as a percentage of GDP is around 3%. In Turkey, R&D expenditures have just reached the 1% level (Table 4).

Regarding global economic competition, it is no longer meaningful to talk about the best university in a country. Worldwide rankings have crucial importance. Higher education institutions now tend to center around geographical clusters or university hubs. Just as the center of gravity in the world economy shifts toward the Asia Pacific region, so the universities of this region are also on the rise. Of the top 200 universities in the world, 5 are from the PRC, 3 are from South Korea, and 2 are from Singapore and Japan. Additionally, it is not only universities but also innovation centers that have been gathering in certain geographical locations. For instance, in South Korea, the R&D headquarters of Samsung is located in Suwon city, which is 1 hour away from Seoul. With its 1 million residents, the city of Suwon is home to 11 universities, and it has Samsung's Digital City, Crystal City, and Nano City campuses.

There is also a sociocultural dimension of innovation. Taking social values and norms into account, the overall picture of entrepreneurship, risk taking, and business administration and similar activities should be examined. Although an important problem in the Turkish context relates to financial limitations, it is reported that some R&D funds have not been used due to a lack of applications. Fikri Işık, Science, Industry and Technology Minister, stated that an innovation culture has not settled well in Turkey; he admitted that the financial aspect of R&D activities has been significantly improved, but the mentality problem still endures (Şeref Oğuz, Sabah, 3 December 2014).

Moreover, the concepts of innovation and the knowledge economy become more meaningful together with sociology and geography. Innovation has a geographical dimension and sociological dynamics. Techno-parks, global cities, "smart cities," "competitiveness of cities," and "viable cities index" – all these novel concepts are related to an innovation ecosystem. In order to be able to attract talent, it is necessary to ensure a livable environment for scholars and researchers (Gill and Kharas 2015). For example, Mercer's Quality of Living Index has been evaluating and ranking 230 cities around the world by over 39 parameters, including politics, economy, environment, safety, health, and transportation, for almost 10 years. According to this ranking, Vienna is at the top of the list as the most livable city.

Human capital is one of the important inputs within the ecosystem of innovation, but it is not sufficient by itself. Additional criteria, such as strategic decision-making mechanisms and an entrepreneurship culture, have also been put in place to grow innovation ecosystems. New concepts such as Mode-1, Mode-2, and "Triple Helix" are concepts designed to develop a culture of innovation and a sociological framework for university-industry-public relations. One such example in Turkey is the Center for Excellence in Composite Technologies, which recently allied with Sabancı University, Kordsa, and the government.

Innovations and patents, which are economic concepts, can only be achieved when they are designed within an ecosystem (Jackson 2011). This includes the harmonized components of a common system with many variables such as sociological parameters, research inputs, material capital (financial supports) and human capital (e.g., students, academics, researchers, laboratory staff), businessmen, public administrators, politicians, centers of excellence, and satellite campuses. One of the successful academics of Harvard University, Prof. Gökhan Hotamışlıgil, in an interview revealed the importance of the ecosystem in science and innovation:

If you draw a circle with a radius of 3 miles in the Cambridge district of Harvard and MIT where I live, you can find 10 thousand research laboratories. This is where researchers in the world demand the most and settle most. Even when you go out and walk in the streets in the evenings you breath science in the air. Continuous interaction is needed in our fields. The intelligence and creative capacity of anyone can never be strong enough to solve the complexity of science. This is all about the environment. You can use your mental liberty here unconditionally. (Milliyet, 1 November 2015)

In Turkey, recently universities have been categorized by TÜBİTAK based on innovation capacity. This is the Ranking of the Entrepreneurial and Innovative University Index that has been prepared by the leadership of TÜBİTAK. This index, which was produced for the last 4 years, is an important step. This initiative might be the first step toward differentiating the leading universities of Turkey (Table 5).

Table 5 Entrepreneurship and innovation index in Turkish universities

2012 Ranking			2014 Ranking			2016 Ranking		
Rank	University	Score	Rank	University	Score	Rank	University	Score
1	Sabancı	84	1	ODTÜ	83	1	Sabancı	95
2	ODTÜ	83	2	Sabancı	81	2	ODTÜ	85
3	Bilkent	70	3	Boğaziçi	76	3	Bilkent	83
4	Özyeğin	69	4	Bilkent	75	4	İTÜ	80
5	İTÜ	67	5	Koç	74	5	Boğaziçi	80
6	Boğaziçi	65	6	Özyeğin	73	6	Koç	79
7	İzmir YTE	58	7	İTÜ	72	7	Gebze YTE	78
8	Koç	57	8	TOBB ETÜ	69	8	Özyeğin	75
9	Gebze YTE	57	9	İzmir YTE	67	9	İzmir YTE	69
10	TOBB ETÜ	54	10	Selçuk	60	10	Yıldız	68
11	Hacettepe	49	11	Yıldız	57	11	TOBB	64
12	Ege	47	12	Gebze YTE	57	12	Selçuk	59
13	Erciyes	46	13	Anadolu	55	13	Ege	55
14	SDÜ	45	14	Hacettepe	54	14	Erciyes	53
15	Gazi	44	15	Ege	49	15	İst. Şehir	53
16	Selçuk	43	16	Gazi	48	16	Gaziantep	52
17	Çankaya	43	17	Atılım	47	17	Hacettepe	52
18	Bahçeşehir	43	18	Çukurova	43	18	Çankaya	51
19	Yıldız	41	19	Uludağ	43	19	Atılım	51
20	Çukurova	41	20	SDÜ	43	20	Anadolu	50

Source: TÜBİTAK 2016

When looking at this ranking, it is clear that the majority of leading universities are in three metropolitan areas. The top ten universities three times in a row are as follows: ODTÜ, Sabancı, Bilkent, Boğaziçi, Özyeğin, ITU, İzmir High Technology, Koç, and TOBB-ETU. There are some break points in this list of rankings. METU and Sabancı Universities, which share the first two ranks, are clearly leading institutions. In the future, this index should be used in connection with Turkey's innovation policies. Priority areas for Turkey's development must be taken into consideration along with this index, and officials should introduce the elite university concept when designing higher education reforms in the future.

3.4 Fourth Pillar: Turkey's Business and Governance Climate

The most important need of Turkey is to come up with a common vision that all stakeholders share and internalize. General strategy and vision documents within a 25- to 50-year time period should be prepared with the participation of all public- and private-sector stakeholders bearing responsibility in national education, higher education, technology, and development areas (Tekneci 2016). Five-year interim plans should be prepared under the guidance of these main documents. Institutions that have become dysfunctional owing to excessive centralized and bloated bureaucratic structures such as YOK must be redesigned in a more integrated, holistic way.

The most critical step Turkey needs to take is the construction of a commonly shared strategic vision. All stakeholders should agree on this vision. All public institutions, predominantly the YÖK, must be redesigned in a holistic policy. The entrepreneurship and innovation index produced by TÜBİTAK for Turkey's universities is an important step. To move into the high-income league, Turkey must focus on the concept of elite universities. In order for Turkey's universities to reach global standards, at least some of them must be able to operate autonomously.

For example, an investigation of the productivity of public universities outside of major cities in Turkey revealed strong organic links between academic administration and local interest groups. In any public university in a small city, the influence of local elites is observed in recruitment, promotion, and appointment in the universities. Özoğlu et al. (2016) reported on intervention by local elites and the public authority to the newly established public universities in the respective cities as an important problem area in research conducted at 12 newly established universities.

One of the important recommendations mentioned in the literature on the middle-income trap and development is the need to change the central government's economic philosophy or mentality. In particular, policies on social programs and income inequality need to be formulated independently of development strategies. With a simple statement, a demand-oriented production structure should be targeted for transition to the category of high-income countries; possible social programs in the transition from poverty to the middle-income level are no longer the main parameters. The tendency to pursue populist politics is one of the biggest hurdles in the transition to a higher income class. In this regard, we can give examples of populist practices such as the elimination of student fees at public universities and the distribution of free milk to elementary school students.

4 Conclusion

For Turkey to advance in the league of knowledge economies the critical reform area is education, and especially higher education. World politics has been witnessing fierce competition, and nations tend to amass power through innovation, education, and knowledge economies. The primary tool for accumulating political and economic power is the production of advanced knowledge. Turkey as a middle power with middle-income levels in world politics has been trying to secure more advantageous positions in the global system. On this matter Turkish officials need first a commonly shared development vision that should contain higher education reform, innovation culture, entrepreneurship, and university-industry-public coordination.

It is important to aim for qualitative and holistic targets. Focusing on narrowly quantitative targets is not a good strategy. Turkey needs to design a *sui generis* development model that is appropriate to its culture, history, demographic structure, and all other sociopolitical realities. In recent times, South Korea, Singapore, Taiwan (PRC), and Japan created successful economic models. However, there have been some negative side effects in these cases. For example, according to World Health Organization data, South Korea is in first place in suicides. According to 2013 data, the number of deaths due to suicide per 100,000 residents is 28.5 in South Korea and 21.4 in Japan, while this figure is around 4 for Turkey (WHO 2014). Likewise, in terms of population growth rate, South Korea, Singapore, and Japan are expected to face serious problems. In sum, in the course of planning and implementing Turkey's economic growth and development policies, special attention should be paid to important social and political parameters such as fertility, suicide, divorce, and social capital, in addition to efficiency and productivity.

References

Açıkgöz, Ömer. 2012. Yükseköğretim Üzerine Bir Değerlendirme: Yeniden Yapılanma Sürecinde Bir Sistem Önerisine Giriş. *Yükseköğretim ve Bilim Dergisi* 2: 11–17.

Agénor, Pierre-Richard, Otaviano Canuto, and Michael Jelenic. 2012. *Avoiding Middle-Income Growth Traps,* World Bank Policy Research Working Paper (WPS 16954), 1–7. Washington, DC: World Bank.

Aiyar, Shekhar, Duval Romain, Puy Damien, Wu Yiqun, and Zhang Longmei. 2013. *Growth Slowdowns and the Middle-Income Trap. No. 13–71.* Washington, DC: International Monetary Fund.

Berg, A., J. Ostry, and J. Zettelmeyer. 2012. What Makes Growth Sustained? *Journal of Development Economics* 98 (2): 149–166.

Brand Finance. 2017. *Global 500–2017: The Annual Report on The World's Most Valuable Brands.* http://brandfinance.com/images/upload/global_500_2017_locked_website.pdf. Accessed 25 May 2017.

British Council. 2016. *The Shape of Global Higher Education National Policies Framework for International Engagement-Emerging Themes.* https://www.britishcouncil.org/education/ihe/knowledge-centre/global-landscape/global-gauge. Accessed 19 May 2017.

Byun, Kiyong, Jae-Eun Jon, and Dongbin Kim. 2013. Quest for Building World-Class Universities in South Korea: Outcomes and Consequences. *Higher Education* 65 (5): 645–659.

Çağlar, Esen, and Ozan Acar. 2013. *An Assessment on the Tenth Development Plan*. TEPAV Evaluation Note, 1–27. http://www.tepav.org.tr/upload/files/1378461158-4.An_Assessment_on_the_Tenth_Development_Plan.pdf. Accessed 12 Mar 2017.

Dixon, Brandon J., and Leah S. Yared. 2017. Harvard Raises $1.19 Billion in Fiscal Year 2016, Topping Stanford. *The Harvard Crimson*, February 8. http://www.thecrimson.com/article/2017/2/8/harvard-fundraising-tops-stanford/. Accessed 29 June 2017.

Felipe, Jesus, Arnelyn Abdon, and Utsav Kumar. 2012. Tracking the Middle Income Trap: What Is It, Who Is in It, and Why? *Levy Economics Institute Working Paper* 715: 1–59.

Gill, Indermit S., and Homi Kharas. 2015. *The Middle-Income Trap Turns Ten*, World Bank Policy Research Working Paper (WPS 7403), 1–27. Washington, DC: World Bank.

Gür, Bekir S., Zafer Çelik, Türker Kurt, and Serkan Yurdakul. 2017. *Yükseköğretime bakış 2017: İzleme ve değerlendirme raporu*. Ankara: Eğitim-Bir-Sen Stratejik Araştırmalar Merkezi.

Hu, Claire, Christine Min Wotipka, and Wen Wen. 2015. International Students in Chinese Higher Education. In *Global Perspectives and Local Challenges Surrounding International Student Mobility*, ed. Krishna Bista and Charlotte Foster, 153–174. Hershey: IGI Global.

Im, Fernando Gabriel, and David Rosenblatt. 2015. Middle-Income Traps: A Conceptual and Empirical Survey. *Journal of International Commerce, Economics and Policy* 6 (3): 1–39.

Interbrand. 2016. *Best Global Brands*. Retrieved http://interbrand.com/best-brands/best-global-brands/2016/ranking/. Accessed 25 May 2017.

Jackson, D. 2011. *What Is an Innovation Ecosystem?* Arlington: National Science Foundation. http://www.erc-assoc.org/docs/innovation_ecosystem.pdf.

Jon, Jae-Eun, and Hae-In Chung. 2014. *STEM Report: Republic of Korea*. Report for the Australian Council of Learned Academies (ACOLA). Melbourne: Australian Council of Learned Academies. http://www.acola.org.au/PDF/SAF02Consultants/Consultant%20Report%20-%20Korea.pdf. Accessed 17 Mar 2017.

MEB. 2013. *PISA 2012 Ulusal Ön Raporu*. Ankara: Milli Eğitim Bakanlığı.

Michalski, Bohdan, Gaja Kołodziej, and Agnieszka Piasecka. 2013. *Organization and Functioning of South Korean Higher Education System*. EU-KOREAN Universities Consortium.

Moon, Mugyeong, and Ki-Seok Kim. 2001. A case of Korean Higher Education Reform: The Brain Korea 21 Project. *Asia Pacific Education Review* 2 (2): 96–105.

NCES (National Center for Education Statistics). 2015. *Trends in International Mathematics and Science Study (TIMSS).* https://nces.ed.gov/timss/timss15advanced.asp. Accessed 12 May 2017.

OECD. 2016a. *OECD Science, Technology and Innovation Outlook 2016*. Paris: OECD Publishing.

———. 2016b. *Education at a Glance 2016*. Paris: OECD Publishing.

Özoğlu, Murat, Bekir S. Gür, and Sedat Gümüs. 2016. Rapid Expansion of Higher Education in Turkey: The Challenges of Recently Established Public Universities (2006–2013). *Higher Education Policy* 29 (1): 21–39.

Şeremet, Mehmet. 2015. Türkiye ve İngiltere Yükseköğretimindeki Uluslararasılaşma Politikalarına Karşılaştırmalı Bir Yaklaşım. *Yükseköğretim ve Bilim Dergisi* 4 (1): 27–31.

Tekneci, Pelin Deniz. 2016. Evolution of Turkish Higher Education System in the Last Decade. *Journal of Higher Education and Science* 6 (3): 277–287.

TÜBİSAD (Türkiye Bilişim Sanayicileri Derneği). 2017. *Bilişim ve Enformasyon Teknolojileri Pazar Verileri.* https://www2.deloitte.com/content/dam/Deloitte/tr/Documents/technology-media-telecommunications/TUBISAD-2017-bit-pazar-verileri.pdf. Accessed 2 Apr 2017.

TÜBİTAK. 2015. *Türkiye Üniversiteleri'nin Bilimsel Yayın Performansı: 2004–2014.* http://ulakbim.tubitak.gov.tr/tr/hizmetlerimiz/turkiye-universitelerinin-bilimsel-yayin-performansi-2004-2014. Accessed 27 Mar 2017.

———. 2016. *Girişimci ve Yenilikçi Üniversite Endeksi-2016*. http://www.tubitak.gov.tr/tr/kurumsal/politikalar/icerik-girisimci-ve-yenilikci-universite-endeksi. Accessed 29 Apr 2017.

Wilson, William T. 2014. *Beating the Middle-Income Trap in Southeast Asia*, Heritage Foundation Special Report (156). Pennsylvania: Heritage Foundation.

World Bank. 2007. *Building Knowledge Economies: Advanced Strategies for Development*. Washington, DC: World Bank Publications.

———. 2017. *World Development Indicators 2016*. Washington, DC: World Bank Publications.

World Health Organization (WHO). 2014. Preventing Suicide: A Global Imperative. Retrieved from http://www.who.int/mental_health/suicide-prevention/world_report_2014/en/.

Yüzak, Özlem. 2014. ODTÜ Rektörü: Değerleri elimizde tutamıyoruz. *Cumhuriyet*, November 8 http://www.cumhuriyet.com.tr/haber/egitim/138673/ODTU_Rektoru__Degerleri_elimizde_tutamiyoruz.html. Accessed 28 Feb 2017.

Part II

Financial System

Financial Openness, Financial Stability, and Macroeconomic Performance in Turkey: A Comparative Perspective

Ali Ari

1 Introduction

Economic theory, based on assumptions of competitive and efficient markets, argues that financial openness and financial development promote economic growth. However, experiences in various developing countries did not always correspond to this theoretical reality since some countries benefited more from financial openness, while others experienced severe crises following financial liberalization. Moreover, the impact of financial openness on growth is not linear. In other words, there is a trade-off between openness and growth over time: a country that experienced crises and recessions in the first years following financial openness had higher growth rates in the long run, or vice versa.

The Turkish liberalization experience also fits the preceding description. Following the capital account liberalization implemented in 1989,

A. Ari (✉)
Department of Political Science and Public Administration, Marmara University, Istanbul, Turkey

A. F. Aysan et al. (eds.), *Turkish Economy*,
https://doi.org/10.1007/978-3-319-70380-0_7

Turkey suffered three full-fledged financial crises in 1994, 1998–1999, and 2000–2001, while economic outcomes such as growth and inflation have improved remarkably in the post-2001 crisis period. This is mainly due to more effective fiscal and monetary management, strengthened banking regulation and supervision, and conservative banking practices (IMF 2012) pursued over the last decade and a half that significantly contributed to greater financial stability. On the other hand, thanks to these policies the Turkish financial system showed great resilience to the 2008–2009 global financial crisis compared to other emerging market economies in Europe, Latin America, and Asia.

This paper aims to show in a descriptive and comparative way the importance of financial stability and financial development in Turkey's macroeconomic performance in the aftermath of the severe financial crisis in 2001. The paper will argue that financial liberalization should be implemented in a well-designed, effective supervisory and regulatory framework and in a sequenced manner in order to allow emerging countries such as Turkey to enjoy the potential benefits of financial openness and development for economic growth.

This chapter is organized as follows. Section 2 presents two opposite faces of financial openness and development from both theoretical and empirical perspectives. Section 3 details the Turkish experience with financial liberalization since the early 1980s. Section 4 concludes with some policy recommendations.

2 Financial Openness: Is It Growth-Enhancing or Crisis-Causing?

Since the pioneering contributions of Patrick (1966), McKinnon (1973), and Shaw (1973), the link between financial development and economic growth remains an important subject in economic literature. Different aspects of this relationship have been extensively analyzed in both theoretical and empirical studies for single countries and across nations as well as at industry and firm levels. According to the theory, a well-developed financial system plays an important role in the growth process because it channels and mobilizes savings into profitable large-scale investments, reduces the costs of acquiring and evaluating information on prospective projects, and helps to monitor investments to reduce the risk of resource mismanagement (OECD 2004; Levine 2005).

On the other hand, financial openness that contributes to financial development (Rajan and Zingales 2003; Baltagi et al. 2009) is a key factor for long-term economic growth. As explained in Stiglitz (2000), free capital mobility offers the opportunity to realize the highest return on savings that is expected to affect capital accumulation, allocation of resources, and technological innovation, to borrow at the most favourable rates, and to diversify away idiosyncratic risk. Moreover, exposure to international competition may improve the efficiency of the domestic financial system through the introduction of international standards and financial innovation, which can directly broaden the scope of financial services (Huang 2010).

However, in less-developed and developing countries where financial markets lack depth, high amounts of capital in- and outflows may lead to financial crises (Aghion et al. 2004; Stiglitz et al. 2006). While foreign capital flows in, the local currency appreciates, leading to an unsustainable expansion of consumption and to changes in the structure of production. The short-term capital generally goes into real estate and equity markets. This leads to price increases in these markets and engenders wealth effects, thereby raising private consumption. The demand boom and overvalued currency encourage growth in domestic non-tradable sectors but lowers exports, causing high current account deficits. When a shift occurs in investors' sentiment towards a certain economic situation, capital inflows suddenly stop and turn into outflows. This leads to a devaluation of the domestic currency, which results in large increases in the domestic value of foreign-currency-denominated debt. Monetary authorities often raise interest rates to stop currency depreciation, but this policy generally worsens the economic situation because aggregate demand drops, forcing a contraction of production and employment. With less tax revenues and less foreign credits, governments are then forced to cut back expenditures, which further aggravates the economic contraction.[1]

Empirical studies are also far from establishing a consensus on the relationship between financial development and economic growth. A large number of empirical studies, using mostly cross-sectional methods, have found that an increase in the level of financial development is associated with higher economic growth (King and Levine 1993; Beck et al. 2000; Edison et al. 2004; Bekaert et al. 2005; Ranciere et al. 2006; Kose et al. 2009a). Alternatively, other cross-sectional studies present a non-linear relationship between financial development and economic growth (Odedokun 1996; Deidda and Fattouh 2002; Andersen and Tarp 2003; Rioja and Valev 2004). This means that financial development is not related to higher growth rates at all levels of economic development. Edwards (2001) shows that financial development is a good predictor of economic growth in developed countries, while Klein (2003) finds that financial development has no impact on growth in the poorest and the richest countries, but a substantial impact in the middle-income ones. Conversely, some empirical papers find no significant effect of financial development on economic growth (Rodrik 1998; Ram 1999; Barro 2003).

On the other hand, some papers focusing on the openness–growth nexus affirm that financial liberalization that greatly contributes to financial development produces financial instability, leading to crises and recessions, particularly in developing countries (Demirguc-Kunt and Detragiache 1998; Kaminsky and Reinhart 1999) because capital flows increase economic and financial volatility and the probability of a crisis by promoting greater risk-taking and leverage, particularly when the financial system is poorly regulated.

However, some others show the non-linearity of the impact of financial openness on growth. For instance, Aizenman (2004), Loayza and Ranciere (2006), and Kaminsky and Schmukler (2008) underline the fact that financial liberalization is followed by more pronounced boom–bust cycles in the short run but leads to more stable markets in the long run. In contrast, Bussiere and Fratzscher (2008) indicate that countries tend to gain in the short term immediately following capital account liberalization but may not grow faster or may even experience temporary growth reversals in the medium to long term. De Gregorio and Guidotti (1995), Levine et al. (2000), Arteta et al. (2001), Eichengreen and Leblang (2003), Kose et al. (2009a, b), and Eichengreen et al. (2011)

assert that the benefits of financial liberalization are likely to outweigh its costs when the domestic financial system is robust.

The preceding discussion illustrates that capital account liberalization and financial development contribute to economic growth if the country puts in place an effective supervisory and regulatory framework. This argument is also valid for the Turkish case since Turkey had two distinct periods of economic development following the financial openness in the 1980s: high instability and three crisis episodes in the 1990s and early 2000s and a relatively stable economy later on when strengthened banking regulation and conservative banking practices were put in place.

3 Turkish Liberalization Experience: From Crises to Growth

Following the severe currency and debt crises in the late 1970s, Turkish authorities reoriented their development strategy by adopting a radical structural adjustment program in January 1980. This program, largely supported by the International Monetary Fund (IMF) and the World Bank, aimed to establish an outward-looking and free-market economy in order to restore growth by improving economic and financial efficiency, increasing domestic savings, and attracting foreign capital.

In the early phase of the programme (1980–1984), Turkish authorities gradually liberalized trade policy and ended interest rate controls (Rodrik 1990), while in the second phase (1985–1989) they facilitated the entry of new banks in the banking system and opened the domestic economy to foreign capital flows (Boratav and Yeldan 2006). These liberalization efforts contributed to increasing economic growth by 5.5% on average in the period 1982–1989, but this early success was overshadowed by the occurrence of severe financial crises in 1994, 1998–1999, and 2000–2001. These crises led to adverse economic consequences in terms of increasing interest rates, excessive output losses, and failure or nationalization of nearly 30 domestic banks (Fig. 1).

These crises were mainly related to rapid financial sector liberalization since excessive short-term capital inflows due to high real interest rates

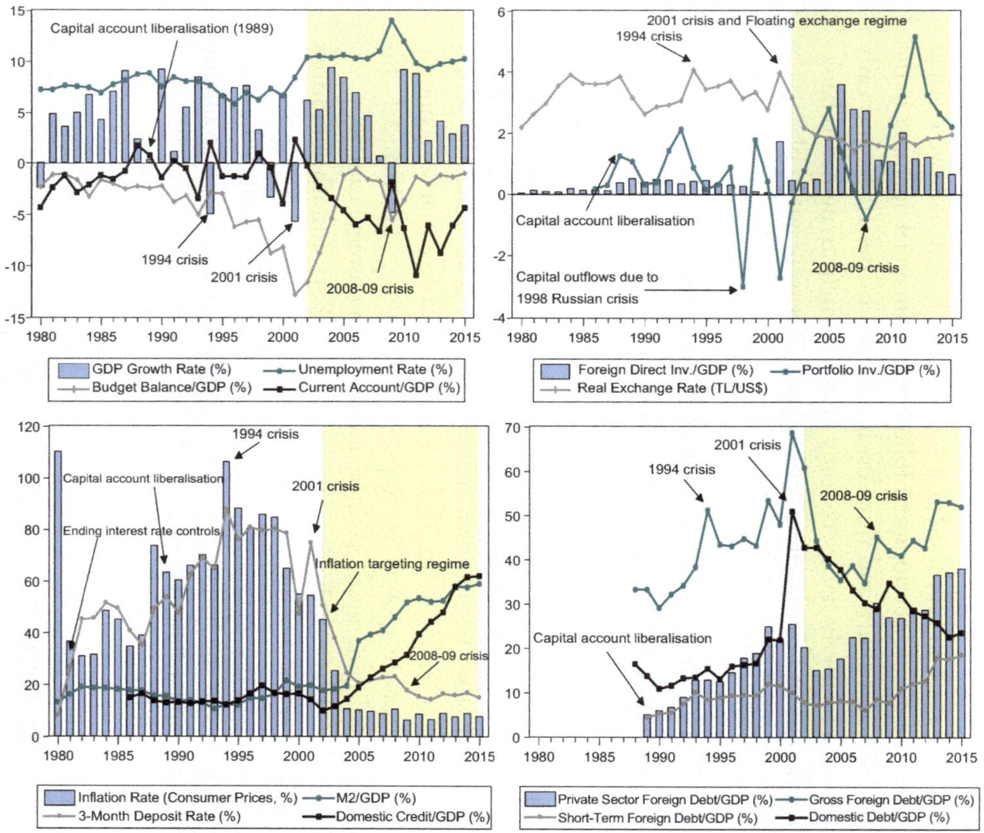

Fig. 1 Macroeconomic indicators of Turkish economy (Source: World Bank-World Development Indicators (WDI), IMF-International Financial Statistics (IFS), Central Bank of Turkey (CBRT), and Turkish Statistical Institute)

led to the overvaluation of the domestic currency, which lowered the competitiveness of exporting firms and, hence, deteriorated the current account balance. To offset current account deficits (nearly 5% of GDP), the country needed more capital inflows, which constantly increased the ratio of short-term foreign debt stock to international reserves.

On the other hand, capital account liberalization, by facilitating borrowing of banks in international capital markets, allowed for rapid growth in lending and a boom in investment, but at the expense of constant increases in bank non-performing loans and bank open positions. Moreover, poor supervision and regulation of the system, since the Banking Regulation and Supervision Agency (BRSA) had effectively been created in May 2001, and close connections between bank conglomerates and political authorities unquestionably fostered this excessive risk-taking setting. Increasing vulnerabilities in the domestic economy then led to high amounts of capital outflows, which triggered the outbreak of financial crises with consequent negative impacts on both the financial sector and real economy.

Stabilization and restructuring efforts, i.e. effective fiscal and monetary management, strengthened banking regulation and supervision, the introduction of a floating exchange rate regime, and an inflation-targeting strategy, implemented following the severe 2001 crisis in the framework of an IMF-backed program, restored relative economic and financial stability: inflation decreased from nearly 60% to single digits, budget deficits plunged from 12% of GDP in 2001 to 2% in 2016, which helped to lower public debt from 80% of GDP in 2001 to 35% in 2016, and output continually increased (around 5% on average), except for the 2008–2009 crisis period.

This performance is also worth highlighting because Turkey was able to reduce high chronic inflation rates together with increasing economic growth and doubled GDP per capita at purchasing power parity (PPP) in less than 15 years, despite the global financial crisis. This growth process is also said to be 'inclusive' since income inequality, measured by the Gini coefficient, fell, but more importantly, poverty was reduced by more than half, access to high-quality health, education, and municipal services expanded, and income gaps between regions narrowed (OECD 2014).

Moreover, as shown in Fig. 2, Turkey outperformed most of its peer countries in terms of economic growth over the last 15-year period. This is mostly due to increasing financial stability, which also increased confidence in the management of the economy. Thus, Turkey could attract significant amounts of foreign direct and portfolio investments to finance high growth rates.

Figure 3 shows the developments of some key banking sector indicators in Turkey. As seen in Fig. 3, bank reserves to assets steadily declined from 1989 (date of capital account liberalization) to 2002; bank return on assets followed a downward trend from 1996 to 2002; bank open positions, measured by bank foreign exchange (FX) assets over FX liabilities, steadily increased from 1997 to the start of the banking crisis in November 2000; bank non-performing loans reached record levels (26% of total loans in 2002) despite the fact that the ratio of loans to deposits decreased from 1997 to 2002 and that low bank loans to private sector reached only 20% of total loans. Although the CBRT massively bailed out the banking sector (the ratio of bank liabilities to CBRT over total liabilities was 6% on average from 1997 to 2001), nearly thirty domestic banks failed and/or transferred to the Savings Deposit Insurance Fund (SDIF) from 1994 to 2003 that cost more than US$50 billion or 25% of GDP at that time.

Since the severe financial crisis in February 2001, Turkey has made remarkable progress in renewing its regulatory and supervisory framework to bring it further in line with international standards. The foundation of politically independent BRSA and the amendment of CBRT law in 2001 that has strengthened central bank independence and powers were key factors behind this effective regulatory framework. Moreover, implementation of conservative banking practices by the BRSA and improvements in the monetary policy framework of the CBRT have substantially increased financial stability: banks have rebuilt capital and reserves to adequate and comfortable levels, bank profitability has been restored, and the ratio of non-performing loans to total loans has plunged, even though bank loans to the private sector have significantly increased. On the other hand, good prospects have attracted large-scale foreign direct investment into the banking sector, and Turkish banks have been able to obtain financing abroad at advantageous rates (IMF 2007). One

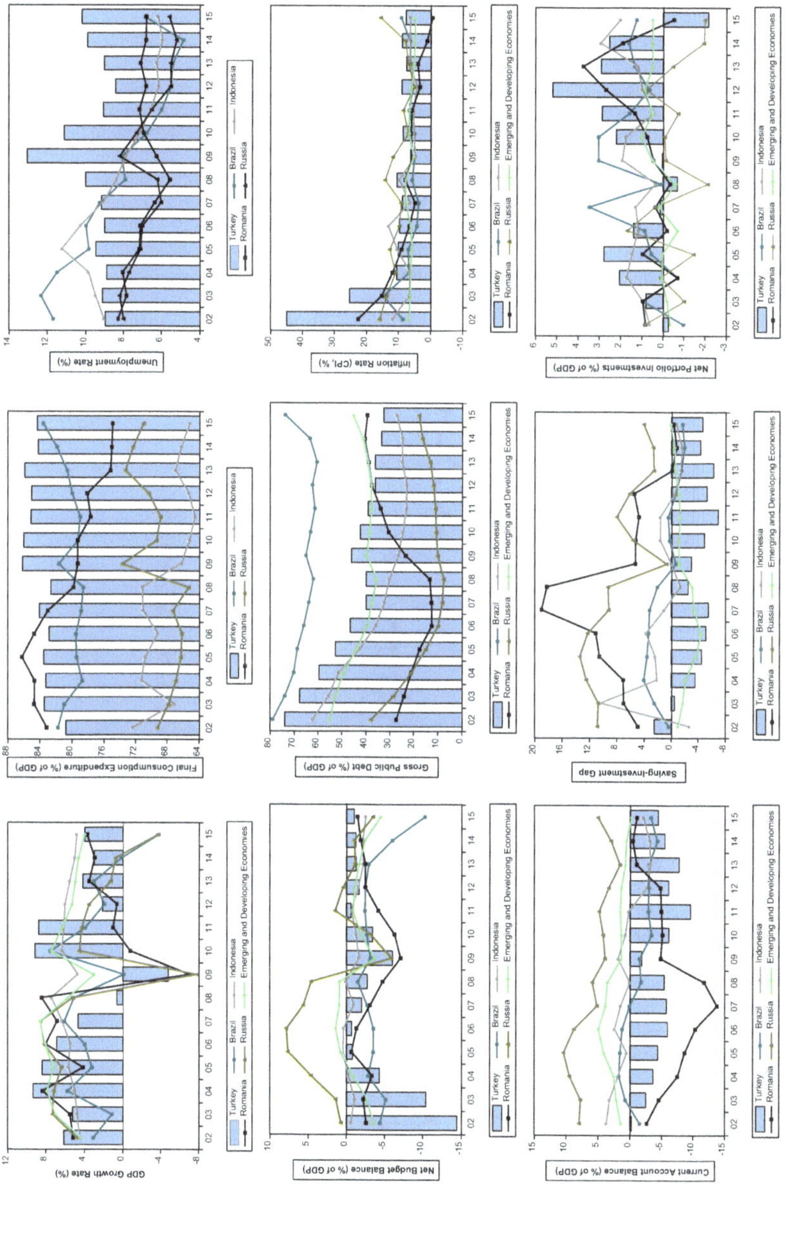

Fig. 2 Macroeconomic indicators for some emerging and developing countries (Source: World Bank-WDI and IMF-IFS)

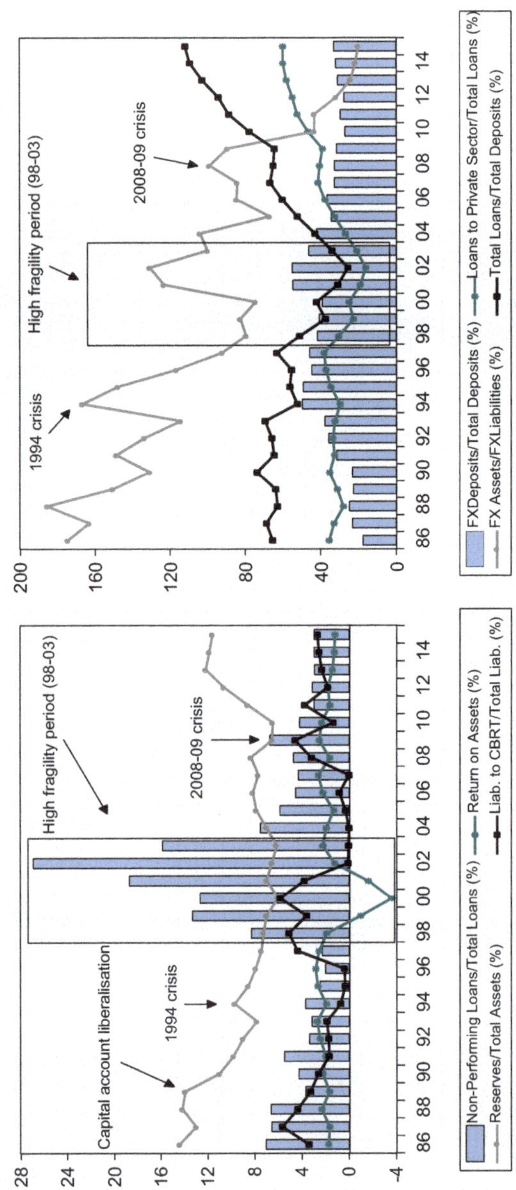

Fig. 3 Turkey's banking sector indicators (Source: IMF-IFS and CBRT)

may thus affirm that assuring financial stability has fully contributed to high growth rates over the last 15-year period.

On the other hand, all these improvements also explain why the Turkish financial system showed great resilience to the 2008–2009 global financial crisis. Following the restructuring and recapitalization of the banking system after the 2000–2001 crisis, the regulatory framework was modernized via passage of a banking law in 2005. The strengthened regulatory framework accompanied by BRSA's conservative banking practices and tight supervision prevented local banks from taking excessive risks like in the USA and the eurozone.[2] To be more precise, by the end of 2007, the ratio of gross non-performing loans to total loans was 3.4%, while the ratio of capital to assets and the ratio of liquid assets to total assets were 12.1% and 54.2%, respectively, and profits were robust. In addition, low financial development, measured frequently by the ratio of credit to the private sector over GDP, which reached only 26.2% in 2008, and very limited use of new financial instruments, such as derivatives, restrained the probable negative effects of the global financial crisis on the Turkish financial sector and real economy.

Moreover, a reactive role played by the CBRT during the global crisis was also quite important. After a reticent approach in the early stage of the global crisis in 2008, the CBRT engaged in unprecedented monetary easing during the crisis by cutting the policy interest rate by 9.5% from September 2008 to September 2009. One of the major factors determining the effectiveness of monetary policy in this period was an expansionary fiscal policy that tended to revive domestic demand and boost investment in order to stimulate economic growth. Thanks to loose monetary and fiscal policies, as well as easy global monetary conditions that led to a surge in short-term capital inflows, Turkey was assured a quick economic recovery compared to other countries from the fourth quarter of 2009. However, rapid credit growth pushed by lower borrowing costs on loan engendered a strong growth in domestic demand, which contributed to the widening of the current account deficit at the end of 2010. The lack of a formal institutional setup to contain increasing macro-financial risks in Turkey drove the CBRT to take a leading role (Kara 2016). Accordingly, the CBRT adopted a new policy strategy by incorporating financial stability into the conventional inflation-targeting framework and redesigning the toolkit to address macro-financial risks such as credit growth, volatility in capital flows, and increasing current account deficits. In this sense, unconventional tools, such as the interest rate corridor and reserve requirements, were jointly used for both monetary policy and macroprudential purposes. Note also that the creation of the Financial Stability Committee (FSC) in June 2011 was another major step towards establishing a formal macroprudential framework in Turkey. The FSC was then charged with assessing systemic risks, identifying necessary measures, and making relevant policy recommendations. One can then affirm that Turkey's macroprudential policy framework, introduced following the Great Recession in late 2010, has provided a basis for timely and coordinated responses to emerging risks.

However, there are still some deep-rooted structural issues that adversely affect financial stability in the Turkish economy, such as high current account deficits, a growing savings–investment gap, consumption-driven growth, high and increasing inflation and unemployment rates (Fig. 2), and recently emerging domestic and international political uncertainty (e.g. failed coup attack in July 2016, change of political system in April 2017 referendum, the war in Syria).

Turkey has a long-term problem with current account deficits, mainly related to its dependence on imported energy sources, import-based, low-value-added production, and low private savings rates that barely reached 13% of GDP in 2016. Hence, higher growth rates lead to higher current account deficits, which necessitate larger capital inflows, which in turn leads to increases in real domestic interest rates. When interest rates are not set in accordance with international financial conditions, the country has difficulties in attracting foreign capital, which puts pressure on the domestic currency, the Turkish lira (TL). The high rate of TL depreciation increases the burden of FX debt both for financial and non-financial corporations, which now stands at a gross level of US$400 billion.

On the other hand, since external demand has been weak in European and oil-exporting trade partners, particularly since 2011, the contribution of net exports to real growth remains close to zero. Hence, the country relies on domestic consumption fuelled by externally financed bank loans to the private sector to assure an acceptable 3% growth rate in the medium term. However, this growth rate, which is far below the long-run growth trend of the Turkish economy (4.5% between the years 1923 and 2016), cannot cover an increasing labour supply and, thus, avoid higher unemployment rates. This domestic demand-driven growth also contributes to inflationist pressures. Hence, Turkey seems to be entering an early stagflation stage, presenting a challenging macro-financial environment.

Moreover, the pattern of economic growth based on domestic demand that is fuelled by externally financed bank loans also leads to banking sector problems (Fig. 3). The most notable issues are large open positions (bank FX assets can only cover 25% of its FX liabilities) and risks of liquidity and non-performing loans, which have built up as a result of increasing reliance on short-term FX financing. In a highly uncertain global environment, there are risks of a collapse of external financing that could lead to a depreciation of the domestic currency – and hence subsequent deterioration in bank balance sheets – and push Turkey into recession.

This scenario actually materialized in 2006, 2008, 2013, and 2016. The fluctuations in the exchange rate in 2006 were mainly caused by international economic developments such as increasing global imbalances, rising commodity and oil prices, and increasing speculative bubbles in the US mortgage market. Contrary to the 2006 episode, the 2008–2009 crisis gravely affected the real economy as the country recorded a recession of nearly 5% of GDP, slumping export revenues (more than US$30 billion), and rising unemployment rates of 14% in 2009. In 2013, political risks increased, which led to high depreciation of the domestic currency (more than 25%), increasing interest rates, and slowing growth rates (about 3%). Again late 2016 and early 2017 saw increasing domestic and international political risks that caused capital outflows and TL depreciation.

4 Conclusion

According to our descriptive study, there exist two distinct periods in the Turkish economy: before and after the 2000–2001 financial crisis. During the pre-2001 crisis period, Turkey displayed important macroeconomic imbalances and significant banking sector weaknesses and underwent some external shocks, mostly related to the 1997–1998 Asian and 1998 Russian crises. However, these domestic problems were related not only to domestic factors but also to volatile capital flows. Of course, the highly unstable and factional political context, excessive public deficits, and excessively risk-taking domestic banks in the poorly supervised and corrupt banking system all created a crisis-prone economy. But significant capital in- and outflows following capital account liberalization in 1989 worsened all these domestic problems. This is consistent with the recent literature, which demonstrates that the sustainability of financial openness necessitates a deep fiscal and financial restructuring before its implementation (Aizenman 2004). In other words, if capital account liberalization is rapidly implemented without an efficient supervisory and regulatory framework, its crisis-causing effect exceeds its growth-enhancing effect.

In the post-2001 crisis period, Turkey managed to restore relative economic and financial stability with a radical structural economic program in a relatively stable political framework. However, the country suffered a severe crisis in 2008–2009 and high fluctuations in its money and currency markets in 2006, 2013, and 2016. A pattern of production that was highly dependent on imported energy and high-tech inputs and economic growth based on domestic demand that was heavily dependent on bank loans and short-term capital inflows were the main reasons behind this external vulnerability and financial fragility. Therefore, structural reforms should focus on decreasing dependence on imported inputs, increasing private savings, and improving labour productivity, which will reduce the dependence of the domestic economy on external financing, sustain investment and output, make the economy more competitive, and help Turkey to reduce its external deficit in order to join the ranks of high-income countries.

Recently, Turkish authorities have taken some measures in that order: voluntary pension accounts, introduced in 2003, have become mandatory in 2016 for both public servants and employees in the private sector, with a government matching contribution of 25% of the investment. Moreover, in the framework of the National Renewable Energy Action Plan implemented in late 2014, Turkish authorities have started to provide subsidies for private investments in renewable energy production that should reduce the country's over-dependence on imported energy sources and support sustainable economic growth under environmental considerations in the long run. But much work remains to be done.

On the other hand, macroprudential policies should take into account increased bank risks associated with FX borrowing and overall indebtedness, and authorities should further raise banking regulation and supervisory effectiveness. In addition, further financial development would contribute to the diversity and efficiency of the financial system and ultimately enhance macroeconomic and financial stability by lowering reliance on FX borrowing (IMF 2017). This is actually confirmed by some empirical papers whose results indicate the existence of a long-run positive relationship between financial development and economic growth in Turkey (Ozturk 2008; Yildirim and Tastan 2012; Arac and Ozcan 2014; Ari and Cergibozan 2017). In this sense, stronger institutions, by providing better protection of property rights, creditor rights and information, and higher regulatory quality and rule of law are necessary for greater financial development and, hence, higher economic growth (Sahay et al. 2015).

Notes

1. Note that we distinguish short-term capital flows from foreign direct investments, which are considered to be more stable long-term investments. Hence, they are less likely to destabilize the domestic economy.
2. Kara (2016) gives some highlights of these prudent banking policies: 'Banks were not allowed to have currency mismatches, foreign currency loans to consumers were prohibited, there were restrictions on foreign currency lending to non-financial firms, and tight restrictions were imposed on distributing bank dividends, new bank entry, branch openings etc.'

References

Aghion, Philippe, Philippe Bacchetta, and Abhijit Banerjee. 2004. *Financial Development and the Instability of Open Economies*, NBER Working Paper 10246. Cambridge, MA: NBER.

Aizenman, Joshua. 2004. Financial Opening: Evidence and Policy Options. In *Challenges to Globalization: Analyzing the Economics*, ed. Robert E. Baldwin and L. Alan Winters, 473–497. Chicago: University of Chicago Press.

Andersen, Thomas B., and Finn Tarp. 2003. Financial Liberalization, Financial Development and Economic Growth in LDCs. *Journal of International Development* 15: 189–209.

Arac, Aysen, and Suleyman Kutalmis Ozcan. 2014. The Causality Between Financial Development and Economic Growth: The Case of Turkey. *Journal of Economic Cooperation and Development* 35: 171–198.

Ari, Ali, and Raif Cergibozan. 2017. Sustainable Growth in Turkey: The Role of Trade Openness, Financial Development, and Renewable Energy Use. In *Industrial Policy and Sustainable Growth*, ed. Murat Yulek, 1–21. Singapore: Springer.

Arteta, Carlos, Barry Eichengreen, and Charles Wyplosz. 2001. *When Does Capital Account Liberalization Help More Than It Hurts*, NBER Working Paper 8414. Cambridge, MA: NBER.

Baltagi, Badi H., Panicos O. Demetriades, and Siong H. Law. 2009. Financial Development and Openness: Evidence from Panel Data. *Journal of Development Economics* 89: 285–296.

Barro, Robert J. 2003. Determinants of Economic Growth in a Panel of Countries. *Annals of Economics and Finance* 4: 231–274.

Beck, Thorsten, Ross Levine, and Norman Loayza. 2000. Finance and the Sources of Growth. *Journal of Financial Economics* 58: 261–300.

Bekaert, Geert, Campbell R. Harvey, and Christian Lundblad. 2005. Does Financial Liberalization Spur Growth? *Journal of Financial Economics* 77: 3–55.

Boratav, Korkut, and Erinc Yeldan. 2006. Turkey, 1980–2000: Financial Liberalization, Macroeconomic (In)stability, and Patterns of Distribution. In *External Liberalization in Asia, Post-socialist Europe, and Brazil*, ed. Lance Taylor, 417–455. Oxford: Oxford University Press.

Bussiere, Mathieu, and Marcel Fratzscher. 2008. Financial Openness and Growth: Short-Run Gain, Long-Run Pain? *Review of International Economics* 16: 69–95.

De Gregorio, Jose, and Pablo E. Guidotti. 1995. Financial Development and Economic Growth. *World Development* 23: 433–448.

Deidda, Luca, and Bassam Fattouh. 2002. Non-Linearity Between Finance and Growth. *Economics Letters* 74: 339–345.

Demirguc-Kunt, Asli, and Enrica Detragiache. 1998. The Determinants of Banking Crises: Evidence from Developing and Developed Countries. *IMF Staff Papers* 45: 81–109.

Edison, Hali J., Michael W. Klein, Luca A. Ricci, and Torsten Slok. 2004. Capital Account Liberalization and Economic Performance: Survey and Synthesis. *IMF Staff Papers* 51: 220–256.

Edwards, Sebastian. 2001. *Capital Mobility and Economic Performance: Are Emerging Economies Different?* NBER Working Paper 8076. Cambridge, MA: NBER.

Eichengreen, Barry, and David Leblang. 2003. Capital Account Liberalization and Growth: Was Mr. Mahathir Right? *International Journal of Finance & Economics* 8: 205–224.

Eichengreen, Barry, Rachita Gullapalli, and Ugo Panizza. 2011. Capital Account Liberalization, Financial Development and Industry Growth: A Synthetic View. *Journal of International Money and Finance* 30: 1090–1106.

Huang, Yongfu. 2010. *Determinants of Financial Development*. Basingstoke: Palgrave Macmillan.

IMF. 2007. *IMF Country Report*: Turkey. 07/361.

———. 2012. *IMF Country Report*: Turkey. 12/261.

———. 2017. *IMF Country Report*: Turkey. 17/35.

Kaminsky, Graciela L., and Carmen M. Reinhart. 1999. The Twin Crises: The Causes of Banking and Balance of Payment Problems. *American Economic Review* 89: 473–500.

Kaminsky, Graciela L., and Sergio L. Schmukler. 2008. Short-Run Pain, Long-Run Gain: Financial Liberalization and Stock Market Cycles. *Review of Finance* 12: 253–292.

Kara, A. Hakan. 2016. A Brief Assessment of Turkey's Macroprudential Policy Approach: 2011–2015. *Central Bank Review* 16: 85–92.

King, Robert G., and Ross Levine. 1993. Finance, Entrepreneurship, and Growth: Theory and Evidence. *Journal of Monetary Economics* 32: 513–542.

Klein, Michael W. 2003. *Capital Account Openness and the Varieties of Growth Experience*, NBER Working Paper 9500. Cambridge, MA: NBER.

Kose, M. Ayhan, Eswar S. Prasad, and Marco E. Terrones. 2009a. Does Openness to International Financial Flows Raise Productivity Growth? *Journal of International Money and Finance* 28: 554–580.

Kose, M. Ayhan, Eswar S. Prasad, Kenneth Rogoff, and Shanjg-Jin Wei. 2009b. Financial Globalization: A Reappraisal. *IMF Staff Papers* 56: 8–62.

Levine, Ross. 2005. Finance and Growth: Theory and Evidence. In *Handbook of Economic Growth Volume 1A*, ed. Philippe Aghion and Steven N. Durlauf, 865–934. Amsterdam: Elsevier.

Levine, Ross, Norman Loayza, and Thorsten Beck. 2000. Financial Intermediation and Growth: Causality and Causes. *Journal of Monetary Economics* 46: 31–77.

Loayza, Norman, and Romain Ranciere. 2006. Financial Development, Financial Fragility, and Growth. *Journal of Money, Credit and Banking* 38: 1051–1076.

McKinnon, Ronald I. 1973. *Money and Capital in Economic Development*. Washington, DC: The Brookings Institution.

Odedokun, Matthew O. 1996. Alternative Econometric Approaches for Analyzing the Role of the Financial Sector in Economic Growth: Time-Series Evidence from LDCs. *Journal of Development Economics* 50: 119–146.

OECD. 2004. *Understanding Economic Growth: Macro-Level, Industry-Level, Firm-Level*. New York: Palgrave Macmillan.

———. 2014. *OECD Economic Surveys*: Turkey.

Ozturk, Ilhan. 2008. Financial Development and Economic Growth: Evidence from Turkey. *Applied Econometrics and International Development* 8: 85–98.

Patrick, Hugh T. 1966. Financial Development and Economic Growth in Underdeveloped Countries. *Economic Development and Cultural Change* 14: 174–189.

Rajan, Raghuram G., and Luigi Zingales. 2003. The Great Reversals: The Politics of Financial Development in the Twentieth Century. *Journal of Financial Economics* 69: 5–50.

Ram, Rati. 1999. Financial Development and Economic Growth: Additional Evidence. *Journal of Development Studies* 35: 164–174.

Ranciere, Romain, Aaron Tornell, and Frank Westermann. 2006. Decomposing the Effects of Financial Liberalization: Crises vs. Growth. *Journal of Banking & Finance* 30: 3331–3348.

Rioja, Felix, and Neven Valev. 2004. Does One Size Fit All? A Reexamination of the Finance and Growth Relationship. *Journal of Development Economics* 74: 429–447.

Rodrik, Dani. 1990. *Premature Liberalization, Incomplete Stabilization: The Özal Decade in Turkey*, NBER Working Paper 3300. Cambridge, MA: NBER.

———. 1998. Who Needs Capital-Account Convertibility? In *Should the IMF Pursue Capital-Account Convertibility?* ed. Stanley Fischer et al., 55–65. Princeton: Princeton University Press.

Sahay, Ratna, et al. 2015. *Rethinking Financial Deepening: Stability and Growth in Emerging Markets*, IMF Staff Discussion Note 15-08. Washington, DC: IMF.

Shaw, Edward S. 1973. *Financial Deepening in Economic Development*. New York: Oxford University Press.

Stiglitz, Joseph E. 2000. Capital Market Liberalization, Economic Growth, and Instability. *World Development* 28: 1075–1086.

Stiglitz, Joseph E., Jose A. Ocampo, Shari Spiegel, Ricardo Ffrench-Davis, and Deepak Nayyar. 2006. *Stability with Growth – Macroeconomics, Liberalization, and Development*. New York: Oxford University Press.

Yildirim, Nuri, and Huseyin Tastan. 2012. Capital Flows and Economic Growth Across Spectral Frequencies: Evidence from Turkey. *Panoeconomicus* 59: 441–462.

Capital Inflows and Banking in the Turkish Economy

Resul Aydemir and Gokhan Ovenc

1 Introduction

The Turkish economy has increasingly become more integrated into the global economy through not just trade but also capital flows. In the aftermath of the 2001 banking and financial crises, the process of capital integration of the Turkish economy with the rest of the world has moved into a new phase supported by structural financial reforms and political stability.

Capital inflows can provide substantial benefits for emerging countries at the expense of additional risks. Capital inflows can stimulate domestic investment through lending, thereby increasing growth rates and living standards. They also supply necessary funds for developing countries that make it easier for them to sustain their budget deficits. On the other

R. Aydemir (✉)
Department of Economics, Istanbul Technical University, Istanbul, Turkey

G. Ovenc
Department of Economics, Istanbul University, Istanbul, Turkey

A. F. Aysan et al. (eds.), *Turkish Economy*,
https://doi.org/10.1007/978-3-319-70380-0_8

hand, capital inflows lead to current account deficits, market bubbles, lending booms, volatile and short-run flows, and exchange rate fluctuations risks, which are even prevalent in countries having sound economic fundamentals (Calvo et al. 1996; Mishkin 2009; Caballero 2016). Emerging market economies (EMEs) have implemented several macroprudential policies to minimize the risks associated with capital flows and increase their potential benefits.

Banks, as intermediaries of financial flows between domestic and global markets, play a significant role in managing the trade-off between these benefits and risks. Banks also act as a bridge between foreign loans (cross-border liability) and domestic lending. In recent years, EMEs have witnessed a rapid growth in bank credits. Simultaneously, there has been an increasing trend towards the internationalization of EMEs banking through cross-border banking (i.e., non-core) liability (Fig. 1) (BIS

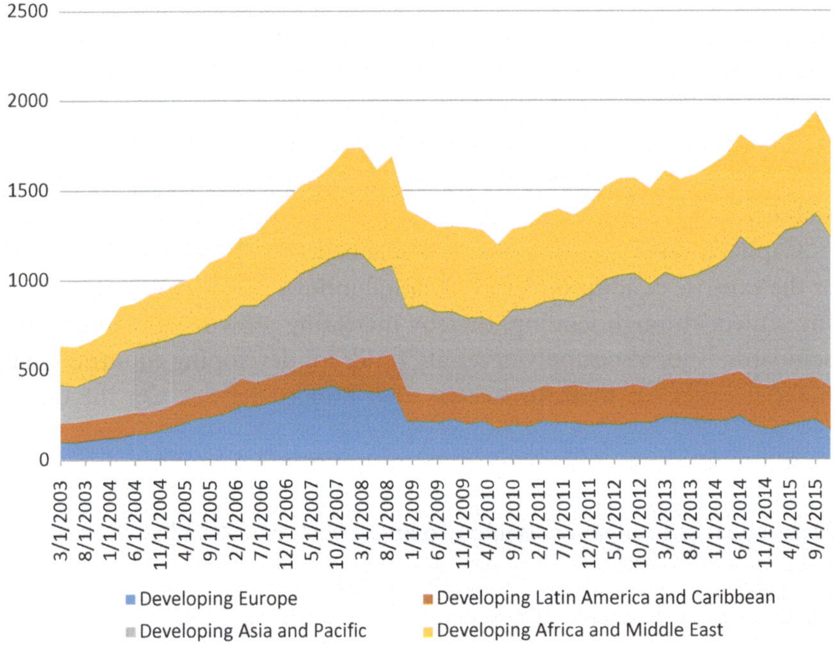

Fig. 1 Cross-border total banking liability by emerging regions (billion USD) (Source: BIS)

2014). Therefore, any overuse or abuse of cross-border liability by EME banks to meet domestic lending demand could create a banking crisis or financial turbulence since cross-border banking liability directly affects the level of domestic lending, especially when the domestic banking sector cannot find enough core liability (i.e. domestic deposit).

Since 2002, Turkish domestic deposits have grown significantly as a result of financial deepening and overall income growth. Likewise, the Turkish economy's credit growth has increased during the same period. However, as the loan-to-deposit ratio exceeded the critical level of one in 2011, the Turkish banking sector gradually started to rely increasingly on cross-border liability.[1] This higher reliance on cross-border liability may have increased banking risks related to maturity mismatch, currency mismatch, liquidity, short-/long-term foreign exchange (FX) liability, and interest and exchange rates. In response to larger access to non-core liability (banking foreign loan inflow) and sudden stop/volatile financial flows, the Central Bank of Turkey (CBRT) started to implement new policies (such as interest rate corridor and reserve option mechanism) and changed its reserve requirement rate for non-deposit FX liability to deal with these potential risks. As a consequence of macroprudential policies, foreign borrowing in the Turkish banking sector creates little short-term risk due to non-deposit FX liability. However, because the loan-to-deposit ratio of the sector exceeds the 100% threshold, there would still be a problem because the higher reliance on foreign sources makes the domestic banking system more vulnerable to external shocks.

In this chapter, we examine the developments in the Turkish banking industry in the context of capital and financial flows, specifically focusing on cross-border banking liability (non-core). In the first part, we briefly analyse how the Turkish economy, as an EME, has been affected by capital and financial inflows. Then, we touch upon how different types of financial inflows and the banking sector are interrelated especially through cross-border liability. In the second part, the transformation of the Turkish banking sector will be described by focusing on the post-2001 period. Then we investigate the association between cross-border liability (non-core) and the performance of Turkish banks. Afterward, we examine the current outlook for the Turkish banking sector. Finally, we conclude with policy recommendations.

2 The Turkish Economy and Financial Inflows

The Turkish economy has demonstrated similar characteristics to other emerging economies. The prevailing facts regarding financial flows observed in the other EMEs and the impacts of these flows specified in the literature, such as lower interest rates, market bubbles, lending booms, and monetary expansion, have been true for the case of Turkey as well (Calvo et al. 1996). As an example, in Fig. 2 we show the first 10 countries with the largest international investment deficits (IIDs) (financial assets: e.g. foreign direct investment (FDI), portfolios, loans). Turkey has the ninth largest international trade deficit in the world economy (ranked between Mexico and Indonesia). More importantly, Turkey has the fifth highest ratio of IID to GDP.[2] We need to look at the composition of financial flows into a country to understand its international investment position.

The composition of financial flows in the Turkish economy can be seen in Fig. 3. The total share of FDI in financial flows is smaller than that of other categories but follows a stable pattern, while portfolio inflows are more volatile compared to other inflows. We observe an increasing trend in financial inflows since 2003, albeit with high volatility.

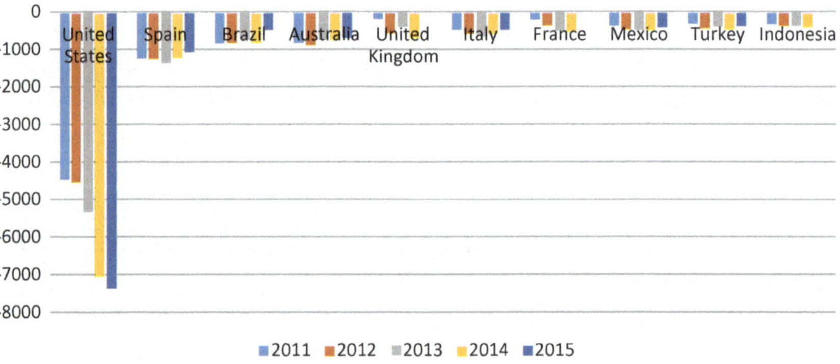

Fig. 2 International investment deficit positions (billion USD) (Source: International Monetary Fund)

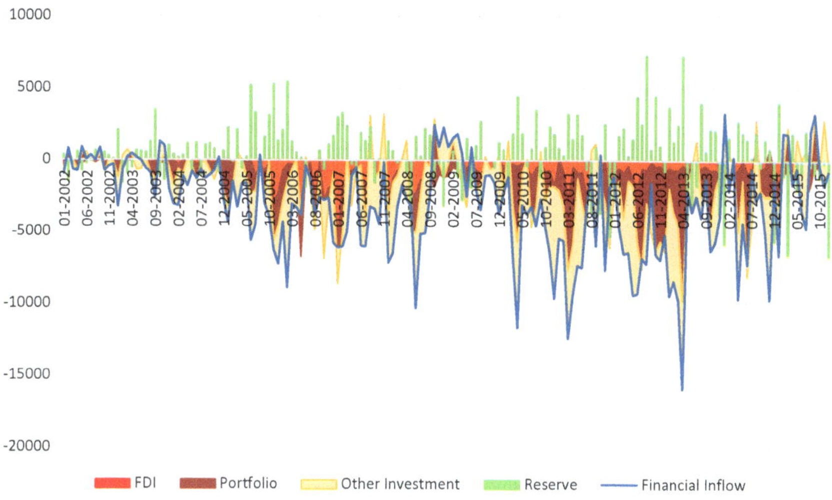

Fig. 3 Turkey's financial account composition (million USD) (Source: CBRT)

The large swings in financial inflows inevitably influence the macroeconomic environment by affecting firms' and banks' balance sheets, their access to credit, lending behaviour, pricing dynamics, and import/export structure. To address potential risks created by short-run/volatile financial flows, which have started to rise again since the 2008 financial crisis, the CBRT has been very actively and successfully managing the volatile and sudden stop in financial flows through traditional and new macroprudential tools. For instance, the active use of the interest rate corridor (widening or narrowing) and the reserve option mechanism by the CBRT in 2010 reduced the lower bound of the interest rate (borrowing rate) and increased the reserve option coefficient during large capital inflows, restricting the supply of foreign currency and its depreciation (Aysan et al. 2015). Moreover, the ratio of current account deficit to GDP was again reduced to a critical level of 5% (CBRT 2016; Roubini and Wachtel 1999).

During the same period, the Borsa Istanbul stock exchange's main BIST 100 index rose about 700% from an average of 10,000 to around 80,000, and the secondary-market bond rate with 2-year maturity decreased from 65% to 9%, while the USD/TL exchange rate was stable between 2002 and 2014. The exchange rate showed a declining trend between 2003 and 2009 but then increased as a result of the US Federal Reserve (Fed)'s announcement of possible systematic interest rate hikes in 2014. Real consumption doubled over 2002 levels. The M1 money supply in the Turkish economy rose about 1700% between 2002 and 2015. One of the main characteristics of this period is the high appreciation of Turkish housing prices, especially in big cities. All these facts are consistent with the financial inflow literature.

3 Types of Financial Flows and Banking Through Non-core Liabilities

Financial flows are comprised of various components such as FDI, portfolios, deposits, credit, and reserves that differ based on the maturity (long, short) or nature of the claim (equity, debt). Each component has a different effect on the financial system and banking industry (Caballero 2016). It is held that equity-based inflow is not damaging compared to debt-based inflow. For instance, equity-based inflow FDI is steady and usually demonstrates long-run characteristics, while debt-type inflows, such as deposits or credit (through banking), have short-run and sudden-stop characteristics. One crucial component of financial inflows is cross-border banking liability (bank loans, debt securities inflows). Although the share of banking industry credit inflow (cross-border loan liability) in overall financial inflow is low, it could adversely affect the financial system stability because of its volatile and procyclical nature, especially in emerging economies depending on the global and domestic risk perceptions (Bruno and Shin 2014; Shin 2014; Cowan et al. 2007). Concerns related to cross-border banking credit inflows can be observed through banks' balance-sheet transactions, and they can influence banks' lending behaviours since they are directly related to how banks manage their external and internal balance-sheet liabilities. The main funding source of domestic banks is domestic savings, which make up the deposit part of the balance-sheet liability, the so-called core liability. However, bank deposits heavily depend on the performance of the domestic economy, specifically on households' savings rates, which constrain the size of the overall internal funding source. If demand for domestic credit grows faster than the supply of total domestic deposits, banks turn to foreign funds to finance the excess demand for domestic credits. Especially during a credit boom period, we observe that banks in emerging economies such as Turkey and Brazil try to increase their lending capacity by borrowing from abroad using the international banking system. Figure 4 shows the cross-border banking liability for some emerging countries.

This kind of credit inflow or wholesale funding from foreign creditors increases the non-core liabilities of banks' balance sheets. It is important to note that banking industry credit inflow (wholesale foreign funding) is unstable compared to domestic deposits since it depends on international capital market conditions and risk perceptions (Hermann and Mihaljek 2010). Therefore, how banks improve their ability to lend through equity and debt (internal or external) is crucial. For example, Hahm et al. (2013) find that the non-core liabilities of banks are the most pronounced indicator of financial vulnerability during lending booms since they directly affect the risk variables of an economy such as maturity mismatch, liquidity, short-/long-term FX liability (non-deposit and deposit), and interest and exchange rates.

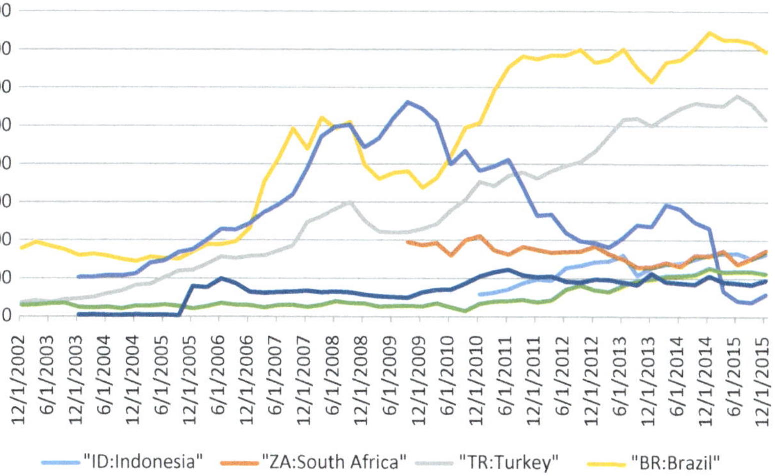

Fig. 4 Cross-border banking liability (all instruments, million USD) (Source: BIS)

One of the main factors affecting domestic banking cross-border liability is exchange rate as domestic banks borrow and pay back foreign wholesale loans in foreign currency, for example in USD and euros. Economists have been studying how financial inflows and exchange rates are interrelated. For instance, Bruno and Shin (2014) show that local currency appreciation has a major impact on the foreign borrowing of domestic banks. Therefore, exchange rate volatility might harm banks' balance sheets through maturity mismatch and the time horizon of their debt positions.

Apart from cross-border liability, normally domestic currency appreciation is expected to reduce the amount of capital inflows since capital inflow would earn a lower return in a non-appreciation period. If policymakers intervene in the foreign exchange market to limit appreciation and control capital inflows, they may encourage additional capital inflows and create extra-market distortions in the short run. Regarding cross-border banking liability and the balance-sheet perspective, domestic currency appreciation is believed to positively affect banking performance since banking credit inflow depends mainly on borrowing in foreign currency and lending in domestic currency. Therefore, policymakers should be very careful in their attempts to control capital inflows and appreciation. Their policies may influence the real economy and financial system in unintended ways. Evidence suggests that EME banks have learned how to deal with or dampen exchange rate fluctuations following the 2008 financial crisis (Brunnermeier et al. 2012). Foreign currency reserves and FX asset/liability composition (long vs. short) in EME banks' balance sheets are shelters against exchange rate fluctuations and financial crises that minimize the damage from external factors.

4 Turkish Banking Sector

4.1 Pre-2001 Developments

After transforming its economy into a fully liberalized market in the 1980s, Turkey began to receive its first huge volume of capital inflows by the end of the 1980s (Agenor et al. 1997). Significant structural economic reforms, such as the convertibility of the domestic currency, free capital movement, and liberalization of loan and deposit rates and the foreign exchange regime were implemented during the middle of the 1980s, and as a result, Turkey has integrated into the global financial system.

Turkey's integration into the global financial system has advantages and risks. As a result of liberal market reforms, the Turkish financial and banking sector made rapid progress. With the entrance of new private and foreign banks, the share of public banks in the total industry fell precipitously. The new entries made the industry more competitive and more institutionalized. Nonetheless, from this point the Turkish economy has had a short-term capital inflow problem. In addition to short-term capital inflows, high inflation, increasing public debt, current account deficits, and dollarization were negative characteristics of the period between 1989 and 2000. During that period, the annual average inflation rate was 72%, distorting the efficiency of monetary/fiscal policy and increasing the uncertainty of economic transactions. The average ratio of external or foreign debt (including public) to GNP was about 47% and increased to 78% for 2000–2001, as a result of public budget deficit financing. During this period, the main objective of the private banks was to provide short-term funds to the public sector by borrowing from abroad, which allowed them to earn the simple interest spread but exposed them to exchange rate risk, while public banks had poor performance mainly because of political intervention and mismanagement. Given all these facts, Turkey experienced several crises resulting from domestic and global events. Among them were the 1991 Gulf War, the 1994 Mexican currency crisis, the 1997 devaluation, the 1997 East Asian financial crisis, the 1998 Russian financial crisis, and the 2000–2001 banking liquidity and FX crises in Turkey (Mercan et al. 2003). In particular, the general outlook and disappointing performance of the Turkish banking industry and political instability were considered to be major consequences of the 2000 and 2001 economic crises. As a result, the primary measures taken to restore the Turkish economy focused on the structural issues of the banking and financial industry.

4.2 Post-2001 Developments

With the Banking Sector Restructuring Programme following the 2001 banking crisis, authorities aimed to increase the efficiency of state banks, solve the problems of the insolvent banks transferred to the Saving Deposit Insurance Fund (SDIF), strengthen the balance sheets of private banks, and broaden the supervisory and regulatory scopes by the Banking Regulatory and Supervisory Agency (BRSA). Certain criteria about deposit insurance, capital adequacy, non-performing loans, ownership, FX position, and liquidity management were established to make the supervisory and regulatory framework function well. For instance, under the new FX regulation, banks were not allowed to increase their FX positions to more than 20% of their equity. In the years following the regulatory and supervisory measures, the overall size of the banking industry shrank. The number of banks, branches, and employees significantly declined. The period between 2001 and 2004 is known as the period of recovery and stabilization of the Turkish banking sector (Akın et al. 2009).

After the recovery and stabilization period, the Turkish banking sector entered a new phase in which political stability, economic growth, and external factors such as EU membership negotiations and global macroeconomic recovery played important roles in this development. From 2004 to 2008, the total USD-valued assets increased by 183% and total equity rose by about 156% (Fig. 5).

The number of employees in the banking industry increased by about 25%, and the number of branches rose by about 80%. During the same period, five additional foreign commercial banks entered the Turkish market, and the Turkish banking industry was able to borrow large amounts of money from international financial markets through syndication and securitization loans in which the total amount of cross-border liabilities rose from 4.3 billion USD in 2004 to 27 billion USD in 2008.

Even though there was an increase in the number of employees and branches in the Turkish banking sector between 2008 and 2011, global economic and financial conditions depressed banking activities. During this period, the total assets, total lending, and cross-border inflows

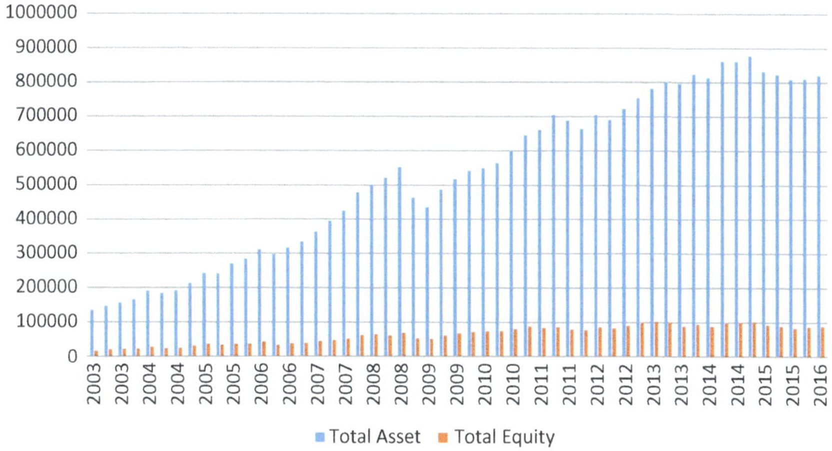

Fig. 5 Turkish banking industry (million USD) (Source: BRSA)

declined. The period between 2011 and 2015 was dominated by internal conflict in 2013, political uncertainties that resulted from governmental elections in 2015, and change in the Fed's interest rate policy. Also, increased risk perception towards EMEs and lower growth rates of the Chinese economy shaped this period. Moreover, tighter domestic prudential regulations on credit, a rise in interest rates, and lower economic growth put pressure on banking activities and lending in the last 2 years of this period (CBRT 2015). Although these internal and external factors might have short-run negative impacts on the banking industry and lending activities, the Turkish banking industry is expected to progress and grow as it has in the past. When global economic and financial conditions improve, rising GDP growth rates and domestic political stability could foster international financial flows into Turkey and stimulate domestic investment.

4.3 The Turkish Banking Sector and Non-core Liabilities

In recent years, EMEs have witnessed rapid growth in bank credit. Simultaneously, emerging economies have faced an increasing trend in cross-border banking credit that has led to greater profitability through higher interest rate spreads but is also a new risk factor for financial intermediation. In EMEs such as Turkey, Korea, and Mexico, the share of wholesale funding in total liabilities has increased in the last decade (BIS 2016). Like other EMEs, total syndication and securitization loans (cross-border liability) in the Turkish banking industry have risen steadily since 2002 (Fig. 6).

Between 2003 and 2008, banks were increasingly able to borrow from abroad, but global financial turbulence reversed this inflow because of changes in the global risk perception. Then the Turkish banking industry started to receive a high volume of foreign credit again from the beginning of the second quarter of 2013 until the second quarter of 2015. The year 2012 and the last two quarters of 2015 were dominated by elections and domestic conflicts, which increased the country's risk level and discouraged international investors' willingness to lend.

Cross-border banking liability is crucial for domestic lending, especially when the banking sector cannot find enough core liability (domestic deposits). Domestic deposit growth has followed a strong path in the Turkish economy, resulting from financial deepening and general income

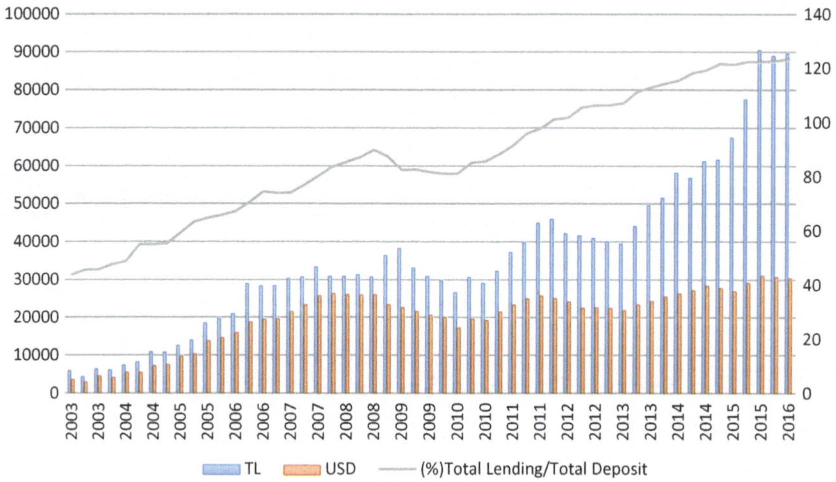

Fig. 6 Syndication and securitization loans (million USD *left axis*) and total lending/total deposits (% *right axis*) (Source: BRSA)

growth since 2002. Simultaneously, the trend in credit growth outpacing domestic deposit growth has also increased during the same period. But the sector's loan-to-deposit ratio exceeded the critical level of one in 2011, which in turn increased banks' reliance on foreign funding. As the domestic credit growth/level has been larger than the domestic deposit growth/level, banks have started to turn to foreign markets (external borrowing) (Fig. 6). The high correlation between *lending to deposit ratio* and *cross-border liability to asset ratio* since 2010 might be a potential risk that should be taken into account. The increasing reliance of the Turkish banking sector on cross-border liability might create risks such as credit risk, funding risk, maturity mismatch, currency mismatch, liquidity, short/long-term FX liability, and interest and exchange rate fluctuations (Adrian and Shin 2009; Hills and Hoggarth 2013; Allen 2011). For instance, when banks expand their balance sheets through cross-border liability, their borrowing has a shorter maturity than lending. This may make banks vulnerable to a maturity mismatch problem.

Banking non-core liability is directly associated with liquidity risk. Concerning liquidity risk, the Turkish banking industry has two concentrations: one around TL assets and core liabilities, the other around FX and non-core liabilities. Generally speaking, Turkish banks seem to be successful at containing their liquidity risk, including TL and FX. However, it is still important to manage the liquidity risk associated with external financing (non-core liabilities). Banking industry USD-valued external debt increased from 2009 but started to decrease in early 2015 owing to internal and external risks. However, the growth rate of foreign debt is still positive under an exchange-rate-adjusted effect (CBRT 2015).

To deal with the potential risks, the monetary authorities in emerging economies may implement policies and regulations to strengthen the resilience of the banking industry against risks associated with non-core liabilities. Monetary authorities in EMEs have carried out macroprudential regulations such as raising non-deposit FX reserve requirement, attracting foreign bank entry, and stronger supervision (BIS 2009). In addition, the interest rate corridor and reserve option mechanism were new policy tools that started to be implemented in 2010 by the CBRT to reduce risks related to volatile short-term capital inflows and control currency appreciation/depreciation (Aysan et al. 2015). These new tools are crucial because when volatile capital flows are not managed properly by monetary authorities, the sudden appreciation or depreciation of foreign exchange might occur. These sudden ups and downs inevitably affect banks' balance sheets and lending activities adversely. Based on the empirical evidence from Turkey, Aysan et al. (2015) show that these new policy tools have been effective at minimizing the impacts of volatile cross-border capital inflows.

The composition of foreign financing also changed owing to the new arrangement of the CBRT that aimed to foster external financing with long-term maturities. The CBRT recently increased the reserve requirement ratios for non-deposit FX liability with a maturity of less than 3 years. In response to this change, there was an increase in long-term external financing and a decrease in foreign funding with short-term maturities. The short-term foreign liabilities as a share of total foreign liabilities decreased from 58% in 2014 to 33% in 2015. Further, the average maturity of foreign liabilities of banks rose to 51 months, and the average maturity of syndicated loans increased from 12 to 15 months (CBRT 2015).

Interest rate and exchange rate fluctuations might create a risk of maturity mismatch between banks' assets and liabilities. Since 2013, the average maturity of banks' assets has been fluctuating between 19 and 21 months, while liabilities exhibit a more stable and smoother pattern at 3 months. During this period, the maturity of loans (interest-rate sensitive) and long-term TL deposits as a share of total deposits have been declining, whereas the share of FX assets and liabilities have been rising. The total amount of FX liabilities is higher than FX assets, and FX liabilities as a share of total liabilities has been increasing. According to the CBRT's 2015 financial report, the impact of exchange rate fluctuations on Turkish banks' balance sheets is very limited since banks take on-balance-sheet short and off-balance-sheet long positions simultaneously. Therefore, net FX positions of the banking industry follow a steady trend (CBRT 2015). Instead, the banking industry's long-term maturity TL assets and liabilities are more sensitive to interest rates compared to maturities up to 1 year (CBRT 2015).

4.4 Overall Outlook and Some Policy Recommendations

As of 2016, 52 banks operate in the Turkish banking industry, including 34 commercial banks (3 publicly owned, 9 privately owned with domestic holders and 15 privately owned with foreign holders), 13 investment and development banks, and 5 participation banks. Six international commercial banks have branches in Turkey (BAT 2016). Over the last 15 years, the total assets of the Turkish banking industry have risen by about 505%, valued at 821 billion USD, and total equities have increased by 416%, valued at over 91 billion USD. As can be seen in Fig. 7, the general profitability of the Turkish banking sector has experienced a noticeable decline in all measures including net interest margin (NIM), return on assets (ROA), and return on equity (ROE) since 2002. During this period, ROE diminished less than ROA since total banking assets grew more than total equities and the steady fall in interest rates kept downward pressure on NIM.

To deal with declining profitability, the banking sector intends to increase efficiency, more effectively use technology, and minimize costs. A closer look at the numbers shows that the strong and well-designed

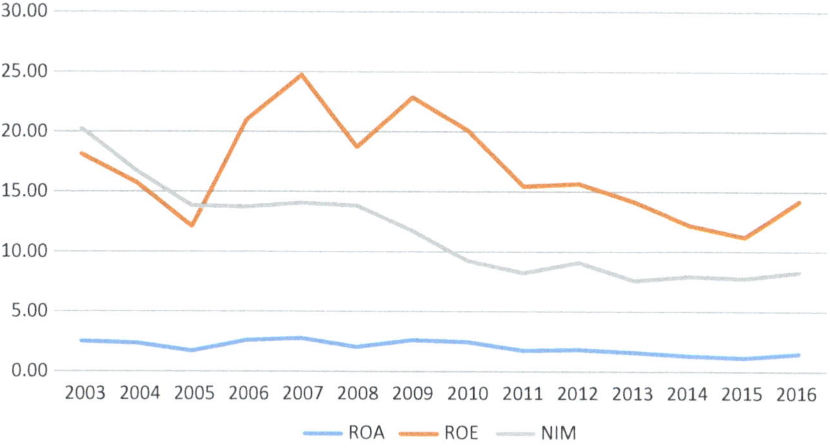

Fig. 7 Turkish banking profitability (%) (Source: BRSA)

domestic supervisory and regulatory framework is likely to support the banking sector's positive outlook. Risk indicators such as liquidity risk, capital adequacy, and non-performing loans reflect a stable and promising signal for the future. Cross-border liability (non-core) will continue to be the primary funding sources for domestic lending given that domestic deposits and the savings rate continue to be low while domestic lending is on an upward trend. Although increased reliance on wholesale foreign borrowing does not create any short-term risk in terms of non-deposit FX liability, it is likely to be one of the risk factors that the banking sector will confront until it finds less risky funding sources, other than foreign funding, for its lending activities. In fact, the Turkish banking sector should devise a new road map, in line with its solid appearance, to be classified as one of the top banking systems among EMEs. In this context, we have some general and specific policy recommendations for the sector.

The interest income of Turkish banks dominates their non-interest income (Aydemir and Ovenc 2016). Unlike EMEs, one of the key features of developed countries' banking sectors is that they have higher trading income compared to interest income to hedge against interest rate risk. Hence, we recommend that the Turkish banking sector increase its trading income capacity through hedging, direct investment, or investment partnerships. These kinds of trading activities and investment partnerships might help the sector to increase its profitability and shield the sector against possible risks.

In today's international financial system, advanced economies and global banks capture the lion's share of cross-border banking inflows. Against this backdrop, increasing the capacity of regional financial integration between the Turkish and other EMEs' banks would be beneficial. This kind of integration, through creative and efficient partnership models, has the potential to instigate a new momentum towards cross-border liability expansion and might eventually reduce the global risks associated with capital flows from advanced economies. In this regard, the Turkish banking sector could seek to enter new markets in countries with which Turkey has historically maintained good relationships and has high levels of economic integration in other sectors. Opening new branches in neighbouring countries that Turkey trades with actively could reduce Turkey's dependence on non-core liabilities from advanced economies.

Given the difficulties in efficiently coordinating cross-border inflows and a lack of global regulation, the CBRT and other authorities should continue to closely monitor cross-border financial inflows. Measures should be pursued vigorously to attract long-term cross-border banking liabilities. Effective policies and regulations that stimulate domestic savings and long-term investment positions might reduce the banking sector's reliance on cross-border foreign funding. Although the macroprudential policies implemented by the CBRT have helped manage capital flows and cross-border banking liability in the short term, we should keep in mind that these policies are only the second-best solutions until long-term structural reforms yield the desired results with respect to increasing savings rates and productivity and lowering inflation and current account deficits (Kara 2016).

To limit the extent to which the banking and financial system is adversely affected by exchange rate fluctuations and outflows, a Tobin tax imposed on short-term financial capital might be considered an option. Indeed, following the East Asian and Latin American crises, Malaysia and Chile successfully implemented such a policy (Rajan 1998). The Malaysian authorities imposed controls on capital flows and foreign exchange transactions to deal with speculative capital movements (Kim 2003). The possibility of levying such a tax on some types of financial flows was discussed in Turkey after the 2001 banking and financial system crisis, and it is a hot topic among economists and authorities whenever current account deficits create a risk for the country. Apart from the current account risk, this kind of tax might dampen speculative flows into the Turkish economy.

Asset price bubbles, especially in real estate markets, have a direct impact on the excessive use of credits and, therefore, on cross-border banking liability. Effective use of monetary policy (i.e. interest rate) and macroprudential regulations could help reduce the systemic risks related to market bubbles. Given the facts that real estate prices vary by region and some cities have different economic fundamentals than others, using a tight monetary policy to address asset price bubbles might cause unintended consequences. For instance, while a rise in the interest rate might limit and control asset prices in some markets, it might also negatively affect real estate markets in cities that do not have bubbles. In such circumstances, in lieu of monetary policy, macroprudential policies such as fine-tuning of loan-to-value ratios would be more effective at dealing with market bubbles (Allen 2011). In this regard, the CBRT should actively continue using these targeted macroprudential policies to address systemic bubble risks.

The problems faced by banks, such as maturity mismatches, currency mismatches, and exchange rate volatility, are partly shaped by the nature of cross-border banking flows. Central banks play a critical role in reducing risks associated with these problems. Specifically, during shortages of foreign reserves, the timely intervention of the central bank to provide adequate reserves to the banking sector is vital, so that attempts to harm the credibility of the central bank should be avoided at all costs. To maintain its credibility, the central bank must not only be independent of outside pressure but also needs to be a good communicator. These qualities would help resolve ambiguities that arise in the course of the central bank's work, especially in dealing with problems related to cross-border banking inflows.

5 Conclusion

Since the early 2000s, the Turkish banking sector has continued to prosper significantly and gradually become more integrated into global financial markets. The strong and well-designed domestic supervisory and regulatory framework is likely to support the banking sector's positive outlook. Risk indicators such as liquidity risk, capital adequacy, and non-performing loans reflect a stable and promising signal for the future. To deal with falling profitability, the banking sector must do its best to minimize costs, increase efficiency, and better utilize technological innovations.

Domestic deposit growth has followed a strong trajectory in the Turkish economy as a result of the financial deepening and overall income growth that have occurred since 2002. Likewise, the Turkish economy's credit growth has also increased during the same period. The high correlation between *lending-to-deposit ratio* and *cross-border-liability-to-asset ratio* since 2010 might be a potential risk that should be taken into account. Cross-border liabilities (non-core) seem to be a key funding source for domestic lending, given that domestic deposit and savings rates in Turkey continue to remain low while domestic demand for lending is on an upward trend.

Although the increased reliance on wholesale foreign borrowing does not create any short-term risk in terms of non-deposit FX liability, maturity mismatch, currency mismatch, and liquidity, it is likely to be one of the risk factors that the banking sector should confront until it finds alternative, less-risky financing sources since higher reliance on foreign wholesale funding makes the domestic banking system more vulnerable to external shocks. In fact, the Turkish banking sector should come up with an updated road map, in line with its solid appearance, to be classified as one of the top banking systems among the EMEs.

Notes

1. Turkish banking sector total cross-border liability has increased from USD 7.3 billion to USD 103 billion since 2002. Especially during the last 5 years, total cross-border banking liability to banking total assets rose on average from 8% to 13%.
2. We calculate the ratio of IID to GDP using a 2014 data set of 15 countries that had the highest international investment deficit. For instance, USA's IID-to-GDP ratio was around 0.4, while Turkey had a ratio of 0.55. Greece, Portugal, and Spain were among the top three countries that had the highest IID to GDP ratio.

References

Adrian, Tobias, and Hyun Song Shin. 2009. *Money, Liquidity, and Monetary Policy*, FRB of New York Staff No. 360. New York: Federal Reserve Bank of New York.

Agenor, Pierre-Richard, C. John McDermott, and Murat Üçer. 1997. Fiscal Imbalances, Capital Inflows, and the Real Exchange Rate: The Case of Turkey. *European Economic Review* 41 (3): 819–825.

Akın, G. Gülsün, Ahmet Faruk Aysan, and Levent Yıldıran. 2009. Transformation of the Turkish Financial Sector in the Aftermath of the 2001 Crisis. In *Turkey and the Global Economy: Neo-Liberal Restructuring and Integration in the Post-Crisis Era 73*.

Allen, Franklin. 2011. *Cross-Border Banking in Europe: Implications for Financial Stability and Macroeconomic Policies*. Washington, DC: CEPR.

Aydemir, Resul, and Gokhan Ovenc. 2016. Interest Rates, the Yield Curve and Bank Profitability in an Emerging Market Economy. *Economic Systems* 40 (4): 670–682.

Aysan, Ahmet Faruk, Salih Fendoğlu, and Mustafa Kilinc. 2015. Macroprudential Policies as Buffer Against Volatile Cross-Border Capital Flows. *The Singapore Economic Review* 60 (01): 1550001.

BAT (The Banks Association of Turkey). 2016. *Banks and Banking Sector Information*. http://www.tbb.org.tr/en/banks-and-banking-sector-information/member-banks/list-of-banks/34. Accessed 15 Sep 2016.

BIS (Bank for International Settlements). 2014. *EME Banking Systems and Regional Financial Integration*, Committee on the Global Financial System, CGFS Papers 51. http://www.bis.org/publ/cgfs51.pdf. Accessed 10 Jan 2016.

———. 2009. *Capital Flows and Emerging Market Economies*, Committee on the Global Financial System, CGFS Papers 33. http://www.bis.org/publ/cgfs33.pdf. Accessed 10 Jan 2016.

———. 2016. *Locational Banking Statistics*. http://www.bis.org/statistics/bankstats.htm?m=6%7C31%7C69. Accessed 15 Apr 2016.

Brunnermeier, Markus, José De Gregorio, Barry Eichengreen, Mohamed El-Erian, Arminio Fraga, Takatoshi Ito, P. R. Lane et al. 2012. *Banks and Cross-Border Capital Flows: Policy Challenges and Regulatory Responses*, Committee on International Economic Policy and Reform. Washington, DC: Brookings.

Bruno, Valentina, and Hyun Song Shin. 2014. Cross-Border Banking and Global Liquidity. *The Review of Economic Studies* 82 (2): 535–564.

Caballero, Julián A. 2016. Do Surges in International Capital Inflows Influence the Likelihood of Banking Crises? *The Economic Journal* 126 (591): 281–316.

Calvo, Guillermo A., Leonardo Leiderman, and Carmen M. Reinhart. 1996. Inflows of Capital to Developing Countries in the 1990s. *The Journal of Economic Perspectives* 10 (2): 123–139.

CBRT (The Central Bank of Turkey). 2015. *Financial Stability Report*. http://www.tcmb.gov.tr/wps/wcm/connect/TCMB+EN/TCMB+EN/Main+Menu/PUBLICATIONS/Reports/Financial+Stability+Report/2015/Financial+Stability+Report-November+2015%2C+Volume+21/. Accessed 5 June 2016.

———. 2016. *Monetary Policy, Interactive Charts, Current Account Balance*. http://www.tcmb.gov.tr/wps/wcm/connect/TCMB+EN/TCMB+EN/Main+Menu/PUBLICATIONS/Reports/Financial+Stability+Report/2016/Volume+23/. Accessed 5 Mar 2017.

Cowan, Kevin, De Jose Gregorio, Alejandro Micco, and Christopher Neilson. 2007. *Financial Diversification, Sudden Stops and Sudden Starts*. Banco Central de Chile. https://core.ac.uk/download/pdf/6642643.pdf. Accessed 22 Aug 2016.

Hahm, Joon-ho, Hyun Song Shin, and Kwanho Shin. 2013. Noncore Bank Liabilities and Financial Vulnerability. *Journal of Money, Credit and Banking* 45 (s1): 3–36.

Herrmann, Sabine, and Dubravko Mihaljek. 2010. *The Determinants of Cross-Border Bank Flows to Emerging Markets: New Empirical Evidence on the Spread of Financial Crises*, Bundesbank Series 1 Discussion Paper No. 2010,17.

Hills, Bob, and Glenn Hoggarth. 2013. Cross-Border Bank Credit and Global Financial Stability. *Bank of England Quarterly Bulletin* Q2: 126–136.

Kara, Hakan. 2016. *Turkey's Experience with Macroprudential Policy*, BIS Paper No. 86q.

Kim, Young-Chul. 2003. Understanding the Silence Amid Turmoil: The Tobin Tax and East Asia. In *Debating the Tobin Tax*, ed. J. Weaver, R. Dodd and J. Baker, 135–150. Washington, DC: New Rules for Global Finance Coalition.

Mercan, Muhammet, Arnold Reisman, Reha Yolalan, and Ahmet Burak Emel. 2003. The Effect of Scale and Mode of Ownership on the Financial Performance of the Turkish Banking Sector: Results of a DEA-Based Analysis. *Socio-Economic Planning Sciences* 37 (3): 185–202.

Mishkin, Frederic S. 2009. Why We Shouldn't Turn Our Backs on Financial Globalization. *IMF Staff Papers* 56 (1): 139–170.

Rajan, Ramkishen. 1998. *Restraints on Capital Flows: What Are They?* No. 22383. East Asian Bureau of Economic Research.

Roubini, Nouriel, and Paul Wachtel. 1999. Current-Account Sustainability in Transition Economies. In *Balance of Payments, Exchange Rates, and Competitiveness in Transition Economies*, ed. M.I. Blejer and M. Škreb, 19–93. Boston: Springer.

Shin, Hyun Song. 2014. The Second Phase of Global Liquidity and Its Impact on Emerging Economies. In *Volatile Capital Flows in Korea*, ed. K. Chung, S. Kim, H. Park, C. Choi, and H.S. Shin, 247–257. New York: Palgrave Macmillan.

Turkish Banking Industry: A CAMELS Analysis

Muhammed Habib Dolgun and Lokman Gündüz

1 Introduction

The Turkish financial system has had a long history of economic and financial crises. However, it experienced remarkable progress in performance following the restructuring programme after the last crisis in the country in 2001. Because weaknesses in the banking sector were considered to be one major culprit of the crisis, efforts to restructure the Turkish economy were particularly focused on the banking industry. Many inefficient banks were closed down or merged with stronger banks. Several foreign players (including Citigroup, Fortis, and BNP Paribas) started to invest in the Turkish banking system after 2004, at which time the

The opinions expressed in this paper are those of the authors and do not necessarily reflect the views of the Central Bank of the Republic of Turkey.

M. H. Dolgun (✉)
CBRT, Ankara, Turkey

L. Gündüz
Department of Management, College of Management and Administrative Sciences, Istanbul Sehir University, İstanbul, Turkey

A. F. Aysan et al. (eds.), *Turkish Economy*,
https://doi.org/10.1007/978-3-319-70380-0_9

banking sector entered a "growth period" (Aysan et al. 2009). The regulatory, supervisory, and macroprudential measures taken by the financial authorities after the global financial crisis also increased the resiliency of the Turkish banking system. In addition to having a resilient asset structure, it also has a sound capital base thanks to restrictive regulatory requirements and a notable, well-developed approach to liquidity management.

The successful implementation of the programme was reflected in the banking sector structure. Private banks increased their regulatory capital, which had eroded during the 2001 crisis. Those banks that failed to underwrite new capital had to merge with other banks or were nationalized by the Savings Deposit Insurance Fund (SDIF). State-owned banks were restructured and recapitalized after the 2001 crisis. Non-performing loans (NPLs) that were on the balance sheets of the state-owned banks were settled against government debt securities, and the financial structures of these banks were strengthened. At the same time, the Banking Supervisory and Regulatory Agency (BRSA) gained greater autonomy with accountability for systemic banking stability. Laws and regulations regarding banks' activities were revised in 2005 and converged with internationally recognized standards. Fukuyama and Matousek (2011) found that Turkish banks positively reacted to this consolidation and restructuring process and that bank efficiency had gradually improved and cost-efficiency scores peaked immediately after the restructuring programme was introduced. However, they found a gradual deterioration of bank efficiency from 2004 to 2007, and they explained this negative trend by the strict regulatory rules imposed by the BRSA.

The Turkish financial system is dominated mainly by the banking sector. As of late 2016, the size of the financial sector reached approximately USD 1.2 trillion. Total banking sector asset size is around USD 780 billion (Table 1), which was only USD 51.6 billion in late 1995. Currently, 51 banks operate in the sector, of which 5 are participation banks, 5 are state banks, and 21 are foreign banks. In 2016, the total assets of the Turkish commercial banks were around USD 700 billion, whereas participation banks had nearly USD 38 billion, and investment and development banks had USD 40 billion in assets.

Table 1 Overview of Turkish banking sector (late 2016, million USD)

	Total assets	Credit	Deposit	Equity
Commercial banks	700,031	444,433	391,580	14,503
Participation banks	37,701	21,536	23,064	2,222
Investment and development banks	40,613	28,558	0	5,667
Banking sector	778,347	494,529	414,916	22,394

Source: Banking Regulation and Supervision Authority (BRSA)

Turkish banks have a strong capital structure and efficient risk management approach. The intermediation function has been performed much more efficiently compared to the pre-2001 crisis era, and the credit-to-deposit ratio reached 123% as of December 2016. The Turkish banking sector has higher profitability ratios than the banking sectors of many countries, including European Union countries. Return on equity is greater than 10%, and return on assets is almost 1.5%. The banking industry as a whole documented an 18.3% rate of growth in deposits and 19.7% increase in credit volumes in 2015. However, owing to geopolitical risks, an attempted military coup, and depreciation of the local currency, the banking sector's asset size, in USD terms, showed a 4.3% rate of decrease at the end of 2016. The Turkish banking sector maintained its robust position during the global financial turmoil as the profitability of the banking sector continued to be quite high in international standards. In the last 12 years, Turkey has improved the regulatory and supervisory framework and harmonized its banking sector with the best international standards. In this regard, Turkey's banking sector was found to be fully compliant with the Basel II and Basel III standards in risk-based capital standards as well as other capital components regulations as of 2016 by the Regulatory Consistency Assessment Programme (RCAP) coordinated by the Basel Committee in 2016.

If the Turkish banking sector is in better shape today, it is mainly due to implementation of the right policies at home at the right time. The Great Moderation also helped significantly when those reforms were under way. However, it still has its weaknesses, most of which stem from structural problems of the Turkish economy such as low savings rates and, hence, a dependence on foreign capital flows. Relatively higher but volatile economic growth rates over the years do not help the banking industry either. The banks continue to move in a procyclical direction, while regulatory authorities are trying to implement a right mix of monetary and macroprudential policies in times of increasing global financial uncertainty. All these factors are reflected in the various indicators of the banking industry. While some of them, like financial performance indicators, are much better relative to the previous decade, others, such as credit-to-deposit ratio and the low level of competition, signal that there are limits to the banks' further growth.

In this paper, we briefly examine the Turkish banking industry by making use of CAMELS analysis. The acronym CAMELS refers to the six component of a bank's condition that is assessed: capital adequacy, asset quality, management, earnings, liquidity, and sensitivity to market risk and interest rate risk. Several academic studies have found CAMELS to be very useful both in summarizing current conditions and in the supervisory monitoring of bank conditions. We then point to the challenges and opportunities facing the Turkish banking industry in the years ahead and conclude with some key lessons.

2 CAMELS

2.1 Capital Structure

The financial reforms implemented following the 2001 crisis and the excessive prudence of the supervisory authorities led banks to hold high capital ratios. Until 2005, the average capital adequacy ratio (CAR) in the banking sector was above 20%. It then continued to perform at these levels, although it showed a slight decrease in 2011. The CAR of the Turkish banking sector has remained around 16% for more than 5 years, above the legal ratio (8%) and the target ratio (12%) of the BRSA as of October 2016 (Graph 1).

The capital structure of the Turkish banking system is much better than that of the banks in most countries. The persistently high proportion of the main capital ratio shows that the prudential approach to banking still continues. There are also some disadvantages of having a high capital ratio. Since the capital ratio is measured in relation to

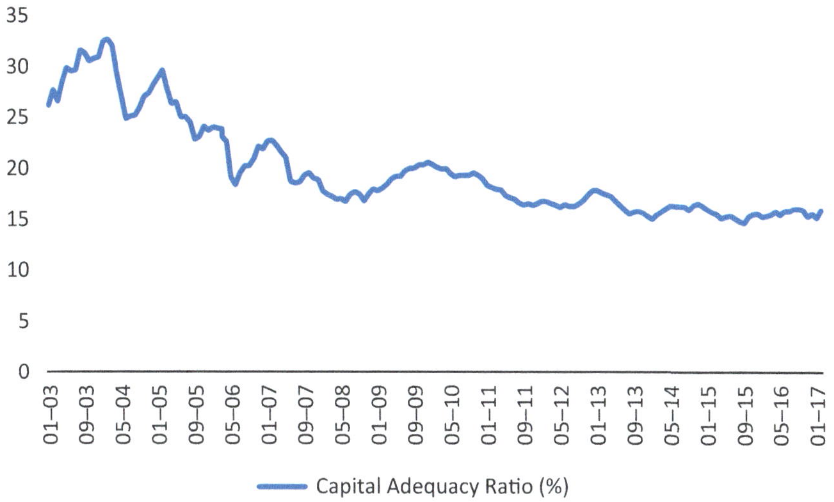

Graph 1 Capital structure of Turkish banks (Source: Central Bank of the Republic of Turkey (CBRT))

risk-sensitive assets, the banks do not give credit to high-risk entities, which may cause harm to real sectors and economic growth. In many countries, banks hold several items as elements of capital such as convertible bonds issued by banks as Tier 2 products or additional Tier 1 instruments. These products are very rare in Turkish banks' capital structure, and the Tier 1 common equity capital has an important share in the capital structure of Turkish banks.

2.2 Asset Quality

Thanks to the Turkish banking sector's strong capital structure and efficient risk management applications, the industry has increased its asset size. In 2016, the banking sector's total assets reached USD 778 billion. Its lending reached 1609 billion Turkish lira (TL) as of October 2016. The cumulative annual credit growth rate in TL was 27% between 2002 and 2016, well above the global average. The average deposit growth rate was 19% between 2002 and 2016 in TL. A rule of thumb suggests that when the sum of the assets in the banking sector in a country exceeds gross national income, the financial wealth of the citizens is also positively influenced by economic growth. In this context, the Turkish banking sector's total assets to total national income exceed 100%. At the end of 2015, the ratio of total assets to gross domestic product (GDP) exceeded 120%, but it then decreased to 105% by the end of 2016 (Graph 2).

However, it is clear that the Turkish banking sector has increased its assets significantly over time. Yener et al. (2007) divide the Turkish banking system into two segments, commercial banks and non-depository banks. Commercial banks have an authority to collect deposits, while the others do not. Yener et al. (2007) claim that commercial banks in Turkey operate as universal banks. In other words, they offer a broad range of products and services to their customers. The second group of banks concentrate on investment activities. Although the shares of development and investment banks and participation banks have increased, the Turkish banking sector is still dominated by deposit banks, which are typically commercial banks.

The Turkish banking sector's total loan ratio has increased in the last 13 years, though its ratio to GDP is far below 100% (Graph 2). In particular, there was massive credit growth in the 2011–2012 period. However, annual credit growth started to decrease after 2012 because of a tight monetary policy stance and the implementation of new macroprudential policies such as higher risk weights and provisions for consumer

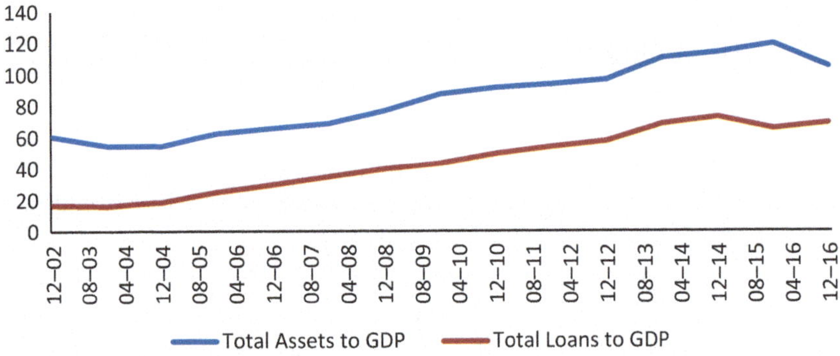

Graph 2 Ratio of total assets and total loans to GDP (Source: CBRT)

loans, an increase in the loan-to-value cap for housing loans and vehicle loans, credit card payment regulation, and maturity restrictions for uncollateralized consumer loans. Hence, it should be noted that the ratio of non-bank corporate credit to GDP remains lower than that of advanced countries, which signals that there is ample room for financial deepening. It is expected that credit will continue to grow at moderate rates owing to the introduction of several macroprudential measures.

One of the most significant problems in fast-growing economies is that the deterioration of NPLs is not easily seen in the good times. Therefore, it is necessary to impose macroprudential measures in a timely manner. The banking sector continued to enjoy high asset quality while the NPL ratio stood at low levels. As of October 2016, the NPL ratio was 3.3% (Banking Regulation and Supervision Agency 2016). Although NPLs have been on a rising trend due to a slowdown in consumer demand and economic growth, the increase in these ratios is low in comparison with the 2009–2010 period (Akıncı et al. 2013). Moreover, it should be stressed that currently, the NPL ratio in the Turkish banking sector is much lower than that of many advanced economies, especially European countries (Graph 3).

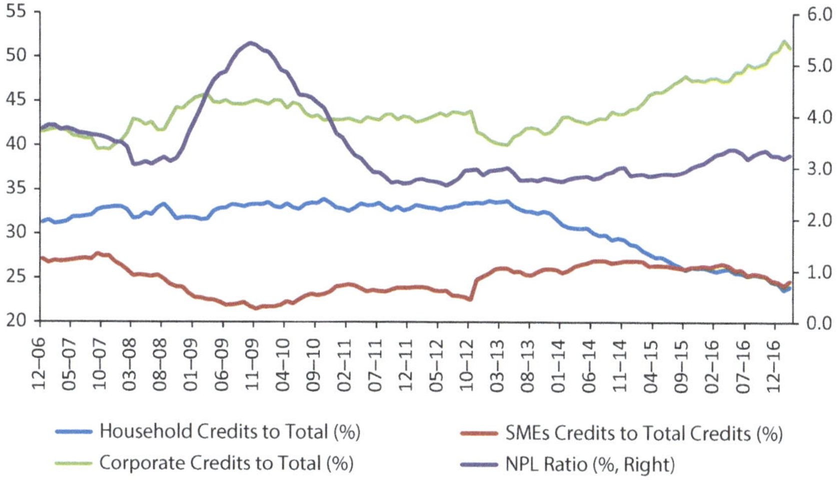

Graph 3 NPLs and credit share of households, corporations, and small and medium-sized enterprises (Source: CBRT)

Managing the balance between costs associated with NPLs and income is and will be an important issue in the years to come. Though macroprudential measures and regulations are very efficient in controlling NPLs, new reforms and other financial stability measures should be taken to mitigate their risks (Aysan et al. 2015). Loan demand decreased compared to 2011 due to the many macroprudential measures taken by the CBRT and BRSA, especially after 2012. Today, Turkish banks' loan growth is more sustainable compared with the higher trend before 2012. The household leverage ratio (liabilities/assets) has also been declining since 2012.

Although there is stability regarding household indebtedness, exchange rate movements increased non-bank corporate debt in 2016. Accordingly, macroprudential measures such as consumer loan risk weights are expected to support credit growth in the upcoming period. On the other hand, the probability of exchange-rate-related risk in the private sector remains low because of the increasing share of long-term foreign-currency-denominated loans in recent years. These loans continue to be concentrated in larger firms that are relatively better at risk management.

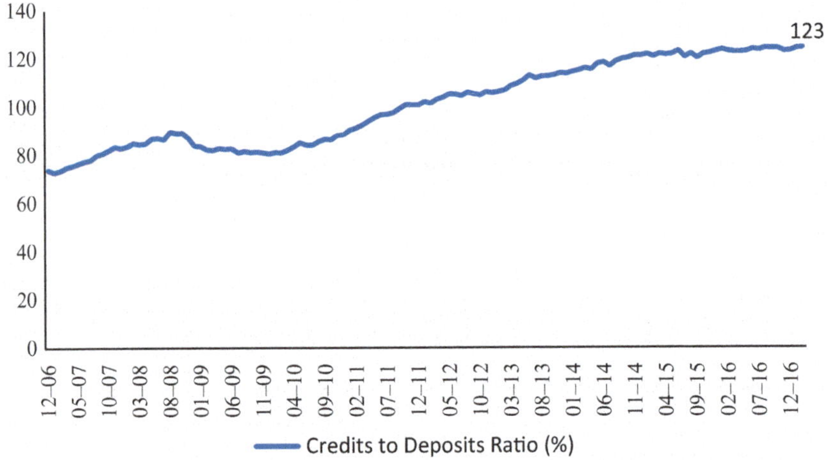

Graph 4 Credit-to-deposit ratio (Source: CBRT)

The ratio of credits to deposits is alarming because it has exceeded the threshold of 100% (Graph 4). Historically it was less than 100% before 2012. Since the Turkish banking sector has a strong capital base, stable funding, and low foreign currency risk, this ratio would not be a big problem in the short run. On the other hand, the Turkish banking system is capable and very careful in managing exchange rate risk. The ratio of foreign-currency-denominated liquid assets to foreign-currency-denominated other resources has not changed much since 2012. Although banks include the exchange rate risk on their balance sheets, they mitigate it via off-balance-sheet operations. In doing so, the banking sector maintains a neutral net general FX position. While external borrowing has declined, favourable borrowing costs and longer maturities signal that banks hold a positive outlook when it comes to accessing external funding sources.

2.3 Management Capabilities (Financial Performance, Governance, and Rating)

A well-educated management team and calibrated good corporate governance rules increase efficiency and decrease idiosyncratic risks. The management system in the Turkish banking sector is very competitive and similar to international counterparts. Turkish banks are aware of the constant need to increase the quality of their services and decrease costs. In this connection, the Turkish banking sector increased the number of ATMs to facilitate banking services and to reduce their costs related to branches and employees. The number of ATMs and branches is increasing, but the employment rate increase is very slow in comparative terms (Graph 5). The recent increase in the number of branches signals a tough competitive environment among banks but also suggests that opening up new branches can increase costs and result in lower efficiency, as argued by Aysan and Ceyhan (2008).

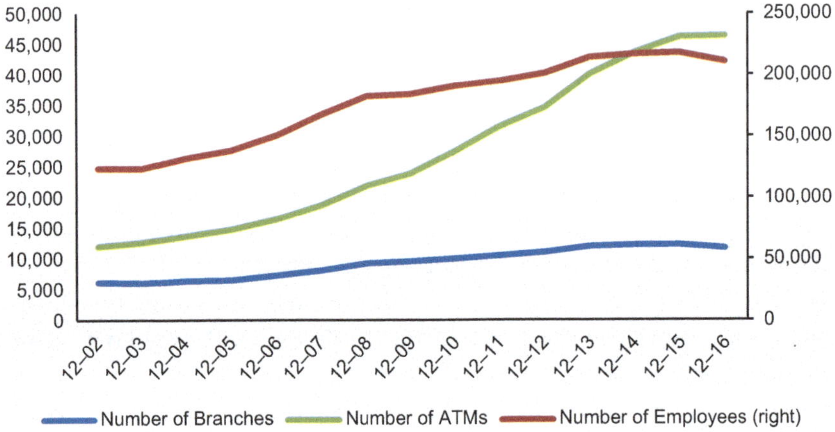

Graph 5 Number of ATMs, employees and branches (Source: CBRT)

2.4 Earnings

In a high-inflation-rate environment with economic growth, the banking sector, based on consumer loans, made huge profits after 2001. After the 2008 crisis it witnessed decreasing profitability. Profitability indicators for the banking sector started to deteriorate by mid-2013, when the U.S. Federal Reserve announced a tapering policy to reduce the amount of money it was feeding into the system, which led to the so-called taper tantrum, and this trend continued until September 2015. Interest expenses increased as a result of rising funding costs, which caused a decline in profitability in the sector. However, the banking sector is still very profitable. A more efficient management of non-interest expenses is the primary element partially limiting the negative effects of rising funding costs. Although there has been a decrease in the return on equity (ROE) and return on assets (ROA) in comparison to 2007, the sector's average ROE and ROA ratios are higher than those of many European banks. By the end of 2016, ROE was around 14 and ROA 1.5% at the end of 2016 (Graph 6).

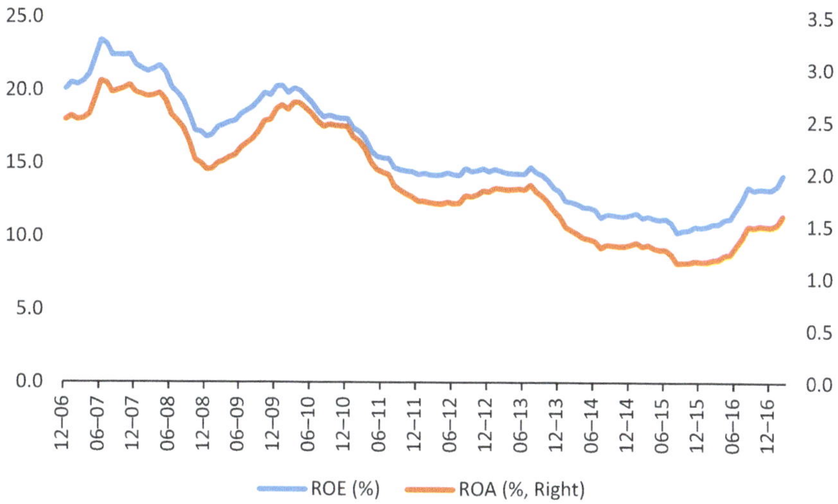

Graph 6 Return on equity and return on assets of Turkish banking system (Source: CBRT)

2.5 Liquidity Structure

The last global financial crisis revealed the importance of liquidity risk management, and many countries have accordingly changed their regulatory framework to mitigate several risks, including liquidity risk. Bank liquidity is a crucial component in managing bank assets. A resilient and robust liquidity management framework can ease the transformation of maturity between liabilities and assets. Without enough liquidity, a bank may face several risks, such as fiduciary risk, operational risk, maturity transformation risk, and other risks that affect the bank's financial stability as a whole. Turkey did not experience a major liquidity problem during the global financial crisis and has not experienced one since the crisis. Currently, the liquidity position of the Turkish banking system is quite strong. The liquidity requirement ratio – up to a month – is more than 100% (Graph 7).

On the other hand, several structural changes have been made to liquidity components. The liquidity structure of the Turkish banking system reflects monetary policy changes made by the CBRT and the

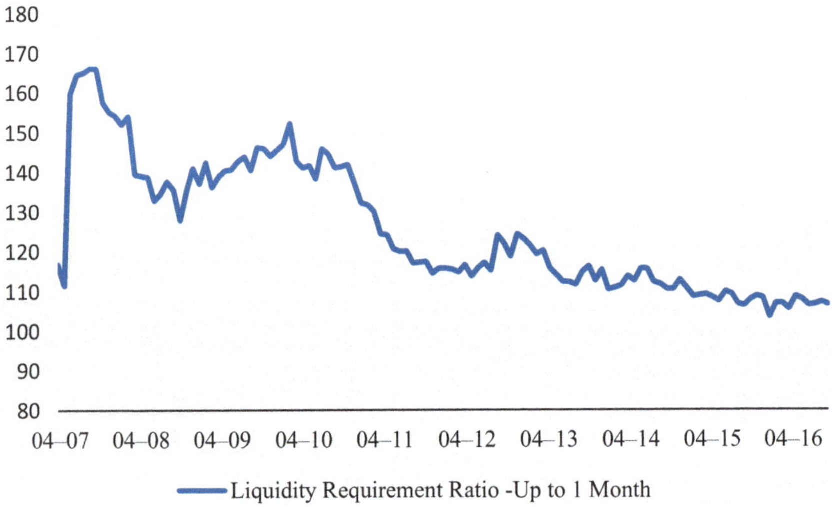

Graph 7 Liquidity requirement ratio (Source: CBRT)

BRSA. As a result of monetary policy and macroprudential policies of regulators, the share of securities available for sale and investment decreased, whereas required reserves increased after 2011. During this time, the main concern was to control credit growth, which was annually more than 40%. The CBRT and the BRSA decided to implement many macroprudential policies for managing credit growth. These attempts have definitely changed the liquidity structure of the banking system.

2.6 Sensitivity to Market Risk and Interest-Rate Risk

The Turkish banking sector's data show that the sensitivity to market risk and interest-rate risk has not increased, though the ratio of foreign debt to bank assets is rising (Graph 8 and Table 2 respectively). The net interest margin ratio of the Turkish banking sector has decreased slightly in recent years thanks to falling interest rates. There is an increase in the ratio of foreign debt to bank assets, but it is around 20% (Graph 8). On the other hand, the net interest margin of the Turkish banking sector was

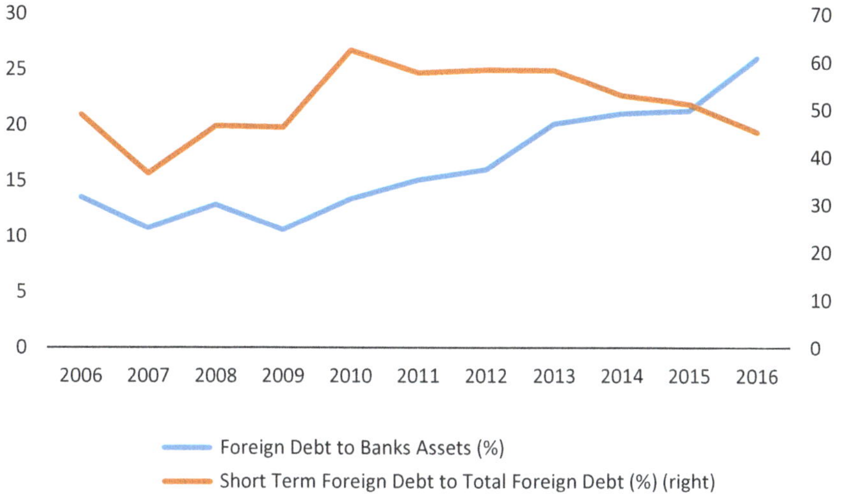

Graph 8 Foreign debt to banks assets (Source: CBRT)

Table 2 FX loans to total loans and FX deposits to total deposits

	Total credit (million TL)	Total deposits (million TL)	FX loans/ total loans (%)	FX deposits/ total deposits (%)	Net interest margin (%)
12.02	48.981	137.973	59	57	5.10
12.03	66.222	155.312	45	49	5.06
12.04	99.342	191.065	35	45	6.36
12.05	156.410	251.490	27	37	5.37
12.06	218.987	307.647	26	39	4.71
12.07	285.616	356.865	24	35	4.88
12.08	367.445	454.599	29	35	4.72
12.09	392.621	514.620	27	34	5.44
12.10	525.851	617.037	27	30	4.30
12.11	682.893	695.496	29	34	3.45
12.12	794.756	772.217	26	33	4.07
12.13	1.047.410	945.770	28	37	3.72
12.14	1.240.708	1.052.693	29	37	3.53
12.15	1.484.960	1.245.428	32	43	3.45
12.16	1.734.342	1.453.632	35	42	3.64

Source: CBRT

3.6%, down from 4.6% in 2006, but still relatively higher than that of its emerging market peers.

Turkish banks' level of exposure to credit risk is low. The Turkish banking sector has almost entirely hedged its FX lending, though the cost of hedging is increasing. The sector has many buffers against the indirect risk caused by the FX liabilities of non-financial corporations thanks to its ability to adapt to global changes and to its high-quality collateral obtained from non-financial corporations.

Macroprudential policies are expected to encourage long-term external funding to reduce the banking sector's susceptibility to adverse developments in global markets by lengthening maturities. The Turkish banks' ratio of FX general positions to regulatory capital remains stable, whereas the ratio of on-balance-sheet foreign currency deficit to regulatory capital keeps increasing. Accordingly, the developments in the global economy, domestic markets, balance of payments, and public sector have proved influential and effective at maintaining financial stability during these times. Global and local markets, as well as the balance of payments and the public sector, have contributed favourably to financial stability.

3 Challenges and Opportunities Ahead

The fact that the rate of increase in deposits continues to slow down while the ratio of credit to deposits is growing presents a major challenge for the Turkish banking sector in the years ahead. Several factors seem to be effective at reducing the rate of increase in deposits. Lower savings and relatively high inflation rates may be among the main reasons. Furthermore, financial inclusion may not enhance the income of depositors. More likely, in an environment where real interest rates are low, people may prefer not to put their deposits in a bank. Another reason may be the increase in construction investment, which means people may prefer to invest in real estate rather than parking their cash in a deposit account. As a result, the growing banking sector is more dependent on outsourcing and syndicated loans. However, the syndication loan cost is linked to credit rating. This implies a more reasonable scenario that either foreign funding needs to be sustainable as previously or domestic savings will increase.

Indeed, a glance at the last three decades reveals how the growth rate of the Turkish economy and Turkish financial sector are sensitive to global conditions. This in large part stems from the fact that the domestic savings rate is low in comparison to many emerging countries. Foreign capital flows thus play a prominent role in explaining both the volatility and growth of the Turkish economy. In a period of high capital inflows, both the real economy and the financial sector benefit and have high growth rates. On the other hand, both suffer and show a slowdown in bad times. Moreover, sometimes a rosy global picture is not enough if the domestic economic and political stability are not maintained. The Turkish economy in the 1990s illustrated this well. It was, after all, a lost decade for Turkey mainly as a result of domestic political uncertainty. A cloudy and cold global climate does not necessarily translate to a worse scenario for the Turkish real economy and the financial sector when local economic and political policies are correct and implemented well. The period after the recent global financial crisis is a case in point. It is striking to note that with a right combination of political and economic decisions, the Turkish economy has rebounded very quickly from the trough of the crisis and performed relatively very well.

Recall that recent global liquidity conditions are indicating a tighter turnaround for many emerging markets, including Turkey. The measures taken in the framework of Basel III and the reforms being carried out should all be in full force soon, which may result in tighter conditions for banks. Moreover, structural conditions no longer make it easy for the banking sector to grow; on the contrary, they make it even more challenging. Regulations implemented in the context of increases in capital market financing arrangements and the Istanbul International Finance Centre project show that banks are likely to enter a more challenging era.

Regarding competition in banking, Turkey is not a good example and differs from other emerging countries. Yıldırım (2014) argued that the level of competition in the Turkish banking system did not increase despite the restructuring undertaken at the time and the increased foreign bank competition. She further found that the level of competition in the sector deteriorated during the global crisis. It seems that strong economic growth in the last decade positively strengthened Turkish banks.[1] Aydemir (2014) also found that the market structure of the Turkish banking industry, which is very concentrated, is conducive to a lack of competition. This is not surprising given the fact that greater concentration in the marketplace is associated with less competition. Foreign bank entry is likely to strengthen competition in banking. Aysan et al. (2014) argued that there are procompetitive spillover effects from foreign banks on their domestic counterparts that boost banking outreach. Süer et al. (2016) also found that increases in foreign ownership lead to a decrease in accounting profits owing to the increased competition and or greater efficiency. In any case, there is ample room for the government to promote banking competition in all parts of Turkey.

From an economic policy perspective, it is clear that there is a need for a more developed and diversified financial sector in Turkey. The dominant role of the banking sector and heavy dependence on bank loans pose threats to long-term macroeconomic stability. Turgutlu (2010), for example, provides strong evidence regarding the counter-cyclicality of Turkish banks' margin. In other words, Turkish banks can easily fail to provide sufficient funds to economic actors when there is an immediate need, especially in times of economic contraction, and hence can delay economic recovery. To overcome the obstacles posed by bank the dominant financial sector, financial instruments should be differentiated further and their use encouraged by authorities.

Accordingly, Turkish banks must find new ways to increase their profits and mitigate their risks while continuing to provide financing to nonfinancial corporations. In this sense, issuing or arranging capital market products and providing more risk-sharing instruments or equity financing seem to be important areas in which banks could expand their activities. Certainly, diversification of income sources would also help banks to mitigate the negative effects of possible economic downturn periods associated with a decline in loan portfolios and an increase in NPLs.

4 Conclusion

In this chapter, we briefly examined the Turkish banking system using a CAMELS approach with a focus on recent developments. The ROA and ROE of the Turkish banking sector are at a comparatively satisfactory level and have been trending higher lately. The increase in profitability in the sector strengthens capital, and the slowdown in the loan growth rate limits risk-weighted asset growth. The Turkish banking system continues to remain resilient to interest-rate shocks and maintains its resilience to exchange-rate risk. Banks' use of foreign resources for the moment remains stable, and their liquidity buffers are adequate to cover shocks in global liquidity conditions. It is fair to say that, overall, the Turkish banking sector has remained resilient and continued to preserve its credibility in domestic and international markets in a period marked by increased volatility in global markets.

The Turkish financial industry faces both opportunities and challenges. After all, it is a concentrated bank-based financial sector. There is ample room for the development and diversification of financial markets, institutions, and instruments. Recent experience suggests that in order to mitigate the risks in an uncertain global economic environment, one should do her homework well and act proactively. Given the structural problems of the economy and its dependence on foreign capital inflows, eventually, the Turkish banking system will need to resolve these fragilities. In the case of a sudden stop in capital flows, the private sector's problems can easily turn into bankers' problems. Prudently, Turkish banks still have some time and capital to prepare for that moment.

Notes

1. See also Aysan et al. 2013. "Bank Competition and Outreach: Evidence from Turkey",

References

Akıncı, Derviş Ahmet, Roman Matousek, Nemanja Radić, and Chris Stewart. 2013. Monetary Policy and the Banking Sector in Turkey. *Journal of International Financial Markets Institutions and Money* 27: 269–285.

Aydemir, Resul. 2014. Competition and Collusion in the Turkish Banking Industry. *Emerging Markets Finance and Trade* 49: 31–40.

Aysan, Ahmet Faruk, and Şanli Pinar Ceyhan. 2008. What Determines the Banking Sector Performance in Globalized Financial Markets? The Case of Turkey. *Physica A: Statistical Mechanics and its Applications* 387 (7): 1593–1602.

Aysan, Ahmet Faruk, Güzin Gülsün Akin, and Levent Yildiran. 2009. Transformation of the Turkish Financial Sector in the Aftermath of the 2001 Crisis. In *Turkish Economy in the Post-Crisis Era: The New Phase of Neo-Liberal Restructuring and Integration to the Global Economy*, ed. Ziya Onis and Fikret Senses, 67–83. London: Routledge.

———. 2013. Demand and Competition Analysis in the Turkish Deposit and Credit Markets. *Emerging Markets Finance and Trade* 49 (5): 41–58.

Aysan, Ahmet Faruk, Mustafa Dişli, and Koen Schoors. 2014. Bank Competition and Outreach: Evidence from Turkey. *Emerging Markets Finance and Trade* 49: 7–30.

Aysan, Ahmet Faruk, Salih Fendoğlu, and Mustafa Kılınç. 2015. Macroprudential Policies as Buffer Against Volatile Cross-border Capital Flows. *The Singapore Economic Review* 62 (01): 5–25.

Banking Regulation and Supervision Agency. 2016. *Turkish Banking Sector Interactive Monthly Bulletin*. www.ebulten.bddk.org.tr

Central Bank of the Republic of Turkey 2015. *Financial Stability Report*, November 2016, www.tcmb.gov.tr.

——— 2016. *Financial Stability Report*, November 2016. www.tcmb.gov.tr

Fukuyama, Hirofumi, and Roman Matousek. 2011. Efficiency of Turkish Banking: Two-Stage Network System Variable Returns to Scale Model. *Journal of International Financial Markets Institutions and Money* 21 (1): 75–91.

Süer, Ömür, Haluk Levent, and Süleyman Şen. 2016. Foreign Entry and the Turkish Banking System. *North American Journal of Economics and Finance* 37: 420–435.

Turgutlu, Evrim. 2010. Cyclical Behaviour of Price-Cost Margins in the Turkish Banking Industry. *Economic Modelling* 27: 368–374.

Yener, Altunbaş, A. Kara, and Özlem Olgu. 2007. *Turkish Banking-Banking Under Political Instability and Chronic High Inflation*. London: Palgrave Macmillan.

Yıldırım, Canan. 2014. Competition in Turkish Banking: Impacts of Restructuring and the Global Financial Crisis. *The Developing Economies* 52: 95–124.

Modern History of Islamic Finance and a Strategic Roadmap for Its Development in Turkey

Murat Yas, Hakan Aslan, and Mucahit Ozdemir

1 Introduction

Unlike many financial centres that have recently been keen to become hubs of Islamic finance by promoting Islamic financial products and services in the last decade, Turkey has more than a 30 year history in Islamic finance. The government of Turgut Özal in the 1980s introduced a number of initiatives as part of the government strategy for developing the Islamic finance industry. However, Turkey, according to an Islamic Finance Development Index report published by Thomson Reuters in 2016, is not among even the top 20 Islamic financial centres. Poor legal and regulatory frameworks and a lack of supportive government policies,

M. Yas (✉)
Islamic Finance, INCEIF, Kuala Lumpur, Malaysia

H. Aslan • M. Ozdemir
Research Center for Islamic Economics and Finance (ISEFAM), Sakarya University, Sakarya, Turkey

A. F. Aysan et al. (eds.), *Turkish Economy*,
https://doi.org/10.1007/978-3-319-70380-0_10

in the period after Turgut Özal, have been major reasons for the stagnation of Islamic finance in Turkey. Moreover, increasing political pressure against Special Finance Houses (SFHs) after the so-called post-modern coup in 1997 that ousted the government at the time led to a bill proposal in 1999 regarding the inclusion of SFHs in the Banking Act aimed at obliging it to follow conventional banking principles. This would have signalled the end of Islamic banking in Turkey in legal terms if some prominent members of parliament members and leading businessmen had not objected so strenuously to the bill.

After the election of the AK Party government in 2002, the removal of political pressures on the Islamic finance industry enabled the achievement of double-digit growth over the next decade. Recently, the government has been keener to promote the development of Islamic finance in Turkey through initial steps aimed at improving legal and regulatory frameworks as well as the establishment of state-owned Islamic banks to enable further growth (Aysan et al. 2013). However, those initiatives are still far from achieving Turkey's potential to expand this market as well as to become a regional and, later, a global hub of Islamic finance.

This chapter contributes to filling the gap in the literature by investigating the modern history of Islamic finance in Turkey in detail to understand its challenges and potential and providing a general framework for designing initiatives and strategies for the development of an Islamic financial services industry in Turkey.

2 Modern History of Islamic Finance in Turkey

2.1 Islamic Banking

The enactment of the Special Finance Houses decree in August 1983 enabled the establishment of Islamic banks under the legal title of Special Finance House (SFH) as part of a plan to attract deposits from religious citizens. Bahrain-based Albaraka Türk, the first Islamic bank in Turkey, acquired a license to begin operations in 1984, while a Saudi-owned

Islamic bank, Faisal Finans, followed it in 1985. In 1988, the assets of SFHs reached 1.3 per cent of total financial assets, despite a market survey showing its potential to be around 15 per cent (Pir 1988). In 1989, another Gulf-based Islamic banking group established Kuveyt Türk (KT) in a partnership with the Directorate General of Foundations in Turkey and Islamic Development Bank based in Saudi Arabia. In 1991, the first domestic SFH, Anadolu Finans, was established by a family business group from Kayseri. In 1991, the total assets of Islamic banks in Turkey reached 2.8 per cent of total banking assets (Milliyet 1991).

In the early 1990s, the Turkish economy suffered severe setbacks from large and volatile international capital flows. Firstly, the embargo on Iraq due to the Gulf War in 1991 and Iran's reorientation of its exports to Asia and Europe led to the loss of a huge export market. Secondly and more importantly, huge requirements for public sector borrowing combined with major policy errors to finance the deficit led to the currency crash in 1994. However, Prime Minister Tansu Çiller stated that SFHs had shown better performance than conventional banks during the currency crisis in 1994 (Özgentürk 1994).

In 1995, Ihlas Finans and, 1 year later, Asya Finans became new domestically owned players in the Islamic banking industry. In 1996, a segment of the Islamic banking sector with six actors increased its penetration to 3 per cent of the industry's total. Meanwhile, MUSIAD, a well-known Islamic business association in Turkey, also attempted, yet failed, to acquire a licence for the establishment of two more SFHs, Genç Finans and Gümüş Finans in 1996 (Güngör 1996). The post-modern coup in February 1997 forced the resignation of Islamist Prime Minister Necmettin Erbakan's Welfare Party and dissolved parliament by ending the coalition government. The establishment of the new Mesut Yılmaz-led government in June 1997 was a sign of an impending period of tremendous political pressure on the Islamic banking industry while deposits, namely participation accounts of SFHs, were at their highest market share of 10 per cent of total banking deposits in 1998 (Sabah 1998). Afterward, the Mesut Yılmaz government also announced stricter regulations and supervision of SFHs not only to ensure the stability and soundness of the sector but also to remove some advantages enjoyed exclusively by SFHs, such as lower reserve ratio requirements, as a response to the political discomfort felt due to the high market penetration of SFHs (Sabah 1998). Meanwhile, Prince Muhammed Al-Faysal, as the owner of Faisal Finans, was summoned to court owing to allegations of the involvement of Faisal Finans in a deal involving fake invoices during one of its purchase and sale transactions. Thus, in 1998, Prince Muhammed Al-Faysal sold Faisal Finans to OLFO AG, a Swiss Company owned by Kombassan Holding in Turkey because of a lawsuit against him (Yeni Şafak 2002). Similarly, 75 per cent of Anadolu Finans's shares has been sold to Boydak Holding in June 1999.

Turkey went through a severe financial crisis between 1999 and 2001 owing to a financing budget deficit and a fragile banking system suffering from lack of prudential regulation and supervision, political instability, and over-reliance on foreign investment in high yield bonds. Consequently, five conventional banks filed for bankruptcy in December 1999 after the closure of interbank credit lines to vulnerable banks ended in a liquidity crisis. At the same time, a bill regarding the abolition of the SFH decree by incorporating it into the Banking Act, which disregards SFHs' need to ensure compliance with Islamic financial principles, was considered as marking the end of Islamic banking in Turkey (Milliyet 1999). However, an objection from some prominent parliament members, including Prime Minister Mesut Yılmaz, as well as complaints from well-known intellectuals and CEOs of the biggest conventional banks, enabled adjustments to the draft of the Banking Act to ensure that Islamic banks could maintain compliance with Shariah principles in business activities.

After the establishment of the Banking Regulatory and Supervision Authority (BRSA) in 2000 to regulate and supervise banks more effectively, BRSA registered 12 more banks for bankruptcy by the end of 2001. In the middle of the financial turbulence, where the soundness and the stability of all banks were called into question, insider sales of 3.79 per cent of total shares by Enver Ören, president of İhlas Finans, and news about its poor performance caused a flurry of rumours about the insolvency of İhlas Finans in November 2000 (Milliyet 2000). Moreover, a lack of corporate governance mechanisms and a large asset–liability mismatch also precipitated a bank panic. After İhlas Finans faced a liquidity crisis and could not meet depositors' withdrawal demands, BRSA revoked its banking licence in February 2001. The cancellation of its banking licence, which required the liquidation of its assets and the bankruptcy of İhlas Finans, spread panic and fear to other Islamic banks. Thus, total deposits of SFHs except İhlas Finans fell from USD1.75 billion to USD1.05 billion in just a few weeks. The lack of deposit insurance in SFHs, unlike conventional banks, incited bank runs during the financial panic, and financial assets of SFHs fell to their lowest level, 1.08 per cent of industry totals. Thus, a bill regarding the establishment of deposit insurance by SFHs was passed in the following year (Yeni şafak 2001). In May 2001, Ülker Group acquired Faisal Finans, and the name of the bank was changed to Family Finans House.

Following improvements in macroeconomic stability, decreasing political uncertainties, and the disappearance of political pressure put on the Islamic banking industry with the victory of the AK Party in the general elections, Islamic banks have enjoyed high rates of growth: the share of total Islamic banking assets rose from 1.08 per cent in 2001 to 1.83 per cent in 2002. In 2003, the establishment of state-owned Islamic banks was put on the agenda of the AK Party government through workshops managed by new board members of Ziraat and Halk Banks with Islamic banking experience (Milliyet 2003a).

In 2005, the Banking Law officially replaced the term *special finance house* with *participation banking* to enable SFHs to equip themselves with major financial instruments peculiar to Islamic banks, yet the law does not define in detail many Islamic financial contracts and products, as well as reporting, auditing, and corporate governance from the perspective of Islamic finance. In the same year, the merger of Anadolu Finans with Family Finans gave birth to Türkiye Finans. In 2007, AlBaraka Türk had its initial public offering, floating 25 per cent of its total shares. Islamic financial assets of Islamic banks rose from USD 2.4 billion in 2002 to USD 16.7 billion in 2007, with an average annual growth rate of 47.4 per cent, while its market share increased from 1.8 per cent to 3.4 per cent. As a result of promising growth rates in the Islamic banking industry and political stability under the AK Party government, investors from Gulf countries were keen to invest in Turkey's Islamic banks again. In 2007, National Commerce Bank, based in Saudi Arabia, acquired 60 per cent of Türkiye Finans.

In 2009, Istanbul International Financial Centre put the promotion of Islamic financial products and the development of Islamic financial institutions on its agenda. Islamic financial assets of Islamic banks increased from USD 16.7 billion in 2007 to USD 45 billion in 2013, with an average annual growth rate of 18 per cent, despite the 2008 global financial crisis, while its market share increased from 3.4 to 5.5 per cent. In early 2013, the government announced that two state-owned conventional banks, Ziraat Bank and Halk Bank, were planning to launch Islamic bank subsidiaries (Sabah 2013). The establishment of state-owned Islamic banks signified the AK Party government's determination not only to develop the Islamic banking industry but also to ensure the future of Islamic banks in Turkey against possible political threats by a secular government. However, the Gezi protests in May 2013, which demanded the downfall of the Erdoğan government, and the 17–25 December political crises organized by the Gülen Movement's arm in the judicial system slowed down this process. The latter event involved demands to arrest several family members of cabinet ministers, pro-Erdoğan businessmen, and the CEO of Halk Bank based on corruption charges; this led to political uncertainties and slowed down the launch of state-owned Islamic banks until the AK Party government scored consecutive victories in general and presidential elections the following year.

Following the AK Party's victory in the presidential election in 2014, state-owned companies and pro-AK Party businessmen also withdrew many deposits from Bank Asya, an Islamic bank associated with the Gülen Movement, and so Bank Asya faced a huge risk of bankruptcy, although it was the largest Islamic bank in Turkey. Consequently, between 2013 and 2015 the Islamic banking industry recorded very low growth in financial assets, at 11.8 per cent annually, and experienced a loss in market share, falling to 5.1 per cent following large-scale deposit withdrawals and political pressure that forced Bank Asya to downsize. Eventually, the banking licence of Bank Asya was revoked by BRSA on 22 July 2016 because of the significant deterioration in its financial figures (Banking Regulation and Supervision Agency 2016).

Recently, the government has become keen to introduce initiatives and launch governmental Islamic financial institutions to spur growth in the Islamic finance industry. Thus, Ziraat Participation was established in

May 2015 as the first state-owned participation bank (PB), followed by the launch of Vakıf Participation in February 2016. In 2017, the total assets of Ziraat and Vakif reached USD 4.28 billion, which represents 11 per cent of total assets of Islamic banks. However, the total share of PBs in the banking sector was still around 5 per cent at the end of 2016.

2.2 Islamic Capital Markets

Capital markets play a crucial role in the economy by channeling savings and investment from those with excess funds (such as retail and institutional investors) to those in need of such funds (such as individuals, companies, and government). This applies especially to developing countries, including Turkey, which are intensively dependent on savings and investments to maintain economic growth. However, domestic savings levels in those countries generally do not furnish the required capital. Therefore, they must develop and differentiate capital market products to attract not only domestic funds but also international savings and investments. On this point, Islamic capital markets in which activities are compliant with Islamic principles, such as the prohibition of *riba* (interest), *maisir* (gambling), and *gharar* (excessive uncertainty), provides the best opportunity to attract foreign investment to not only Muslim-majority countries but also to other non-Muslim-majority countries. In this section, the progress of Islamic capital markets in Turkey will be investigated from a historical perspective, especially focusing on recent developments, dividing the discussion into two categories: *sukuk* and Islamic indices and funds.

Sukuk

The Islamic capital market is the fastest growing constituent of the overall Islamic finance system, although it has been a late entrant into the industry, starting only in the mid-1990s. Islamic capital market instruments consist of three main sectors: Shariah-compatible indices (equities), sukuk (Islamic bond market), and Islamic funds market (e.g. mutual, pension funds) (IFSB 2015). The sukuk market comprises 15 per cent of the Islamic financial services industry and is the most widespread and known Islamic capital market instrument (IFSB 2016). Global sukuk issuances in 2012 (USD 138 billion) and in 2013 (USD 136 billion) reached peak levels; however, the market witnessed sharp decrease (43 per cent fall compared to 2014) in 2015, with only USD 61 billion sukuk being issued. The reason behind this major decline is the strategic decision of Bank Negara Malaysia to discontinue issuance of short-term investment sukuk (International Islamic Financial Market 2016). Apart from sukuk, other Islamic capital markets, such as Islamic indices and funds, have been showing significant development in recent years.

Although Turkey has recently embraced Islamic capital markets by issuing its first sovereign dollar currency sukuk in 2012, major attempts to introduce Islamic capital market products began in the 1980s. In particular, the Legislation to Promote Savings and Acceleration of Public Investment was issued in 1984 so that state institutions and organizations could issue revenue sharing certificates (RSCs), which entitle certificate holders to the revenues of publicly held infrastructure facilities such as those related to transportation and communication. The Turgut Özal government issued the first RSCs supported by revenues of Bosporus Bridge tolls in 1984 (Milliyet 1984) and later Keban and Oymapinar barrage RSCs in 1985 (Milliyet 1985).

In 2003, the AK Party government also attempted to issue new RSCs supported by the revenues from several barrages (Radikal 2003a), bridges, and highways (Radikal 2003b), but the draft legislation was merely issued in 2005 as a result of asset extensions with hydroelectric plans (Hürriyet 2005). Although there has been significant progress with new RSC issuances, the size of the RSC market continues to fall short of its potential. Another kind of interest-free certificate that is issuable by joint stock companies is the profit and loss sharing certificate (PLSC). Unfortunately, PLSCs and RSCs have not been issued since 1995 and 1996 (Capital Market Board of Turkey 2017) respectively, and these products have not been used effectively by the government or companies.

The most significant and controversial interest-free certificate is the revenue indexed bond (RIB), which was first issued by the Turkish treasury on 28 January 2009, with the aim of encouraging domestic savings, broadening the investor base, and diversifying borrowing instruments. The coupon payments on these instruments are indexed to the revenues of some state-owned enterprises including Turkish Petroleum Corporation, State Procurement Office, General Directorate of State Airports Authority, and General Directorate of Coast Safety, which is transferred to the state's budget as "Treasury Levy Payments" (REVENUE INDEXED BONDS 2017). Moreover, the yields of these securities are guaranteed within a certain range for eliminating uncertainty over fluctuations of revenues during the lifetime of the bond.

The first issuance of RIBs was followed by new issuances on 29 April 2009, 24 February 2010, 11 August 2010, 23 February 2011, and 24 August 2011. PBs were the main investors behind the RIBs, and the total amount of RIBs in their portfolios reached USD 1 billion by the end of 2011. This new instrument allowed PBs to diversify their asset structure and was used as collateral to obtain funds from the Central Bank of the Republic of Turkey (CBRT) through weekly repo transactions starting in the third quarter of 2011. However, Hayrettin Karaman, who is one of the most prominent Shariah scholars in Turkey and a member of some Shariah boards of Islamic banks, declared in his article (Karaman 2012) on 19 February 2012 that RIBs do not comply with Shariah since they are not backed by assets that create a cash flow but by coupon payments linked to an index, and therefore their return is treated as interest until they are converted into RSCs. PBs did not participate in the RIB issuance by the Treasury on 17 February 2012 because they had been informed before the article became publicly available. After this article, PBs were seen as investing in interest-based securities with ongoing 1 billion RIB portfolios and facing a Shariah risk. The uncertainty regarding Shariah compliance of RIBs continued for several months, and the Participation Banks Association of Turkey has made some announcements in order to mitigate Shariah risk ("Karaman: GES'ler devlet tahvilinden farksız" [Karaman: RIB'S are no different from government bonds.] 2018). Although this undesirable development has negatively affected PBs' credibility in the eyes of customers, it has accelerated the long-awaited sovereign sukuk issuance. The AK Party government (Hürriyet 2003) and KT (Milliyet 2003b) made some attempts to issue the first sovereign and corporate sukuks in Turkey in 2003 to attract funds from Gulf countries.

However, corporate and sovereign sukuks were not realized until 2010 and 2012 respectively by Islamic banks and the government.

Turkey was very late in entering the global sukuk market – so much so that the first sukuk issuance was done by the KT participation bank only in 2010 with USD 100 million. KT used KT Turkey Sukuk Limited as an special purpose vehicle (SPV) that was registered not in Turkey but in the Cayman Islands because of a lack of legislative infrastructure for sukuk issuance in Turkey. The Turkish government introduced legislation regarding sukuk just in 2010 and called it a 'lease certificate' since it only has to do with Ijarah Sukuk (Official Gazette of the Republic of Turkey 2010). Some amendments were made in the income tax law, corporate tax law, VAT law, stamp duty law, and charges law to eliminate tax obstacles for the issuance of sukuk in Turkey through the Finance Bill legislation for sukuks in 2011 (Official Gazette of the Republic of Turkey 2011).

A high-performing economy and close relationship, especially with Gulf countries, enabled Turkey to issue its first sovereign sukuk of USD 1.5 billion with 5.5-year maturity on 18 September 2012. The demand for the issuance was almost five times more than the actual amount. Two hundred fifty international investors (58 per cent from the Middle East, 13 per cent from Europe, and 12 per cent from Asia) invested in the sukuk. This successful issuance and strong demand directed the government to issue sukuks in USD and TRY currency regularly. The Turkish Treasury has issued 10 sukuks (three of them in USD) between 2012 and 2015. The size of the sukuk market in Turkey has reached USD 11.5 billion and TRY 3.8 billion at the end of 2015. The type of all issued sukuks is Ijara sukuk since an abundance of tangible assets of the Treasury such as public buildings enabled them the Treasury to securitize them. The issuance of sovereign sukuk had a very positive effect on the issuance of corporate sukuk and thus directed the attention of international investors to Turkey.

The Turkish government also introduced legislation to support sovereign and corporate sukuk issuances. On 7 June 2013, a communiqué ("Sukuk communiqué") prepared by Capital Markets Board (CMB) was published in Official Gazette and went into effect (Official Gazette of the Republic of Turkey 2013). The new legislation defined and enabled corporations to make use of different sukuk structures such as *mudaraba*, *musharaka*, *murabaha*, *salam*, and *istithna*. Thanks to these regulations and issuances by the Turkish Treasury, PBs have accelerated sukuk issuance in different types such as *Ijarah*, *Wakalah*, and Tier 2 and in currencies such as TRY, USD, and the Malaysian Ringgit (MYR). The total issuance of sukuk by the private sector registered with the Capital Market Board of Turkey (CMBT) between the first quarter of 2011 and second quarter of 2016 reached USD 8 billion. The positive trend in the growth of the Turkish sukuk market is expected to continue, and new actors in the market such as state-owned PBs will contribute to the growth of the market (Aysan Dolgun and Turhan 2013).

Islamic Indices and Funds

Islamic indices are a subset of global stock market securities and include securities that are free from prohibited activities and elements such as riba, maisir, and gharar, *haram* (or forbidden) business activities. The Shariah screening attempts to exclude those securities that contravene these Shariah principles. The first Islamic index was established in 1998 in collaboration with Kuwait and FTSE Group and was followed by the Dow Jones Islamic Market Index the following year. Today, there are more than a hundred Islamic indices all over the world. The volume of these indices is very low compared with conventional securities; however, they have been outperforming conventional ones in recent years.

The Dow Jones Islamic Market Turkey Index was first calculated on 30 September 2004, with companies trading on the Istanbul Stock Exchange (Borsa Istanbul-BIST) and compatible with Shariah investment guidelines. However, this index was not registered with BIST. Some attempts were made to establish an Islamic index in Turkey by BIST, but they did not work out and were postponed because of the global financial crises. The first Islamic index that was created domestically and registered with Borsa Istanbul, namely Participation Index 30 (PI30), was established in 2007. It is composed of 30 companies traded on the Borsa Istanbul and complies with Islamic banking principles. This PI30 was followed by the PI50, introduced in 2014. PI30 has outperformed the BIST 100 index in the period 2011–2015, and the compound annual growth rate (CAGR) was 10.6 per cent (CAGR of BIST 100 was 8.8 per cent during the same period).

The availability of sukuk and Islamic equity indices has accelerated the formation and development of Islamic funds. More than a thousand Islamic funds operate in the world with assets under management valued at over USD 70 billion (IFSB 2016). In Turkey, the Islamic funds market has gained momentum thanks to the development of Islamic capital market instruments such as lease certificates and a participation index (PI).

Kuveyt Türk is very active in gold banking and has channelized this experience to the Islamic funds market. It has established two exchange-traded funds (ETFs), a type B gold ETF and type B silver ETF. In 2015, KT also established KT Portfoy as a fully owned subsidiary, which has become the first portfolio management firm ever to be established by an Islamic bank in Turkey. Apart from providing private portfolio management and investment consultancy services to its clients, KT Portfoy also deals in collective investment products. KT has been forming various types of mutual funds such as global (foreign currency) and local (TRL) lease certificate funds, participation funds, and others. Another important market player in Islamic capital markets is Bizim Securities Inc. This company also manages a wide range of mutual funds such as a participation fund, lease certificate fund, participation stock fund, PI30 fund, and gold ETFs. Apart from these two companies, leading conventional asset management companies have also formed interest-free mutual funds ranging from lease certificate to participation stock funds.

2.3 Takaful (Islamic Insurance)

While the first implementation of *takaful* started in Sudan in 1979, Malaysia, Saudi Arabia, and other Gulf countries also launched takaful businesses in subsequent years. Global takaful assets reached USD 38 billion in 2015 and were mainly driven by the top three countries, Saudi Arabia, Iran, and Malaysia, which together hold 85 per cent of total global assets. Saudi Arabia is the largest takaful market, and its insurance market is based fully on a cooperative insurance model, after the conversion of its insurance sector and the introduction of the law on the Supervision of Cooperative Insurance Companies in 2002 (World Takaful Report 2016). Considering that total Islamic financial assets reached USD 2 trillion, the takaful market has only around a 1.5 per cent share of the total market, yet it has enjoyed double-digit growth in the insurance and takaful markets, especially in Malaysia and Gulf countries.

In Turkey, the takaful concept was initially discussed by the Congress of International Islamic Commercial Law in 1996 (Yusuf 1996). In 1995, Işık Insurance was the first company to apply takaful in its business. However, it was only able to invest in interest-free financial instruments for the collected funds, yet there has been no official announcement regarding whether the company applies the takaful concept in its business model or not. The first takaful company in Turkey was Neova, a subsidiary of KT, established in late 2009. The takaful assets of Neova reached almost 2 per cent of the Turkish insurance market within 7 years. What is more, the higher-than-average growth rate of takaful premium payments as a share of Neova's business in the insurance industry holds great potential for the takaful market in Turkey. Doğa Insurance, a cooperative insurance company, began to offer takaful products through its takaful window in 2015 (Milliyet 2015). Shortly after its establishment, Ziraat Participation also started to offer takaful products by acting as an agent of Ziraat Insurance's takaful window (Katılım Sigortacılığı [Participation Insurance] – Ziraat Sigorta A.Ş. 2016).

Even though potential is assumed to exist for the Turkish takaful market (EY Takaful Insight 2014), there is as of yet no law or regulation governing takaful companies. Thus, no company is defined as takaful under Turkey's insurance law. However, the lack of a legal infrastructure poses no legal obstacles for the operation of takaful companies and takaful windows in Turkey. However, the reputation and public image of current takaful companies and windows can be damaged unless government immediately issues comprehensive legislation and regulations to define business model and activities regarding takaful companies. Takaful companies were defined as 'participation insurance companies' in the proposed omnibus bill in 2014. However, Article 29, which covers this definition, was removed before passage of the omnibus bill.

2.4 Islamic Pension Funds

A private pension system (PPS) was introduced in Turkey as an alternative to the governmental social security system in 2003. A total of 3.1 million individuals subscribed to the PPS between 2003 and 2013, in addition to the 2 million people who enrolled after major amendments were made to the system in 2013. The government has considered the PPS one of the best instruments contributing to Turkey's economic growth using savings in pension funds. Therefore, the PPS is a win-win system that will benefit both the country and retirees. Thus, the government has also provided an incentive to PPS participants with a 25 per cent contribution. Recently, the government established a new system called 'automatic participation', which obliges companies with more than 250 employees to participate in the PPS. Enforcement of the mandatory PPS commenced in early 2017 (Milliyet 2016).

An Islamic private pension fund was first launched in Turkey by Türkiye Finans under the name Organic PPS. The company cooperated with Garanti Private Pension, a conventional private pension company that offers fund management for Türkiye Finans, in 2010 (Milliyet 2010). Several conventional companies, such as Anadolu Hayat Pension, also started offering Islamic funds in 2010 (Alternative Earning Fund – Anadolu Hayat 2016). The first Islamic private pension company, Asya Pension, was established in 2011. Katılım Pension was established in collaboration with Albaraka Türk and KT in 2013. The Capital Markets Board passed important regulations governing PPS in 2013, one of which is the introduction of non-interest methods as seen in the participation banking system. Although the system is quite new, 370,000 individuals are now increasing the value of their savings with such accounts. There is a fund of around TRY 1 billion in these accounts alone; it was launched in 2015 (Daily Sabah 2015). Two state-owned Islamic banks also started offering Islamic PPS products in collaboration with their conventional counterparts in 2016.

Life insurance and private pension products are generally offered by the same companies in Turkey. The issue of life insurance is more controversial than non-life insurance in terms of Islamic law. Vakıf Pension offers some products for Türkiye Finans called profit sharing participation insurance (Kâr Paylaşımlı Finansman Güvence Sigortası [Profit Sharing Financial Security Insurance] Türkiye Finans 2016). This product targets those who use Islamic financing but may face default risk. Other Islamic private pension companies also offer a similar product that mainly offers protection against default risk. Life takaful products are not well developed in Turkey compared to other Islamic countries. Islamic PPS is more popular for long-term investments and savings. However, the PPS cannot offer insurance in case of death or accident. Thus, family takaful products need further development in Turkey.

Insurance and PP companies are regulated and supervised by the Turkish Treasury. Recently, Osman Çelik (Habertürk 2016), whose background is in Islamic finance, was appointed head of the Turkish Treasury. This new assignment is expected to bring new regulations for takaful and Islamic pension companies.

2.5 Islamic Microfinance

Today eradicating poverty is on the agendas not only of the least developed or developing countries but even of developed countries. Various policies and development strategies of banks have already been implemented by governmental and international institutions and monitored to reduce the poverty level. Microfinance is seen as a significant tool for poverty reduction through the financial empowerment of entrepreneurs and small businesses, which are generally excluded from financial services by conventional financial institutions because of their high-risk profile. Microfinance has proved that the poor can also be financed with a low rate of default, contrary to the general perception, and it can be profitable for financial institutions. Although microfinance started in the 1970s as non-governmental organization (NGOs) with the support of donors but was ignored by formal financial institutions, today even commercial banks are providing small loans especially for the economically active poor through their subsidiaries. It is estimated that more than 10,000 microfinance institutions (responsAbility 2014) ranging from NGOs to microfinance banks are operating and serving millions of people.

While some state-owned banks such as Ziraat and Halk Bank have been providing microcredit to low-income people, especially microenterprises, for a long time, there are two so-called microfinance institutions, MAYA and Turkey Grameen Microfinance Programme, in Turkey. Microfinance institutions in Turkey provide not only financial services such as credit and savings to their clients but also other non-financial services such as education and training. In addition, some public institutions provide loans and charitable donations to low-income people and microenterprises.

One of the main objectives of Islamic finance is to enable distributions of wealth justly by providing financial services not only for wealthy people but also for all segments of society. However, Islamic financial institutions have been diverging from this objective by becoming more like their conventional competitors, although the first modern Islamic bank, Mit Ghamr in Eygpt, was very similar to today's microfinance institutions in terms of providing financial services to low-income people. However, current Islamic banks ignore poor people as conventional counterparts and exclude them from financial services. Therefore, Islamic microfinance institutions have been developed especially in Muslim countries to fill the gap between poor people and Islamic finance.

Although it is asserted by Çizakça (2003) that the first microfinance institutions in the world are cash *waqfs*, an institution what dates back to the fifteenth century under the Ottoman Empire, Islamic microfinance in Turkey is a very new concept and no institution exists for the sole purpose of extending interest-free microfinance to low-income people. Some institutions, such as KOSGEB, extend interest-free credit to microenterprises/small and medium-sized enterprises and insure credit without interest. PBs currently provide financial services to small and medium-sized enterprises; however, there is a need for a more strategic perspective that includes operational adjustments (Aysan et al. 2016). PBs also have small microloan portfolios in their total credit profiles. However, their strategy of targeting the upper segment of poor people, not the poorest of the poor, is one of the most significant criticisms of microfinance institutions globally.

3 Policy Recommendations

Although the Islamic banking industry, with its more than 30-year history, has proved so far that it holds great potential in Turkey, its market share was still less than 6 per cent in 2016. As we have seen, many large-scale failures have led to severe shocks in Turkey's Islamic banking industry and damaged confidence that prevented it from gaining further momentum. Many problems in the Islamic finance industry still need to be addressed by actors in the industry and by government. That is why the market share of Islamic banks is still much lower than past forecasts and polls of market potential had predicted.

In the first decade of Islamic banking, high demand and lax regulations enabled high growth in the industry; at the same time, these very features exposed SFHs to higher risks through the use of a wide range of Islamic financial products whose risks were poorly understood because of poor corporate governance and low capital holdings.

Initially, the Islamic banking industry in Turkey went through a period of high volatility in assets as a result of losses due to poor management of liquidity risk, Shariah non-compliance risk, investment risk, operational risk, and credit risk. Since a lack of familiarity with the inherent risk of Islamic financial products and the absence of tools and control mechanisms to manage those risks decrease the profitability and damage the reputation of the industry, Islamic banks, regulatory bodies, and universities must conduct comprehensive research and policy analysis over the relevant risks of Islamic financial products and improve appropriate risk management mechanisms to ensure the financial stability and sustainable growth of the industry.

Risk sharing is a significant concept in Islamic finance, yet the early development of the Islamic banking industry in Turkey pushed the excessive use of debt-based contracts of *murabahah* and *ijarah*, particularly for more than 90 per cent of funding activities. On a relevant note, fixed-return investment products were almost the only option for investors.

Thus, improvement of higher profit-loss-sharing-oriented products on the liability side and providing more *mudharabah*- and *musharakah*-based financing on the asset side will attract more borrowers and lenders with higher risk appetites.

Since Islamic banking is based on trading such as the purchase, sale, or lease of assets, Islamic banks are exposed to tax disadvantages compared to conventional banks. Tax disadvantages arising from the asset-based structure of Islamic banking should be removed to ensure a competitive environment for Islamic banks in Turkey. Moreover, some Islamic financial products can be promoted by the government by providing special tax benefits as part of relevant tax reforms.

In the Turkish secularist narrative, the word 'Shariah' has always been a buzz-word that has generated fear. That is why, although all activities of Islamic banks must be consistent with Shariah principles, even referring to them as Islamic banks has led to legal concerns in the context of Turkey's brand of secularism. Similarly, such a concern regarding infringements on secularism led PBs to use the term 'advisory committee' rather than 'Shariah Board' and 'Shariah Advisory Council'. Moreover, advisory committees and their fatwas, which plays a key role in ensuring compliance of financial activities with Shariah law, are mostly not publicly available, even though their members are supposed to be well known and fatwas regarding Islamic financial products and activities must have been more transparent and in harmony with the majority rulings of other Islamic banks in the Gulf and South-East Asia regions. However, the presence of contrasting fatwas by different Islamic banks in Turkey and Islamic financial products that are available only in Turkey is also common. That is why Shariah non-compliance risk is one major issue facing Islamic banks and has not only caused financial losses so far but has also severely damaged the reputation of the industry. Therefore, the establishment of a central Shariah authority, implementing external Shariah audits and standardization of Islamic financial products, would facilitate the growth of Islamic banking in Turkey.

Although Islamic and conventional banks seem to have a similar function as financial intermediaries by channeling funds from savers to spenders indirectly, the majority of Islamic financial products and types of contracts are different from their conventional counterparts. However,

Islamic banks in Turkey use International Financial Reporting Standards (IFRS) as accounting standards to record Islamic financial transactions, despite the fact that IFRS does not have accounting rules for many types of Islamic financial contracts. What is more, IFRS accounting statements for conventional banks are heavily reliant on the concept of the time value of money, and such a practice is strictly forbidden under Shariah law. For this reason, other countries such as Pakistan and Malaysia use additional Islamic accounting standards alongside IFRS for Islamic banks, while some Gulf countries prefer to apply the guidelines of the Accounting and Auditing Organization for Islamic Financial Institutions as a completely separate set of Islamic accounting standards.

The development of Islamic financial institutions in Turkey is closely related to government support in various aspects. Firstly, the improvement of the legal framework for Islamic financial institutions will make it possible to resolve current legal disputes more effectively. Secondly, more engagement by state-owned companies with Islamic banks in their financial activities will help spur the growth of Islamic finance. The Treasury and central bank should use Islamic financial products more to improve risk management mechanisms and catalyze the growth of the industry. Government should support the establishment of Islamic finance programmes in universities to fill the skills gap in human resources and improve Islamic finance practices through academic researchers. Attracting foreign Islamic banks and increasing the number of state-owned banks will also enable the further penetration of the market since Turkey has the lowest number of Islamic banks compared to its peers in South-East Asia and the Middle East. Finally, the government must ensure that in the context of secularism in Turkey, Islamic financial institutions are never considered a threat to secularism by clarifying the concept of secularism more precisely since Islamic banks suffered severely from political risks in the past.

Compared to Islamic banking, less attention has been paid to Islamic capital markets in promoting Islamic finance in Turkey. However, recent initiatives such as sukuk issuances and incentives for the PPS have shown that developments in capital markets are quite positively affecting Islamic banking and complement each other. Although the Islamic capital market of Turkey has been showing remarkable growth rates in recent years –

which is expected because of a very niche market that values this –much remains to be done to reach the desired level in the development of the Islamic finance industry and particularly in the Islamic capital markets in Turkey.

Private-sector companies such as Islamic banks, asset management companies, and pension funds are making efforts to diversify their products and increase their market penetration. However, new financial service providers, especially in the Islamic fund market, which is relatively niche, offer significant opportunities for attracting foreign investment and catalyzing economic growth. The private sector should also take more responsibility for the development of new products through their relatively greater openness to innovation compared to state-owned financial institutions. South-East Asian countries, especially Indonesia and Malaysia, are very innovative in Islamic capital market products and should be emulated in Turkish regulations and structures. Not only the private sector but also the government has a great responsibility to ensure positive trends in the Islamic capital markets of Turkey. Supporting the role of government is the key determinant in the progress of Islamic capital markets. The Malaysian experience – a pioneer in Islamic finance, especially in capital markets – shows the key role of government in promoting the sector by, for example, introducing needed regulations, providing services as a market player, and issuing capital market instruments with high credit ratings. In recent years, the Turkish government has indeed begun working hard to formulate a strategic role of Islamic finance in its development programme and in supporting the sector.

Sukuk issuances by the Turkish Treasury have played a significant role in deepening the sukuk market and triggering the formation of a secondary market, which is vital, especially for PBs, for liquidity management. New state-owned PBs will also contribute to the sukuk market by being not only suppliers but also investors. Legislation governing sukuk issuances introduced by the CMBT has paved the way for new issuances and the establishment of SPVs; however, the private sukuk market has still been driven by Islamic banks, which make up the demand and supply sides. Other corporations have not shown the expected interest in sukuk, and corporate sukuk issuances are very low. The main reason behind this is that legislation, especially tax law and procedures, is not easy to understand, and Islamic banks have had difficulties in clarifying the process. This problem has had two negative results for corporate sukuk issuance. Firstly, it has prevented companies from issuing sukuk; secondly, uncertainties increase the cost of issuing because of consultancy fees. Therefore, legislation especially regarding tax issues should be simplified and clarified, on top of incentives such as tax reductions. It should also be noted that companies must make issuance through SPVs, which also increases costs, bureaucracy, and the issuance period. This should also be reviewed by taking into consideration the stability of the market and the health and needs of companies.

The volume of the sukuk market in Turkey is very low. Thus, the secondary market of sukuk has not been developed as expected and remains far from desired levels. New strategies must be developed for domestic and international issuances in order to deepen the market. In recent years, Turkey has carried out high-budget projects such as a third airport, a bridge, and an undersea tunnel. At least some part of these should be financed by issuing Islamic capital market products such as sukuk and RSCs to entice international and domestic investors into contributing to and strengthening the market. Also, issued sukuk for the financing of infrastructure projects should be traded on the Borsa Istanbul. Investing on a secondary sukuk market should be encouraged by introducing tax advantages, especially for individual investors.

Although Islamic equity and fund markets in Turkey are new, market is still in its infancy compared to its potential. A PI provides Shariah-compliant investment opportunities in a stock market, which the majority of Muslims have avoided for many years. Moreover, the fact that Shariah-compliant equities can outperform their conventional competitors will attract more investment into the PI. However, the features and performance of the PI are not well known, and many people are not even aware of its existence. Thus, education and awareness regarding Islamic equity markets are critical for the development and growth of the market.

Capital market investors are quite sensitive to macroeconomic developments. Apart from the evaluation of a company/product, they analyse macro variables such as political stability, legal infrastructure, and credit ratings in detail. All relevant stakeholders ranging from government to

PBs have great responsibilities for the development of the Islamic finance industry in Turkey. In particular, the coordination of related public institutions such as the Treasury, CBRT, BRSA, CMBT, and BIST has a vital role since regulations or incentives may not be effective without price stability or an investable credit rating. Some board members and presidents of three key institutions, CBRT, BRSA, and Treasury, have many years of experience in Islamic banking and they can play a significant role in promoting the development of Islamic finance in Turkey more effectively.

Turkey has significant potential for Islamic microfinance, and 36 per cent of the population is economically vulnerable (Grossman 2006) – the main target of microfinance. Moreover, around 3 million Syrian refugees live in Turkey, and the government is planning to grant citizenship to some of them, which may add to the demand potential of microfinance. PBs can benefit from this potential and develop suitable products for the refugee population. In the short run, it may be expected that there will be limited return, yet in the medium to long run, some of them may turn into profitable customers. Thus, the objective of PBs is to attain a 15 per cent market share in the total banking sector, and this can be achieved by appealing to low-income people. A new state-owned PB, Vakıf Katılım, which was established by charity endowments to have a social impact and earn spiritual rewards for its founders, should serve the poor not only by spending company profits but also by extending them credit as customers.

In Turkey, takaful has a very low market share, around 1 per cent, of the insurance industry. Thus, the development of takaful in Turkey will take longer than other Islamic financial institutions. The situation is similar in the conventional finance sector. Firstly, takaful companies need a legal definition that differentiates them from other insurance companies. Secondly, agency training is very important in takaful, considering that contracts have an important role in the takaful business. Insurance and takaful agents should provide information that clarifies the differences between takaful and conventional insurance. This issue can be resolved easily by adding a module to the agency technical personnel exam, which is obligatory for all insurance agents. Several PBs still work as agents for conventional insurance companies. To develop a better image in society and eliminate misconceptions, PBs should provide takaful products only at their branches. Retakaful, which is a kind of Islamic counterpart to reinsurance, needs to be established in Turkey. The government may lead the establishment of the first retakaful company not only to increase the number of takaful companies for catalysing growth of the takaful market but also to improve the public image of and trust in the takaful market. Deepened Islamic capital markets are a necessity for family takaful and private pension funds. In particular, long-term sukuks can greatly contribute to the development of takaful and a PPS.

References

Alternative Earning Fund – Anadolu Hayat. 2016. http://www.anadoluhayat.com.tr/bireysel-emeklilik/emeklilik-yatirim-fonlari/orta-riskli-fonlar/age-ahe-alternatif-kazanc-fonu. Accessed 18 Feb 2017.

Aysan, Ahmet Faruk, Muhammed Habib Dolgun, and M. Ibrahim Turhan. 2013. Assessment of the Participation Banks and Their Role in Financial Inclusion in Turkey. *Emerging Markets Finance and Trade* 49 (s5): 99–111. https://doi.org/10.2753/ree1540-496x4905s506.

Aysan, Ahmet F., Mustafa Disli, Adam Ng, and Huseyin Ozturk. 2016. Is Small the New Big? Islamic Banking for Smes in Turkey. *Economic Modelling* 54: 187–194. https://doi.org/10.1016/j.econmod.2015.12.031.

Banking Regulation and Supervision Agency. 2016. *Announcement on the Revocation of the Banking Licence of Bank Asya* [online]. Available at: http://www.bddk.org.tr/WebSitesi/turkce/Duyurular/BDDK_Kurul_Kararlari/153626947.pdf. Accessed 1 Jun 2017.

Capital Market Board of Turkey. 2017. *Monthly Statistical Bulletin APRIL 2017*. Monthly Statistical Bulletin. CMBT.

Çizakça, Murat. 2003. Tekerlegin Yeniden Kesfi: Mikro Finansman Kuruluslari Yasa Tasarisi [Re-Inventing the Wheel: The Micro-Finance Institutions Bill]. *Zaman*, March 16.

Daily Sabah. 2015. State Incentives Have Discernible Effect on Private Pension System. January 7.

Ernst & Young. 2014. *EY Global Takaful Insights 2014* [online]. Ernst & Young. Available at: http://www.ey.com/Publication/vwLUAssets/EY_Global_Takaful_Insights_2014/$FILE/EY-global-takaful-insights-2014.pdf. Accessed 1 July 2017.

Finanstrend. 2018. Karaman: GES'ler devlet tahvilinden farksız [Karaman: RIB'S Are No Different from Government Bonds]. [online] Available at: http://www.finanstrend.com/haber/97465/karaman-ges-ler-devlettahvilinden-farksiz/1. Accessed 3 July 2017.

Grossman, Helmut. 2006. *Demand Study for Micro-Finance in Turkey*. Frankfurt: Bankakademie International. http://www.tr.undp.org/content/dam/turkey/docs/Publications/PovRed/MFDEMANDShortReport.pdf. Accessed 15 Dec 2016.

Güngör, Z. 1996. Faizsiz bankalar izin için sırada bekliyor [Interest-Free Banks Are in Queue for License]. *Milliyet*, August 15.

Habertürk. 2016. Yeni Hazine Müsteşarı Osman Çelik Oldu [Osman Çelik Was Appointed as New Undersecretary of Turkish Treasury]. June 28.

Hürriyet. 2003. Sukuk İcara Ile 10 Milyar Dolar Gelecek [10 Billion Dollar Will Come with Sukuk Al-Ijarah]. June 30.

———. 2005. 4,7 Milyar Dolarlık Baraj Senedi Geliyor [4.7 Billion Barrage Bond Is Coming]. March 4.

International Islamic Financial Market. 2016. *Sukuk Report: A Comprehensive Study of the Global Sukuk Market*, 5th ed. Sukuk Report [online]. IIFM. Available at: http://www.iifm.net/system/files/private/en/IIFM%20Sukuk%20Report%20%285th%20Edition%29%20A%20Comprehensive%20study%20of%20the%20Global%20Sukuk%20Market_0.pdf. Accessed 29 July 2017.

Islamic Financial Services Board. 2015. *Islamic Financial Services Industry Stability Report 2015* [online]. Kuala Lumpur: IFSB. Available at: http://www.ifsb.org/docs/IFSB%20Islamic%20Financial%20Services%20Industry%20Stability%20Report%202015_final.pdf. Accessed 1 Jul 2017.

———. 2016. *Islamic Financial Services Industry Stability Report 2016* [online]. Kuala Lumpur. Available at: http://www.ifsb.org/docs/IFSI%20Stability%20Report%202016%20(final).pdf. Accessed 1 Jul 2017.

Kâr Paylaşımlı Finansman Güvence Sigortası [Profit Sharing Financial Security Insurance] | Türkiye Finans. 2016. *Türkiye Finans*. http://www.turkiyefinans.com.tr/tr-tr/bireysel/sigortacilik-hizmetleri/Sayfalar/Kar-Paylasimli-Finansman-Guvence-Sigortasi.aspx. Accessed 12 Jan 2017.

Karaman, Hayrettin. 2012. Devletin Borç Senetleri [Government Debt Securities]. *Yeni Şafak*, February 19.

Katılım Sigortacılığı [Participation Insurance] – Ziraat Sigorta A.Ş. 2016. *Ziraatsigorta.Com.Tr*. https://www.ziraatsigorta.com.tr/katilim_sigortacil-igi_.html. Accessed 15 Feb 2017.

ME Global Advisors. 2016. *World Takaful Report 2016* [online]. ME Global Advisors. Available at: http://www.takafulprimer.com/main/downloads/ms_5860.pdf. Accessed 2 July 2017.

Milliyet. 1984. Köprü Senetleri Piyasada [Bridge Certificates in the Market]. December 3.

———. 1985. Barajlar "Az" Sattı [Barrages Were Sold Low]. July 11.

———. 1991. Faizsiz bankalar 7 trilyon toplar [Interest-Free Banks Can Collect TL7 Trillion]. August 8.

———. 1999. İslami Finans Tarih oluyor [Islamic Finance Will Disappear]. December 4.

———. 2000. Enver Ören İhlas holding hissesini sattı [Enver Ören Sold His Stocks of Ihlas Finans]. October 25.

———. 2003a. Kamu bankaları da islami bankacılık yapacak [State-Owned Banks Will Start Islamic Banking]. March 31.

———. 2003b. Faizsiz Tahvil Eylülde Geliyor [Interest Free Bond Comes in September]. July 22.

———. 2010. Katılım Bankacılığı Müşterilerine BES Imkânı [PPS Opportunity for Clients of Participation Banks]. August 18.

———. 2015. Türkıyede İlk Kez İslami Sigorta Hizmete Sunuldu [First Islamic Insurance Have Been Introduced]. June 5.

———. 2016. 13 Milyon Çalışan, Aylık 100 Lira Kesintiyle Zorunlu BES'E Girecek [13 Million Employees Will Be Registered To Mandatory PPS by 100TL Fee]. June 15.

Official Gazette of the Republic of Turkey. 2010. *Principles Regarding Lease Certificates and Asset Lease Companies*. Capital Market Board of Turkey.

———. 2011. *A Bill Related To Baking Amendments On Some Regulations*. Council of Ministers.

———. 2013. *Lease Certificates Communique*. Capital Market Boards of Turkey.

Özgentürk, J. 1994. Kriz, İslami Bankacılığı da vurdu [Crisis Hit the Islamic Banking]. *Milliyet*, February 18.

Pir, C. 1988. Müslüman bankacılık üç aylarda [Islamic Banking in Holy Months]. *Milliyet*, September 17.

Radikal. 2003a. Barajlar Para Basacak [Barrages Will Print Money]. May 2.

———. 2003b. Gelir Ortaklığı Senedi Yolda [Revenue Sharing Bond on Way]. March 27.

ResponsAbility. 2014. *Microfinance Market Outlook 2015*. ResponsAbility.

REVENUE INDEXED BONDS. 2017. Treasury.Gov.Tr. http://www.treasury.gov.tr/en-US/Undesigned-General-Content/REVENUE-INDEXED-BONDS. Accessed 26 Feb 2017.

Sabah. 1998. Faizsiz bankacılığa sıkıyönetim geliyor [Strict regulations are coming for Interest-free banks]. March 25.

———. 2013. Ziraat ve Halk'a Katılım Talimatı [Order to Establish Ziraat and Halk Participation]. March 29.

Tasarrufların Teşviki ve Kamu Yatırımlarının Hızlandırılması Hakkında Kanun. 1984. *[Legislation of Promotion of Savings and Acceleration of Public Investment].* No.18335. 29 Feb 1984.

Yeni Şafak. 2001. Faizsiz finansa garanti çatısı geldi [Interest-free Finance Now Has Deposit Guarantee]. October 27.

———. 2002. Çağlar: Özel Finans Kurumları atakta [Çağlar: Special Financial Institutions Penetrate the Market]. April 14.

Yusuf, Muhammad Fazlı. 1996. Brief Outline of the Concept and Operational System of Takaful Business (Islamic Insurance). In *1. Uluslararasi İslam Ticaret Hukukunun Günümüzdeki Meseleleri Kongresi [1St International Congress of Modern Issues of Islamic Law in Business]*, 931–944. Konya: KOMBAD.

Saving Behaviour in Turkey: Where Are We? And What Can We Do About It?

Mevlüt Tatlıyer

1 Introduction

After the tumultuous decade of the 1990s, the Turkish economy evolved dramatically in the 2000s (economic performance recovered significantly, inflation rate plummeted from very high levels to below 10 per cent, fiscal deficits – one of the defining features of the 1990s – have been eliminated, the financial sector has expanded tremendously, social expenditures have dramatically increased, and the current account balance has significantly worsened). This period also witnessed the rapid decline of the Turkish saving rate from well over 20 per cent to below 15 per cent. This caused concern among policymakers and academics in Turkey due to the strong correlation between saving rates and economic growth. Motivated by the perceived importance of saving and the rapid decline of this rate in the 2000s, this study aims to uncover how the Turkish saving rate declined in the first place, determine where this rate is headed in the future, and address what can be done about it.

M. Tatlıyer (✉)
Department of Economics and Finance, Istanbul Medipol University, Istanbul, Turkey

A. F. Aysan et al. (eds.), *Turkish Economy*,
https://doi.org/10.1007/978-3-319-70380-0_11

Saving is one of the fundamental concepts in economics due to its alleged importance as the source of investment and, hence, productive capital. Saving seems to be correlated strongly with economic growth, and empirical findings indicate, though tentatively, that countries with higher economic growth rates tend to have higher saving rates. However, the direction of causation between saving and economic growth is ambiguous both theoretically and empirically.

Firstly, in the theoretical sense, while neoclassical economists regard saving as a key driver of economic growth and thrift as a valuable trait for the whole economy, on the other hand, Keynesians believe that *more* saving *ceteris paribus* is a drain on effective demand and actually disrupts the economy and paves the way to economic stagnation (Keynes 1936; Modigliani 1986). From a different perspective, while saving is, for the first camp, an exogenous variable affecting the real economy and hence the growth potential, the other camp argues that saving is actually an endogenous variable and its level is determined mainly by income level.

Secondly, in the empirical sense, while some studies report that saving precedes economic growth (e.g. Tang and Tan 2014; Mehta and Rami 2014; Odionye et al. 2016), others consistently find that economic growth precedes saving (e.g. Andrei and Huidumac-Petrescu 2013; Waithima 2008; Odhiambo 2009; Ekinci and Gül 2007). Yet others find a two-way relationship between these variables (e.g. Jouini 2016; Singh 2010; Najarzadeh et al. 2014). Lastly, some studies show one- and two-way relationships between these variables for different countries (e.g. Kónya 2004). However, note that empirical studies have mostly been in favour of the causal relationship running from economic growth to saving (Mohan 2006). Whatever the direction of causation, nevertheless, the strong correlation between these variables highlight the importance of saving in the pursuit of prosperity, and the direction of causation comes into prominence only when deriving policy conclusions regarding saving.

2 Methodology

Aggregate saving is a rather elusive concept both to define and calculate. From the standpoint of individuals, saving is just the money they did not spend from their income in a given period. However, for the whole economy, saving does not mean the money that is not spent, but the money that is not *consumed* for immediate needs, in other words, money that *is* spent on investments that generate future income. That means, in a closed economy, all income is spent *by definition* for either consumption or investment and saving level simply corresponds to investment level.

Therefore, how to demarcate the boundary between consumption and investment is of paramount importance, and the decision regarding this amounts to no less than the decision between what amount is consumed or saved *by definition*. For example, some argue that expenditures on durable goods should be regarded as investment, since these are not perishable goods and can last years and even decades. Others argue the same for education and research and development (R&D) expenditures since these are actually long-term investments that greatly increase the productive capacity of the economy and so cannot be regarded as part of consumption. Yet some advocate that health expenditures too should be considered as investment, since these increase health levels and life expectancy and, hence, productive human capital. In a nutshell, *any* expenditure on goods that are not consumed and exhausted immediately could be regarded as investment and, hence, saving (Reinsdorf 2004; Audenis et al. 2002; Gorman et al. 2013; Orthofer 2015; Rocher and Stierle 2015; Claus and Scobie 2002).

On the other hand, defining and calculating income represents another challenge, mostly for practical reasons on how to calculate the overall income level and how to derive the saving level from that. First of all, higher inflation distorts real income and saving levels for both borrowers and lenders. In an inflationary and high nominal interest rate environment, capital gains of lenders seem higher than the actual level, since capital gains consist of both real interest gains and interest gains for the compensation of the expected inflation rate. The converse holds true for borrowers: their income level seems lower because of interest payments that stem from the expected inflation rate. Secondly, there is the dilemma of whether rising asset prices should be regarded as capital gains and, hence, income. Under fixed consumption, if these capital gains on paper are assumed to be income, then the overall saving rate of these investors will be higher. On the other hand, if only *realized* capital gains are regarded as income, then the saving rate of the investors will be lower.

Thirdly, tax composition constitutes another challenge for the calculation of income level. When calculating disposable income for households, direct taxes are subtracted from the gross income. However, this subtraction is not the case for *indirect* taxes such as a value-added tax (VAT). This creates a problem when comparing household saving rates across countries and time periods. For example, in countries that rely mostly on indirect taxes, households will pay lower income taxes and their income levels will seem higher. However, they will have to spend more because of higher indirect taxes. That means, when calculating their saving rates, their income or expenditure levels will be exaggerated and their saving rate will seem lower than it actually is. Likewise, if the composition of tax revenues changes in a way that lowering or increasing the share of direct taxes in favour of or against indirect taxes over time, then the household saving rate will seem to be declining or increasing, even though there is no change in household saving behaviour.

Fourthly, the health system and social security contribution structure have an important impact on the perceived household saving level. In countries with a more universal health system and inevitably a higher level of social contribution level, household saving rates tend to seem more than what they actually are since both the denominator (net disposable income) and the numerator (expenditure) decline by the same amount, resulting in a seemingly higher saving rate. For example, suppose that net disposable income declines from 100 to 90 units and health expenditure decreases from 85 to 75 units; then the saving rate increases from 15 per cent to 17 per cent, although household health expenditures did not change at all.

All in all, one needs to be very careful when assessing saving behaviour and comparing saving rates across time and space because of these methodological difficulties.

3 Potential Determinants of Saving

Although there is a vast empirical literature on saving behaviour for different time periods and different countries or country groups, no consensus has emerged regarding the main determinants of saving. This is partly due to the chosen estimation technique (cross-sectional or time-series estimation) or the analysed time period or the countries or country groups being examined. For example, demographic variables tend to have more significant effects on saving rates in cross-sectional analyses than in time-series estimations since these variables tend to change very slowly. Moreover, there are some theoretical ambiguities concerning some potential determinants of saving as to their overall effect on saving such as real interest rate. In addition, there are well-known technical and practical drawbacks regarding the estimation of saving rates, as mentioned in the previous section.

The literature shows that there exist several potential determinants of saving in. Of these, income growth and the real interest rate are theoretically ambiguous and empirically inconclusive (Loayza et al. 2000a, b; Edwards 1996). On the other hand, income level, inflation rate, favourable terms of trade, and current account surplus have a positive impact on saving rate theoretically and somewhat empirically. While a higher income level means a higher saving rate due to the Keynesian decreasing marginal propensity to consume (Hondroyiannis 2006; Attanasio et al. 2000), a higher inflation rate prompts saving by increasing uncertainty (Bérubé and Côté 2000; Hüfner and Koske 2010). In addition, favourable terms of trade (Hevia 2010) and a current account surplus (Loayza et al. 2000b) mean higher income levels, so more saving.

Lastly, credit expansion, elderly and youth dependency ratios, social security level, and public saving have a negative effect on saving both theoretically and more or less empirically. While credit expansion prompts households to spend more and save less (Zeldes 1989; Bayoumi 1993), increasing elderly and youth dependency ratios put a downward pressure on the saving rate thanks to the increasing burden on the workforce (Agrawal et al. 2009; Kim and Lee 2008; Li et al. 2007). In addition, a higher social security level tends to decrease saving rates by mitigating uncertainty (Horioka and Yin 2009; Feldstein 1980). Lastly, there is an apparent trade-off between public and private saving rates, i.e. increasing public saving rates tend to be accompanied by decreasing private saving rates, though this trade-off is by no means perfect (Masson et al. 1998; Matur et al. 2012; Schrooten and Stephan 2002).

4 Stylized Facts Regarding Saving Rates in Turkey

In order to be able to evaluate saving behaviour, one needs to understand how the private saving rate is calculated in Turkey. An economy consists of three major groups: households, firms, and government. While it is relatively easy to calculate the saving rate of the government, the saving rates of households and firms are not easy to determine. In this respect, as in some countries, the private saving rates – the saving rates of households plus firms, in other words, non-government saving rate – is calculated not directly but as a double residual in Turkey, and because of this there is no way to differentiate between savings of households and firms. When calculating private saving, private disposable income is first calculated as a residual by subtracting public disposable income from gross national product (GNP) prior to 1998 or from gross national disposable income (GNDI) since that time. Second, private consumption is also calculated as a residual by subtracting public expenditures (consumption and investment) from gross domestic product (GDP) and then decomposing the remaining part into consumption and investment. In the end, the private saving ratio is obtained as a ratio of two residuals, private consumption and income levels. In addition, relatively reliable and comparable private saving rate figures date back to only 1975, and prior to 1963 it was impossible to calculate this variable since no disposable income or private consumption expenditure data series existed (Uygur 2012; Alkin 1970; DPT 2010).

Historical saving rates in Turkey are shown in Fig. 1. First, the public saving rate was on the order of 5 per cent from 1975 to the late 1980s. It declined rapidly after 1988, reaching zero in 1991 and hovering around

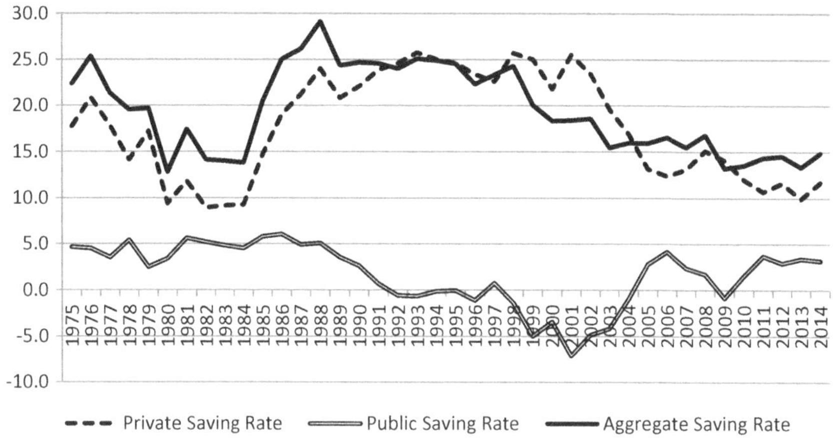

Fig. 1 Saving rates in Turkey (1975–2014) (Source: Ministry of Development of Turkey)

there for half a decade. With the escalating political turmoil and particularly the 28 February *coup d'état* and resulting budget deficits, this ratio began to plummet in 1997, reaching an all-time trough with a 7.1 dissaving ratio in 2001, thanks partly to a devastating financial crisis in that year. However, the public saving ratio quickly recovered in the 2000s thanks to political and economic stability in that period and has been on the order of 3–4 per cent since 2006, except during the 2008–2009 global financial crisis period.

On the other hand, the private saving rate was in a downward trend between 1975 and 1982 and declined from over 20 per cent to below 10 per cent. In the second half of the 1980s this rate began to climb and reached well over 20 per cent and stayed there in the entire decade of the 1990s. However, it plunged after the 2001 financial crisis and hit just 13 per cent from over 25 per cent in just four years. It more or less stabilized after the 2008–2009 global financial crisis at around just over 10 per cent. The aggregate saving rate mostly followed a trajectory over time similar to that of the private saving rate. This ratio was also around well over 20 per cent in the 1990s, only declining rapidly after 1997 to just over 15 per cent in 2003, almost totally thanks to the rapid rise in the public saving rate. After that year, the aggregate saving rate more or less stabilized at around 14 per cent, except during the 2008–2009 global financial crisis period.

5 Saving Behaviour in Turkey

Several factors account for the substantial decline in the Turkish aggregate saving rate in the late 1990s and first half of the 2000s. The initial decrease in the aggregate saving rate was on the order of 6 percentage points and is explained by the rapid decline of the public saving rate owing to a marked deterioration in public finances in the 1997–2001 period, wherein the private saving rate was relatively stable, hovering around 25 per cent. The second decrease in the aggregate saving rate happened in the 2001–2006 period and was milder (around 2.5 percentage points) compared to the first one. In this period, the public saving rate rose rapidly and the private saving rate plummeted, offsetting each other to a certain extent and limiting the fall in the overall saving rate. This rate fell a little bit further (1–2 percentage points) with the 2008–2009 global financial crisis owing both to a rapid decrease in the public saving rate and a more gradual decrease in the private saving rate. While the public saving rate has more or less reached pre-1988 levels in recent years, the private saving rate has decreased dramatically from around 24 to 12 per cent in the 2000s, due mostly to the rapid decline in the 2001–2006 period.

While the public saving rate is determined primarily by the decisions of policymakers, explaining changes in the private saving rate is not an easy task. Why did the private saving rate fall so dramatically in just five years between 2001 and 2006, and why did it remain at those levels afterwards, albeit fluctuating in the 2008–2009 global financial crisis period? There are several possible reasons behind this spectacular decrease, including an increased public saving rate due to the significant recovery in public finances, rapid financialization, a notable decline in the inflation rate, and a steep increase in social expenditures (Tatliyer 2017).

Firstly, the Turkish case confirms the well-documented trade-off between public and private saving rates in the literature, such that while the public saving rate increased markedly between 2001 and 2006, the private saving rate decreased dramatically. Secondly, credit volume expanded immensely after 2001, increasing consumption and depressing the private saving rate. While the ratio of credit volume to GDP was around 9 per cent in 2002, it skyrocketed to 26 per cent in 2007 and over 70 per cent as of 2015 by accelerating after 2008. In particular, household credit volume to GDP steeply increased from 2 per cent in 2001 to 11 per cent in 2007 and around 19 per cent as of 2015.

Thirdly, the inflation rate decreased dramatically in the 2000s, from well over 50 to below 10 per cent in just a few years as of 2004, and nominal interest rates declined tremendously in the following years, reflecting rapidly diminishing uncertainty regarding the Turkish economy. Theoretically, the higher the uncertainty, the more people, both households and investors, tend to save for precautionary reasons. Therefore, a rapidly decreasing inflation rate should have a downward pressure on the private saving rate if this theoretical insight holds for Turkey. In addition, the almost perfect concurrence of these developments lends further support to this argument.

Fourthly, social expenditures in Turkey greatly expanded in the 2000s. The ratio of social expenditures to GDP was only 8.5 per cent in 2000. This ratio increased to 11.6 per cent in 2007 and 14.3 per cent as of 2014, while the Turkish economy grew by 4.7 per cent annually on average in that period. Numerically, real social expenditures at 2014 prices increased from 95 billion to around a stunning 250 billion Turkish liras, almost tripling in just 14 years. As with a decreasing inflation rate, rapidly increasing social expenditures too should weaken uncertainty and insecurity among households, thereby decreasing the need to save for precautionary reasons and prompting people to spend more.

On the other hand, there are important income- or expenditure-related factors that have a bearing on *the calculated* private saving rate, but not necessarily on *the real* private saving rate (depending on the definition of *saving* that is adopted), including a changed tax structure, increased social security payments and contributions, and a decreased inflation rate through an inflation effect.

Firstly, the ratio of indirect to direct taxes collected was 1.3 in 1990 and stood at 1.5 on average in the 1990s, despite some fluctuations, indicating a more or less stable and relatively fair tax composition. However, the tax composition has deteriorated markedly in the 2000s, with this ratio increasing from 1.5 to a stunning 2.4 in just six years between 2001 and 2006, which is the same period in which the private saving rate plummeted. Therefore, relying much more heavily on indirect taxes has biased private saving rates downwardly to a marked extent. For example, if this ratio were 1.3 in 2006 as in 1990, then private disposable income *and* private expenditures would be 37.3 billion Turkish liras lower and the private saving rate would be 0.7 percentage points higher, not 12.4 but 13.1 per cent. The effect of the tax structure on the private saving rate has been around 0.7 per cent on average for the entire period between 2000 and 2013, reaching around 1 percentage point as of 2013. Note that this is *a real effect*; private disposable income was indeed not as high as it seems to have been in the 2000s compared to the 1990s, thus, in the same way, the private saving rate was not as low as it seems to have been. Overall, a rapidly changing tax composition accounts for a portion of the decrease in the private saving rate in the 2000s (Fig. 2).

Secondly, in the 1990s, one of the major reasons behind the low and even negative public savings was the expanding wedge between social security contributions and social expenditures, an exemple of the bad governance of the period. In that period, while governments were providing porous and limited social security to the public both quantitatively and qualitatively, a high level of corruption and ineffectiveness in the system resulted in ever-increasing public debts and even monetization of the debt to a significant degree and, hence, among other reasons, a plummeting public saving rate. However, in the 2000s, this outlook rapidly changed and the low efficiency level of the system quickly improved to a marked extent, while the social benefits increased significantly, as mentioned earlier. Therefore, as social security has begun to take root in Turkey, social security contributions have increased dramatically from around 3 per cent in the 1990s to around 7.8 per cent as of 2014. That means for households that they happened to be in a position that they have now been enjoying *more* social benefits in exchange for higher contributions to the system. Therefore, a downward pressure emerged in the 2000s on *both* private disposable income (denominator) and private expenditures (numerator), which meant a downward pressure on the private consumption rate and, consequently, an upward pressure on the

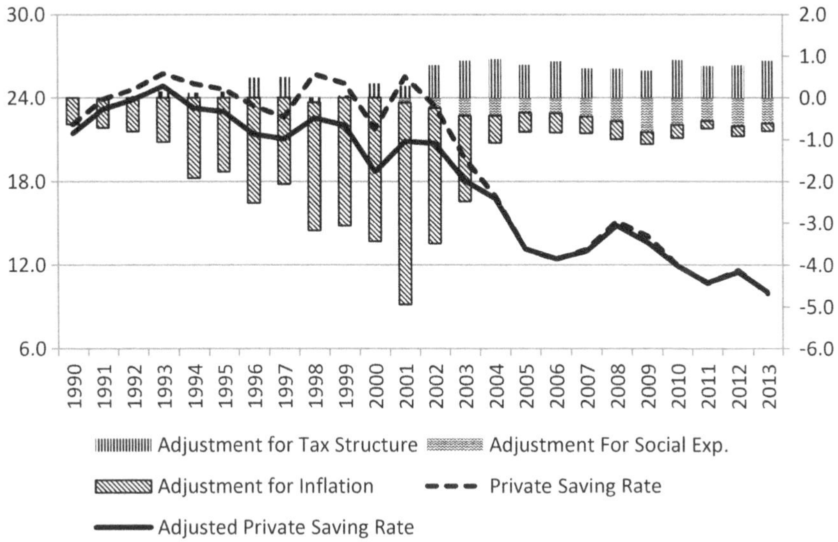

Fig. 2 Adjusted and original private saving rates (1990–2013) (Note: the adjusted private saving rate denotes the private saving rate plus adjustments for tax structure, social expenditures, and inflation. While the *left side* of the vertical axis in the left is for original and adjusted private saving rate figures, the *right side* of the vertical axis is for the adjustments. The base year for the calculation of the adjustments for the tax structure and inflation is the beginning year, 1990. However, it is 2000 for social expenditures because the Turkish Statistical Institute has been publishing social expenditures series only since that year. The tax-structure-adjusted private saving rate was calculated as 1 minus the tax-structure-adjusted private consumption rate (the ratio of private expenditures plus extra collected indirect taxes in excess of 1.3 times collected direct taxes in a given year to private disposable income plus the extra collected indirect taxes in the same year). The social-expenditure-adjusted private saving rate was calculated as 1 minus social-expenditure-adjusted private consumption rate (the ratio of private expenditures plus extra social expenditures in excess of the 2000 level to private disposable income plus extra collected social contributions in excess of the 2000 level). Lastly, the inflation-adjusted private saving rate was calculated as 1 minus the inflation-adjusted private consumption rate (which was calculated by subtracting the realized inflation part of the interest payments made by the government from private disposable income). We are subtracting interest payments from income. The wedge between the original and adjusted private saving rates expands as the inflation effect strengthens in the second half of the 1990s; however, in the 2000s this effect dwindles substantially. While all three of these factors affect the *calculated* private saving rate, only the effect of inflation has an impact on the public saving rate. Therefore, the aggregate saving rate is also affected owing to the other two effects. However, these two effects cancel each other out almost completely, thereby exerting a negligible effect on the aggregate saving rate. Source: Ministry of Development of Turkey, Turkish Statistical Institute, and the author's own calculations)

private saving rate, owing to the fact that if both the denominator and numerator decrease by the same amount, then the overall rate too decreases *mathematically*. As a result, the effect of social expenditures on the private saving rate stood at around 0.5 percentage points on average. That means the social-expenditure-adjusted private saving rate was actually lower by some 0.5 percentage points in the last decade.

Thirdly, inflation plays a distinct, albeit indirect, role in affecting the *calculated* or *perceived* saving rate, apart from its role in prompting households to save more owing to higher uncertainty. Theoretically, the nominal interest consists of two parts, the real interest rate and expected inflation rate. That means realized nominal interest income consists of two parts, real interest income and realized inflation rate. However, not real but nominal interest income counts as capital income. Thus, while the income level of lenders seems higher than it actually is, borrowers face the opposite situation: Their income level seems lower than it is in reality. However, for the whole economy this does not constitute a problem: These two distortionary effects cancel each other out, and overall the saving rate does not change in the end. Yet, if lenders and borrowers are different in nature from a saving behaviour perspective, then the inflation effect looms large. Firstly, if a country is a net borrower in a local currency from abroad, then its overall saving rate seems higher than what it actually is. However, Turkish net foreign debt did not change significantly, though there were some fluctuations, in the 1990s and 2000s. Therefore, the inflation effect is negligible in that dimension. Secondly, if the government is a net borrower chiefly from private individuals in a highly inflationary environment, then while the overall saving rate stands still, the private saving rate seems higher and the public saving rate seems lower than what they actually are. The inflation effect in this dimension is sizeable in Turkey, since both net public debt and the inflation rate were very high in the 1990s compared to the very low levels seen in the 2000s. Numerically, the ratio of net public debt to GDP plummeted from 80 per cent in 2001 to the historically low level of 37 per cent as of 2015. Moreover, the inflation rate was some 77 per cent on average, while the public borrowing rate was roughly 109 per cent in the 1990s. Both rates declined dramatically in the 2000s, eventually falling below 10 per cent. Thus, the inflation effect greatly diminished as the ratio of net public debt to GDP, the inflation rate, and the nominal interest rate plummeted. Therefore, the high level of private and low level of public saving in the 1990s emanates partly from that inflation effect. Consequently, the private saving rate was roughly 3.5 percentage points higher than what it actually was between 1998 and 2002 thanks to the inflation effect at its height. This difference diminished rapidly to only 0.4 percentage points on average between 2004 and 2013, eventually reaching a mere 0.2 percentage points in 2013.

Taken all together, one-third of the decrease in the private saving rate for the periods 2001–2006 and 2001–2013 becomes spurious mostly thanks to the inflation effect since the effects of the changed tax structure and social expenditure pattern on the private saving rate in the 2000s roughly cancel each other out.

6 Different Definitions of Saving

On the other hand, as mentioned earlier, there is no standard agreed-upon definition of *saving*. In this sense, some expenditures can be regarded as investments, not consumption, on the grounds that these expenditures are made not for immediate consumption but for future benefits that will emerge, such as expenditures for education, health, durable goods, and R&D. Therefore, two kinds of saving definitions emerge. Narrowly defined, the saving ratio is the officially calculated rate, while broadly defined the saving ratio corresponds to the saving ratio in which expenditures on education, health, R&D, and even (partly) durable goods are treated as investments.

In fact, expenditures in these categories have expanded tremendously in the 2000s, reflecting the increasingly stronger Turkish economy. Firstly, while education expenditures had been around 2.5 per cent of GDP in the 1990s, it increased significantly in the 2000s, averaging roughly 3.7 per cent and reaching over 4 per cent in 2013. Moreover, the ratio of private education expenditures to GDP first declined and then slightly increased by 0.3 percentage points in the 2000s. Overall, if education expenditures are regarded as expenditures, then the overall saving rate increases by around 4 per cent from 13.4 to around 17.4 per cent as of

2013, and the difference between aggregate saving rates in the 1990s and 2000s diminishes by around 1.5 percentage points.

Secondly, overall health expenditures increased significantly in the 2000s, rising from 3.5 to 4.2 per cent of GDP, a 20 per cent increase in just 14 years between 2000 and 2014. On the other hand, the ratio of private health expenditures to GDP first stagnated and then slightly declined by some 0.1 percentage points in the 2000s, owing to the introduction of near-universal health coverage. Overall, if one regards health expenditures as investments, then the overall saving rate increased by around 4.4 per cent in the 2000s, while the difference between aggregate saving rates in the 1990s and 2000s decreased by some 0.7 percentage points.

Thirdly, the ratio of durable goods consumption to GDP increased significantly, from around 12 per cent on average in the 1990s to some 16 per cent in the 2000s, reaching a stunning 20 per cent in 2014. When the depreciation of durable goods is taken into account, the contribution of durable goods consumption to the overall and private saving rates were around 9 percentage points on average in the 1990s and 14 percentage points between 2004 and 2014. This means that the difference between aggregate saving rates in the 1990s and 2000s diminished by some 5 percentage points under this extended definition of saving.

Lastly, the ratio of R&D expenditures to GDP was around a mere 0.5 per cent in the 1990s. Though not sufficient, this ratio increased steadily in the 2000s, averaging some 0.8 per cent between 2005 and 2013 and reaching around 1 per cent as of 2013. If R&D expenditures are regarded as investments, then the difference in the overall saving rate between the 1990s and 2000s dwindled by another 0.3 percentage points.

As can be seen in Fig. 3, BDASR+D was around 40 per cent in the 1990s and declined significantly from 40.9 per cent to 32.5 per cent between 1998 and 2003; however, the ratio then recovered quickly and increased to some 39 per cent in 2013, reaching the levels attained in the 1990s. On the other hand, the course of BDASR largely resembles that of NDASR, though the decrease in BDASR was only 31 and 29 per cent respectively for the periods 1998–2003 and 1998–2013, compared to 58 and 45 per cent decreases in NDASR for the same periods respectively. Consequently, the decrease in BDASR was around one-half that of

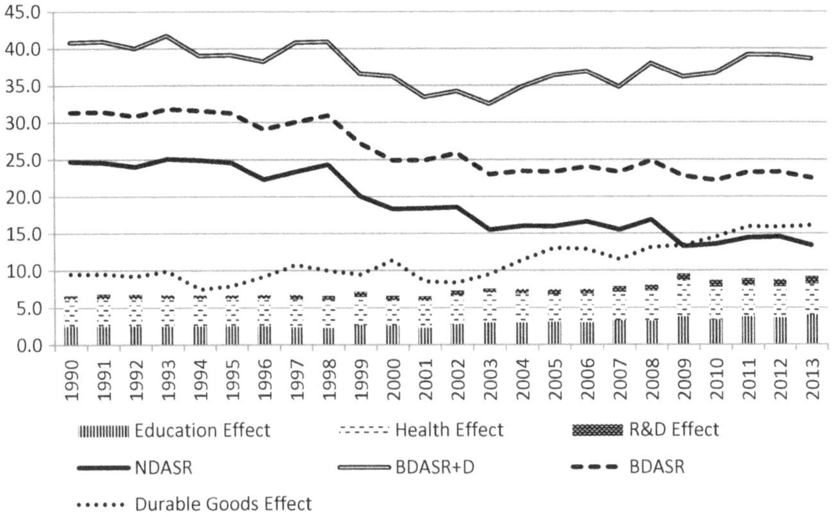

Fig. 3 Narrowly and broadly defined saving ratios (1990–2013) (Note: While NDASR denotes narrowly defined aggregate saving rate, BDASR designates broadly defined aggregate saving rate with education, health, and R&D effects. Lastly, BDASR+D denotes BDASR plus durable goods effect. While BDASR+D has returned roughly to the levels seen in the 1990s in recent years, BDASR declined in the late 1990s and in the early 2000s, as did NDASR, though much less pronouncedly. In the end, while NDASR was below 15 per cent, BDASR stood at 22.5 per cent, and BDASR+D was nearly 40 per cent in the 1990s. On the other hand, education data start in 1997 and health data in 2000. Because of this, the corresponding series were constructed through extrapolation using averages of the next five years for the entire missing period. In addition, there are no direct data for the share of the durable goods in GDP after 2006. Because of this, the series from 1990 to 2006 were extrapolated for the 2007–2013 period using the durable goods expenditure share in household consumption expenditures multiplied by household final consumption share in GDP as a proxy; using this method, the durable goods expenditure share in the overall economy was obtained. Source: Ministry of Development of Turkey, Turkish Statistical Institute, and the author's own calculations)

NDASR for the period 1998–2003 and one-third that for the period 1998–2013.

When all these figures are taken together, it becomes obvious that the rapid decrease in the private and aggregate saving rates in the 2000s cannot be attributed to only increases in perishable consumption. On the contrary, a sizeable portion of the decrease could be accounted for by the significant increase in education and health expenditures, which are both very important for society as a whole as well as for the economy and can easily be regarded as investments. On the other hand, while one-third of the decrease in the private saving rate in the 2000s relative to the 1990s is spurious, the bulk of the decrease in the remaining two-thirds can be attributed to the rapid increase in expenditures on durable goods, which can partly be regarded as investment.

7 Where Are We and What Can We Do About It?

Although the definition of saving seems straightforward, as stated by Crossley et al. (2010, 36), 'there is no single "correct" definition of saving', and the definition of saving simply changes as 'the issue under investigation' changes and dictates its own terms. For example, education expenditures can easily be regarded as saving from the standpoint of policymakers and people who are trying to increase their human capital; however, it also can be regarded as sheer consumption for financial and affordability reasons in the short run. Therefore, policy conclusions regarding saving will largely be contingent upon the circumstances and priorities, such as financing and the need for development.

Therefore, although the Turkish aggregate saving rate plummeted in the late 1990s and in the early 2000s, and has not recovered fully since then, roughly one-half of the fall in the aggregate saving rate in the 2000s can be attributed to the rapid increase in education and health expenditures, which can easily be regarded as investments under broader definitions of saving. Nevertheless, the other half is still an important matter to be dealt with, not to mention there is no unique definition of saving to which everyone subscribes. In addition, one-third of the decrease in the private saving rate in the 2000s is spurious, and the other two-thirds are mostly associated with durable goods consumption, though counting durable goods as investment has its downsides as well as upsides.

Moreover, it is hard to argue that the factors behind the decrease in the saving rate in the 2000s represent generally negative developments. Actually, except for the rapid expansion of credit volumes, other proposed reasons are rather positive developments *in nature*, i.e. decreased inflation rate, expanded social expenditures, and increased public saving.

Therefore, as stressed earlier, the saving rate figure results from a myriad of economic processes, and it is an end product of the real economy. Because of this, any attempt to increase the saving rate *directly* will have numerous unexpected and possibly undesirable consequences. Moreover, empirical evidence in the literature is tilted towards a causality running from economic growth to saving, though there is no consensus on that. Therefore, when all things are considered, rather than trying to increase the saving rate *per se*, one could argue that it would make more sense to focus on economic growth and development, not just because higher income levels will free up more savings and investment, but also because trying to increase savings directly can have detrimental effects on both levels of private consumption, which is the backbone of the real economy with around a 60 per cent share in GDP, and investments on education, R&D, health, and the like, which are of paramount importance for the future trajectory of the economy.

On the other hand, while financial deepening can have a considerably positive impact on the real economy, rapid credit expansion and deteriorating credit composition, i.e. higher share of credit directed to unproductive areas, can significantly harm the economy. In this sense, in an empirical study, Cecchetti and Kharroubi (2015) conclude that

> the faster the financial sector expands, the slower the real economy grows … [and] financial growth disproportionately harms industries *the less tangible their assets or the more R&D intensive* they are. [Italics added]

Therefore, limiting credit expansion and, maybe more importantly, improving credit composition by directing much more credit to productive industries away from unproductive ones and the bubble-prone housing sector with smart financial policies is of paramount importance. Such a policy will have the potential to create two desirable outcomes: on the one hand, it will induce households to save more, for *the betterment of the economy*, and on the other hand, it will increase the productivity level of the entire economy, greatly contributing to economic growth and income levels and, hence, the saving rate.

A desirable and enhanced credit composition can be achieved through several policies, such as developing Islamic financial instruments and creating wealth and pension funds, among others. Islamic finance, which has the built-in advantage of being *directly* connected to the real economy, offers important opportunities in this regard. Developing carefully designed financial instruments via financial engineering within the tradition of Islamic finance can contribute greatly to the real economy and improve credit composition to a remarkable extent. Moreover, wealth and pension funds, which can be founded and run by either state or state-sponsored private enterprises, have the potential to channel funds to much-needed projects and industries much more directly and swiftly and for a much longer period than the traditional banking industry is willing to do. The Turkish state, actually, took important *preliminary* steps in this direction by founding the Turkish Wealth Fund, whose portfolio value reached USD 160 billion within just six months after its creation in August 2016, and by introducing a mandatory pension fund, BES (Bireysel Emeklilik Sistemi, or Individual Pension System), with the option of opting-out in January 2017.

Another factor presumably contributing to the decreasing saving rate in the 2000s is the global liquidity abundance, first in the early 2000s and then in the aftermath of the global financial crisis of 2008–2009, which almost perfectly overlaps with the decreasing saving rates in Turkey. Actually, this abundance of liquidity is one of the major factors of the rapid credit expansion in Turkey in the 2000s, among other reasons. In addition, it is now perfectly clear that the total elimination of barriers to international capital flows resulted in a much less stable global economy with numerous financial crisis.

In this regard, capital controls, which had been an integral part of the global financial structure under the Bretton Woods system and which was abandoned almost totally in the neoliberal era, has made a curious comeback in the wake of the global financial crisis. Several mainstream economists began to question the existing financial structure and address the possible benefits of some sort of capital controls. Shockingly, even the International Monetary Fund, once an ardent promoter of unfettered financial markets, has begun to advocate some sort of capital controls, among numerous others (Ostry et al. 2016; Magud et al. 2011; Kim and Doo Yong Yang 2012). Thus, implementing some sort of capital controls can mitigate both financial instability in an era of very high current account deficits and unproductive credit expansion in Turkey. In the end, the saving rate would be affected rather positively, both directly and indirectly.

References

Agrawal, Pradeep, Pravakar Sahoo, and Ranjan Kumar Dash. 2009. Savings Behaviour in South Asia. *Journal of Policy Modeling* 31 (2): 208–224.

Alkin, Erdoğan. 1970. 1951–1971 Dönemi Yatırım, Tasarruf ve Sermaye-Hasıla Oranları. *İktisat Fakültesi Mecmuası* 30 (1–4): 141–161.

Andrei, Elena-Adriana, and Cătălin-Emilian Huidumac-Petrescu. 2013. Saving and Economic Growth: An Empirical Analysis for Euro Area Countries. *Theoretical and Applied Economics* 20 (7): 43–58.

Attanasio, Orazio P., Lucio Picci, and Antonello E. Scorcu. 2000. Saving, Growth, and Investment: A Macroeconomic Analysis Using a Panel of Countries. *Review of Economics and Statistics* 82 (2): 182–211.

Audenis, Cédric, Stephane Grégoir, and Claudie Louvot. 2002. *The Various Measures of the Saving Rate and Their Interpretation*. Meeting of the OECD National Accounts Experts, OECD.

Bayoumi, Tamim. 1993. Financial Deregulation and Household Saving. *The Economic Journal* 103 (421): 1432–1443.

Bérubé, Gilles, and Denise Côté. 2000. Long-term Determinants of the Personal Savings Rate: Literature Review and Some Empirical Results for Canada. *Bank of Canada Working Paper* 3: 1–58.

Cecchetti, Stephen G., and Enisse Kharroubi. 2015. Why Does Financial Sector Growth Crowd Out Real Economic Growth? *CEPR Discussion Papers* 10642: 1–28.

Claus, Iris, and Grant Scobie. 2002. Saving in New Zealand: Measurement and Trends. *New Zealand Treasury Working Paper* 02 (02): 1–41.

Crossley, Thomas F., Cormac O'Dea, and Lionel Browne. 2010. *The Wealth and Saving of UK Families on the Eve of the Crisis*. London: Institute for Fiscal Studies.

DPT. 2010. *9th Development Plan (2007–2013)*: State Planning Organization of Turkey (T.C. Devlet Planlama Teşkilatı – DPT).
Edwards, Sebastian. 1996. Why Are Latin America's Savings Rates So Low? An International Comparative Analysis. *Journal of Development Economics* 51 (1): 5–44.
Ekinci, Aykut, and Ekrem Gül. 2007. Türkiye'de Yurtiçi Tasarruflar ve Ekonomik Büyüme Arasındaki İlişki: Uygulamalı Bir Analiz (1960–2004). *Dumlupınar Üniversitesi Sosyal Bilimler Dergisi* 19: 167–184.
Feldstein, Martin. 1980. International Differences in Social Security and Saving. *Journal of Public Economics* 14 (2): 225–244.
Gorman, Emma, Grant M. Scobie, and Yongjoon Paek. 2013. Measuring Saving Rates in New Zealand: An Update. *New Zealand Treasury Working Paper* 13 (04): 1–62.
Hevia, Constantino. 2010. Saving in Turkey: An International Comparison. In *Background Study for the CEM*. Ankara: World Bank.
Hondroyiannis, George. 2006. Private Saving Determinants in European Countries: A Panel Cointegration Approach. *The Social Science Journal* 43 (4): 553–569.
Horioka, Charles Yuji, and Ting Yin. 2009. Household Saving Rates and Social Benefit Ratios: Country Comparisons. In *Effects of Social Policy on Domestic Demand: Annual Conference*, Tokyo.
Hüfner, Felix, and Isabell Koske. 2010. *Explaining Household Saving Rates in G7 Countries*. Paris: OECD Publishing.
Jouini, Jamel. 2016. Economic Growth and Savings in Saudi Arabia: Empirical Evidence from Cointegration and Causality Analysis. *Asia-Pacific Journal of Accounting & Economics* 23 (4): 478–495.
Keynes, John Maynard. 1936. *The General Theory of Interest, Employment and Money*. London: Macmillan.
Kim, Soyoung, and Jong-Wha Lee. 2008. Demographic Changes, Saving, and Current Account: An Analysis Based on a Panel VAR Model. *Japan and the World Economy* 20 (2): 236–256.
Kim, Soyoung, and Doo Yong Yang. 2012. Are Capital Controls Effective? The Case of the Republic of Korea. *Asian Development Review* 29 (2): 96–135.
Kónya, László. 2004. *Saving and Growth: Granger Causality Analysis with Bootstrapping on Panels of Countries*. Bundoora: La Trobe University, School of Business.
Li, Hongbin, Jie Zhang, and Junsen Zhang. 2007. Effects of Longevity and Dependency Rates on Saving and Growth: Evidence from a Panel of Cross Countries. *Journal of Development Economics* 84 (1): 138–154.

Loayza, Norman, Klaus Schmidt-Hebbel, and Luis Servén. 2000a. Saving in Developing Countries: An Overview. *The World Bank Economic Review* 14 (3): 393–414.

———. 2000b. What Drives Private Saving Across the World? *Review of Economics and Statistics* 82 (2): 165–181.

Magud, Nicolas E., Carmen M. Reinhart, and Kenneth S. Rogoff. 2011. *Capital Controls: Myth and Reality-a Portfolio Balance Approach*, 1–46, NBER Working Papers (16805).

Masson, Paul R., Tamim Bayoumi, and Hossein Samiei. 1998. International Evidence on the Determinants of Private Saving. *The World Bank Economic Review* 12 (3): 483–501.

Matur, Eser Pirgan, Ali Sabuncu, and Sema Bahçeci. 2012. Determinants of Private Saving and Interaction Between Public and Private Savings in Turkey. *Topics in Middle Eastern and North African Economies* 14: 102–125.

Mehta, Sachin N., and Gaurang D. Rami. 2014. Nexus Between Savings, Investment and Economic Growth in India. *Voice of Research* 3 (3): 37–40.

Modigliani, Franco. 1986. Life Cycle, Individual Thrift, and the Wealth of Nations. *The American Economic Review* 76 (3): 297–313.

Mohan, Ramesh. 2006. Causal Relationship Between Savings and Economic Growth in Countries with Different Income Levels. *Economics Bulletin* 5 (3): 1–12.

Najarzadeh, Reza, Michael Reed, and Mona Tasan. 2014. Relationship Between Savings and Economic Growth: The Case for Iran. *Journal of International Business and Economics* 2 (4): 107–124.

Odhiambo, Nicholas M. 2009. Savings and Economic Growth in South Africa: A Multivariate Causality Test. *Journal of Policy Modeling* 31 (5): 708–718.

Odionye, Joseph Chukwudi, Okwudili Beede Emerole, and Ugochukwu Sebastine Ugwuebe. 2016. Savings and Economic Growth Nexus: Evidence from Nigeria. *Developing Country Studies* 6 (4): 112–118.

Orthofer, Anna. 2015. What We Talk About When We Talk About Saving: Concepts and Measures of Household Saving and Their Application to South Africa. *Economic Research Southern Africa Working Paper* 530: 1–39.

Ostry, Jonathan D., Prakash Loungani, and Davide Furceri. 2016. Neoliberalism: Oversold? *Finance & Development* 53 (2): 38–41.

Reinsdorf, Marshall B. 2004. Alternative Measures of Personal Saving. *Survey of Current Business* 84 (9): 17–27.

Rocher, Stijn, and Michael Stierle. 2015. Household Saving Rates in the EU: Why Do They Differ So Much? *European Commission Discussion Papers* 005: 1–30.

Schrooten, Mechthild, and Sabine Stephan. 2002. Back on Track? Savings Puzzles in EU-Accession Countries. *DIW Discussion Papers* 306: 1–31.
Singh, Tarlok. 2010. Does Domestic Saving Cause Economic Growth? A Time-Series Evidence from India. *Journal of Policy Modeling* 32 (2): 231–253.
Tang, Chor Foon, and Bee Wah Tan. 2014. A Revalidation of the Savings–Growth Nexus in Pakistan. *Economic Modelling* 36: 370–377.
Tatliyer, Mevlüt. 2017. Determinants of Private Saving Level: Evidence from Turkey. *Sosyoekonomi* 25 (32): 149–167.
Uygur, Ercan. 2012. Türkiye'de Tasarrufların Seyri ve Etkileyen Bazı Unsurlar. *Turkish Economic Association Discussion Paper* 108: 1–17.
Waithima, Abraham K. 2008. The Egg or the Chick First, Saving or GDP Growth: Case for Kenya. *KCA Journal of Business Management* 1 (1): 1–10.
Zeldes, Stephen P. 1989. Consumption and Liquidity Constraints: An Empirical Investigation. *The Journal of Political Economy* 97 (2): 305–346.

Part III

Real Economy, Trade and Energy

Towards Inclusive Growth and Sustainable Development: Science, Technology, and Innovation Strategies and Policy Implications

Emine Nur Ozkan-Gunay
and Gozde Nur Kazazoglu-Sahin

1 Introduction

Economic and social development, which is also called 'inclusive growth', occurs when the standard of living and welfare improve in all dimensions of life – real income, education, health, infrastructure, and political representation. Therefore, the concept of inclusive growth is multidimensional and multisectional, capturing all segments of the society. The main questions for sustainable development are why inclusive growth is important and how it can be achieved.

E. N. Ozkan-Gunay (✉)
Grand National Assembly of Turkey, Ankara, Turkey

G. N. Kazazoglu-Sahin
Istanbul Technical University, Istanbul, Turkey

A. F. Aysan et al. (eds.), *Turkish Economy*,
https://doi.org/10.1007/978-3-319-70380-0_12

First of all, inclusive growth is important because rising inequality in earnings and standard of living is a major concern all around the world. Oxfam (2017) states that a world in which 1 per cent of humanity controls as much wealth as the other 99 per cent will never be stable. Since 2015, the richest 1 per cent has owned more wealth than the rest of the planet. The top segment capturing the lion's share of growth is a worldwide problem as much as it is a regional and national one.

Multidimensional inclusive policies aim to raise the pace of growth and expand the size of the economy, while all segments benefit fairly. Therefore, it depends on increasing international competitiveness by improving productivity in employment, investing in research and development (R&D) and innovation, producing high-value-added products, and changing income redistribution schemes. Here, the key concept is knowledge, where technology, creativity, and innovation are cultivated to strengthen global competitiveness.

Secondly, the transition from middle-income to high-income levels has become an increasingly universal phenomenon especially among emerging economies. Many emerging market economies grew rapidly during the first decade of the twenty-first century, advancing from the ranks of low-income to middle-income countries. However, the transition from middle-income to high-income status is much harder to achieve. Since the 1960s just 13 out of 101 middle-income economies have managed to move from middle-income to high-income status, accounting for slightly over 4 per cent of the world's population (World Bank 2017). The main reason for this difficulty in transition is the so-called middle-income trap, an economic development stage in which a country's growth slows down after reaching middle-income levels. Escaping the middle-income trap has become harder since the global economic crisis owing to a slowdown in global economic growth and trade.

Science, technology, and innovation (STI) are the main pillars of a knowledge-based economy and sustainable development (Fig. 1). It is found that countries that have STI-oriented global competitiveness strategies demonstrate sustainable competitiveness, growth, and development. Therefore, STI-oriented economic strategies and policies should inform structural reforms to achieve sustainable global competitiveness.

Fig. 1 Innovation policy (World Bank 2010)

These developments in emerging economies in the first decade of the twenty-first century and the challenge of escaping the middle-income trap in this post–global economic crisis age has become the driving force for this study. We believe that STI and inclusive growth will be major drivers fostering sustainable development in emerging economies. The purpose of the study is to analyse the national science, technology, and innovation (NSTI) policies in Turkey, to reveal the implications of NSTI policies for society, to compare Turkey's current status with that of Organisation for Economic Co-operation and Development (OECD) and European Union (EU) countries, to develop custom-made policy recommendations as second-generation STI reforms based on the economic and social realities of Turkey to meet 2023 Goals.

This chapter is organized as follows. Section 2 introduces the NSTI policies and their impacts in Turkey, and Section 3 provides a brief comparison of Turkey, OECD countries, and the EU based on STI performance indicators. The final part proposes policy recommendations as second-generation STI reforms that are designed around inclusive growth.

2 STI Policies in Turkey

Turkey is a fast-growing and promising middle-income emerging country at the crossroads of Europe and Asia that is dealing with the middle-income trap and income inequality. The Turkish economy ranks 17th among 196 countries with a gross domestic product (GDP) of USD 850 billion. The income per capita over the past 14 years has risen from USD 3,580 to nearly USD 10,800 in 2016. The increasing trend in GDP and GDP per capita is amazing when we compare the data with those from 2002 and 2008, USD 3,580 and USD 10,930, respectively. This improvement is based on sectoral reforms, including the restructuring of the banking and financial system and prudent macroeconomic policies. Unfortunately, Turkey has also been experiencing the middle-income trap since the early 2010s. Turkey has apparently hit a milestone in its dynamic transformation from traditional resource-based growth to knowledge-based growth, where comparative advantage is based on productivity, innovation, and R&D.

The government's broad-based goals, which are known as Vision 2023, are to more than double GDP to USD 2 trillion, triple Turkish exports to USD 500 billion, and increase the employment rate to 55 per cent. These ambitious goals can only be realized by focusing on knowledge-based inclusive growth with a concrete roadmap and an action plan. A number of STI policies to foster the integration of research and entrepreneurial activities have been implemented since 2004. The Turkish Research Area (TARAL) was introduced to focus on the mobilization and collaboration of R&D and innovation among business and public sectors, together with non-governmental organizations. The specific TARAL objectives are to enhance the quality of life, find innovative solutions to societal needs, increase the competitiveness of the country, and foster and diffuse STI awareness in society. The main policy tools for reaching TARAL targets are relate to the share of R&D expenditures in GDP, the demand for R&D, and the number of qualified R&D personnel.

Turkey's NSTI policy is based on the National Science, Technology, and Innovation Strategy (NSTIS) 2011–2016 and the Tenth Development Plan 2014–18. The vision of the NSTIS (2011–2016) is 'to contribute to new knowledge and develop innovative technologies to improve the quality of life by transforming the former into products, processes, and services for the benefit of the country and humanity' (TUBITAK 2010). Targets for gross expenditure on R&D (GERD) and business expenditure on R&D (BERD) were set by the Supreme Council for Science and Technology (SCST) to reach 3 per cent and 2 per cent of GDP respectively by 2023.

The main indicators of STI policies are defined as GERD as a percentage of GDP, GERD by sector performance, percentage of GERD by sector performance, percentage of GERD by source of funds, R&D human resources, number of scientific publications and the ranking of Turkey with respect to scientific publications. Progress in the main indicators of STI policies are summarized in Table 1.

R&D expenditures have increased significantly from USD 5.4 billion in 2006 to USD 16.2 billion in 2015, jumping by 322 per cent. The highest spending in R&D belongs to the private sector, with USD 8 billion, showing impressive progress since 2006. This is followed by the government sector, with 176 per cent, and higher education, with 124 per cent. Consequently, GERD as a share of GDP has almost doubled, reaching 1.06 per cent in 2015. The business sector led until 2012, but later private-sector R&D expenditures exceeded that of the other two sectors, signalling a new phase in R&D investments. Government R&D expenditures stayed relatively low throughout the period.

In 2006, total R&D personnel were around 54,000 people, which increased to 122,000 in 2015. Full-time equivalent (FTE) R&D personnel increased by 126 per cent from 2006 to 2015, while a striking increase of 322 per cent was seen between 2002 and 2015. On the other hand, FTE researchers more than doubled in number, from 43,000 in 2006 to 95,000 researchers in 2015. The distribution of FTE R&D personnel among sectors in 2015 was as follows: 54.5 per cent in business, 35.4 per cent in higher education, and 10.1 per cent in the government sector. With respect to gender employment, the ratio of female R&D personnel was 31 per cent in 2015. The highest female R&D personnel employment was in higher education, at 42 per cent, then government at 26 per cent, and business at 24 per cent.

Table 1 Main indicators of STI policies in Turkey

Indicator	2006	2015	Change, 2006–2015 (%)
GERD as a Percentage of GDP	0.60	1.06	77
GERD by Sector Performance (million PPP$)			
GERD by Business Sector	1,923	8,117	322
GERD by Higher Education Sector	2,879	6,438	124
GERD by Government Sector	607	1,678	176
Percentage of GERD by Performance of Sectors			
GERD share of Private Sector[a]	24.20	49.80	106
GERD share of Higher Education Sector[a]	67.90	40.50	−40
GERD share of Government Sector[a]	8.00	9.70	21
Percentage of GERD by Source of Funds			
Percentage of GERD by Industry	44.30	50.10	13
Percentage of GERD by Government	34.60	27.60	−20
Percentage of GERD by Higher Education	15.70	18.10	15
Percentage of GERD by Other National Sources	4.80	3.20	−33
Percentage of GERD by Foreign Sources	0.60	1.00	67
Number of R&D Human Resources (in thousands)			
FTE[b] R&D Personnel	54	122	126
FTE Researcher	43	95	121
Number of Scientific Publications	15,344	29,319	91

Source: TUBITAK 2017

[a]The GERD share of the private sector, higher education sector, and government sector starts from 2004

[b]FTE stands for Full Time Equivalent

As the main output of R&D investments, the number of scientific publications increased by 204 per cent between 2002 and 2014 and 91 per cent between 2006 and 2015. However, the rank of Turkey with respect to scientific publications has not changed much. Turkey ranks 18th in 2015, ranging between 18th and 20th since 2006.

R&D expenditures as a share of GDP by sector confirm the trend of R&D expenditures by sector. The share of government R&D expenditures shows a stable trend, whereas the share of higher education R&D expenditures declined from 67.9 per cent in 2004 to 40.5 per cent in 2014 (Fig. 2). On the other hand, the share of private sector climbed

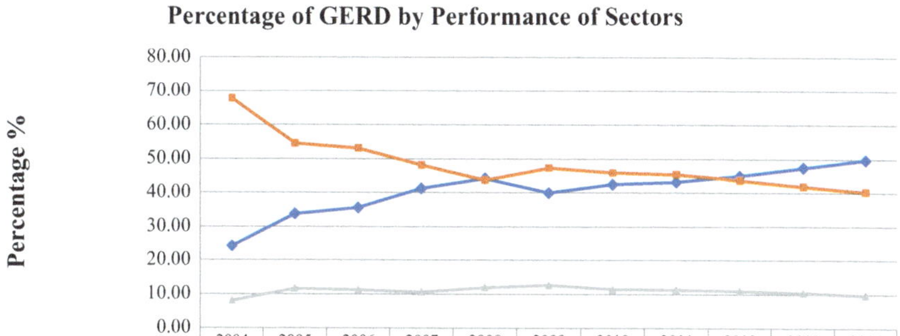

	2004	2005	2006	2007	2008	2009	2010	2011	2012	2013	2014
Business Enterprise	24.20	33.80	35.60	41.30	44.20	40.00	42.50	43.20	45.10	47.50	49.80
Higher Education	67.90	54.60	53.20	48.20	43.80	47.40	46.00	45.50	43.90	42.10	40.50
Government	8.00	11.60	11.20	10.60	11.90	12.60	11.40	11.30	11.00	10.40	9.70

Fig. 2 Percentage of GERD by sector performance (TUBITAK 2017)

from 24.2 per cent in 2004 to 49.8 per cent in 2014. Half of the total R&D expenditures was made by the business enterprise sector. This represents promising progress because the private sector is the engine of R&D expenditures in most developed countries. According to OECD data, by 2015 private-sector R&D as a share of total R&D expenditures was 77 per cent in Japan, 64 per cent in the USA, and 61 per cent in Sweden.

The business sector ranks first, with 50.1 per cent among R&D financers. This is followed by the government sector at 27.6 per cent, and then higher education sector at 18.1 per cent, with other national sources at 3.2 per cent and foreign funds at 1.1 per cent (Fig. 3). These figures show that R&D expenditures by international financers are the lowest. In developed countries, however, according to OECD data, by 2015 the share of international financers was 10.3 per cent in Sweden, 5 per cent in the USA, and 4.7 per cent in Japan. This can be interpreted as indicating that Turkey as a developing country needs to invest in its clustering and specialization mechanisms in certain R&D sectors so that it can become a globally known hub in certain sectors that can attract foreign funds like the developed countries.

Moreover, the share of scientific publications and patents produced domestically with at least one co-author abroad is weak compared to other OECD countries. Therefore, four measures have been taken to

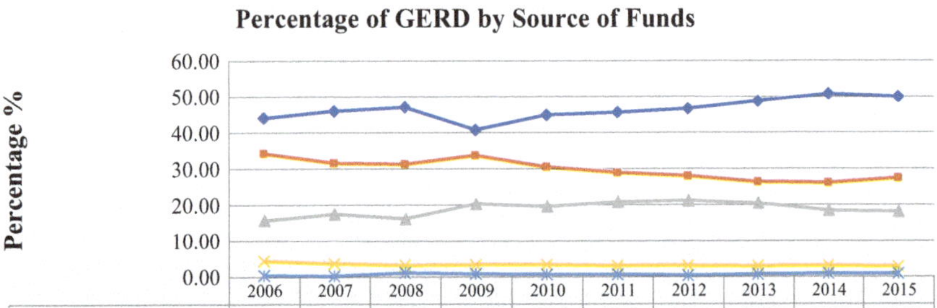

	2006	2007	2008	2009	2010	2011	2012	2013	2014	2015
Industry	44.30	46.20	47.30	41.00	45.10	45.80	46.80	48.90	50.90	50.10
Government	34.60	31.90	31.60	34.00	30.80	29.20	28.20	26.60	26.30	27.60
Higher Education	15.70	17.50	16.20	20.30	19.60	20.80	21.10	20.40	18.40	18.10
Other National Sources	4.80	4.00	3.60	3.70	3.70	3.40	3.40	3.30	3.40	3.20
Abroad	0.60	0.40	1.30	1.00	0.80	0.80	0.50	0.80	1.00	1.00

Fig. 3 Percentage of GERD by source of funds (TUBITAK 2017)

improve cooperation among Turkish and international researchers and the penetration of Turkish companies in global markets. Firstly, the Turkish National Researcher Information System (ARBIS) was developed to create an ecosystem for research personnel in universities and the public and private sectors in Turkey and Turkish researchers serving abroad (ARBIS 2017). ARBIS is a dynamic system that provides national scientists a database and information exchange platform. Secondly, the TUBITAK National Research Infrastructure Information System (TARABIS) was designed as a web-based application to foster collaboration and communication in product and technology development activities between laboratories and industry (TARABIS 2017). Thirdly, the Incubation and Accelerator Support Program was introduced to support Turkish companies globally by the SME Development Organization. The aim is to accelerate Turkish companies' penetration in international markets, to support start-ups, and to form a bridge between domestic companies and Turkish researchers abroad. KOSGEB provided USD 4 million for the establishment of incubation centres in the USA in 2016. There are five incubation centres in the USA. Lastly, the Investment Support and Promotion Agency of Turkey (ISPAT) was established to attract foreign R&D investments.

In short, Turkey has made significant progress in building up its STI capacities and improved international STI cooperation with the rest of the world and is committed to sustaining its investment in STI.

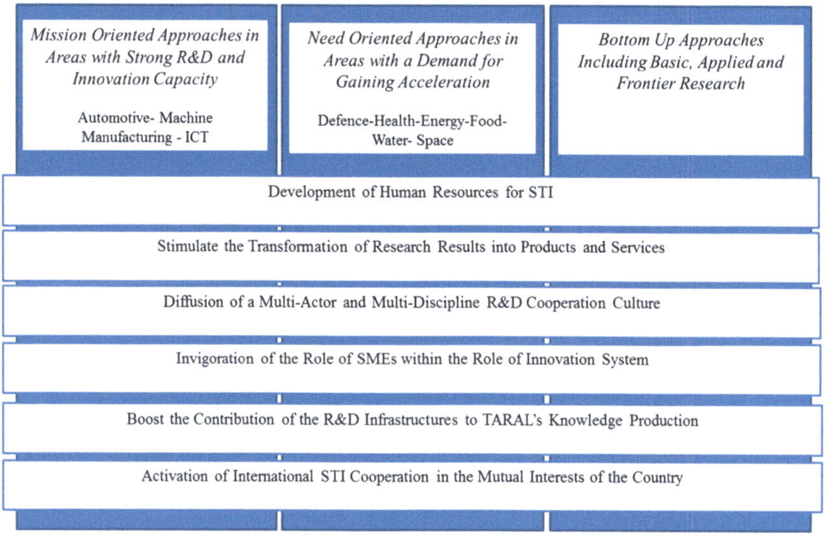

Fig. 4 NSTIS for 2011–2016 (TUBITAK 2010)

The NSTIS for 2011–2016 focuses on disseminating a culture of multilateral and multidisciplinary RDI cooperation, stimulating sectoral and regional RDI dynamics, encouraging SMEs to become stronger actors within the national innovation system, and enhancing the contribution of research infrastructures to the knowledge-creation capacity within the national innovation system. The strategic framework of the NSTIS (2011–2016) is composed of three vertical axes and six horizontal axes that intersect with the vertical ones (Fig. 4).

As an important follow-up phase to improve STI policy, an impact assessment of support programmes was conducted. The lessons learned during the implementation of the NSTIS 2011–2016 and ongoing impact assessment exercises will form the basis of the new NSTIS 2017–2023. The Coordination Council for R&D was founded in 2011 to evaluate all national support schemes and mechanisms for research commercialization. Performance indices for techno-parks, universities, and R&D centres in the business sector were introduced by the Minister of Development and TUBITAK in 2011 and the monitoring process was implemented starting at that time.

It is obvious that a significant improvement in the NSTI system in Turkey took place in the 2000s. However, a comparative approach may provide a better understanding of Turkey's competitiveness at the international level.

3 Comparative Performance of NSTI Systems

Innovation and R&D policies are vital at all stages of development. The creation and diffusion of technologies across all regions represent the most important phase of a knowledge-based economy and improvement of wealth. To see the current situation about the impact of STI policies and to design additional STI policies in Turkey, benchmarking Turkey against the OECD and EU may provide a foundation.

The comparative approach is based on eight dimensions to evaluate Turkey's progress with respect to OECD and EU averages (OECD 2012, 2016). Innovation competence and capacity constitute the first dimension of comparative performance, innovation skills and interaction the second dimension, economic and environmental performance the third, structural aspects and specialization of STI policies the fourth, and the NSTI policy mix the fifth dimension.

OECD Science, Technology and Innovation Outlook 2016 (OECD STI 2016) presents a comparison of Turkey with the EU28 average and middle range of OECD values with respect to the performance of national science and innovation systems. Based on 10 parameters – public R&D expenditures, scientific publications, top 500 universities per GDP, business R&D expenditure, triadic patent families and trademarks per GDP, top 500 corporate R&D investors per GDP, venture capital per GDP, young patenting firms per GDP and ease of entrepreneurship index, innovation competence, and capacity – Turkey is compared with the OECD median and EU average in terms of universities and public research, R&D and innovation in firms, and innovative entrepreneurship. While the EU and OECD show similar patterns, Turkey performs poorly with respect to almost all subparameters compared to the EU average and OECD median. EU shows a better performance in terms of top 500 universities, top 500 corporate R&D investors, triadic patent families, and young patenting firms. In that regard, Turkey has increased its support for R&D, mainly through tax incentives. Between 2002 and 2012, R&D spending as a share of GDP nearly doubled. Meanwhile, patent applications increased by a factor of six, trademark applications increased by a factor of three, and industrial design applications doubled. In fact, Turkey received the third most applications in accordance with the Patent Cooperation Treaty (PCT) among middle-income countries in 2013. These will all feed into a larger share of medium- and high-technology intensive production of goods and services and exports in the Turkish economy.

Turkey lags behind OECD and EU countries, especially in the innovative entrepreneurship component. Even though there is increased interest from international angel investor networks and domestic investors, venture capital investment in Turkey is still in its infancy. There are many start-up companies with innovative ideas, but access to financing is very limited in the early stage. Thus, several tech and incubation centres, especially at universities, have been established to develop an entrepreneurial ecosystem in Turkey. On the other hand, entrepreneurship conditions in Turkey have improved significantly according to the World Bank's Ease of Doing Business Index and the Global Competitiveness Index since 2002 owing to STI reforms over the past decade. The goal is to design a well-functioning STI ecosystem around the business sector and entrepreneurs.

The Ministry of Science, Industry and Technology created a support mechanism for the promotion and marketing of technological products in 2013, and then a technological product investment support programme was launched in 2014. Recently, many support mechanisms and policy initiatives have been introduced for SMEs and entrepreneurs. The acquisition of foreign high-tech companies and R&D centres was allowed in 2014; international incubation centres were established in 2015, and the scope of business-sector R&D centres was expanded to R&D design issues in 2016.

Another aspect of the knowledge-based economy is the commercialization of ideas through patents and trademarks. Even though there is a close relation between universities and industry in Turkey, patent application is poor in number. A series of initiatives has been introduced. TUBITAK introduced special support programmes for industry–science collaboration through large-scale R&D projects and temporary employment opportunities at research centres for academic staff. The Technology Development Foundation of Turkey (TTGV) was founded for the purpose of providing financial assistance to firms willing to develop prototypes and providing training programmes on technology assessment, the management of intellectual property and licences, business development, and alternative funding models for start-ups. One of the most important steps strengthening Turkey's high-tech base was the launch of the Public-University-Industry Partnership Strategy and Action Plan (2015–2018). Moreover, Turkey implemented three initiatives related to intellectual property rights.

In terms of the interactions and skills innovation subparameters, which is the second dimension of the comparison, Turkey placed in the bottom half of the OECD median, except industry-financed public R&D expenditures and tertiary education expenditures per GDP. Turkey underperforms on information and communications technology (ICT) and Internet performance indicators as well as the number of fixed and wireless broadband subscriptions per capita and e-government indices (OECD 2016). The EU average is also in the bottom half of the OECD median with respect to ICT investment, fixed broadband subscriptions, wireless broadband subscriptions, tertiary education, and adult population in tertiary education.

To improve IT infrastructure, the 2015–2018 Information Society Strategy and Action Plan were launched to meet Turkey's information society goals, including expansion of its broadband infrastructure, distribution of more effective public services, improvement of the diffusion of ICT, and support of e-commerce.

Turkey showed better performance than the EU average in industry-financed public R&D expenditures and tertiary education expenditures. It is not just the expenditures, but the quality of education and training has improved based on the requirements of the labour market. In July 2017, a new national curriculum at both the primary and secondary education levels was introduced to establish essential knowledge in reading, writing, science, and mathematics. Turkey also collaborates in a European-wide support programme for science, technology, engineering, and mathematics (STEM) teachers and researchers. The Ministry of Education introduced the Fatih Project to integrate state-of-the-art computer technology into Turkey's public education system to improve ICT competences and skills. It is the greatest and most comprehensive educational reform with respect to education technology use in the world. Another bit of important progress is that Turkey has quadrupled the number of FTE researchers since 2002 from almost nothing.

It is obvious that, according to the OECD STI 2012 data, Turkey outpaces OECD and EU averages in terms of economic performance, as indicated by labour productivity and GDP per hour worked. However, Turkey's productivity performance is less than half that of the USA in 2012. This shows the need for further reforms and investments to boost productivity. On the other hand, Turkey underperforms in terms of environmental performance, measured by green productivity (GDP per unit of CO2 emitted) with respect to the OECD and EU averages. However, a sharp increase after 2012 is noticeable in Turkey. The gap between the OECD and Turkey in terms of environmental performance is shrinking. Turkey's unemployment and youth unemployment rates were slightly higher than the OECD and EU averages, 10.3 per cent and 18.5 per cent respectively by 2015, whereas vulnerable unemployment was much higher in Turkey at 29.4 per cent by 2015 (OECD STI 2016). Vulnerable employment is usually associated with inadequate earnings, low productivity and difficult working conditions, and the unregistered economy.

Structural aspects and specialization is represented by GERD in selected areas such as biotechnologies, ICT, and environment-related technologies; Turkey's performance is again compared with the OECD median and EU28.

According to the OECD STI 2012 data, the EU has an advantage in biotechnologies and environment-related technologies compared to the OECD median. Turkey underperforms in all three sectors but has a better positioning in biotechnologies than in environment-related technologies versus ICT. Therefore, Turkey established its priority sectors with high value added in its Tenth Development Plan 2014–2018 and the Turkish Industry Strategy 2015–2018. Nano- and biotechnology industries were identified as priority sectors among other high-tech industries.

OECD STI 2012 also represents a cobweb plot presenting Turkey's structural composition of business R&D with respect to the OECD median and Turkey's position in 2007. With respect to the OECD median, Turkey outperforms in the services industry, medium- to low-tech manufacturing, and knowledge-intensive market services and underperforms in industry, high-tech manufacturing, and non-knowledge-intensive services. Turkey is close to the OECD median in non-resource-based manufacturing and primary and resource-based industries. When Turkey's progress from 2007 to 2013 is considered, a significant improvement is noticed in industry and knowledge-intensive market services. Conversely, deterioration in the same period is observed in industry, non-resource-based manufacturing, and high-tech manufacturing.

Therefore, Turkey identified its priority sectors with high value added in its Tenth Development Plan 2014–2018 and Turkish Industry Strategy 2015–2018. Energy, IT, health, automotive, aviation, railway, defence, and nano- and biotechnology industries were identified as 'targeted sectors' to boost Turkey's efficiency and competitiveness in medium- and high-tech manufacturing, which would allow it to become one of the leading production bases in Eurasia and Africa in medium- and high-tech products. The Tenth Development Plan also encourages a cluster-oriented and entrepreneurship-focused innovation system.

OECD STI 2016 maintains a comparison of the Turkey's 2015 national STI policy mix with the country's 2007 performance and OECD median in terms of allocation of public funds to R&D. A similar pattern is observed for Turkey and the EU with respect to balance in higher education R&D expenditures, funding of national performers, and public funding. Firstly, university research activities dominate public research in Turkey, the EU, and the OECD. Secondly, research oriented towards civil society counterbalances defence-oriented research. Direct funding dominates in the EU, whereas Turkey presents a more balanced position between direct and indirect funding. Publicly funded R&D research dominates private-sector-funded R&D in Turkey, the EU, and the OECD. Currently, initiatives and measures are being taken to improve the quality of public research in collaboration with the private sector. Performance-based funding models were introduced in 2014 in the universities to establish a sustainable research infrastructure and environment.

In addition, according to Turkey's self-assessment index, in most relevant instruments of public funding of business R&D by 2016, direct funding instruments, such as competitive grants, debt financing and risk-sharing mechanisms, repayable advances, and public procurement, are more functional in Turkey in comparison to the OECD median, whereas tax incentives for business R&D is preferred as the form of indirect funding.

Based on the findings of the comparative approach presented in this section, recommendations for STI policies are proposed in the next section.

4 Policy Recommendation for Second Phase of NSTI Strategy

Turkey has strong macroeconomic fundamentals and is committed to making structural reforms in its STI capacities in collaboration with the rest of the world. Turkey has made significant progress in building up its STI capacities since 2007. Gross expenditures on R&D expanded by 9.7 per cent annually over 2009–2014. Still, Turkey underperforms in many key STI performance indicators compared to the OECD median and the EU. Turkey's rankings in ease of doing business and the Global Competitiveness index has improved significantly since 2002 owing to the STI reforms implemented over the past decade. According to the United Nations Development Programme's Human Development Index, Turkey's ranking increased from 88 to 69 in 2013, although the sample size increased to 187 countries.

Currently, the NSTI Strategy 2011–2016 and the Tenth Development Plan 2014–2018 provide guidelines for Turkey's national STI policy. An impact assessment analysis of NSTI Strategy 2011–2016 along with the introduction and implementation of second-generation reforms will provide the basis for the new NSTI Strategy 2017–2023. The ultimate goal is to foster a highly productive and competitive economy through *innovative production, sustainability,* and *high growth.* Industrial policy will be boosted towards generating higher domestic value added and transitioning to high-tech production schemes that will move Turkey up in the global value chain.

However, the major challenge for innovation and R&D policy in emerging countries is to encourage inclusive growth and support research addressing major social challenges, so these countries can also escape the middle-income trap. Hence, Turkey should design NSTI strategies based on inclusive growth, embracing all firms and sectors, known as 'industrial inclusiveness', all regions and places, known as 'territorial inclusiveness', and all people and segments, referred to as 'social inclusiveness' (OECD 2017). Industrial inclusiveness will close the gap between high-tech/innovative industries and traditional industries, improve the competitiveness of disadvantaged firms, and stimulate new ideas and entrepreneurship (OECD 2017). Territorial inclusiveness will close the economic gap between developed regions and lagging regions and bolster regions' economic resilience and reduce their dependence on transfers from the central government (OECD 2017). Social inclusiveness will close the social gap among different segments of people and regions and reduce economic, social, and cultural discrimination, especially towards disadvantaged groups (OECD 2017). The basis for diversity can be inherent, such as due to race and gender, or acquired, such as due to experience, education, and or cultural background.

These three components of inclusiveness are essential for improving economic performance and social well-being. They are closely related and overlap with each other. However, the crucial move in this phase is to design correct reform policies and implement them with appropriate action plans.

The ultimate goals of NSTI policies are to become competent in science and technology by establishing a cultivated national research ecosystem, adopt acquired technology effectively and develop new national technologies, and convert technological developments into social and economic benefits. Globally, STI policy has slightly changed focus, form, and objective in recent years. A growing share of public spending on

R&D has been allocated to the business sector instead of public research, signalling a shift in strategic objectives (to increasing industry capacity to innovate) and targets (firms) and requiring a change in instruments.

Policy areas to achieve inclusive growth through STI policies can be grouped by *industrial inclusiveness*, *territorial inclusiveness*, and *social inclusiveness*.

In the context of *industrial inclusiveness*, decision makers should identify strategic technologies and priority sectors, encourage public-private partnerships (PPPs), assist SMEs and start-ups in accessing global markets, establish clusters of SMEs for connecting to global knowledge networks, foster the integration of under-represented industrial groups in innovation, research, and entrepreneurial activities, and promote diversity in these activities. With the shift from closed innovation to open innovation, efforts towards open science have focused on the creation of enabling legal frameworks and policy guidance for open access and open data. The number of countries with mandatory open access provisions is increasing. Open science, maintaining open data and encouraging interdisciplinary research, and open innovation, fostering cooperation and knowledge sharing, together with proper levels of funding and governmental incentives, should lead to internationalization. With the internationalization of industry, the adoption and adaptation of foreign technologies increase. The adoption of foreign technologies can yield high payoffs, because technology adoption requires adaptation to local economic, technological, or environmental conditions. This can lead to the development and accumulation of innovation capabilities. There is evidence that domestic innovation played a greater role than imports of knowledge in the rise of emerging Asian economies (Ang and Madsen 2011).

In the context of *territorial inclusiveness*, decision makers should identify intraregional and interregional dynamics, as well as competitive advantages and disadvantages, and reinvigorate economic potential by restructuring regional funding policies. According to the Classification of Statistical Regions (SR) Level-1, R&D expenditures in 2015 were highest, at 28 per cent, in (TR5) West Anatolia, which consists of Ankara, Konya, and Karaman (Turkstat 2016). This region was followed by (TR1) Istanbul at 21.6 per cent and (TR4) East Marmara at 21 per cent (Turkstat

2016). Even though the highest R&D expenditures were in the TR5 region, the cities are categorized at different levels according to the Government Incentive Scheme: Ankara in Region 1, Konya in Region 2, and Karaman in Region 3. Thus, these cities receive different levels of support from the government. On the other hand, there are 8 technology development regions (TDRs) in Ankara, 2 in Konya, and 1 in Karaman, out of a total of 66. The second R&D investment region has seven TDRs. It is apparent that there is a close correlation between R&D investments and TDRs. However, no study has been conducted analyzing the impact of support policies regarding the performance of TDRs. Based on the findings of impact analysis, the correct approach is the so-called smart specialization approach. Smart specialization can be used as a policy tool to boost regional innovation to achieve economic growth and prosperity by enabling regions to focus on their strengths (reference). There are 12 statistical regions at Level 1 and 26 at Level 2 by geographic location in Turkey. However, geographic proximity does not necessarily mean that these cities/regions have similar dynamics for competitive advantage. A smart specialization strategy needs to be built on a sound analysis of regional assets and technology, including an analysis of potential partners in other regions, and should avoid unnecessary duplication (European Commission 2017). Later on, smart specialization centres can be copied in other regions with similar internal dynamics. Consequently, the waste of scarce human and capital resources will be avoided by efficient allocation based on competitive advantage.

A similar concentration is seen in human capital in R&D. According to R&D personnel percentage, Istanbul (TR1), at 24.1 per cent, was in first place. This region was followed by West Anatolia (TR5), at 21.4 per cent, and East Marmara (TR4), at 14.2 per cent. It is crucial for the central government to be guided in the process of restructuring funding policies by the expertise of the regional development agencies to minimize intraregional and interregional differences. Thus, establishing effective governance of STI policies and improving STI policy governance, with strong attention given to policy evaluation and the design of responsible research and innovation policies (RRI) with regional bodies, are crucial to maintaining territorial inclusiveness. Consequently, development agencies must be restructured according to the regional needs. Currently, all development agencies implement the same funding mechanisms but with different expected outputs without regarding local dynamics and beneficiaries.

The context of social inclusiveness can be the most difficult part of inclusiveness. Making changes in the social context should proceed hand in hand with territorial and industrial inclusiveness. The most crucial problem that must be understood deeply and resolved in social inclusiveness is discrimination in all areas of social and economic life. Discrimination has negative impacts on individuals and entire economies. Individuals suffering discrimination also suffer from lower incomes and poorer health status, stemming from higher psychological distress, lower self-esteem, and related mental health problems (Choi et al. 2013; Versey and Curtin 2016). At the aggregate level, discrimination can lead to depressed wages and underemployment for a large portion of the discriminated population (Baldwin and Johnson 1996). That might create a disincentive for these groups to invest in further education and training because their (average) return on such investments is below that of non-discriminated groups, thereby limiting future opportunities for those individuals and aggregate economic growth (Milgrom and Oster 1997). This is because individuals who are being discriminated against will receive less for the same productivity, qualifications, and skills and will not have the same opportunities in labour markets owing to some identity factor, such as gender, race, age, disability status, or place of residence.

Inclusive innovation policies can foster both social mobility and inclusion by integrating disadvantaged groups into more productive activities of the economy, by (1) enhancing their innovation-related skills and (2) facilitating their access to opportunities, particularly by addressing specific barriers faced by these groups (e.g. when establishing their own businesses). The successful integration of disadvantaged groups in innovative activities can be expected to improve their economic status and general well-being (including in terms of job satisfaction) and increase their chances for upward social mobility. Intergenerational upward social mobility is also expected to have positive effects on economic growth by improving the allocation of talents and abilities in the economy (Galor and Tsiddon 1997; Causa et al. 2009). A number of inclusive innovation policies, by fostering the integration of under-represented groups in innovation, research, and entrepreneurial activities, promote diversity in those activities. This is particularly the case with policies aimed at increasing the participation of women and minority groups in public research activities.

The integration of disadvantaged groups into productive activities is also likely to increase their involvement in the social, political, and cultural life of society and to strengthen their sense of belonging to a community. Social cohesion in turn benefits norms and institutional rules, leading to less risky cooperation, increased innovation and creativity, and higher participation in civil society. Higher social cohesion can strongly enhance people's well-being (Bertelsmann et al. 2014) and have positive impacts on the economy (Birdsall et al. 1995; Easterly et al. 2006).

In the context of social inclusiveness, which is also highly correlated with territorial inclusiveness, decision makers should restructure the education system ensuring a future supply of talent and building a culture for STI. Turkey's priority should be to enhance the quality of the human capital stock. High-income countries rely more on high-skilled labour, and this is where Turkey needs to make the most progress. Average schooling years of people over 25 years old is 7.6 years in Turkey, nearly 4 years less than the OECD average. Turkey, though, has made great strides in increasing access to education and, crucially, between boys and girls. With these policies, the gross schooling ratio has increased by 56.3 percentage points to 92.1 per cent in higher education over the last decade (Simsek 2014). In terms of school registrations, the ratio of girls to boys has increased from around 90 per cent to 102 per cent.

Even so, Turkey has further to go. Despite some improvement in recent years, Turkey's test scores in mathematics, reading, and science are still below the OECD average. To improve in this area, Turkey made education the number one spending item in its national budget, amounting to nearly a quarter of tax revenues. With these resources, Turkey has hired nearly half a million teachers over the past 12 years and made better use of technology, such as by providing free tablets to students and furnishing classrooms with smart boards and broadband Internet connection. With the evolution of society from a strictly consumer society to a make- or do-it-yourself society, developing skills for innovation and entrepreneurship becomes more important for the future supply of talent. Increasing budgets to boost STEM education, putting forth initiatives to make STEM more attractive to young people, or revising curricula to develop generic skills, problem-solving capability, and entrepreneurial behaviour are fundamental in the future supply of talent.

Under the three dimensions mentioned earlier, STI policy instruments can be categorized under research capacity, funding, education, governance, commercialization, and internationalization as (1) boosting research capacity, (2) improving governance and the regulatory framework of STIS, (3) strengthening the skills base for STI, and (4) establishing appropriate channels and institutions for financial access.

5 Conclusion

Most of the world's poor population lives in middle-income countries where the inequalities in income and job opportunities are stunningly obvious. Therefore, inclusive growth is central to addressing social challenges, improving economic performance, creating jobs, and achieving sustainable development in middle-income countries because the impacts are 'socially' inclusive. Thus, NSTI policies can help address the challenge of inequalities, especially in middle-income emerging countries. For decision makers, it is essential to focus policies on improving research capacities and the ability of firms to invest in R&D and innovation to escape the middle-income trap.

Middle-income economies usually have a basic industrial base, a growing research capacity, and innovation capabilities. The initial stage of this process includes a range of activities, from technology learning and adopting existing technologies to building innovation and R&D capacity for leading technologies. During the first stage, governments engage in a learning process in building institutions and competences needed for an STI ecosystem. The first policy implication drawn from experiences and implications is to lay the groundwork for a new STI landscape necessary for the second phase of the STI strategy. Therefore, the second phase should also include societal as well as economic challenges, defined as 'inclusive growth'.

Innovation dynamics and STI policies have impacts on industrial inclusiveness, capturing differences among firms and industries with diverse innovation and productivity performances; territorial inclusiveness, capturing diversity in the geographic dimensions of industry; and social inclusiveness, capturing diverse social groups with inequalities. Under the three dimensions mentioned earlier, in summary, this section recommends implementing immediately the following second-phase NSTI policies:

- Foster international cooperation and coordination to form global knowledge networks through open science and open innovation policies and incentives;
- Conduct economic and social impact analyses of TDRs to develop additional second-phase efficiency policies;
- Engage in smart specialization and the diffusion of TDRs in the context of local economic and social dynamics;
- Engage in interregional cooperation and coordination in terms of the similarities among the regions' competitive advantages rather than solely concentrating on geographic proximity;
- Restructure regional development agencies in terms of funding mechanisms regarding the regions' economic and social dynamics;
- Implement inclusive innovation policies minimizing ongoing discrimination against disadvantaged groups and maintaining higher social cohesion.

This second phase of NSTI policies, designed based on the economic and social realities in Turkey, will be essential for meeting the ambitious goals of Vision 2023. Thus, in summary, this section strictly recommends implementing the foregoing policy actions to forge a highly productive and competitive economy through innovative and high-tech production and stable and high growth in the context of inclusive growth.

References

Ang, James, and Jakob B. Madsen. 2011. Can Second Generation Endogenous Growth Models Explain the Productivity Trends and Knowledge Production in Asian Miracle Economics? *Review of Economics and Statistics* 93 (4): 1360–1373.

ARBIS. 2017. https://arbis.tubitak.gov.tr/.

Baldwin, Marjorie L., and William G. Johnson. 1996. The Employment Effects of Wage Discrimination Against Black Men. *ILR Review* 49 (2): 302–316.

Bertelsmann Shiftung and Eurofound. 2014. *Social Cohesion and Well-Being in the EU*. https://www.eurofound.europa.eu/sites/default/files/ef_publication/field_ef_document/ef1472en.pdf.

Birdsall, Nancy, David Ross, and Richard Sabot. 1995. Inequality and Growth Reconsidered: Lessons from East Asia. *World Bank Economic Review* 9 (3): 477–508.

Causa, Orsetta, Sophie Dantan, and Asa Johansson. 2009. *Intergenerational Social Mobility in European OECD Countries*, OECD Economics Department Working Papers 706.

Choi, Kyung-Hee, et al. 2013. Experiences of Discrimination and Their Impact on the Mental Health Among African American, Asian and Pacific Islander, and Latino Men Who Have Sex with Men. *American Journal of Public Health* 103 (5): 868–874.

Easterly, William, Jozef Ritzen, and Michael Woolcock. 2006. Social Cohesion, Institutions and Growth. *Economics and Politics* 18 (2): 103–120.

European Commission. 2017. *Smart Specialisation*. https://ec.europa.eu/research/regions/index.cfm?pg=smart_specialisation. Accessed 28 June 2017.

Galor, Oded, and Daniel Tsiddon. 1997. The Distribution of Human Capital and Economic Growth. *Journal of Economic Growth* 2 (1): 93–124.

Milgrom, Paul, and Sharon Oster. 1997. Job Discrimination, Market Forces, and the Invisibility Hypothesis. *Quarterly Journal of Economics* 102 (3): 453–476.

OECD. 2012. *OECD Science, Technology and Industry Outlook 2012*. Paris: OECD Publishing. https://doi.org/10.1787/sti_outlook-2012-en.

———. 2016. *OECD Science, Technology and Innovation Outlook 2016*. Paris: OECD Publishing. https://doi.org/10.1787/sti_in_outlook-2016-en.

———. 2017. *Making Innovation Benefit All: Policies for Inclusive Growth*. Paris: OECD Publishing. https://www.innovationpolicyplatform.org/system/files/Inclusive%20Growth%20publication%20FULL%20for%20web.pdf.

Oxfam. 2017. *Just 8 Men Own Same Wealth as Half the World*. https://www.oxfam.org/en/pressroom/pressreleases/2017-01-16/just-8-men-own-same-wealth-half-world. Accessed 16 Jan 2017.

Simsek, Mehmet. 2014. Escaping the Middle Income Trap: Turkey's Strategy. *Global Economic Symposium 2014 Proposals*. http://www.global-economic-symposium.org/knowledgebase/escaping-the-middle-income-trap/proposals/escaping-the-middle-income-trap-turkey2019s-strategy/#_ftn3.

TARABIS. 2017. http://tarabis.tubitak.gov.tr. Accessed 28 June 2017.

TUBITAK. 2010. *National STI Strategy 2011–2016*. https://www.tubitak.gov.tr/en/about-us/policies/content-national-sti-strategy-2011-2016.

———. 2017. *National Science, Technology and Innovation Statistics of Turkey*. http://www.tubitak.gov.tr/en/content-national-science-technology-and-innovation-statistics-of-turkey.

TURKSTAT. 2016. *R&D Activities Survey 2015*. http://www.turkstat.gov.tr/PreHaberBultenleri.do?id=21782.

Versey, Shellea, and Nicola Curtin. 2016. The Differential Impact of Discrimination on Health Among Black and White Women. *Social Science Research* 57: 99–115.

World Bank. 2010. *Innovation Policy: A Guide for Developing Countries*. https://openknowledge.worldbank.org/handle/10986/2460.

———. 2017. http://data.worldbank.org/. Accessed 12 June 2017.

Thinking About a New Industrial Policy Framework for Turkey

Murat A. Yülek

1 Introduction

The positive and sustained association between the manufacturing sector and per-capita income, as well as their growth, suggests that manufacturing can act as an engine of growth, as Kaldor (1967) suggested. Figure 1 shows that there is a direct relationship between the levels of per-capita GDP and per-capita manufacturing value added even in developed countries, which have long become service-based economies. Thus one could infer that industrial policies may generate economic growth even in more developed, service-based economies. This is supported by the positive relationship between growth of per-capita GDP and growth of manufacturing value added (Fig. 2). Further, industrial policy can be instrumental

I thank Lorna Girayalp, Elif Tıpır, and Sena Nur Tozoğlu for their valuable assistance.

M. A. Yülek (✉)
Center for Industrial Policy and Development, Istanbul Commerce University, Istanbul, Turkey

A. F. Aysan et al. (eds.), *Turkish Economy*,
https://doi.org/10.1007/978-3-319-70380-0_13

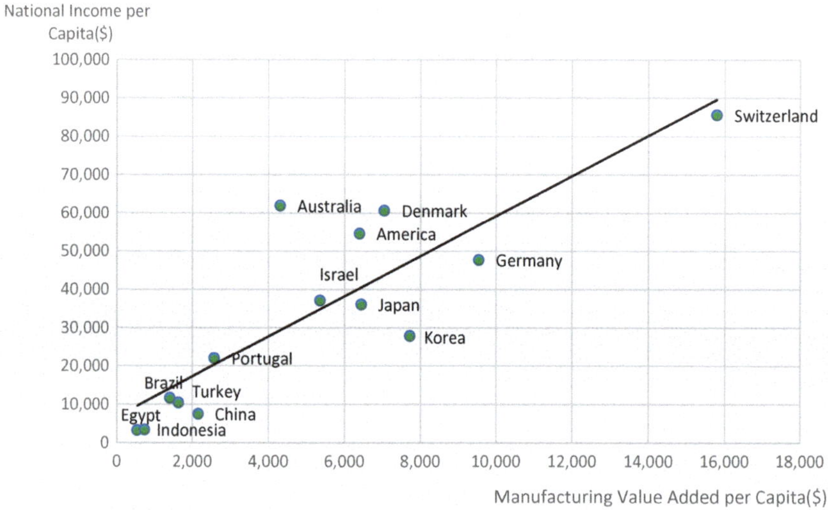

Fig. 1 Manufacturing value added and GDP per capita by country (2014) (Source: World Economic Outlook, IMF and World Bank)

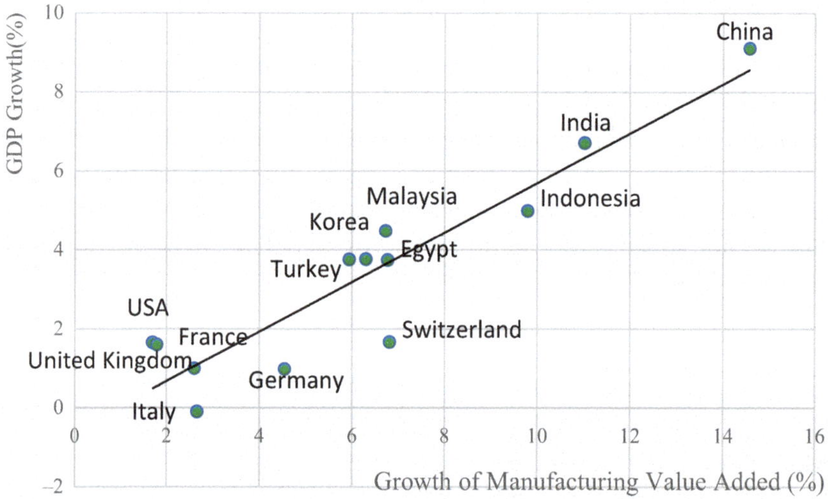

Fig. 2 Growth of manufacturing value added and GDP per capita by country (2000–2014) (Source: Çukurova Genç İşadamları Derneği 2016, IMF and World Bank)

in a country's breaking out of the middle-income trap (Yülek 2016a), which means reduced growth rates once the country reaches middle-income levels.

Turkey's industrialization process started in the late nineteenth century. Since then, with a volatile record, it has been among the relatively faster growing and industrializing countries. Meanwhile, however, other countries in the world have experienced their own industrialization processes determining the conditions of the global industrial and economic environment for Turkish firms and policies. Among these countries are newly industrializing East Asian countries, most importantly China, which have recorded phenomenal growth and development records more impressive than Turkey's.

More recently, administrations in developed and developing countries alike have been discussing the need for new industrial policies or science technology and innovation policies that have relevance to the industrial sector.[1] It is thus evident that there is a perceived need for strengthening the industrial sector in both sets of countries.

With this in mind, this chapter first reviews the industrialization process in Turkey. It then assesses Turkey's current level of industrialization and its features by implementing metrics of manufacturing value added and export sophistication. Next, it places Turkey and a set of comparators on a streamlined industrialization process map. Based on the findings and assessment, this chapter finally proposes the main features of an appropriate industrial policy for Turkey that would address the identified deficiencies. In doing so, the paper considers the policies as well as the administrative structure that would be conducive to the design and implementation of such policies.

2 Industrialization and Industrial Policies in Turkey: Background

Industrialization in the Ottoman Empire started in the late nineteenth century and was insufficient compared to UK or continental Europe. There were state-led attempts at industrialization and educational reform with an emphasis on technical education. All in all, the newly established republic at the outset of the twentieth century did not inherit a significant manufacturing industrial base from the Ottoman Empire.

The early administrators of the republic, in particular Mustafa Kemal Atatürk, tried to find a way to accelerate economic development and industrialization. In the Izmir Economic Congress (1923), the necessity for industrialization was discussed, but no significant and specific policy measures were developed except, again, the discussion of the need to protect and encourage industries. In 1927, a significant move came with the enactment of the Industrial Encouragement Law (Teşvik-i Sanayi Kanunu) on 28 May 1927. The main objective of the law was to incentivize private-sector manufacturing investments. The implementation of the law was successful; in the first five years, the number of private industrial firms and industrial employment quadrupled (Sanayi ve Teknoloji Bakanlığı 1973). In the 1930s, the need for direct government intervention was felt more and more; in order to extend financing to the private sector, two state-owned banks (Sümerbank and Etibank) were established to support, primarily, textiles, mining, and metallurgical industries. Although both were officially deposit-collecting banks, their objectives related more to development banking by channelling financial savings into industrialization and development.

In the subsequent years of the 1930s, the statist tone in economic policy intensified as the private sector was rightly seen to be insufficient in bringing about the desired growth and development. In 1934, the First Five-Year Industrial Plan was launched. The plan included 20 specific industrial investments to be undertaken by the government in cotton and woolen textiles, paper and cardboard, and iron and steel sectors (Appendix 1 presents a list of the industrial facilities). At the background of the plan were (1) "The Report on Our Economic Situation" ("İktisadi Vaziyetimize Dair Rapor") prepared by the Ministry of Economics and (2) two separate economic reports by Russian and American experts (Yücel 2014). Etibank and Sümerbank also contributed to the plan. Total projected investment on the factories under the plan was quite large, 44 million Turkish lira (TL), while the actual investment cost reached TL 100 million (3 and 8 per cent of 1934 GDP, respectively). The plan was ultimately successful in the sense that the facilities were completed and became operative.

The plan was quite focused sectorally and carried a significant tone of import substitution, although it was not accompanied by protective measures. It had three principal strategic priorities. Firstly, the factories would be in sectors that used domestically produced raw materials; secondly, they would require high capital expenditures, scale, and technology; and thirdly, their capacities would be adequate in meeting domestic demand.

Following the first industrial plan, a second plan was formulated in the late 1940s. It was more comprehensive than the first one in terms of covering the mining, combustibles, energy, food, chemical, and machinery industries. The second plan, however, was never implemented because of the Second World War, during which industrialization almost stopped.

In the 1950s, a new and democratically elected government came to power with liberal economic policies. The key economic strategies of the new government were the encouragement of agriculture growth leading to self-sufficiency, infrastructure development, and private-sector-led industrial development. Banking and liberal foreign direct investment policies were introduced, aimed at supporting industrialization. An industrial development bank was established, with the World Bank as a shareholder. The Law to Encourage Foreign Investment was enacted in 1951. The liberal policies continued until the 1960s. During this period, private-sector-led industrialization (e.g. textiles, tiles) was achieved, though without a focused or sectoral policy.

Following the coup in 1960, the State Planning Organization was established in 1961. The subsequent period, 'the planned period' until the 1980s, was characterized by five-year development plans and a strong import substitution policy with significantly protectionist measures. The plans included macroeconomic general equilibrium models and carried compulsory policies for the state-owned companies and ministries. For the private sector they were 'indicative', which meant the industrial incentives and financial policies would be formed and implemented accordingly.

The protectionist import substitution policy aimed at directing the private sector principally towards consumption goods, such as food and textiles (Eşiyok 2004, 4) and the state enterprises towards heavier industry such as petrochemicals, iron and steel, and paper. During the 1960s, however, unlike Korea, Turkey did not simultaneously pursue export-led growth (Yülek 2016b), although exports for some sectors were targeted. This policy (along with other policies such as in the financial sector) ultimately led to a balance-of-payments crisis in the late 1970s as sustained import dependency led to increasing demand for foreign currency, which was not balanced by the foreign currency earnings from exports.

During the 'planned period', a certain amount of sector targeting was conducted. In the first, second, and third plans (1963–1967, 1968–1972, and 1973–1977), residential construction, agriculture, manufacturing, and transportation were the high-level priorities. However, economic growth was predicated mainly on the industrial sector. In the manufacturing sector, machinery, metallurgy, and chemicals were emphasized. The protectionist policies meant that if a product was manufactured by domestic companies, its imports would be restricted or banned. In the assembly industries, local content would be increased with the aim of attaining complete domestic manufacturing in the future. However, with reference to international division of labor, 'not all products had to be manufactured domestically'.

The plans included detailed production and investment targets for selected manufacturing subsectors (Table 1). In some subsectors such as ceramics, some plans discouraged greenfield investments and limited new investments to the expansion of existing plants. In others, such as textiles and garments, in addition to import substitution, policies encouraged exports. The plans also included policies shaping the market structure with some measures aimed at regulating the market structure and preventing monopolistic tendencies and rents. On the other hand, in subsectors such as textiles and garments, achievement of scale by defragmentation of the many small enterprises in operation was targeted. The plans also targeted technological progress and development by firms, reduction of vulnerabilities to economic and technical external shocks, and increasing production of intermediate and capital goods. In this respect, the chemical, petrochemical, metal, and electronics industries were among the priorities.

In 1960, the new president following the coup, Cemal Gürsel, took an initiative to ensure local automobile manufacturing. While a prototype, 'Devrim' (Revolution), was successfully built, the initiative was not successful in establishing a commercial industry. The main reason was that

Table 1 Manufacturing subsector plans with production and investment targets

	Five-year development plans				
Industry	I	II	III	IV	V
Food, beverage, and tobacco	●	●	●	●	●
Textile and clothing	●	●	●	●	●
Paper	●	●	●	●	●
Tyre	●	●	●	●	●
Plastics processing	●	●	●	●	●
Chemicals	●	●	●	●	●
Glass	●	●	●	●	●
Chine and porcelain	●	●	●	●	●
Cement	●	●	●	●	●
Iron, steel, and metallurgy	●	●	●	●	●
Metalware and steel construction	●	●	●	●	●
Machine manufacturing	●	●	●	●	●
Vehicle repair and manufacturing	●	●			
Handicrafts	●	●			
Leather		●	●	●	●
Petroleum products		●	●	●	●
Electronics		●	●	●	●
Road vehicle manufacturing		●	●	●	●
Railway vehicle manufacturing		●	●	●	●
Ship manufacturing		●	●	●	●
Aircraft manufacturing and repair		●	●	●	●
Agricultural equipment and machinery manufacturing			●		●
Non-electrical machinery				●	●

Source: Turkey's Five-Year Development Plan text and author

the idea of industrialization did not win the confidence of the dominant actors in society. For example, well-known editors and columnists such as Nadir Nadi, Çetin Emeç, Esin Talu, and Çetin Altan, among others, wrote strong 'anti-automobile manufacturing' pieces in their newspapers (Sanır 2011, 148–157).

In the mid-1970s, narrowly targeted industrial policies were implemented under the leadership of Necmettin Erbakan, who acted as Deputy Prime Minister in the period 1974–1978. The main strategy was again state-led: a number of state enterprises were formed to make physical investments in electronics, heavy industry, aeronautics, and machinery industries (Table 2). The locations of the facilities were spread out around the country for regional development purposes. The results of the implementation of

Table 2 Industrial targeting in Erbakan period

State enterprise	Sector	Number of factories: In 1975	Number of factories: Additional by 1982	Selected provinces of new factories
TESTAŞ	Electronics	0	4	Pasinler, Erzurum, Aydın, Ankara
Turkish Iron Steel Co.	Iron and Steel	2	4	Karabük, Sivas, Divriği, İskenderun
TAKSAN	Machine Tools	0	4	Tokat, Kayseri, Erzincan, Yerköy
TÜMOSAN	Engine	0	5	Konya, Uşak, İzmit, Eskişehir, Bursa
TEMSAN	Electromechanics	0	11	Malatya, Diyarbakır, Elazığ, Yozgat
TUSAŞ	Aircraft	0	1	Ankara
MKE	Machinery and Chemicals	18	50	Yozgat, Kütahya, Kayseri, Konya
Turkish Cement Industry Inc.	Cement	13	33	Ergani, Kahramanmaraş, Lalapaşa
Turkish Sugar Factories	Sugar	17	31	Muş, Konya, Çorum, Niğde
Turkish Nitrogen Industry Inc.	Nitrogen	5	21	Mersin, Manisa, Şırnak, Mazıdağı
SEKA	Cellulose and Paper	4	10	Afyon, Balıkesir, Kastamonu

Source: Sanayi ve Teknoloji Bakanlığı (1977)

the programme were mixed largely owing to the volatile political environment. Some investments were successfully completed while others, such as aeronautics, were restarted and completed after a decade. Still others were cancelled in the initial phases owing to political problems of the government.

In January 1980, in a major shift of policies, the liberalization of the Turkish economy was launched under the leadership of Turgut Özal, who subsequently became Turkey's prime minister and president. The policies addressed the liberalization of state controls on prices, privatization, liberalization, financial sector liberalization, and the liberalization of capital movement (Yülek 1998). Under trade liberalization, the import substitution policy was abolished in favour of export promotion. Sector targeting was also abolished; industrial incentives were designed to achieve general industrialization without sectoral preference and to direct physical investments towards underdeveloped regions.

During the 1990s, Turkey had experienced a number of financial and economic crises as well as political instability. After 2001 political and economic stability was restored. Macroeconomic accounts strengthened, and inflation rates were reduced and fiscal balance improved. However, the current account deficit increased on the back of increasing income levels driving up imports. Industrial incentives were used increasingly as a tool of policy in the 2000s, and this pushed up exports; between 2002 and 2011 Turkey's exports multiplied five times. After 2001 the government supported manufacturing in defence industries. This led to the local production of military vehicles, aircraft, and ships. On the civilian front, government aimed at developing a locally designed and manufactured automobile, but there was little success in the actual implementation of the idea.

High current account deficits were also linked to high import dependency as Turkey's export and domestic manufacturing industries were dependent on intermediate and raw materials imported from abroad (Senesen and Günlük-Senesen 2003; Aydoğuş et al. 2015). Starting in 2011, the Ministry of Science, Industry, and Technology issued sectoral strategy documents for several sectors including automobiles, machinery, and textiles. The strategy documents included action plans that included measures to be taken by various ministries and governmental units. However, the action plans mostly lacked enforcement that would enable the ministry to take action in case the measures were not undertaken.

2.1 A Summary of Industrial Policies and Outcomes in Turkey

As a summary, various industrial policy approaches have been pursued since the founding of the republic (Table 3). These approaches aimed at addressing the challenges of the specific period. In general, however,

Table 3 Evolution of industrial policy in Turkey

Period	Industrial policy
1923–1933	General industrialization policies
1933–1940	Sector targeting supported by financial sector policies; state-led industrialization
1950–1960	General industrial policies supported by financial sector policies; increasing private-sector participation in physical investments
1960–1980	Economic planning; sector targeting; import substitution industrialization with very little export orientation
1980–2011	Export-led growth; trade liberalization; general industrialization policies
From 2011	Export led growth; trade liberalization; general industrialization polices; industrial strategy documents

Turkish industrial policies lacked the focus that some of the more successful industrializers, such as South Korea, pursued.

As a result, while Turkey has achieved some level of industrialization, its performance falls behind stars such as South Korea. The latter started with much more modest initial conditions but ended up with a more impressive outcome (Fig. 3). Turkey's per-capita GDP and its exports were significantly higher than South Korea's in 1960. Korea's industrial policies led to a rapid expansion of exports in absolute terms compared to Turkey, triggering the impressive growth of per-capita income. Korea's export orientation and focused industrial policies were instrumental in the achievement of sustained growth and industrialization (Yülek 2016b).

However, the GDP growth record has been quite volatile historically and falling more recently. Per-capita GDP time series in the last four decades show three plateaus that can be identified as middle-income traps. The first two were during 1980–1988 and 1990–2001 at around USD 1,500 and USD 3,000 respectively. The third one started in 2008 and continues to the present, at around USD 10,000 (Fig. 4). During these periods, per-capita GDP stagnated for relatively long periods of time.

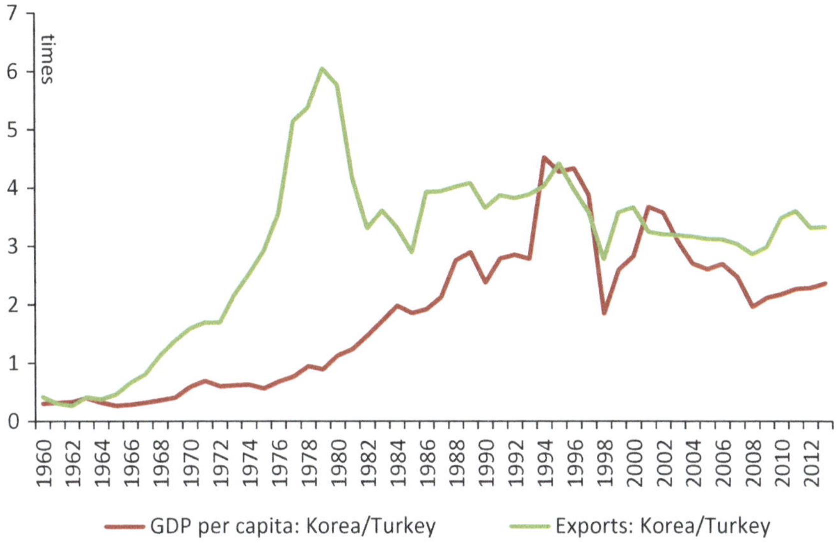

Fig. 3 Comparison of performances of Turkey and South Korea (Source: Yülek 2016b)

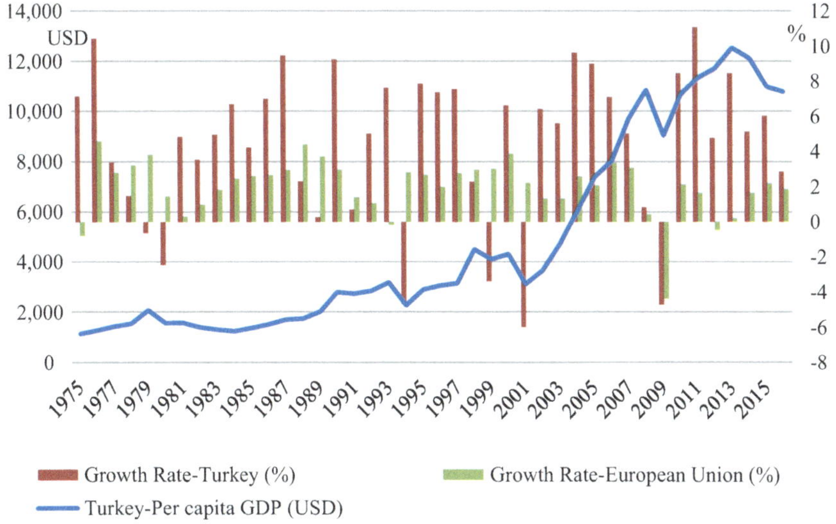

Fig. 4 Turkey: GDP growth rates and per-capita GDP (Source: IMF)

3 Current Level of Industrialization in Turkey

The preceding sections looked at past industrial policies; this section first discusses the level of industrialization in Turkey using some relevant metrics. Then it briefly discusses the effect of industrialization process on Turkey's exports, its export diversification and sophistication. It then introduces a streamlined process of industrialization for developing countries with a view to classifying Turkey and some other countries.

3.1 Manufacturing Value Added: Turkey and Some Comparators

Turkish manufacturing sector growth rates have improved rapidly since 2001, but a stagnation has set in more recently. Overall, the average growth rate of Turkey's manufacturing value added is among the highest in the world (Table 4). This was reflected in the rapid expansion of exports between 2001 and 2012 despite a significant contraction in 2009 following the global financial crisis.

However, although Turkish manufacturing value added per annum is among the top 20 in the world, it is still small compared to that of the large industrial economies. Turkey's manufacturing sector generated a total value added of USD 126 billion in 2014. That makes the country the 16th largest manufacturer in the world.

The manufactured goods market is in fact quite concentrated; the world's four largest manufacturers generate a total of USD 7.35 trillion in manufacturing value added per annum. The information in Table 5 shows that there is a gap in the size of manufacturing value added after Germany, the fourth largest manufacturer in the world. An indicative classification is also presented in Table 5 defining USD 200 billion to USD 399 billion in manufacturing value added as the upper-medium group and USD 100 billion to USD 199 billion as medium-low group. On that basis, Turkey can be considered a lower-medium-sized manufacturer.

Table 4 Average growth of manufacturing value added per annum: selected countries (billion USD unless otherwise indicated)

Country name	2000	2014	Average nominal growth rate (%)
China	482	3,713	14.6
India	67	322	11.0
Indonesia	46	187	9.8
Switzerland	48	129	6.8
Malaysia	29	77	6.7
Egypt	18	45	6.3
Turkey	53	126	5.9
Germany	404	788	4.6
Italy	200	297	2.7
France	193	284	2.6
USA	1,509	1,944	1.7
Korea	146	390	6.8
United Kingdom	217	283	1.8

Source: Çukurova Genç İşadamları Derneği (2016), IMF, and World Bank

However, in terms of per-capita manufacturing value added, perhaps a better indicator of the level of industrialization, Turkey ranks poorly (Table 6). It is the 56th country in the world with USD 1,632 as compared to USD 7,720 for Korea and USD 15,793 for Switzerland.

3.2 Exports and Export Sophistication

Exports reveal a country's competitiveness. Turkey's exports are constituted predominantly by manufactured products (Table 7). Thus the industrial sector plays an important role in foreign currency earnings. Turkey has diversified its export markets significantly in the 2000s relative to BRICS or eastern European peers. While Turkey had the second highest level of market concentration of exports in 1999, within the next decade it was one of the most diversified (World Bank 2014a, b, 8–11). During the same period, export product diversification also proceeded rapidly and surpassed that of BRICS and eastern European countries (World Bank 2014a, b, 8–11).

However, Turkey's export sophistication is still limited; its exports comprise mostly low- and middle-technology products. Compared to high-income countries (Table 7), the composition of Turkey's exports

Table 5 Total manufacturing value added (2014)

	Country name	Billion USD
Large manufacturers		
1	China	3,713
2	USA	1,944
3	Japan	905
4	Germany	788
Upper-medium manufacturers		
5	Korea	390
6	India	322
7	Italy	297
8	France	284
9	United Kingdom	283
10	Russia	249
11	Brazil	219
12	Mexico	217
13	Indonesia	187
Lower-medium manufacturers		
14	Spain	167
15	Switzerland	129
16	Turkey	126
17	Thailand	112
18	Holland	96
19	Australia	94
20	Sweden	93

Source: Çukurova Genç İşadamları Derneği (2016), IMF, and World Bank

reveals some key disadvantages. For high-income countries and S. Korea, the majority of exports are composed of chemical products (HS 1988/2 product groups 28–38), electrical and non-electrical machinery (HS 1988/2 product groups 84–85) and transportation equipment (86–89), and miscellaneous manufactured goods, including high-value items such as optical and music equipment, arms, and toys (HS 1988/2 product groups 90–99). The share of Turkey's exports in these categories is significantly smaller than those of high-income countries and shares common features with medium- and lower-income countries such as Mexico, Brazil, China, and India. Export sophistication studies show that although the share of medium-technology exports in total increased during the last decade, their level is still around one-third of the total. More importantly, the share of high-technology exports remained at lower than 5 per cent of the total (World Bank 2014a, b, 14).

Table 6 Manufacturing value added per capita by selected countries (2014, USD)

Rank	Country name	Manufacturing value added per capita	Rank	Country name	Manufacturing value added per capita
1	Switzerland	15,793	23	Italy	4,962
2	Ireland	11,062	25	United Kingdom	4,476
3	Singapore	10,022	28	France	4,209
4	Germany	9,546	30	Slovakia	3,627
5	Monaco	9,049	31	Spain	3,537
6	Austria	8,484	34	Hungary	2,896
7	Sweden	8,238	36	Malaysia	2,713
8	Korea	7,720	37	Portugal	2,589
9	Luxemburg	7,624	38	Saudi Arabia	2,578
10	Finland	7,173	39	Poland	2,411
12	Denmark	7,043	42	China	2,161
15	Japan	6,443	43	Romania	1,939
16	America	6,392	44	Russia	1,796
18	Belgium	5,745	45	Mexico	1,789
19	Holland	5,602	46	Greece	1,771
20	Israel	5,361	47	Thailand	1,754
21	Canada	5,094	48	Turkey	1,632
22	Czech Republic	5,027			

Source: Çukurova Genç İşadamları Derneği (2016), IMF, and World Bank
Note: Smaller economier such Lichtenstein, Puerto Rico, San Marino, Qatar, New Caledonia and Trinidad Tobago which appeared among the top manufacturers have been excluded from table

3.3 Positioning Turkey in a Streamlined Industrialization Process Map

As discussed earlier, Turkey has pursued various industrial policies over the decades. Where have these policies taken Turkey in terms of industrialization? And where does Turkey stand in the industrialization process compared to other countries? These questions are important for discussions about Turkey's path forward. Furthermore, it would be useful to compare Turkey's position in the industrialization process with that of other countries.

Table 7 Composition of exports: selected countries

HS 1988/92 Product Group		France	Germany	USA	S. Korea	Turkey	Mexico	Brazil	China	Indonesia
	01–05_Animal	3.02	1.74	1.92	0.34	1.35	0.88	7.79	0.8	3.48
	28–38_ Chemicals	15.13	12.15	10.11	6.86	3.32	2.82	5.08	4.67	10.51
	16–24_ FoodProd	6.59	2.95	2.84	0.74	4.76	2.67	11.56	1.24	2.06
	64–67_ Footwear	0.63	0.42	0.12	0.13	0.48	0.19	0.55	3.01	1.04
	27–27_Fuels	3.88	2.68	9.61	9.67	3.74	10.61	9.17	1.47	19.63
	41–43_ HidesSkin	1.41	0.26	0.37	0.3	0.57	0.2	1.35	1.5	1.23
	84–85_ MachElec	19.33	26.35	23.72	34.56	14.77	35.29	7.53	41.44	7.12
	72–83_Metals	6.87	7.5	4.87	8.23	13.21	4.39	7.17	7.87	8.06
	25–26_Minerals	0.24	0.19	0.69	0.12	2.51	1.3	12.97	0.18	1.05
	90–99_ Miscellan	7.83	11.76	17.65	7.43	4.38	7.69	3.2	9.8	1.8
	39–40_ PlastiRub	5.05	5.25	4.84	7.06	5.52	2.83	2.46	3.87	2.6
	68–71_ StoneGlas	2.3	1.95	4.67	1.08	7.12	2.88	2.11	4.79	13.72
	50–63_ TextCloth	2.91	2.33	1.62	2.81	18.42	1.76	1.13	12.28	12.15
	86–89_ Transport	18.99	20.61	9.6	19.81	12.58	22.9	7.17	4.47	8.16
	06–15_ Vegetable	3.52	1.24	4.83	0.17	5.33	2.87	16.52	0.93	6.81
	44–49_Wood	2.3	2.61	2.54	0.7	1.95	0.73	4.25	1.68	0.57
	01_99_All Products	100	100	100	100	100	100	100	100	100
	Top 5 export products	84, 88, 87, 85, 30	87, 84, 85, 30, 99	84, 85, 99, 27, 87	85, 87, 84, 27, 89	87, 84, 61, 85, 72	87, 85, 84, 27, 90	26, 12, 27, 2, 84	85, 84, 94, 61, 62	27, 71, 87, 84, 29

Source: Çukurova Genç İşadamları Derneği (2016), World Integrated Trade Solutions database (World Bank)

We will locate Turkey on a simple four-stage streamlined process map developed by Yülek (2016a). In the first stage, capital deepening occurs in the form of production by imported machinery replacing manual production (Fig. 5). This leads to a jump in labour productivity. However, technical skill accumulation remains quite limited. Over time, firms and the labour force start to develop skills that help them run machinery better and more efficiently. This is the 'adoption' stage, Stage II, where new technology is not developed but the technology embedded in the imported machinery is appropriated by the local manpower. In the next stage, Stage III, the importing country furthers technology adoption by gaining skills to service and repair imported machinery. This leads to further productivity gains by a smaller amount of downtime or lower maintenance/repair costs.

Most countries remain somewhere between Stages II and III. Few countries achieve the imitation stage (Stage III) and new products stage (Stage IV). Yülek (2016a) describes these stages as follows:

> If Stage III is reached, a country's firms (through its firms and human resources) reverse-engineer some of the imported machinery and build similar or slightly different ones. This is a new sector for the country. For example, starting with firms that produce textiles, now the country has firms that manufacture textile machinery. The next and ultimate step in the industrialization process is developing new products (Stage IV in Fig. 4). This can be either through formal or informal R&D or through incremental innovation. Both unleash TFP-based GDP growth. They might also lead to new capital deepening and productivity-enhancing avenues owing to the machinery developed. This stage requires properly skilled human resources, such as research and development engineers in the firms and/or in the universities. Countries that have reached this stage have firms at the boundaries of commercialized products. In order to compete, they need to develop new products that are costly but at the same time that provide them with a certain period of pricing power.

Locating countries on the process map is rather subjective. Perhaps a scoring tool could be developed for this purpose, but even that might yield controversial results. Thus a country may be in Stage IV, whereas Fig. 5 identifies it as a Stage III country. Nevertheless, such an exercise could help

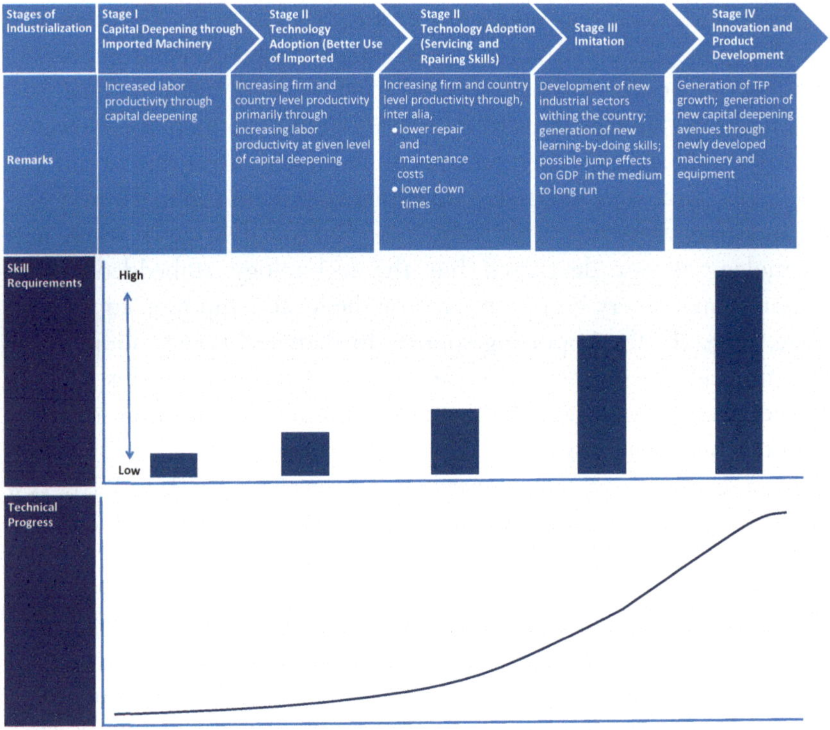

Fig. 5 Industrialization, technical progress, and skills (Source: Yülek 2016a)

fine-tune needed policies to take the country to more advanced stages. In such an analysis, some countries can be identified as being in more than one stage. There are two reasons for this. Firstly, if the assignment of a country to a certain stage is not done on the basis of the 'centre of gravity' of its manufacturing industries, its industrial standing can be different for different manufacturing sectors. For example, Korea can be considered a Stage II country in aviation equipment, a Stage III country in synthetic textiles, and a Stage IV country in electronics. Secondly, it may simply not be possible to assign a specific stage to a country's 'centre of gravity' in the manufacturing sector before a detailed sectoral analysis is completed.

Table 8 presents some tentative placements of selected countries on the industrialization process map. Turkey is listed as a Stage II country.

Table 8 Classification of countries in terms of industrialization

Stage of industrialization	Stage I	Stage II	Stage III	Stage IV
Features	Using imported machinery (capital deepening); this leads to an initial jump in the (per hour) productivity of domestic labour	Adoption of technology; the importing country, through its firms and labour force, develops skills to run the machinery more efficiently. Labour productivity continues to rise	Imitation of sophisticated industrial products of other countries; locally branded industrial goods	Development of new and sophisticated industrial products
Product examples	Textiles and garments, plastics	Textiles and garments, plastics, automobiles, or aircraft under licence, assembly of electrical and non-electrical equipment, assembly of electronic equipment	Technical textiles, locally branded automobiles or aircraft; flat screen for TVs, GSM* equipment, electronic equipment	Branded textile and garments, technical textiles, locally branded automobiles, new medical equipment, branded GSM equipment
Selected countries	Bangladesh	Turkey, Pakistan, Brazil, India, China, Malaysia, Iran	Korea, China	Switzerland, USA, Germany, Japan, S. Korea

Note: Some countries are purposely classified in two different stages
*GSM: Global System for Mobile Communications

Looking at a major comparator, South Korea is identified as an either Stage III or Stage IV country. The reason for this selection for Turkey is that Turkey has so far industrialized primarily on the back of imported equipment. At the moment it is a country that manufactures goods by using this equipment. Its products are mostly standard, undifferentiated ones with medium-technology content. The country's exports mainly consist of industrial goods. The country has not ventured adequately into imitating higher-technology products or developing relatively more sophisticated products such as flat screens, smartphones, tomography equipment, or computer numerical control machines. Moreover, it has not been able to develop locally developed or branded automobiles or aircraft.

4 Thinking About a New Industrial Policy for Turkey

This section starts with a brief summary of the current state of industrialization and the main deficiencies to be addressed. It then discusses the features of an appropriate industrial policy for Turkey with a view to accelerating the industrialization process from where it is now, as reviewed in the previous section. This section considers the administrative structure under which policies will be both designed and implemented.

The foregoing discussion in Sects. 2 and 3 indicated that while Turkey has recorded relatively high growth rates in the manufacturing sector, the level of industrialization is still behind that of the top manufacturers of the world and it is experiencing a middle-income trap. Moreover, as illustrated by its export performance, the country suffers from low sophistication and, thus, low value of exports. The design and implementation of an appropriate industrial policy should be based on these initial conditions.

Thus, one can infer that Turkish industrial policy should address the existing key deficiencies. The key pillars of such an industrial policy are taken up in the rest of this section. This can help the country escape the middle-income trap, as suggested by the positive relationship between the growth of manufacturing output and per-capita income, as well as per-capita manufacturing output and per-capita GDP (Yülek 2016a).

4.1 Concentration on Technical Capabilities of Industrial Layer

Industrialization is a process of building on technical capabilities (Yülek 2016a). Technical capabilities comprise three components: productive, technological, and R&D capabilities (Fig. 6). Productive capabilities refer to 'producing with a given level of technology at world levels of efficiency or productivity' (Radošević and Yoruk 2015: 5). Technological capabilities, on the other hand, refer to making use of 'technological knowledge in an effort to assimilate, use, adapt and change existing technologies in order to sustain competitiveness' (Yun 2007; Kim 2001). R&D capabilities, on the other hand, refer to making deliberate and effective use of R&D activities in order to develop new products and processes. R&D activities become more significant as a firm approaches the world technology frontier when its own R&D substitutes technology transfer activities.

The industrial policy should concentrate first and foremost on building these capabilities across manufacturing firms, public and private research institutions and universities, and human resources. Together, these form an ecosystem that can be called the 'industrial layer' (Yülek 2016a). In other words, Turkish industrial policy covering the next ten to twenty years should aim at forming a strong industrial layer that can accelerate the industrialization process and make the country among the top manufacturers of the world.

Currently, the country lacks an adequately strong industrial layer in some manufacturing subsectors, especially those subsectors that higher-

Fig. 6 Capabilities necessary for the formation of an industrial layer

income countries currently specialize in, namely electrical and non-electrical machinery, chemicals, transport equipment (other than automobiles), certain other machinery such as optical and precision equipment, pharmaceuticals, and health and personal care goods. Hausman et al. (2007) suggest that increasing export sophistication, which can be achieved by extending a product range towards that of the higher-income countries, would lead to higher growth rates in developing economies.

With the objective of forming a strong industrial layer, the prospective industrial policy can concentrate on the number of pillars to build or strengthen technical capabilities. Firstly, enhancing the productive capabilities of firms should be an important objective of the policy. Learning by doing leads to diminishing unit costs, informal training of the workforce, formation of an ecosystem of suppliers, and small-scale innovations.

A diminished manufacturing base due to 'premature deindustrialization' (Dasgupta and Singh 2007) in developing countries may thus lead to a loss of valuable time. Some manufacturing is better than no manufacturing, whatever the level of sophistication of the products is, because forces such as learning-by-doing-induced unit cost reductions are at play. Furthermore, manufacturing highly sophisticated and priced products starts with manufacturing products of low- or medium-level sophistication.

A drive to increase the sophistication of a product pattern will obviously benefit from the build-up of productive capabilities. In any case, competition in low-sophistication products are fiercer, and it is not sustainable for countries like Turkey with relatively high wages compared to low-cost producers to compete in such products in the global market.

4.2 Sector Targeting

Shifting towards more sophisticated products necessitates a well-focused sector based on industrial policy for a mid-level industrialized country such as Turkey. The answer to the question of whether a sector-targeting industrial policy is necessary for Turkey is yes, in order to overcome market failures leading to artificially high barriers of entry to more sophisticated industrial products.

4.3 Branding for Product Differentiation

Turkey has experimented with branding programmes such as Turquality. In some subsectors where Turkey has a relatively stronger industrial layer (such as textiles and apparel), the country needs to improve its national- and firm-level branding. This will, again, help raise export prices in global and local markets and support economic growth. Branding is important not only for consumer goods but also for capital goods industries; thus, machinery and intermediate goods industries should also benefit from branding efforts.

4.4 Science, Technology, and Innovation Policies and Innovation in Product Differentiation

Science, technology, and innovation (STI) policies, as a category distinct from industrial policies, would also play a role for a mid-level industrial country, if not for a low-level one. Even if the overall industrial layer needs to be strengthened in Turkey, there are industrial sectors such as automotive spare parts, defence, software, or medical equipment, where certain firms have built up competitive advantages. These sectors would appropriately need support that would fall into the realm of STI policies, which would bolster the technological and R&D capabilities of firms.

One of the key difficulties of such firms is commercialization. They develop prototypes of products but may have difficulty in launching production for domestic and international markets, which would require industrial-scale production facilities as well as successful branding, marketing, and distributing of commercial products. This should be an important component of STI policies. TUBITAK rightly considers commercialization a key activity to be supported. But the success of its support initiatives in this field has not yet been monitored and assessed.

In subsectors in which Turkey has a relatively strong industrial layer, firms' technological and R&D capabilities need to be developed to facilitate innovation. That, in turn, will help raise export prices in global and local markets and, thus, the manufacturing value added. Cooperation between industry and universities, which is manifestly weak, needs to be strengthened so that firms can benefit from the university resources to upgrade their technological and R&D capabilities.

4.5 Development-Based Public Procurement Policy

Public procurement policy should be used actively to foster productive and technological capabilities (Yülek and Taylor 2011). Industrialization efforts in developing countries face considerable barriers from manufacturers in both low-cost countries (in less sophisticated industrial products) and developed countries (in sophisticated industrial products). Obstacles impeding the access of local companies to public and private markets (such as low or negative recognition, inadequate scale effects, or technological barriers) act as typical market failures necessitating government action.

Development-based public procurement provides market and commercialization opportunities to local firms in developing countries, including Turkey, that can be more effective than financial support in developing productive and technological capabilities for firms, especially small and medium-sized enterprises (SMEs). Development-based public procurement policies may assist those efforts by enhancing market opportunities for firms of less industrialized countries (Yülek and Tiryakioğlu 2014; Tiryakioğlu and Yülek 2015).

In Turkey there is a growing awareness about the need for development-based public procurement. However, it is still the case that international firms are favoured in the public procurement of civilian manufactured goods such as elevators, health equipment, and transportation equipment despite growing local manufacturing.

4.6 Reorganization of Industrial Policy Related to Public Entities

Public-sector organization is critical in the development of technical capabilities and industrialization in Turkey. In the current, de facto, situation, the public administration that handles industrial-policy-related matters is quite fragmented, which leads to inefficiencies in the design and implementation of policy. The Ministry of Economy (MoE) handles international trade policy, in particular international commercial agreements and anti-dumping taxes. As the majority of Turkey's international trade is made up of industrial products, the ministry is in fact highly involved in the industrial sector.

MoE also regulates and implements industrial incentives through the General Directorate of Incentives. In Turkey, industrial incentives are considered mostly as a tool of regional development. The incentives decree encourages industrial investments in backward regions by providing tax and social security advantages to firms investing in those regions.

The Ministry of Development (MoD) in its current form draws up multiyear development plans, develops strategies for regional development, and makes approval decisions on line ministries' physical capital investments. The General Directorate of Incentives was first established as a department in the Ministry of Development, formerly called the State Planning Organization in the 1960s.

The Ministry of Science, Industry and Technology (MSIT) has a number of responsibilities. Firstly, it regulates and supervises the safety of industrial products. Secondly, it is responsible for approving the establishment of industrial zones and technoparks, which are mostly undertaken by private-sector agents. Thirdly, it develops industrial strategy documents; however, it does not have direct authority over most strategic measures. Fourthly, it develops science and technology policies and runs certain financial support programmes. Fifthly, it oversees the establishment of R&D centres by firms. R&D centres are encouraged by the ministry by certain tax and social security incentives. The MSIT has recently developed regulations for an industrial participation programme, which establishes the rules for industrial participation in publicly procured industrial products. However, the programme is optional for procuring public entities. Thus, the ministry does not have a tool to enforce the selection of this mode by any public entity.

MSIT has three major related entities. The Scientific and Technological Research Council of Turkey (TUBITAK), SME Promotion and Support Institution (KOSGEB), and the Turkish Patent Institution. Through these institutions the ministry supports R&D efforts and smaller businesses in the country and regulates patenting services.

The Defence Industry Undersecretariat is the procuring body for defence products. It is linked to the Ministry of Defence. It makes decisions on how procurement will be made and establishes offset rules. The defence industry purchases sophisticated industrial products. Thus, the undersecretariat's responsibility extends to industrial policy.

In its current form, industrial policy is thus developed and implemented by a host of different bodies, which leads to inefficiencies, as well as effectiveness problems. The reorganization of these entities could enhance the effectiveness of industrial policy and its outcomes and impacts.

Manpower is critical to the competitiveness of industrial firms. Currently, tertiary educational institutions are regulated and supervised by the Higher Education Council, which is an independent body. Vocational high schools, which provide mid-level technical manpower to industry, on the other hand, are under the jurisdiction of the Ministry of Education. MSIT has no influence over universities and vocational high schools.

A blueprint for reorganization can consist of the following:

- Merging MoE and MIST along the lines of MITI in Japan following the Second World War: Because the country's international trade consists mostly of industrial products, and because trade issues mostly involve the same products, such a merger would increase coordination in the industrial sector. In non-industrial fields such as agriculture, the relevant ministry would coordinate policies with MIST.
- Merging the regional development functions of MoD with MIST: Industrial incentives (currently under MoE) under the new MIST

could be designed both from the perspective of both regional development and industrial development.

- Putting the Undersecretariat of Defence under MSIT: This would also bring about efficiency and coordination gains in the industrial sector.
- Heavy representation of MIST in the Higher Education Council, which regulates and supervises tertiary education in Turkey: This would be necessary to encourage academia–industry relations, including on university curricula.
- Encouraging MIST representation in Ministry of Education's vocational high school policy and implementation.

5 Conclusions

Turkey has utilized different industrial policy sets with varying success. One outcome was that it has fallen into three middle-income traps since 1980 and has been in the third one since 2008. Currently, the country can be considered a medium-level industrialized economy. Under mounting pressure from other competing nations in both its domestic and international markets, the country faces difficulties in progressing from Stage II to Stage III in the industrialization process.

Industrialization is a complex capability-building process requiring appropriate responses to challenges faced and the stage of industrialization. Furthering the level of industrialization in Turkey is likely to help boost overall economic growth rates, increase export earnings, and get the country out of the current middle-income trap.

We conclude that, to continue its rise in the industrialization process, Turkey's industrial policy framework and its administrative structure should be reviewed. The key policy suggestions developed in this chapter are as follows:

- Concentrate on technical capabilities to strengthen the industrial layer;
- Introduce focused sector-targeting industrial policies with a view to developing productive capabilities in the relatively less-developed

industrial firms in addition to implementing STI policies that target technological and R&D capabilities for more developed firms;
- Strengthen cooperation between academia and industry;
- Undertake focused public procurement policies enhancing market potential for local industrial firms and SMEs that are negatively discriminated against;
- Perform an overhaul of institutional structures by reorganizing ministerial organizations.

Appendix 1: Industrial Facilities Included in First Five-Year Industrial Plan (1934–1938) and Their Year of Establishment

Textiles

a) Taşköprü Cannabis Factory (1946)
b) Bursa Merinos Woolen Woven Fabric Factory (1938)
c) Bodrum Sponge Factory (1934)
d) Bakırköy Cotton Weaving Factory (1934)
e) Kayseri Weaving Factory (1935)
f) Ereğli Cloth Weaving Factory (1937)
g) Nazilli Cloth Factory (1937)
h) Malatya Cotton Weaving Factory (1940)
i) Gemlik Silk Fabric Factory (1938)

Mining and Metallurgy

a) Karabük Iron and Steel Factory (1938)
b) Keçiborlu Sulphur Factory (1935)
c) Zonguldak Semicoke Factory (1935)
d) Izmit Paper and Cellulose Factory (1941)

Ceramics

a) Kütahya Ceramic Factory (1940)
b) Beykoz Glass and Bottle Factory (1935)
c) Sivas Cement Factory (1943)

Chemicals

a) İzmit Chlorine and Sodium Hydroxide Factory (1945)
b) Karabük Superphosphate Factory (1944)
c) Isparta Rose Oil Factory (1935)
d) Izmit Hamza Match Factory (1940)

Notes

1. Among many examples in a range of countries are the discussions of encouraging advanced manufacturing methods in the USA, the new industrial policy in the European Union, and the new industrial policy in South Africa.

References

Aydoğuş, Osman, Çağaçan Değer, Elif Tunalı Çalışkan, and Gülçin Gürel Günal. 2015. Import Dependency in Turkey: An Input-Output Analysis. *Ege University Working Papers* 2015/5: 1–9.

Çukurova Genç İşadamları Derneği. 2016. *İmalat Sanayinde Küresel Eğilimler ve Adana: Analiz ve Öneriler*, Report Prepared by PGlobal Global Advisory and Training Services Inc.

Dasgupta, Sukti, and Ajit Singh. 2007. Manufacturing, Services and Premature Deindustrialization in Developing Countries: A Kaldorian Analysis. In *Advancing Development*, ed. George Mavrotas and Anthony Shorrocks, 435–454. London: Palgrave.

Eşiyok, B. Ali. 2004. *Türkiye ekonomisinde kalkinma stratejileri ve sanayileşme (Dün-Bugün-Yarın).* Ankara: Türkiye Kalkınma Bankası Araştırma Müdürlüğü Yayını.

Hausmann, Ricardo, Jason Hwang, and Dani Rodrik. 2007. What You Export Matters. *Journal of Economic Growth* 12 (1): 1–25.

Kaldor, Nicholas. 1967. *Strategic Factors in Economic Development.* New York: Cornell University Press.

Kim, L. 2001. The Dynamics of Technological Learning in Industrialisation. *International Social Science Journal 53* (168): 297–308.

Radošević, Slavo, and Esin Yoruk. 2015. *A New Metrics of Technology Upgrading: The Central and East European Countries in a Comparative Perspective,* GRINCOH Working Paper Series 3.04.

Sanayi ve Teknoloji Bakanlığı. 1973. 50. Yılda Türk Sanayii. Ankara.

———. 1977. *Ağır Sanayi.* Ankara.

Sanır, Arslan Bekir. 2011. *Türk Otomotiv Sanayii Kuruluş ve Gelişim Sürecinde Yazılanlar, Belgeler ve Yorumlar.* Ankara.

Senesen, Ümit, and Gülay Günlük-Senesen. 2003. Import Dependency of Production in Turkey: Structural Change from 1970s to 1990s. In *10th Annual Conference of the Economic Research Forum*, Cairo.

Tiryakioğlu, Murat, and Murat Ali Yülek. 2015. Development-Based Public Procurement Policies: A Selective Survey of Literature, Cross-Country Policy Experience and the Turkish Experience. *Innovation: The European Journal of Social Science Research* 28 (3): 344–359.

World Bank. 2014a. *Trading Up to High Income: Turkey Country Economic Memorandum.* Washington, DC: World Bank Report 82307-TR.

———. 2014b. *Trading Up to High Income.* Washington, DC: World Bank Country Economic Memorandum.

Yücel, Fikret. 2014. *Cumhuriyet Türkiye'sinin sanayileşmede ilk önemli adımı: birinci beş yıllık sanayi planı* 1934–1938.

Yülek, Murat Ali. 1998. *Financial Liberalization and the Real Economy: The Turkish Case,* PhD Dissertation. Ankara: Capital Market Board of Turkey.

———. 2016a. On the Middle Income Trap, the Industrialization Process and Appropriate Industrial Policy. *Journal of Industry, Competition and Trade* 17 (3): 325–348.

———. 2016b. Industrial Policies and Outcomes: A Comparison of Pre-liberalized Korean and Turkish Economies. *Journal of Comparative Asian Development* 15 (1): 179–200.

Yülek, Murat Ali, and Travis K. Taylor, eds. 2011. *Designing Public Procurement Policy in Developing Countries: How to Foster Technology Transfer and Industrialization in the Global Economy*. New York: Springer.

Yülek, Murat Ali, and Murat Tiryakioğlu. 2014. Development-Based Public Procurement Policies: A Selective Survey of Policy Experience. In *Supplement to the 2013 Annual Statistical Report on United Nations Procurement: Procurement for Innovation*. Copenhagen: UNOPS.

Yun, J.J. 2007. The Development of Technological Capability and the Transformation of Inward FDI in Korea from 1962 to 2000. In *Innovation and Technology in Korea: Challenges of a Newly Advanced Economy*, ed. J. Machlich and W. Pascha. Heidelberg: Physika Verlag.

Turkish Labour Market: Outlook, Key Challenges, and Policy Recommendations

Mehmet Huseyin Bilgin and Hakan Danis

1 Introduction

Today, one of the most important economic and social issues facing Turkey is the high unemployment rate; its importance will be revealed only under a detailed analysis of the structure of unemployment and labour market dynamics. The unemployment rate, which has settled around 7–8 per cent for many years, rose gradually with the economic crisis in 2001 and became "structural" almost at the 10 per cent level. While the unemployment rate was 6.5 per cent in 2000, it increased to 8.4 per cent in 2001. In the following years, it continued to increase and reached 10.3 per cent in 2002 and 10.5 per cent in 2003. It decreased slightly, to 10.3 per cent, in 2004 and held steady in 2005. Then it

M. H. Bilgin (✉)
Istanbul Medeniyet University, Istanbul, Turkey

H. Danis
MUFG Union Bank, San Francisco, CA, USA

A. F. Aysan et al. (eds.), *Turkish Economy*,
https://doi.org/10.1007/978-3-319-70380-0_14

decreased to 9.9 per cent in the following two years and remained stable.

Owing to the global financial crisis, however, the unemployment rate jumped significantly, hitting 14.8 per cent in 2009. In subsequent years, this trend reversed, and the unemployment rate retreated to 11.1 per cent in 2010, 9.1 per cent in 2011, and 8.4 per cent in 2012. However, because of the modest slowdown of the Turkish economy after 2013, the unemployment rate gradually increased to 9 per cent in 2013 and 10.9 per cent on average in 2016. In December 2016, the unemployment rate stood at 12.7 per cent.

Despite the rapid growth in the economy following the 2001 crisis, failure to achieve permanent and necessary improvements in the unemployment rate and its structural nature revealed the need for a comprehensive reform of the Turkish labour market. Because the unemployment rate in recent years has started to increase again as a result of the slowdown in the Turkish economy, the necessity of reforms in the labour market gained importance. To become more competitive, flexible, and high value-added, Turkey's labour market is in need of long-lasting, efficient reforms.

In this chapter, we first examine labour market dynamics in Turkey and then discuss labour market reform and make some proposals for Turkey. Finally, we evaluate our main findings.

2 Turkish Labour Market Dynamics

Some details in the Turkish unemployment data are worth noting. Table 1 summarizes the 2016 Turkish labour force indicators and shows the unemployment rate reached 10.9 per cent owing to the modest slowdown in the economy in recent years. Recent statistics indicate that the unemployment rate among females is higher, the non-agricultural unemployment rate is higher than the overall unemployment rate (13 per cent), and youth unemployment (i.e. 15–24 age group) is quite high (19.6 per cent). In addition, the employment rate is 46.3 per cent and is higher among men than women. The labour force participation rate, one of the important labour market indicators, is 52 per cent; broken down

Table 1 Basic labour force indicators, 2016

	Total	Male	Female
15+ age group			
Population (K)	58,720	29,031	29,689
Labour force (K)	30,535	20,899	9,637
Employment (K)	27,205	18,893	8,312
Agriculture (K)	5,305	2,920	2,384
Non-agriculture (K)	21,900	15,973	5,928
Unemployed (K)	3,330	2,006	1,324
Not in labour force (K)	28,185	8,133	20,052
Labour force participation rate (%)	52.0	72.0	32.5
Employment rate (%)	46.3	65.1	28.0
Unemployment rate (%)	10.9	9.6	13.7
Non-agricultural unemployment rate (%)	13.0	10.9	18.1
15–64 age group			
Labour force participation rate (%)	57.0	77.6	36.2
Employment rate (%)	50.6	70.0	31.2
Unemployment rate (%)	11.1	9.8	14.0
Non-agricultural unemployment rate (%)	13.0	10.9	18.2
Youth population (15–24 age) unemployment rate	**19.6**	**17.4**	**23.7**

The figures in the table may not sum to 100 per cent owing to rounding

Source: TURKSTAT (2017)

into rates for men and women, though, the labour force participation rate of men is 72 per cent, which is significantly higher than that of women, which stands at 32.5 per cent.

It can be argued that the main reason behind the high unemployment rates in Turkey is the continuous expansion of the labour force as a result of rapid population growth and insufficient job creation in the economy. Even as the economy recovers and creates new jobs, the unemployment rate slowly falls because people become more optimistic about the economy and many of the marginally attached or discouraged workers re-enter the labour market, which keeps the unemployment rate high. Therefore, the unemployment rate converges to a level higher than its pre-crisis level. The rapid dissolution of jobs in the agricultural sector in recent years has also led to high unemployment rates in Turkey. In particular, despite the robust economic growth between 2002 and 2007, lack of progress in unemployment during the same period can be explained by the rapid population growth and increase in the labour force and decline in agricultural employment. According to data from the Organisation for Economic Co-operation and Development (OECD), from 2004 to 2013, the share of employment in the agricultural sector declined from 29.1 to 23.6 per cent, And data from late 2016 show further declines in the agricultural sector, falling below 20 per cent (19.4 per cent). However, it is still significantly higher than the OECD average of 4.6 per cent in the same period. All these data indicate that while the decline in agricultural employment is an inevitable result of development, employment growth in other sectors has not been sufficient to compensate for the decline (World Bank 2006).

There are also structural issues in the Turkish labour market. The labour market rigidity and educational system in Turkey are the key structural factors. In fact, the current educational system has fallen far short of increasing the labour force to the extent needed by the economy. Although it is not possible to solve the unemployment problem in Turkey solely through economic growth, the main reason why the unemployment rate has started to increase again in recent years is undoubtedly the observed slowdown in the economy. While the Turkish economy grew 8.5 per cent, 5.2 per cent, and 6.1 per cent in 2013, 2014, and 2015 respectively, real economic growth stalled in 2016, growing only 2.9 per cent. In particular, the unemployment rate declined to 9.3 per cent in April 2016 and then steadily increased up to 13 per cent in January 2017. In the same period, real GDP growth slowed down, growing 2.5 per cent on average in the third quarter (2Q16-4Q16).

Moreover, Turkey has among the lowest employment rates in the world (Fig. 1). In particular, according to the World Bank (2006), employment rates in many countries are above 50 per cent and 65 per cent on average in the EU-15, which are significantly higher than levels in Turkey. Selamoglu and Lordoglu (2006) listed structural factors, such as an inability to create sufficient jobs in cities for unskilled workers coming from agriculture, a higher growth rate of the working-age population than total population growth, a lack of ability of the labour force to meet the needs of the economy, and a failure to establish a relationship between the labour market and education, as the main reasons for the low employment rates.

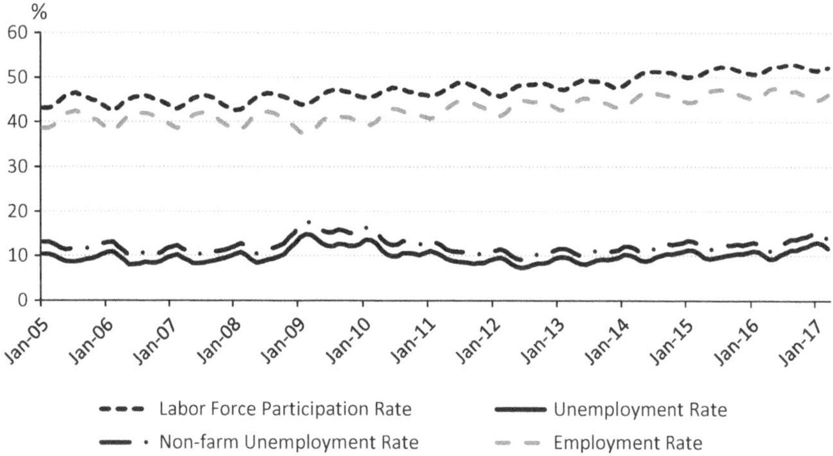

Fig. 1 Basic labour market indicators, 2005–2017 (Source: TURKSTAT; data were retrieved from the Central Bank of the Republic of Turkey (CBRT))

Furthermore, it appears that the composition of the unemployment rate is also of concern. The unemployment rate among young people makes the problem even more worrisome. In 2016, the unemployment rate among the youth was 19.6 per cent (1.4 percentage points higher than the previous year), which demonstrates that the young population is the group most affected by labour market issues. The main reasons for high young unemployment rates are (1) the fact that the 15–24 age group is the first age group to enter the labour market, and they are not preferred by employers because this age group has no or limited work experience; (2) youth have limited knowledge or expertise; (3) employers have higher expectations; and (4) young people have not been trained to meet the needs of the labour market (Selamoglu and Lordoglu 2006). In addition, Sengul (2014) estimated that young workers are almost twice as likely to be unemployed than older workers and young workers are almost three times more likely to lose their jobs. Therefore, the author also argues that high separation rates are the main reason for the relatively high youth unemployment rate compared to adults.

As depicted in Fig. 1, the labour force participation rate in Turkey is also quite low, and this leads to a lower official unemployment rate.

Considering that the average labour force participation rate in OECD countries is 68–70 per cent, the labour force participation rate in Turkey (52 per cent in 2016) is far below the OECD and EU averages. Moreover, while the rate of participation in the female labour force in OECD countries has increased since the 1980s, the labour force participation rate for both men and women gradually declined in the 1990s and 2000s due to increases in schooling and urbanization in Turkey. In particular, as Lordoglu (2006) points out, with the increase of urbanization, women have separated from unpaid family workers and earned a "housewife" status, which is not included in labour force statistics. However, as educated female workers in urban areas began to join the labour force, the labour force participation rate among women has started to increase in recent years (Onder 2013). With the upward trend in the labour force participation rate, the economy needs to generate more employment opportunities to even keep unemployment rate at current levels.[1]

In addition, a high number of discouraged workers, or those not currently looking for work because they believe no jobs are available for them or there are none for which they qualify, reduces the labour force participation rate in Turkey and, therefore, lowers the official unemployment rate. For example, in 2016, the share of workers marginally attached to the labour force was measured at 8.6 per cent. In the same period, according to TURKSTAT, more than two million people were not looking for jobs and thus were out of the labour force, though they are willing to work.

Other important details in the Turkish unemployment data are worth noting. While the unemployment rate in 2016 was 10.9 per cent, detailed labour market statistics point to inefficiencies in the Turkish labour market. While the participation rate has been gradually increasing since 2007 (Fig. 1), the high underemployment rate indicates inefficiencies in the labour market. The underemployed are those who are employed but working less than 40 hours per week for two reasons: economic and non-economic reasons. The statistics show that while workers working part-time for non-economic reasons fluctuate between 1 and 2 per cent (of the total labour force), there have been some improvements in the ratio of those working part-time for economic reasons (Fig. 2). In total, the trend in the underemployment rate in Turkey indicates that the Turkish economy has not been entirely successful to shrink its underemployment problem and it must find other ways to resolve this issue.

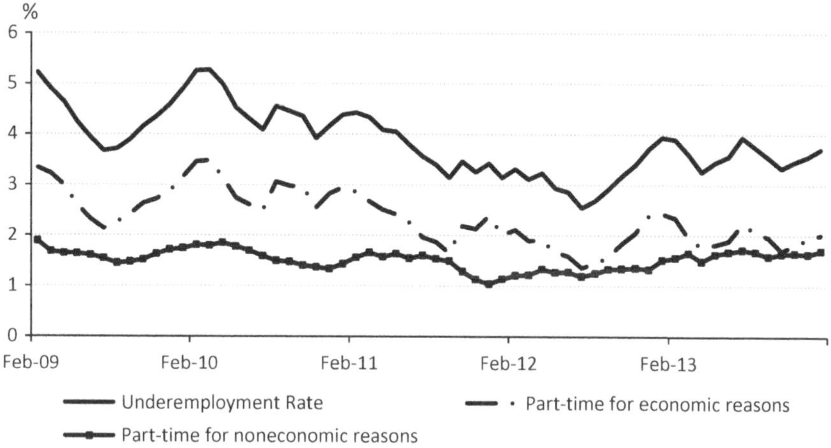

Fig. 2 Underemployment in Turkish labour market, 2009–2014 (Source: TURKSTAT (Data is retrieved from CBRT))

Furthermore, in Turkey, the rates of unpaid family workers, employers and the own account workers are well above the EU and OECD averages. According to TURKSTAT's 2016 statistics; the rate of the regular employee in the labour force in Turkey is 67.8 per cent, the rate of own account workers is 17.1 per cent, the rate of unpaid family worker is 10.5 per cent and the rate of employer is 4.6 per cent. In addition, in 2015, the ratio of self-employed (sum of unpaid family workers, own account workers and employers) to total employment in Turkey was 33.0 per cent while it was 15.6 per cent in the Euro area (OECD 2017). Considering that this ratio was 45.5 per cent in Turkey in 2004, it is self-evident that the share of self-employed has declined rapidly in recent years.

Although under Turkish law women and men enjoy equal opportunity, the employment rate among women is very low. For example, Lordoglu (2006) examines employment rates and asserts that women are mostly in the labour force in rural areas and mostly in skilled jobs in urban areas, or they are completely out of the labour force because they are recorded as housewives. Additionally, the labour force participation rate among women is lower than it is among men. Bilgin and Kilicarslan (2008) mention that the low rate of labour participation among women can be partially explained by social and cultural factors. In other words, cultural and educational traditions could be the major reasons that prevent women from participating in working life. The dense rural-to-urban labour migration and the fact that women living in cities do not have the necessary skills also limit their employment opportunities (Turkiye Kamu-Sen 2004). Furthermore, general unemployment, non-agricultural unemployment, and youth unemployment rates are also higher among women than men.

Furthermore, as TUSIAD (2002) points out, high population growth and an insufficient increase in employment opportunities in the formal sector (which remains below population growth) push people out of the formal sector and into the informal sector with low productivity and low wages. Therefore, unemployment in Turkey is able to hide within 'artificial employment forms' by creating low income and little contribution to national income (Ekin 1997). While in Western countries government and special employment agencies and unemployment insurance schemes that fully encompass labour markets have transformed various types of unemployment into involuntary unemployment, the various socio-economic features that exist in developing countries like Turkey have forced people to 'work in non-productive artificial and informal forms of employment' (Ekin 2003). Therefore, there is a large informal sector in Turkey, including in urban areas.

Indeed, it is understood that informal employment is still a major problem, although it has declined significantly in recent years. The official statistics in Turkey indicate that 32.7 per cent of workers had no form of social security in December 2016, a 0.6 percentage point increase compared to the same period in the previous year. It can be argued that the main reason why the informal labour market is so large is the high cost of non-wage labour costs. The burdens on employment have both adversely affected employment and increased the informal sector. In this framework, it is estimated that employment taxes have a larger impact on employment in labour-intensive sectors, in other words, where labour costs represent a greater share of total costs (TUSIAD 2004).

In addition, there is also the case of rapidly growing 'illegal immigrant worker' in Turkey in the 1990s. Immigrant workers, especially from neighbouring countries including eastern European countries, the former Soviet Union, and Iraq, are working illegally in sectors such as construction, weaving, leather, and hospitality. Since 2000, immigrant workers have come increasingly from African countries. In the last few years, it can be argued that more than two million Syrians who have escaped from the civil war in Syria and sought shelter in Turkey shook up Turkey's labour market dynamics. It is estimated that hundreds of thousands of Syrians are working in low-skill jobs in the informal service sector.

3 Labour Market Reform to Boost Employment and Suggestions for Turkey

In this section, we discuss what Turkey needs to do in combating unemployment and make some suggestions. Within this framework, we list the necessary steps to take.[2]

The main reasons behind the high unemployment rate in Turkey are the rigidities on both the supply and demand sides of the labour market. In other words, as Bilgin (2008) discusses, the main reason for the so-called structural unemployment is the inability to match labour supply with demand. This finding also indicates that a low unemployment rate cannot be achieved through mere economic growth (TUSIAD 2004). Thus, policies should focus on the labour market, which should be made more flexible, and encourage more employment with a comprehensive reform of the labour market, as suggested by the World Bank (2006) in its "Turkish Labour Market Report."

In fact, in recent years, some steps have been taken towards creating employment in Turkey, and some have become law. For example, the 2008 Employment Package aimed at increasing employment among women and youth. In addition, many active and passive labour market policies, including unemployment insurance and education opportunities for young people, were also implemented (Duman 2014). Despite the so-called employment packages, however, limited progress has been made (Maliye Bakanligi 2011). In addition, after experiencing an upward trend in the unemployment rate in recent quarters, the Turkish government introduced new measures to stimulate employment in early 2017.

To reduce the unemployment rate, resolve the structural problems in the labour market, and increase productivity with higher employment in the coming period, the following regulations could be revised: minimum wages, severance pay, social security premiums, shortening of weekly average working hours, and flexible work contracts (Maliye Bakanligi 2011). In addition, the creation and development of human capital, along with regional minimum wage and comprehensive education reforms, are of great importance in this framework.

Economic growth is crucial to combat cyclical unemployment. However, dealing with unemployment at the macro level alone is not enough to address the unemployment problem. Indeed, structural unemployment is unlikely to be solved only though economic growth. On the other hand, as suggested by TUSIAD (2004), it is necessary to make growth 'employment-friendly', and this is possible only if the rigidities in the labour market are tackled. The growth performance of Turkey during the 2002–2007 period and the course of unemployment suggest that the solution should be sought elsewhere. The growth–unemployment relationship, like the countries of continental Europe, shows that the main reason for unemployment in Turkey lies far beyond growth.

In the context of a labour market reform, employment protection should transit from "protecting jobs" to "protecting workers". In the current system, the barriers to offering severance packages and flexible work protect mainly those workers who actually have a job, not workers in general. Reforms should cover flexibility in hiring, setting wages, working time and forms and firing employees at will. Labour laws should focus on not only protecting jobs and employees but also creating employment. The idea put forward at this point is called 'flexicurity' (Tatlioglu 2012). This strategy, often referred to as 'flexible security', on the one hand, strengthens employees' adaptability and improves their skills and, on the other hand, improves the flexibility of the labour market through regulatory reforms (Dunya Bankasi 2008).

One of the main reasons for structural unemployment in Turkey is that the legal framework and institutional structure are not 'employment-friendly'. Existing legal frameworks – legislation and institutional structures – hinder job creation rather than encourage it. Therefore, it is also of great importance to make the legal and institutional structure employment-friendly. Although there is flexibility in hiring and firing, severance package and termination benefits severely limit this flexibility (Bilgin and Ari 2010). Furthermore, the law on severance payments, which was enacted in a period when where there was no disability and unemployment insurance and job security were provided only by the Labour Law, becomes a heavy burden for enterprises over time and causes employers to fall into payment difficulties, especially during economic downturns. It could also be argued that severance pay, which compels dismissals, negatively affects job creation. In particular, current job-security regulations both increase informal employment and hinder employment growth. Therefore, introducing more flexible legislation and reducing burdens on employers would reduce informal employment.

In terms of non-wage labour costs, Turkey's labour market is also far from flexible. The data show that there are heavy burdens on employment. With regard to the mechanism of wage determination, there is also some rigidity in the labour market. As Selamoglu (2002) points out, while the inadequacy of wage flexibility causes an increase in the wage level, it makes it particularly difficult for groups such as low-skilled, young, and women to find jobs. Therefore, the wage determination mechanisms should be made more flexible by considering the realities of the economy, market, and competition conditions in the global economy. Karaca and Kocabas (2011) also found that inequality in education exists between men and women. On the other hand, the tax burden on the minimum wage should also be carefully assessed. As the gap between the cost of the minimum wage to employers and the income of employees grows, restrictions on employment opportunities for the low-skilled labour force become inevitable (Selamoglu 2002).

One of the most important structural reforms, especially stemming from regional differences, is the regional minimum wage. In this context, a new reform could be implemented that would set the regional minimum wage closer to the average wage in that region rather than a single nationwide minimum wage. In areas with low living standards and productivity levels, the transition to a regional minimum wage may be useful in combating unemployment (Maliye Bakanligi 2011).

Regarding flexible working styles, the Turkish labour market is far from flexible. Unlike in OECD countries, the share of part-time employees in Turkey is low. Employers and employees have not yet fully utilized the Turkish Labour Law 4857 (which came into force in 2003) on flexible jobs such as part-time work, temporary work, on-call work, and so forth. Hence, flexible forms of work should be facilitated and promoted. As seen from a global perspective, private employment agencies can play an important role in the fight against unemployment, so in Turkey private employment agencies should be used to increase employment. For example, according to TISK (2004), private employment agencies, which are permitted to operate under Turkish Labour Law 4857, can make important contributions to increasing the dynamism and effectiveness of the labour market by assuming an important role in the implementation of active labour market policies in Turkey through vocational education, retraining, adaptation training, and consultancy services over time. This is consistent with what Hirshleifer et al. (2016) found in their empirical paper. Their analysis indicates that the impact of training on employment is stronger when training is offered by private agencies.

The potential benefits of having a young population are quite large. However, if this large group of young people cannot find a place in the labour market and society today, risks will increase in coming years (Dunya Bankasi 2008). For example, high youth unemployment would urge young adults to postpone getting married, buying homes and begin families. In the long run, this trend would lead to slower economic growth, lower tax receipts and could cause social instability. In this context, an educational system that provides young people with new skills is one of the goals of youth employment policies in many countries. In reality, a lack of skills serves as a barrier preventing many young people entering the labour market. A better employment target for the future requires educational reforms that will equip all young people with the skills they need to find good jobs following graduation (Dunya Bankasi 2008).

In this context, it can also be stated that one of the major causes of unemployment in Turkey is the job-skills mismatch. Especially in recent years, the high unemployment rate among new graduates shows the necessity to focus on the seriousness of this situation. There is no doubt that this is due to poor planning in higher education and vocational-technical education in Turkey. Indeed, the current educational system falls far short of providing the kinds of qualifications needed in the economy and being compatible with the new technology (Bilgin 2008). A more recent empirical study by Hirshleifer et al. (2016) also found that Turkey's vocational training programmes for the unemployed have statistically significant effects on the quality of employment, but after three years these effects disappear. Therefore, to meet the demand of the economy and labour market, and especially to improve the employability of young people, Turkey needs new employment mechanisms (DPT 2006).

In the fight against structural unemployment, educational reforms must be designed to resolve the mismatch between labour supply and demand, create and develop human capital, bring higher education and vocational-technical education to levels that create a workforce that meets the needs of the economy and business world. For this purpose, a plan should be made by taking into account future needs with the participation of relevant ministries, non-governmental organizations, the Union of Chambers and Commodity Exchanges of Turkey (TOBB), and the Council of Higher Education (YOK). In this context, cooperation between educational institutions and the private sector should be expanded, and models that encourage practical or on-the-job training should be developed. Also, in vocational education, practical education, which has an important place in the training of a qualified labour force, should be given priority. Such steps may contribute to reducing youth unemployment, in particular by harmonizing education with the needs of the labour market.

Various active labour market policies applied in many countries, especially in OECD and EU countries, should also be implemented in the fight against unemployment. Within these policies, projects for education and vocational training and retraining should be developed, and certain unemployed groups should be ensured that they will be able to find work. For example, unemployed people who lose their jobs during an economic recession or whose skills become obsolete owing to advances in technology or changes in market conditions should be trained in areas where they are needed and assisted in their job search. However, in practice, it could be more effective to subsidize private-sector companies that provide training and education rather than the public sector (Bilgin 2008).

Active labour market policies aim to increase employability by improving the skills and competence of the workforce. These policies include the development of workforce training, vocational education and workforce adjustment programmes, vocational guidance and counselling services, development of job search strategies, assistance to disadvantaged groups such as the unemployed, the disabled, women, and youth in job searches, and provision of entrepreneurship training and employment-guaranteed training programmes.

Within this framework, new active labour market programmes should be used, or resources allocated to these programmes should be increased, to improve the qualifications and skill sets of the unemployed, disadvantaged, and existing workers to free them up from the agricultural sector (DPT 2006).

On the other hand, country experiences show that active labour market policies are effective at decreasing unemployment. Within the framework of active labour market policies, Layard et al. (2005) recommend the following policies to combat unemployment:

- Decrease duration of unemployment benefit,
- Provide job-search assistance to unemployed workers,
- Offer training programmes that target adults to increase the employability of unemployed workers and implement active policies to provide placement in high-quality jobs,
- Revise employment protection laws.

In addition, as TISK (2004) suggested, the Turkish Labour Agency (IS-KUR) should move in the direction of active labour market policies. IS-KUR, which is responsible for implementing active labour force programmes, should be given sufficient funding and its institutional capacity should be expanded. In addition to supporting private offices that execute agency business, improvements in IS-KUR's infrastructure and capacity would be crucial in the fight against unemployment by increasing IS-KUR's effectiveness.

4 Conclusion

Today, Turkey's most important economic and social problem is high unemployment. When the structure of the existing unemployment and labour market dynamics is examined, its importance becomes more apparent. While economic growth is crucial in fighting unemployment and creating jobs, it is unlikely that Turkey will be able resolve its unemployment problem solely through economic growth, since a significant portion of the current unemployment issue is structural in nature.

Despite its flexibility in some areas, the rigid structure of the Turkish labour market and the inability of the economy to generate sufficient employment make structural reform of the labour market inevitable. Moreover, the Turkish labour market has problems such as rigidities in both supply and demand. It is clear that these problems can only be overcome by structural reforms. Therefore, policymakers should focus on the labour market, implementing various labour market reform measures to make the market more flexible and encourage job creation. The first thing that Turkey needs to do is to make the labour market more employment-friendly. Comprehensive educational reform should also accompany labour market reforms in order to resolve the structural unemployment issue and increase job opportunities for certain groups such as young people. Furthermore, programmes that target bringing down the cost of employment by providing support and incentives to employers could be successful in the short term at fighting cyclical unemployment. However, it seems unrealistic that structural unemployment could be reduced without increasing labour market flexibility and undertaking comprehensive labour market reform.

Because economic activity in the Turkish economy slowed down in 2016 and current policies have failed to bring the unemployment rate closer to the natural rate, the Turkish government has focused on fighting unemployment and launched some sort of economic campaign. This campaign, which aims to reduce the cost of employment and provide incentives to employers, could reduce cyclical unemployment.

Notes

1. Although this is true for the short term, Tansel et al. (2016) found empirical support (i.e. cointegration between the labour force participation rate and the unemployment rate) for *the unemployment invariance hypothesis* in Turkey, which suggests that the long-run unemployment rate is independent of the labour force.
2. For more information on labour market flexibility and reforms, see MUSIAD (2015).

References

Bilgin, M. Huseyin. 2008. Artan issizlige karsi ne yapilabilir? *Radikal Gazetesi*, December 1.

Bilgin, M. Huseyin, and Ismihan N. Kilicarslan. 2008. An Analysis of the Unemployment in Selected MENA Countries and Turkey. *Journal of Third World Studies* 25: 189–205.

Bilgin, M. Huseyin, and Selcuk Ari. 2010. *ABD Deneyimi Isiginda Emek Piyasasi Reformu ve Issizligi Azaltici Politikalar*. Istanbul: TUSIAD Yayinlari.

DPT. 2006. *Dokuzuncu Kalkinma Plani: 2007–2013*. Ankara: Devlet Planlama Teskilati Yayini.

Duman, Anil. 2014. *Labor Market Institutions, Policies, and Performance: Flexibility and Security in Turkey*. Istanbul: TUSIAD Yayinlari.

Dunya Bankasi. 2008. *Türkiye'nin Gelecek Nesillerine Yatirim Yapmak: Okuldan Ise Gecis ve Türkiye'nin Kalkinmasi*, Report No: 44048-TU. http://siteresources.worldbank.org/TURKEYEXTN/Resources/361711-1216301653427/5218036-1216302388732/Youth_Employment_Study-tr.pdf. Accessed 28 June 2016.

Ekin, Nusret. 1997. *Kuresel Bilgi Caginda Egitim-Verimlilik-Istihdam*. Istanbul: Istanbul Ticaret Odası Yayini.

———. 2003. Turkiye'de Issizlik: Is Aramayan Issizler - Kirsal Yoksullar - Kentsel Kayitdisi Yapay Istihdamdakiler - Acik Issizler. *Kamu-Is Dergisi* 7(2). http://www.kamu-is.org.tr/pdf/729.pdf. Accessed 28 June 2016.

Hirshleifer, Sarojini, David McKenzie, Rita Almeida, and Cristobal Ridao-Cano. 2016. The Impact of Vocational Training for the Unemployed: Experimental Evidence from Turkey. *The Economic Journal* 126 (597): 2115–2146.

Karaca, Nuray Gokcek, and Fatma Kocabas. 2011. The Position of Women in Social and Economic Life: A Comparison between the EU and Turkey. *Eurasian Economic Review* 1 (1): 66–94.

Layard, Richard, Stephen Nickell, and Richard Jackman. 2005. *Unemployment: Macroeconomic Performance and the Labour Market*. 2nd ed. New York: Oxford University Press.

Lordoglu, Kuvvet. 2006. *Turkiye Isgucu Piyasalari (Durum Raporu)*. Istanbul: Istanbul Serbest Muhasebeci Mali Musavirler Odası.

Maliye Bakanligi. 2011. *Turkiye'de Isgucu Piyasasi Sorunlari ve Cozum Onerileri*. Strateji Gelistirme Baskanligi Arastirma Raporu.

MUSIAD. 2015. *Isgucu Piyasalari: Issizlik-Esitsizlik*, 2015 Turkiye Ekonomisi Raporu, 97.

OECD. 2017. *OECD Labour Force Statistics 2016*. Paris: OECD Publishing. https://doi.org/10.1787/oecd_lfs-2016-en.

Onder, Nurcan. 2013. Turkiye'de Kadin Isgucunun Gorunumu. *CSGB Calisma Dunyasi Dergisi* 1: 35–61.

Selamoglu, Ahmet. 2002. Gelismis Ulkelerde Istihdam Politikalari, Esneklik Arayisi ve Etkileri. *Kocaeli Universitesi Sosyal Bilimler Enstitusu Dergisi* 4: 33–63.

Selamoglu, Ahmet, and Kuvvet Lordoglu. 2006. *Katilim Surecinde Avrupa Birligi ve Turkiye'de Isgucu ve Istihdamin Gorunumu*. Ankara: Belediye-Is Yayinlari.

Sengul, Gonul. 2014. Ins and Outs of Unemployment in Turkey. *Emerging Markets Finance and Trade* 50 (3): 28–44.

Tansel, Aysit, Zeynel Abidin Ozdemir, and Emre Aksoy. 2016. Unemployment and Labour Force Participation in Turkey. *Applied Economics Letters* 23 (3): 184–187.

Tatlioglu, Ezgi. 2012. Guvenceli Esneklik Cercevesinde Esnek Calismanin Uygulanabilirligi. *Electronic Journal of Vocational Colleges* 2: 69–84.

TISK. 2004. Ulkemizin En Onemli Sorunu: Issizlikle Mucadele. *Isveren Dergisi* September.

TURKSTAT. 2017 *Labor Force Statistics, 2016*, Turkish Statistical Institute, No. 24635, March 23, 2017.

Turkiye Kamu-Sen. 2004. *Istihdam, Issizlik ve Ucret Sorunlarina Cozum Arayislari*. Ankara: Turkiye Kamu-Sen AR-GE Yayinlari.

TUSIAD. 2002. *Turkiye'de Isgucu Piyasasi ve Issizlik*. Istanbul: TUSIAD Yayinlari.

———. 2004. *Turkiye'de Isgücü Piyasasinin Kurumsal Yapisi ve Issizlik*. Istanbul: TUSIAD Yayinlari.

World Bank. 2006. *Turkey: Labor Market Study*, Report No: 33254-TR. http://siteresources.worldbank.org/INTTURKEY/Resources/361616-1144320150009/Labor_Study.pdf. Accessed 28 June 2016.

Developing National Competence in Nuclear Energy: The Case of Turkey

Hatice Karahan

Abbreviations

AFP	Atoms for Peace
BOO	Build-Own-Operate
CBRT	Central Bank of the Republic of Turkey
EC	European Commission
GW	Gigawatt
IAEA	International Atomic Energy Agency
MW	Megawatt
NIMBY	Not in My Backyard
NPP	Nuclear Power Plant
OECD	Organisation for Economic Co-operation and Development
TAEK	Turkish Atomic Energy Authority
TETAS	Turkish Electricity Trade and Contract Corporation
TUBITAK	Scientific and Technological Research Council of Turkey
TurkStat	Turkish Statistical Institute
WNA	World Nuclear Association.

H. Karahan (✉)
Department of Economics and Finance, School of Business, Istanbul Medipol University, Istanbul, Turkey

A. F. Aysan et al. (eds.), *Turkish Economy*,
https://doi.org/10.1007/978-3-319-70380-0_15

1 Introduction

Energy security, which is defined as the continuous availability of reasonably priced energy sources, is a very critical matter today for a number of countries around the world. As a developing and populous economy with an ever-growing need for energy, Turkey serves as an example in this context. Statistics on energy dependence, indicating the extent to which an economy relies upon imports to meet its energy demand, clearly reveal the country's urgent need for action. Owing to its considerable economic and demographic growth, Turkey's energy dependence has increased in the 2000s, reaching 77.5 per cent in 2015 (Fig. 1). Such a level of reliance, which demonstrates the low sufficiency of national energy resources, implies potential future risks concerning the dynamics of national energy security as well as the economy.

As depicted in Fig. 2, the current account deficit problem experienced by the Turkish economy stems mainly from its energy dependence. When (net) energy imports[1] are excluded, the current account balance of the economy exhibits much more sustainable levels of deficits or even some surpluses from time to time. Thus, the graph clearly shows the structural importance of energy for Turkey to reduce the risks in this context. At this point, it should be emphasized that a sizable portion of Turkish

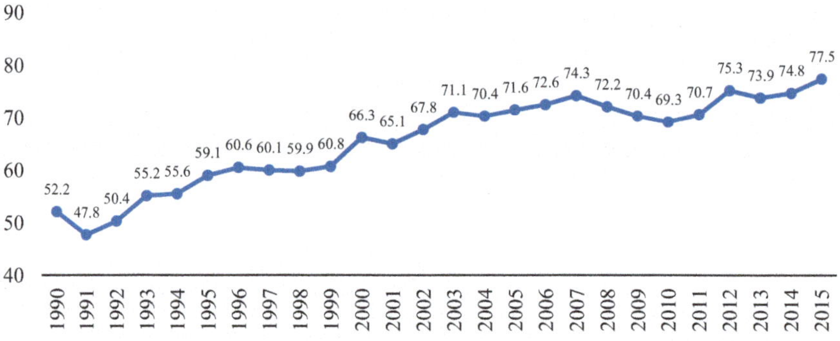

Fig. 1 Energy dependence (Calculated by Eurostat as net imports divided by the sum of gross inland energy consumption plus bunkers) of Turkey (%) (*Data Source: EuroStat*)

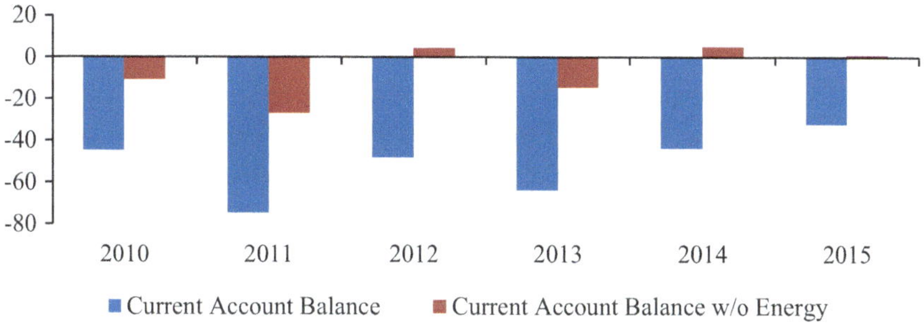

Fig. 2 Current account balance in Turkish economy (billion USD) (Data Source: CBRT, TurkStat, author's calculations)

energy imports is composed of natural gas, which is used largely for power generation in the country.

Hence, accompanied by certain necessary measures to improve energy efficiency and saving, it is essential for Turkey to increase its use of national resources in an effective way. Being aware of this need, recent governments have focused on formulating policies involving the use of alternative sources of energy, renewables and nuclear foremost among them. This chapter intends to discuss the developments in the nuclear space in the country.

As is well known, many countries in the world have been using nuclear power for decades to meet their pressing energy needs. Nuclear power generates electricity by boiling water into steam to drive turbines through the heat produced by nuclear fission that is created by uranium fuel. Providing constant and reliable supplies of electricity on a large scale with relatively benign environmental impacts, nuclear has undeniably been an attractive option for global energy supply despite the safety concerns that have arisen from time to time.

Nuclear energy provides more than 10 per cent of global electricity. Based on data from the World Nuclear Association (WNA), 31 countries use nuclear power to obtain up to three-quarters of their electricity, and a substantial number of these economies rely on it for one-quarter to one-third of their supply. International Atomic Energy Agency (IAEA) statistics show that as of December 2016, 450 reactors operate worldwide, delivering an electrical capacity of 391.9 GW in total (IAEA PRIS). More than three-quarters of those operating reactors are located in Northern America, Western Europe, and Far East Asia. Plus, in parallel to the projections of substantially increasing global electricity demand in the coming decades, new nuclear investments are being made in various countries, particularly the developing ones. Data as of December 2016 reveal that 60 new reactors around the world are under construction, while some additional reactors are being planned.

In this framework, although some countries are quite experienced with nuclear power generation, some are taking relatively newer steps. Turkey is in the latter group. In fact, the country has long considered taking advantage of nuclear energy but failed to take the necessary steps for quite some time, for a variety of reasons. As will be discussed in the next section, the nuclear story of Turkey finally emerged in a concrete way in May 2010, when an intergovernmental agreement was signed with Russia for a nuclear power plant (NPP) in Akkuyu, a province of Mersin located on the southern coast of Turkey. The Akkuyu project was followed by a second agreement signed with Japan in 2013 for the construction of a NPP in the city of Sinop, situated on the northern coast of the country. While studies for a third plant are currently under way, the Akkuyu and Sinop projects seem to have made significant strides towards preparation. Those two power plants are planned to have a capacity of 4800 and 4480 MW respectively, which would help reduce the country's dependence on imported natural gas for generating electricity.

As in a number of earlier examples worldwide, international collaboration on NPPs is a rational shortcut to salvation for countries with insufficient indigenous energy resources and a lack of nuclear knowledge. On the other hand, to have sustainable nuclear energy policies, including aspects ranging from the management of plants to planning for new ones, countries need to develop their own national competence. A crucial attribute in this respect is the responsibility for ensuring nuclear safety. In terms of long-term planning, certain actors like South Korea and India serve as successful examples that launched nuclear programmes with external support and ended up with extensive technical skills among their own workers allowing them to advise newcomers to the field.

All in all, it is widely accepted that countries relying on external expertise on NPPs must do their best to be intelligent consumers (IAEA 2011a) and adopt national energy strategies that include plans to acquire nuclear know-how over time. Experience indicates that a truly successful nuclear programme goes beyond buying relevant technology from abroad and necessitates building up national competences in a comprehensive way. At this point, there is no doubt that Turkey, as a new player entering the field, should embrace this universal approach in order to implement a rewarding nuclear programme.

Nuclear competence building is admittedly a complex job that requires a simplified and well-defined plan initially. This certainly applies to Turkey, as well. In an attempt to shed light on the matter, the rest of this chapter will discuss the features of a desirable nuclear adoption plan, with a focus on Turkey. For this purpose, nuclear developments in the country are briefly discussed, after which a framework for the pillars of an appropriate strategy is drawn up.

2 Background Information: Turkey's Nuclear Story

Nuclear energy is not a new concept for Turkey. In fact, the country has the honour of being the first state in the world to sign the Atoms for Peace (AFP) agreement with the USA in 1955, which had launched an era promoting global cooperation in nuclear technology. A year later, the General Secretariat of the Atomic Energy Commission was founded in Ankara, while the project to build a nuclear reactor for research purposes in the Çekmece region of Istanbul was also launched. By 1962, the reactor was ready to operate within the Çekmece Nuclear Research and Training Centre surrounding it. In the early years of the atomic excitement, Turkey's efforts at accelerating scientific studies in the field proceeded at a notable speed and led to the establishment of the Ankara Nuclear Research and Training Centre in 1967. In 1969, the country signed the international

Non-Proliferation Treaty that would support its national plans on producing nuclear energy and even the relevant fuel for peaceful uses, aside from conducting research and development (R&D) in the area.

As indicated by this enthusiasm, Turkey was a leading and eager promoter of nuclear power intending to generate nuclear energy since the 1960s. However, the country's earnestly launched nuclear story began to crack in the late 1970s in the wake of the disappointment over the first NPP to be constructed by a Swedish firm. Three later attempts with different partners and models in the 1980s, 1990s, and early 2000s failed as well, delaying the nuclear dreams of the country for decades. While numerous governments that took office in this period continuously expressed their interest in nuclear energy and included relevant policies in the five-year national development plans, none of them was able to make tangible progress.

The frustrations over the decades stemmed from a range of factors, including bilateral disagreements, legal issues, and economic circumstances. Moreover, it should be noted that, considering the minimum amount of time required for the successful activation of a nuclear power project, nothing less than a long-term vision and determination would have been acceptable. At this point, one dominant cause lying behind the failures in Turkey's nuclear history was indisputably the political instability the country faced in certain periods, associated with relatively short-term governments and several military coups. As a consequence, the "Atoms for Turkey" ambitions were shelved for nearly half a century, paving the way for prompter and more practical energy solutions, in particular natural gas.

In 2006, a new page was turned in the country's nuclear story, when the sitting government announced plans to build three NPPs and initiated relevant negotiations. In the meantime, a new law regarding the construction and operation of NPPs and energy sale was ratified in 2007, followed by the publication of the regulations and criteria for investors (WNA 2015). Afterwards, TETAS, the Turkish Electricity Trade and Contract Corporation, called for tenders in 2008 for the first power plant to be built in Akkuyu. Following a new series of complications, the decades-long adventure ended up with an intergovernmental agreement signed with Russia in 2010.

According to the agreement, Rosatom, the State Atomic Energy Corporation of Russia, was to become the contractor of the Akkuyu NPP project based on a Build-Own-Operate (BOO) model. Here it should be underlined that the BOO plan settled upon for Akkuyu is in fact a scheme unusual for NPP deals and also a first for Rosatom. The contract, consisting of all phases extending to decommissioning, envisages a seven-year period for the system to launch upon the completion of the preparation stage. In this context, the first unit at the Akkuyu NPP is expected to be commissioned in the year 2022, with the remaining three reactors to be online at one-year intervals thereafter.

Meanwhile, negotiations for a second NPP went forward as well. The proposal offered by a consortium headed by Mitsubishi Heavy Industries of Japan and Areva of France for an NPP in the city of Sinop concluded with an intergovernmental agreement signed between Turkey and Japan in 2013. The Sinop project is designed to have four reactors, the first of which is expected to start operating in the year 2023. Furthermore, plans for a third NPP are on the table to broaden the country's nuclear capacity.

In consequence, the nuclear story of Turkey finally seems to be moving forward through international collaborations as is being done in many countries throughout the world. However, global decades-long experience also reveals that for any starter, implementing a successful nuclear programme is a complicated issue that demands acquiring comprehensive knowledge and skills beyond importing systems. Therefore, Turkey at this stage also needs to take into account the further chapters of its nuclear story that definitely require the development of national competencies in nuclear. The following section draws up a basic framework for that necessity.

3 Discussion: Main Pillars of Nuclear Strategy

Establishing a strategy to develop national proficiencies is the key to a successful nuclear programme. South Korea serves as an ideal example of that. History shows that Turkey had started its nuclear attempts no later than South Korea, but while the former fought various problems delaying the progress, the latter gradually advanced in the field following a decent long-term strategy that eventually led to exporting nuclear technology. As witnessed in the case of South Korea, nuclear planning has multidimensional aspects. That is why it is helpful to proceed with the discussion based on a basic framework for the nuclear strategy needed. In this respect, Fig. 3 illustrates the main pillars of the strategy, each of which is critical for a national nuclear strategy. As will be explained, those pillars are also interconnected to a certain extent.

3.1 Human Capital

Within this framework, human capital is undoubtedly an integral part. The significance of education in the nuclear field cannot be overestimated, considering the requirements of high-level competence and safety.

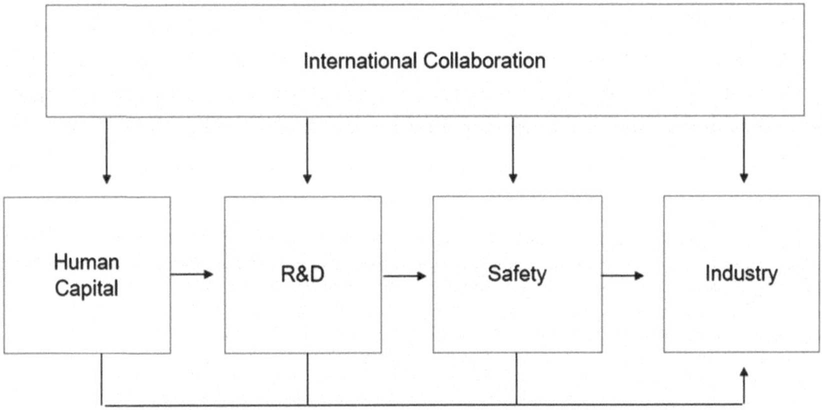

Fig. 3 A framework for nuclear strategy

At this point, it should be emphasized that a nuclear programme is a long-term venture from the construction of a power plant to its decommissioning. There is a saying that nuclear power plants run on money and expertise (Kara and Mattila 1996). In this context, it should be noted that the nuclear sector includes a wide range of tasks and, hence, employs specialists from various fields. Therefore, for a sustainable nuclear programme, a detailed labour force plan should be developed in the early stages, in which job descriptions and the associated education channels must be well defined.

For this purpose, it makes sense to start with a classification of the nuclear jobs required. This is because, whereas some jobs for running an NPP necessitate a high level of competence in nuclear, others are performed by non-nuclear personnel. In this regard, the categorization devised by the Nuclear Energy Agency based on the degrees of so-called nuclearization within the industry can be used as a practical guide.

According to this classification, the top level of competence is fulfilled by 'nuclear' people, such as nuclear engineers and radiochemists, who are educated in pure nuclear fields. The smaller group of high-level professionals placed at this level are associated with long periods of specialized education or experience (OECD 2012). The second layer consists of the 'nuclearized' people from non-nuclear engineering fields who are equipped with nuclear knowledge. At the bottom of the categorization, on the other hand, are the 'nuclear aware' people that serve as craft and administrative personnel who have the nuclear awareness needed to work in the industry. These categories should also be defined based on functions related to power plants, which can be split into construction, operation, and decommissioning. Such a taxonomy helps clarify the job roles required for each function and determine the educational needs of the country (OECD 2012). On the other hand, aside from NPPs, a workforce would also be needed for developing the pillars of R&D, safety, and industry. Hence, similar taxonomies are necessary for the job roles that would support the remaining pillars as well.

Once the job descriptions have been drawn up, the next step would be checking the demand and supply balance in the country for such a workforce in order to reveal the gaps that need to be filled. Accordingly, the government would have to focus on a systematic education plan for a competent labour force essential for the national nuclear programme, which should last for decades. In this framework, educational capabilities of the national universities must be assessed in order to be able to effectively design and offer the programmes needed. Moreover, relevant on-the-job training and continuous educational support would be needed. Nuclear education and training is indeed a multidimensional issue (EC 2015).

As for nuclear education in Turkey, history dates back to 1961 when Istanbul Technical University launched a postgraduate programme in nuclear engineering; followed by an undergraduate programme at Hacettepe University in 1982. Those two programmes were later followed by master's and PhD programmes offered by Ege University and Ankara University respectively. It should however be noted that part of those academic programmes was closed or lost popularity over time. Hence, despite such attempts at building educational programmes in the past, Turkey was unable to develop and retain qualified human capital in the field. A basic reason for that was the unavailability or limitedness of nuclear work opportunities in the country.

Based on this experience, ensuring a plan that will help Turkey reach a sustainable human capital capacity is urgent for an ideal national nuclear strategy. There is no doubt that the country's ongoing cooperation with foreign academic institutions will contribute to the development of the human resources required for nuclear goals. However, considering the decades-long requirements of a national nuclear strategy, Turkey must rebuild its relevant education system.

For this purpose, relevant national institutes, centres, or programmes need to be invigorated. In this respect, selected academic institutions must intensify their efforts in collaboration with the government for all levels of associated degrees, including, in particular, nuclear physics and nuclear engineering. In addition, the importance of establishing a workforce composed of nuclearized and nuclear-aware staff cannot be ignored. On the other hand, it should be borne in mind that providing adequate or attractive job opportunities will be imperative for strengthening the demand for nuclear education in the country.

3.2 Research and Development

The human resource built in the field also serves as the basis for the R&D projects conducted in nuclear science. While the first NPPs are usually turnkey projects delivered by a nuclear-experienced partner, conducting research in certain key areas is of critical importance to the technology importing countries for a sustainable nuclear programme. There is no doubt that developing national competence in nuclear is best supported by R&D activities. It should also be stated that many countries expand their nuclear energy experience into wider technological aspects in different sectors. Therefore, R&D constitutes an integral part of national nuclear strategies. For this reason, an R&D plan incorporating NPPs, directly or indirectly, must be carefully designed.

A number of chapters could be opened within a national R&D plan. A leading one would be on nuclear reactors, dealing with current or next-generation technologies. In this sense, two aspects can be emphasized: reactor safety and use of fuel. This is basically due to the fact that the performance of any reactor depends on its reliability and efficiency. Further improvements in these dimensions can be largely achieved with an R&D focus. Various dynamics of NPPs, including thermal-hydraulics and coolant systems, can also be addressed in this respect (TUBITAK 2012). In terms of nuclear safety, on the other hand, waste management stands out as a fundamental field of research.

One other relevant area of research for building national competence in the field is *nuclear materials*. Considering the fact that the components of power plants are produced based on high technical standards, R&D efforts towards developing nuclear materials hold the key to meeting strategic targets, particularly for an ideally capable national industry. Furthermore, as an indirect added value of relevant studies, national nuclear programmes preferably feature R&D plans in radiation sciences for spillover effects on non-energy sectors such as agriculture, medicine, and metrology.

When it comes to Turkey, however, R&D activities have been quite limited throughout its nuclear history, mainly due to the inadequacy of human capital in the area. The activities have also been constrained by the lack of funding supports as well as the insufficient infrastructure. Therefore, along with the launch of its NPP plans, Turkey has to frame its needs for improving its nuclear competence through R&D.

A critical item that would be included in such an action plan is having an active nuclear research institution that coordinates relevant projects. Plus, the funding problem has to be resolved by establishing support mechanisms for nuclear R&D projects. The mechanism could also be strengthened by encouraging domestic scholars and researchers to participate in international projects and exchange programmes. In fact, problems regarding human resources can be ameliorated through the mobility of researchers (OECD 2004). Furthermore, as mentioned earlier, infrastructure is undeniably an essential element for effective R&D studies. Having nuclear facilities for this purpose would not only help advance nuclear studies but also provide work and training opportunities for the human capital the country needs.

3.3 Safety

A vital aspect of any nuclear power strategy is undoubtedly nuclear safety, which is defined as the achievement of proper operating conditions, prevention of accidents, and mitigation of accident consequences, resulting in the protection of workers, the public, and the environment from undue radiation hazards (IAEA 2016). The NPP accidents that happened in the past have proved the significance of high safety standards for nuclear-energy-producing countries. Nuclear safety is not only a national but also an international responsibility and constitutes a decades-long commitment. In this respect, establishing a solid framework long before the launch of nuclear power production and implementing it effectively is particularly critical for newcomers like Turkey.

In fact, the fundamental safety principles recommended by the International Atomic Energy Agency in SSG-16 (IAEA 2011b) serve as a useful guide. In an attempt to provide a basic outline inspired by the guide, a principal duty can be defined as ensuring the *safety of nuclear infrastructure* throughout the design and construction phases. This is because a main aspect of nuclear safety relates to the safe operation of power plants, which also includes the ability to sort out any problems causing ionizing radiation risks. On the other hand, being prepared for *emergency situations and reacting to incidents* in an effective and prompt manner is another required aspect of nuclear safety.

Crucial to achieving a safe nuclear programme is also the prudent *handling of nuclear waste*. Nuclear fuel used in a reactor is stored to be recycled for supply security purposes or to be disposed of after a while. So it is important to plan the management of the back end of the nuclear fuel cycle, which starts with the removal of fuel from reactors and continues with its treatment and disposal. While the amount of fuel consumed in nuclear reactors is relatively small, the radioactive nature of its waste requires cautious management.

Nonetheless, nuclear waste constitutes not only the used fuel but also various elements contained in an NPP. In this context, clothing and tools from reactor operations serve as examples of low-level radwastes and account for the majority in terms of volume. Intermediate-level wastes, such as components in reactors and resins, are more radioactive-contaminated and pose greater risks (WNA 2012). High-level radioactivity, on the other hand, comes from spent fuel and its waste. Therefore, the management required for the back end should be planned according to the categorization of wastes based on not only their amount but also their radioactivity level. National policies in this context matter.

Safe handling of radioactive materials also requires well-established security protocols. Moreover, security issues can in fact be considered a subset of nuclear safety planning in general. NPPs must be designed with comprehensive security measures that prevent unauthorized access and malevolent intervention. In this framework, it is also a must for NPPs to establish the rigour, culture, ethics, and discipline needed for effective management in nuclear power (IAEA 2007)

Aside from technical and administrative responsibilities, a complementary aspect of nuclear safety for a country is creating a compelling legal and regulatory framework. Experience shows that weaknesses in this regard increase the possibility of accidents and relevant public costs (EDAM 2011). At this point, another critical matter is the independence of national regulatory and supervisory bodies to put in place responsible and effective nuclear energy programmes.

This important detail should be focused on in Turkey because the regulatory agency, the Turkish Atomic Energy Authority (TAEK), has also been dealing with R&D activities in the nuclear space. Although related activities at TAEK's facilities, such as the Çekmece Nuclear Research and Training Centre have been limited, a distinction regarding the mission and activities of the agency must be made. At the time of writing of this chapter, the Turkish government was in the process of making certain adjustments to address the issue. The Turkish nuclear strategy also needs to align its regulatory agency with international standards.

One other task of the Turkish government is to reduce the anxiety related to nuclear power prevalent within society. Social resistance to nuclear energy production is not a new concept, however. The so-called Not in My Backyard (NIMBY) attitude experienced around the NPP regions in particular can be softened by informative awareness-raising activities with contributions from scholars in the field. In other words, public acceptance of nuclear energy must be taken into account as a fundamental dynamic of the process, and government should play a constructive and active role in this regard.

And last but not least, the two previously discussed pillars of the nuclear strategy, human capital and R&D, should be underlined as fundamental elements in the basis for achieving a safe national nuclear programme.

3.4 Industry

Most countries around the world establish their initial NPPs through foreign expertise, and they also happen to consider increasing the role of the domestic industry in future projects. However, nuclear energy production necessitates top quality standards and special techniques for the sophisticated technology it entails. In this sense, on the path towards a nationalized nuclear programme lies also, to a considerable extent, the involvement of domestic industry. Hence, for a country with a long-term nuclear vision, industrial planning should form part of the national nuclear strategy. South Korea, for example, is well known to have integrated its local industry into the country's NPPs and presented a successful model of 'learning by participation'.

In this respect, an assessment of national capabilities based on the requirements of the nuclear programme in terms of goods and services is an initial step for newcomers. Thus, an inventory of national industry needs to be taken by the government and matched up with the requirements specified. For planning purposes, prospective stakeholders can be classified mainly into mechanical equipment producers, electrical equipment producers, and construction/architecture companies. Establishing an NPP, on the other hand, can roughly be considered in two aspects: the reactor and the ancillary infrastructure/components (TUBITAK 2012). Because most of these elements demand highly sensitive production processes, industrial stakeholders must possess/obtain the relevant skills and infrastructure in accordance with international norms. In this framework, developing procurement management procedures and a quality assurance programme, including the establishment of approved vendor lists (IAEA 2011a), is a typical function.

As for Turkey, an inventory-based assessment is known to have been initiated along with the Akkuyu process. What can be highlighted for Turkey as an advantage in the first place are its proven construction skills, which can be integrated with NPP specifications. When it comes to materials, on the other hand, Turkey needs to *improve its capabilities* in order to produce reactor-quality materials for use in steam turbines as well. These include materials like flat steel, tool steel, advanced ceramic materials, and components such as metallic volute pumps, pipes, and valves.

For this reason, the manufacturing capabilities and capacities of the related sectors/firms in Turkish industry that own promising infrastructure need to be developed based on internationally recognized nuclear codes and standards. An ideal portfolio of participants also consists of those that deal with information and communications technology and advanced materials technology.

Considering the available basic infrastructure in certain subsectors, smart planning compatible with inventory could yield a relatively fast adaptation process for Turkish industry. However, one critical aspect to be emphasized at this point is the economic sustainability of investing in nuclear skills. This is because a nuclear industry requires very high capital investments, and in order for a firm to undertake that burden, feasibility must be considered; otherwise, investors will be aggrieved. Therefore, in any economy that attempts to develop nuclear technology, the industry must have guarantees that the government will purchase its products. Moreover, for sector players to make good on their investments, sustainability is a vital issue. If future sales are not accurately forecast, then it is not rational for firms to invest in nuclear technology. Hence developing a nuclear industry requires a long-term perspective. These concerns regarding investment planning matter especially for relatively small-scaled nuclear-power-producing countries and relate to certain parts of power plants such as reactor pressure vessels.

What these details imply for Turkey is that sectors/firms considering investing in nuclear should cooperate with the government as well as national and international shareholders, let alone receive subsidies. Collaboration with the government can provide practical opportunities, including the use of public infrastructure and expertise. There is no doubt that developing national nuclear capabilities will require that the Turkish government create a low-risk environment for investors while playing an active role in coordination. In order for a prospective Turkish nuclear industry to be sustainable, developing economic cooperation in the field with international markets would also be a significant step in the long run. Furthermore, a nuclear strategy should include a carefully considered plan on developing skills in relevant technologies that are not available in the country.

4 Conclusion

Turkey, as a country that imports a substantial portion of the energy it consumes, admittedly needs to diminish its dependence on foreign energy resources. This is required for both shrinking its current account deficit and strengthening its energy security. Hence, considering also the projections indicating a growing electricity demand for the country in the decades to come, Turkey has been searching for ways to develop national competence in alternative sources of energy. While increasing the share of renewable energy in the mix is a part of the action plan, nuclear power is still deemed necessary for satisfying the huge volume required.

The ambition for nuclear power has in fact a long story in Turkey that goes back to the 1950s. Nevertheless, the country had failed to take concrete steps until 2010, when an intergovernmental agreement was signed with Russia on the Akkuyu NPP. This was followed by a deal with Japan in 2013 for another power plant to be constructed in Sinop. While Turkey has understandably launched its nuclear adventure under international collaboration, it is widely accepted that countries relying on external expertise in NPPs must do their best to become intelligent customers and, hence, adopt national energy strategies. This is mainly because nuclear power involves a decades-long commitment.

This chapter outlines the basic framework of a nuclear strategy for newcomers and discusses the case of Turkey in that connection. Beyond the BOO models it adopts, Turkey apparently needs to come up with a well-organized plan for developing its nuclear competence. To be an intelligent customer and perform good nuclear governance, Turkey must focus intently on the issues of human capital and safety, not to mention make strategic plans regarding nuclear R&D and industry.

Notes

1. Calculated using foreign trade statistics from the chapter of mineral fuels and oils.

References

CBRT (Central Bank of the Republic of Turkey). http://www.tcmb.gov.tr. Accessed 1 Oct 2016.

EC. 2015. *Retaining Critical Competencies in Nuclear Energy Sector: National Initiatives and Best Practices, Instruments and Tools*, JRC Science and Policy Report.

EDAM. 2011. *The Turkish Model for Transition to Nuclear Energy–II*. Centre for Economics and Foreign Policy Studies.

EUROSTAT. http://www.ec.europa.eu/eurostat. Accessed 1 Oct 2016.

IAEA. 2007. *Considerations to Launch a Nuclear Power Programme*. Vienna: International Atomic Energy Agency.

———. 2011a. *Workforce Planning for New Nuclear Power Programmes*, IAEA Nuclear Energy Series No. NG-T-3.10.

———. 2011b. *Establishing the Safety Infrastructure for a Nuclear Power Programme*, Specific Safety Guide No. SSG-16.

———. 2016. *IAEA Safety Glossary: Terminology Used in Nuclear Safety and Radiation Protection*, 2016 Revision.

IAEA PRIS. http://www.iaea.org/PRIS/WorldStatistics/OperationalReactorsByCountry.aspx. Accessed 10 Dec 2016.

Kara, Mikko, and Lasse Mattila. 1996. Finnish Nuclear Power Development: Experiences and Lessons Learned. In *Proceedings from the Conference on Nuclear Option in Countries with Small and Medium Electricity Grid*, Opatija, Croatia, October 7–9.

OECD. 2004. *Nuclear Competence Building*. Paris: Nuclear Energy Agency, Organisation for Economic Co-operation and Development.

———. 2012. *Nuclear Education and Training: From Concern to Capability*. Paris: OECD.

TUBITAK. 2012. *Nükleer Santral Yerlileştirme Çalıştayı Sonuç Raporu*. The Marmara Research Center (MAM) of the Scientific and Technological Research Council of Turkey.

TURKSTAT. *Turkish Statistical Institute*. http://www.tuik.gov.tr. Accessed 1 Oct 2016.

WNA. *How a Nuclear Reactor Makes Electricity*. http://www.world-nuclear.org/nuclear-basics/how-does-a-nuclear-reactor-make-electricity.aspx. Accessed 1 Nov 2016.

———. 2012. *Waste Management: Overview*. World Nuclear Association. http://www.world-nuclear.org/information-library/nuclear-fuel-cycle/nuclear-wastes/waste-management-overview.aspx. Accessed 10 Sept 2016.

———. 2015. *Nuclear Power in Turkey*. World Nuclear Association. http://www.world-nuclear.org/information-library/country-profiles/countries-t-z/turkey.aspx. Accessed 10 Sept 2016.

Beyond Planning and Liberalization: Foreign Trade and Industrial Development in Turkey

Mehmet Babacan

1 Introduction

What drives countries to engage in trade with each other the most? The international trade literature has provided many answers to this long-standing question. Technology (i.e. specialization) and factor endowment differences, the economic size of countries, and geographical and industrial proximity, among many other factors, together with institutional-social features, are described as the most important components of trade share of gross domestic product (GDP). The industrial and institutional basis in a country and the rules set-up are accordingly described as significant out of the many possible explanations for cross-country income-level differences and the level of bilateral trade. For the case of Turkey, many studies, including those by Babacan (2011) and Civan et al. (2013),

M. Babacan (✉)
Department of Economics and Finance, School of Business, Istanbul Medipol University, Istanbul, Turkey

A. F. Aysan et al. (eds.), *Turkish Economy*,
https://doi.org/10.1007/978-3-319-70380-0_16

have sought an answer to the recent performance in the country's trade volume. In this chapter, we aim to examine the strong relation, whether cyclical or countercyclical, between industrialization and foreign trade regime/set-up in the case of Turkey.

Turkish industrialization efforts have been strongly related to its bilateral ties to European economies for more than 500 years. Having played a significant role in the economic history of Europe, Turkey's openness towards West and East has long defined its domestic industry, as reflected in resource allocation, modes of production, real wages, and return to capital.

For the entire twentieth century, especially after the customs union agreement signed in 1995, the country's longstanding relationship with the European economies (its largest economic partners) has provided a quality ladder for Turkish export sectors while favourable global economic conditions with relatively low-cost financing in the mid-2000s opened up new spaces for business expansion and specialization. Since the global financial crisis of 2008, despite the contraction in world demand, export sectors have managed to navigate the unchartered waters thanks to diversification in terms of goods and partner countries. Table 1 shows the rising share of Asian countries, including the Middle Eastern economies despite regional turmoil during the last six years, while EU-28 countries continue to hold the majority share of Turkey's total export volume.

Turkey's recent diplomacy efforts to gain further influence in and around its region are strongly connected to its foreign trade diversification in terms of partner and source countries. Among many other scholarly works, what Civan et al. (2013) suggest is that Turkey's newly adopted foreign policy orientation towards fostering diplomatic relations through established missions increases trade with other countries. Strengthening the Middle East and North Africa (MENA)'s trade and investment ties with Turkey is not only an option but a win–win strategy and a real opportunity for the diversification of MENA's exports basket, according to Alaya and Mezghani (2013: 13).

As Babacan (2011: 147) states, Turkey's emerging trade destinations provide a relative advantage for the smaller size entrepreneurs owing to their firm size while yielding significant amounts of positive externalities

Table 1 Turkey's annual exports by country group (2011–2016)

Million USD	2011	% Share	2012	% Share	2013	% Share	2014	% Share	2015	% Share	2016	% Share	% Change
Total exports	**134,907**	**100.0**	**152,462**	**100.0**	**151,803**	**100.0**	**157,610**	**100.0**	**143,839**	**100.0**	**142,530**	**100.0**	**–0.9**
EU countries (28)	62,589	46.4	59,398	39.0	63,040	41.5	68,514	43.5	63,998	44.5	68,344	48.0	6.8
Free zones in Turkey	2,545	1.9	2,295	1.5	2,413	1.6	2,270	1.4	1,907	1.3	1,822	1.3	–4.5
Other countries	69,773	51.7	90,768	59.5	86,350	56.9	86,826	55.1	77,934	54.2	72,364	50.8	–7.1
Other European countries	12,735	9.4	14,167	9.3	14,214	9.4	15,184	9.6	14,141	9.8	9,736	6.8	–31.1
African countries	10,334	7.7	13,357	8.8	14,146	9.3	13,754	8.7	12,449	8.7	11,406	8.0	–8.4
North Africa	6,701	5.0	9,444	6.2	10,042	6.6	9,758	6.2	8,527	5.9	7,755	5.4	–9.1
Other Africa	3,633	2.7	3,913	2.6	4,104	2.7	3,996	2.5	3,922	2.7	3,651	2.6	–6.9
American countries	7,926	5.9	9,623	6.3	9,711	6.4	10,083	6.4	9,225	6.4	9,345	6.6	1.3
North America	5,459	4.0	6,663	4.4	6,580	4.3	7,292	4.6	7,067	4.9	7,404	5.2	4.8
Central America	626	0.5	770	0.5	1,004	0.7	938	0.6	849	0.6	846	0.6	–0.3
South America	1,840	1.4	2,191	1.4	2,127	1.4	1,852	1.2	1,310	0.9	1,095	0.8	–16.4
Asian countries	38,134	28.3	53,026	34.8	47,591	31.4	46,974	29.8	41,393	28.8	40,988	28.8	–1.0
Near and Middle Eastern countries	27,935	20.7	42,451	27.8	35,575	23.4	35,384	22.5	31,086	21.6	31,304	22.0	0.7

(*continued*)

Table 1 (continued)

Million USD	2011	% Share	2012	% Share	2013	% Share	2014	% Share	2015	% Share	2016	% Share	% Change
Other Asian countries	10,199	7.6	10,575	6.9	12,017	7.9	11,591	7.4	10,307	7.2	9,684	6.8	–6.0
Australia and New Zealand	481	0.4	490	0.3	538	0.4	600	0.4	619	0.4	736	0.5	18.8
Other countries	164	0.1	105	0.1	149	0.1	231	0.1	106	0.1	152	0.1	43.9
Selected country groups													
OECD countries	67,114	49.7	66,290	43.5	68,684	45.2	76,675	48.6	75,368	52.4	77,420	54.3	2.7
EFTA	1,887	1.4	2,601	1.7	1,662	1.1	3,795	2.4	6,202	4.3	3,267	2.3	–47.3
Blacksea Economic Cooperation	17,768	13.2	18,791	12.3	20,368	13.4	19,687	12.5	14,590	10.1	13,078	9.2	–10.4
Economic Cooperation Organization	9,292	6.9	16,563	10.9	11,898	7.8	11,717	7.4	9,567	6.7	9,603	6.7	0.4
Commonwealth of Independent States	13,377	9.9	15,075	9.9	16,924	11.1	15,616	9.9	10,569	7.3	7,750	5.4	–26.7
Turkic Republics	5,040	3.7	5,841	3.8	6,908	4.6	7,108	4.5	5,290	3.7	3,992	2.8	–24.5
Organization of Islamic Conference	37,325	27.7	55,218	36.2	49,371	32.5	48,625	30.9	42,738	29.7	41,232	28.9	–3.5
D–8 Organization for Economic Cooperation		–	–	–	8,790	–	8,574	5.4	8,156	5.7	9,127	6.4	11.9

Source: TurkStat

for the conglomerates in their increased bilateral economic ties as well. In return, export sectors are now more capable of product and market diversification than ever. At a rather slow pace, the content factor in Turkish industrial production and exports is developing in favour of mostly middle but also higher technology over the last couple of decades.

In parallel to other success stories from infrastructure to construction, Turkey's trade volume has shown a significant increase during the last couple decades, under AK Party governments. Considering the technology factor in exports, the stability in export performance in terms of its volume over the years, terms of trade, and relative wage issues due to a reallocation of resources, one might conclude that Turkey's current course of navigating in an increasingly unstable economic environment across the world has reached its limits. Despite facing relatively stable terms of trade levels over the last decade, the volatility in the exchange rate (the Turkish lira first appreciated and then depreciated significantly within the same decade) has produced relatively unfavourable results with exports. Within the G-20 countries, Turkey seems to be one of the most stable in its terms of trade ratio, while oil-rich Russia and primary-sector-strong Indonesia face the largest declines (Table 2).

Intergovernmental relations pave the way for exporters to reach new markets while a comprehensive trade strategy is still far from implementation. Turkish exporters are still highly dependent on state policies, and the possible agency problems might hinder further economic development as bureaucratic and administrative quality is the key to success in such a framework. Despite the recent rise in Turkey's trade performance, we may conclude that it is too early to suggest an 'axis shift' in the modes of production and the relative roles of small and middle-sized enterprises (SMEs) versus conglomerates (Babacan 2011: 148).

Based on the trend over the last decade, we could argue that Turkey continues to promote new development in terms of its foreign trade, according to Babacan (2011: 148). Its significant dependence on imports of intermediate goods and the lack of a proper research and development (R&D) strategy, however, are among the factors that hinder more rapid economic growth in the country. In the meantime, Turkey needs to develop a long-term strategic trade plan to address current weaknesses in

Table 2 G-20 countries' terms of trade (2002–2016)

	2002	2003	2004	2005	2006	2007	2008	2009	2010	2011	2012	2013	2014	2015	2016
Australia	54.3	58.4	64	70.9	76	80.3	86.4	82.9	100	100.4	90.7	87.4	78.2	70.2	
Canada	84.3	89	93	96.2	97.2	100.2	104.5	95	100	103.4	101.8	101.8	100.4	93.5	91.7
France	102.1	102.1	101.2	99.8	98.3	99.5	98.8	101.4	100	97.6	97.3	98.4	99.6	102.7	103.5
Germany	101.4	102.6	102.8	101	99.4	99.5	97.9	102.4	100	97.3	97.1	98.2	99.5	102	103.6
Indonesia	110.1	112.3	111.2	109.4	115.5	111.1	99.7	101.8	100	102	96.7	93	94	94.4	
Italy	104.8	106.5	105.5	102.2	99.1	100.1	98	104.2	100	97.4	95.9	97.4	100	102.3	104.9
Japan	134.1	130	124.5	116.6	108.4	104.1	94.5	106.1	100	92.4	91.3	90.4	89.9	97.9	
Korea	117.2	115.3	112	107.9	103.2	103.1	96.1	99.8	100	95.5	95.3	97.3	98.1	106.1	
Mexico	94	92.9	92.6	95.5	98.6	99.6	103	98.8	100	99.9	100.1	100.9	99.4	95.9	
OECD - Total	102.1	102.2	102	101.1	100.3	100.5	97.9	100.7	100	97.9	97.5	98.2	98.3	100.4	
Russia	63.1	67.3	78	90.1	99.9	103.4	119.6	83.9	100	120.8	123.8	116.6	111.5	84.7	71.1
South Africa	76.1	79.3	80.8	82.1	86.2	88.8	89.6	94.4	100	104.3	102.9	97.4	95.6		
Turkey	101.1	104.4	106.8	106.3	101.6	103.4	100.3	102.3	100	92.7	91.9	94.1	93.9	95.9	
United Kingdom	101	102.2	102.7	102	101.1	100.4	97	98.7	100	99	99.3	101.5	103.1	103.8	103.9
United States	106.9	105.4	104.2	102.5	101.8	101.6	96.2	101.5	100	98.8	99.1	100.1	100.4	103.5	

Source: OECD

the production, marketing, and other segments of its trade structure (Babacan 2011: 148).

Therefore, a sustainable trade scheme should incorporate a solution to remedy the structural deficit problem, which stems from the mode of production and low levels of technology, and as a result, Turkey produces products with low value added (Babacan 2011: 155). At this point, a discussion arises on the possibility of reindustrialization following the rise of the services sector, making it predominate both in terms of GDP share and Turkey's export content. We argue that Turkey faces new opportunities ahead given its industrial, financial, and institutional capacity to cope with various challenges over the last decade. Table 3 indicates a sort of stagnation in terms of industrial upgrade, except construction (from 5.13 per cent in 2002 up to 9.25 per cent in 2015). Thus, factor mobility among sectors is affected by relative wages and returns owing to the declining or increasing share of sectors in the GDP value added.

2 A Tale of Industrialization and Deindustrialization in Turkey

From the 1920s to the 1950s, Turkey adopted industrial plans targeting state-led industrialization. Plans represented narrower industrial policy tools and were technically not economic plans because they lacked the wider economic scope of the post-war economic plans in France and Holland, with their macroeconomic targets or forecasts (Yülek 2015: 21–22). In the meantime, foreign trade and integration into the world economy were limited owing to international crises, terms of trade differences, and the changing nature of domestic politics, which in turn fostered Turkey's efforts at industrialization via five-year development plans initiated first in 1934.

Taking a foreign trade perspective, Baysan and Blitzer (1991: 288–290) categorize Turkey's foreign trade between 1950 and 1984 into four distinct subperiods. The first subperiod of 1950–1962 is referred to as *ad hoc* nationalism, whereas the second subperiod of 1963–1973 is considered planned industrialization characterized by central planning and import

Table 3 Sectoral share as value added in Turkey's GDP (%) (2002–2015)

	2002	2003	2004	2005	2006	2007	2008	2009	2010	2011	2012	2013	2014	2015
Agriculture, Forestry, and Fishing	11.634	11.278	10.781	10.598	9.332	8.484	8.407	9.116	10.266	9.362	8.784	7.677	7.451	7.824
Industry including energy	22.75	23.06	22.64	22.59	22.64	22.19	21.79	20.67	21.05	22.47	21.86	22.41	22.72	22.42
Manufacturing	19.16	19.54	19.39	19.36	19.52	18.98	18.3	16.99	17.18	18.73	17.99	18.54	18.99	18.97
Services	60.48	60.38	60.46	60.43	60.82	61.66	62.12	63.91	61.75	60.02	60.88	60.71	60.67	60.5
Construction	5.13	5.28	6.11	6.39	7.22	7.66	7.68	6.3	6.93	8.15	8.48	9.2	9.16	9.25

Source: OECD

substitutive foreign trade policies. The third subperiod is described as one of external shock and domestic turmoil; it covers the years 1974–1979. The subperiod of 1979–1984 is known as a time of economic liberalization that saw extensive measures of openness in all aspects.

Discussion around whether the economic liberalization period after the 1980s was successful or not in terms of export performance mostly yields a positive answer, as Baysan and Blitzer (1991: 391) assert, stating that the growth of manufactured exports in particular was impressive in that period. Thus, one could easily draw the conclusion that deindustrialization in Turkey mostly coincides with periods of political and macroeconomic instability and uncertainty. The 1990s, therefore, would be best described as a lost decade during which industry faced both declines in its share of GDP and total exports. Manufacturing, however, continues to have the predominant share (around 75 per cent) of industrial exports, at least giving some hope for the future with regard to an upgrade in Turkish industry. Table 4 gives the essence of Turkey's industrial breakdown in terms of sectors from 1997 to 2016, which points to manufacturing as the stronghold, while the others are relatively stable in terms of share of exports.

For most of the 2000s, industrial production in Turkey also enjoyed an increasingly favourable domestic and world economic environment. Easier and less costly access to finance could be counted among the factors leading the currently stagnant industrial capacity. Increases in industrial output were based on dramatic increases in imports, thereby yielding a deteriorating current account balance.

Aydın et al. (2007: 48–49) show that even though Turkish exports underwent a transformation after the 2001 banking crisis, Turkey is still short of building any comparative advantage in these new commodities. The rising industries of the post-crisis (2001 banking crisis included) period are considered to be relatively more capital- and high-technology-intensive commodities compared to the popular industries of the 1980s and 1990s. These new industries also have high intra-industry trade. The classification of exports in terms of factor intensity reveals that concentration occurs in high-technology products around the world. Although the share of R&D-intensive product exports was below the world and emerg-

Table 4 Sectoral breakdown of Turkey's exports (% of total)

Sector	1997	2011	2012	2013	2014	2015	2016
Agriculture, Forestry, and Fishing	29.69393	11.32569	10.49027	11.68575	11.89447	12.12759	11.82672
Mining	5.38399	9202541	8.999786	8.86169	7.925127	6.893093	5.921741
Manufacturing	64.76178	77.94259	71.33259	76.67416	77.34	75.15002	75.77687
Other	0.160292	1.5291781	9.177352	2.778402	2.840401	5.829299	6.474669

Source: Turkish Statistical Institute (TurkStat)

ing market averages, Turkey ranked first in growth of R&D product exports among the emerging market economies in the 2001–2004 period.

Both measures of country concentration ratios, weighted spread of Turkish exports by country and share of top 10 and 20 countries in total exports, indicate an increasing trend in country concentration of Turkish exports. Analysis of exports shows that the high import dependence of overall Turkish exports is not exceptional. Indeed, the import dependency of exports is higher in new EU members as well. Sectoral analysis shows that the import dependency rate increased much faster in Turkish manufacturing sectors, particularly in motor vehicles and electrical machinery and apparatus sectors (Aydın et al. 2007: 48).

The issues of industrialization, deindustrialization, and probability of reindustrialization are quite similar to both the developed and developing countries under the G-20 umbrella. Most recent data indicate that with a few exceptions, import share of gross exports for the G-20 countries has been on the rise in the last decade (Table 5).

The latest shift towards the services sector in Turkish exports has many explanations as it does the solution offers to revitalize industrial production. So-called deindustrialization in Turkey could be a legitimate argument after a brief look at the total share of manufacturing in GDP, gross export volume, and employment composition in the country. The question is how to deal with the structural causes of deindustrialization, like education and technological progress through innovation. Trade policy in coordination with all actors could meet some of the needs in connection with reindustrialization and the direction of the country in its modes of production for different sectors. Spillover effects might play a positive role in fostering the value-added component of Turkish exports, given an improved institutional setting to coordinate efforts by government, private investors, capital and labour owners, and bureaucracy.

3 Setting the Stage: Foreign Trade for Industrial Development

Spatial economics, cluster analysis and gravity models, based on location theory might provide an understanding to the effects of different parameters on trade volume. Isard (1954) for instance states that the influence

Table 5 G-20 countries' import share of gross exports (%) (2002–2014)

	2002	2003	2004	2005	2006	2007	2008	2009	2010	2011	2012	2013	2014
Argentina	8.25	9.5	12.32	13.27	13.59	13.76	14.84	11.95	13	14.07	13.14	13.07	12.45
Australia	15.04	12.46	11.86	11.97	13.28	13.45	13.52	12.78	12.77	13.91	13.86	14	14.69
Brazil	12.94	12.57	12.71	11.7	11.63	11.75	12.5	10.14	10.53	10.72	11.73	12.42	12.42
Canada	25.33	23.37	23.89	23.43	22.85	22.36	22.91	22.38	23.46	23.56	24.55	23.86	23.26
China (People's Republic of)	36.71	38.7	38.16	37.37	36.18	34.17	31.67	30.75	31.94	32.11	31.15	30.85	29.35
France	21.93	21.21	22.22	23.39	24.97	25.29	24.68	21.54	23.67	25.01	25.9	25.81	26.27
Germany	18.7	18.97	19.58	21.29	23.31	24.18	24.67	21.78	23.25	25.62	26.03	25.78	25.35
India	12.68	13.33	15.75	17.45	19.5	19.08	22.53	20.91	22.25	24.03	23.39	22.3	20.98
Indonesia	14.63	14.22	16.14	16.15	14.65	14.1	14.61	11.08	11.08	11.98	11.55	11.57	12
Italy	19.15	19.18	20.26	22.01	24.35	25.08	25.68	21.12	24.85	26.41	26.64	25.77	25.36
Japan	7.98	8.24	9.09	11.09	13.22	14.54	15.71	11.18	12.69	14.7	14.8	16.92	18.19
Korea	27.33	30.69	32.39	32.97	34.45	35.4	41.64	37.45	39.16	41.63	41.86	39.43	37.84
Mexico	33.29	33.42	34.37	33	33.45	33.75	32.7	33.51	34.44	31.69	33	33.08	33.5
Russia	16.24	16.57	14.01	13.03	13.31	13.01	13.83	12.64	13.03	13.65	13.54	14	13.65
Saudi Arabia	3.82	3.67	3.6	3.74	4.7	4.51	4.52	4.61	3.9	3.31	2.78	3.19	3.55
South Africa	20.3	17.84	18.9	19.44	21.56	21.65	23.74	18.78	17.94	19.51	19.83	20.92	20.67
Turkey	18.33	19.59	21.13	20.88	23.26	24.13	24.9	21.54	22.6	25.68	24.06	22.25	21.79
United Kingdom	16.86	16.6	16.91	17.02	17.54	17.96	19.34	18.75	21	22.93	23.95	23.21	21.87
United States	11.08	11.57	12.34	13.01	13.76	14.02	15.54	11.54	13.38	14.97	15.52	15.27	15.28

Source: OECD

and an explicit consideration of distance is important as a variable in trade analysis. Agglomeration theory and trade theory both make use of distance as a key element driving cost and demand functions respectively. A more assertive result of his work is his conclusion that a general and comprehensive location theory and a general and comprehensive trade theory are one and the same (Isard 1954: 319).

Chenery (1961: 47) suggests that the commodities that need to be produced and traded cannot be determined by a simple ranking procedure along the lines of comparative advantage owing to the interdependence of sectors. The importance attached to balanced growth and its relation to trade balance on the other hand might differ in accordance with countries' experiences with export markets, foreign exchange reserves, and borrowing capacity (Chenery 1961: 46).

Countries' investment decisions and economic policymaking processes also need to be aligned with their business environment (i.e. clusters, specialization, export markets, institutional quality, regulations) in order to develop their unique strengths, as stated by Porter (2009). Clusters and diversification are argued to be complementary and non-contradictory (Rosenfeld 1997: 21), which suggests successful clusters could both generate specialization and considerable social capital to extend companies' competencies into new markets or products. Therefore, business clusters that yield dynamic economic gains are complete systems with local production facilities along with local social structures.

The development of a robust export industry could lead to better business clusters, which in turn would pave the way to the emergence of other subsectors via backward and forward linkages. A variety of intermediate goods produced on larger scales is expected to create positive externalities in an economy. Whether based on neoclassical assumptions of competitive markets or Dixit–Stiglitz type imperfect markets with monopolistic competition, theories of international trade and spatial economics that envision industrial clustering should include a guiding principle or at least a strategic industrial policymaking component in it (Babacan 2015: 54). Empirical evidence suggests that income differentials between some nations and others are widening over time despite the dominant growth theories with assumptions of economic convergence. Industrial agglomeration across regional or national entities therefore provides a neat explanation for such a divergence. Along with interindustry trade, the intra-industry level of trade is another determining factor in the regional concentration of certain industries (Babacan 2015: 56).

Agglomeration and clustering to enjoy economies-of-scale effects and interindustry and intra-industry spillovers all enhance a country's competitiveness. An external factor that has a significant impact on industrialization through trade is the level of integration with world markets. Terms of trade shocks as well as exchange rate volatility are among many other challenges that export industries have to face. There is, however, mixed evidence regarding the role of foreign trade engagement in industrial development for different groups of countries. Mevel et al. (2016) for instance indicate that reindustrialization in the case of North African countries could be triggered via free trade agreements at the regional or inter-regional scale. In addition to these arguments, the removal of barriers to trade and to foreign direct investment (FDI) are complementary in boosting total factor productivity levels (Ahn et al. 2016: 6).

Counterfactual evidence from recent research by Johnson and Noguera (2016: 2) suggests that the ratio of value added to gross exports was reduced by 10 per cent between 1970 and 2009, while the ratio of value added declined by 20 per cent in manufacturing but increased in non-manufacturing sectors. Impacting factors are being a fast-growing economy, engaging in regional trade agreements, and trading with neighbouring countries as partners. With the removal of trade frictions, Johnson and Noguera (2016: 21) say, the service industry and agricultural products exports seem to benefit while manufacturing industries suffer losses.

All in all, foreign trade regimes are important to the industrial make-up of a country. Foreign trade regimes, according to Bhagwati (1978: 192), may influence growth not only through their direct impact on growth but also the quality of entrepreneurship and degree of innovativeness and technical change. Bhagwati (1978: 198) asserts that unequal opportunities arise from a basic, unequal distribution of wealth and status, and that, whether the foreign trade regime is Phase II (continued reliance on quantitative restrictions in trade) or Phase IV (the effective exchange rate for exports comes closer to the effective exchange rate for imports), the inequalities of access by small-scale and underprivileged enterprises will persist and only their outward manifestation will change.

In a broad sense, Anne Krueger (1974) argues that the impact of foreign trade regime is reflected, not in the income differences between capital and labour owners in a broad sense, but rather within these categories in Turkey.

Bhagwati (1978: 192–194) argues that if developing countries going through a five-phase liberalization process as indicated by the World Bank should finalize the process as a Phase II country with automatic protection of domestic industry to foster domestic entrepreneurship, then it might lead to a rentier state, lower-quality institutions, and overall inefficient resource allocation. As a follow-up to the intuition behind Krueger and Bhagwati's arguments in favour of trade liberalization that leads to import-substitutive industries having to face external competition, Rodrik (1992: 100) puts forward the argument that benefits from liberalization are enhanced by markets, which become or remain imperfect. Domestic firms' output expands under imperfect market conditions, and one possible channel to such a scenario is so-called industry-rationalization theory, which relies on relatively unhindered entry and exit of firms into affected industries. The Turkish case, in this sense, could fit well into Rodrik's arguments.

Turkey has managed to diversify its export markets and manufactured goods in the exporting industries during the last quarter century. However, the technology content of exports remains limited, as indicated by various studies since the 2000s. Turkey's mid-technology share has shown an increase from some 19 per cent of the total in 1990 up to 39 per cent by 2010, while the high-technology component has shown little improvement compared to 1990 and a serious decline since year 2000, from 9 to 5 per cent by 2010. Figure 1 shows a steady rise in the per-kilogram value (in USD) of Turkish exports, an almost 40 per cent increase over the last decade.

In parallel, Fig. 2 implies around a 70 per cent rise in Turkey's share of total world exports within the last 15 years. Provided by Turkish Exporters Assembly's (TIM) 2016 report on export development, evidence from the share of Turkish exports of GDP over the last 15 years suggests that the share of total commodity and service exports declined from 25.1 per

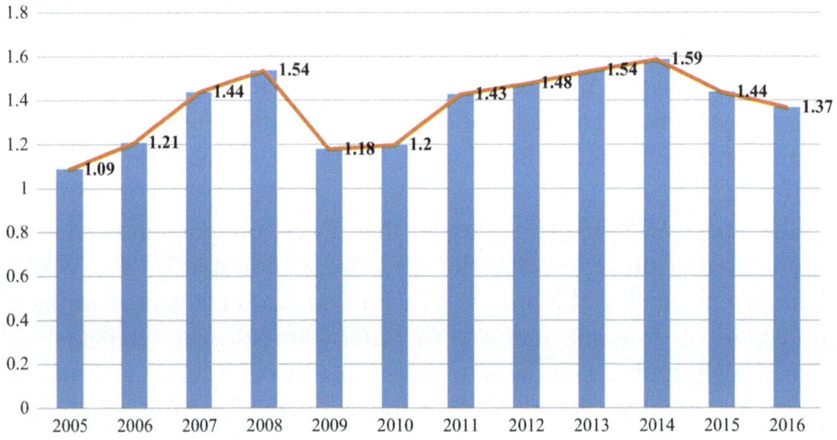

Fig. 1 Turkey's exports per kilogram (in USD) (Source: TurkStat, Turkish Exporters Assembly (TIM))

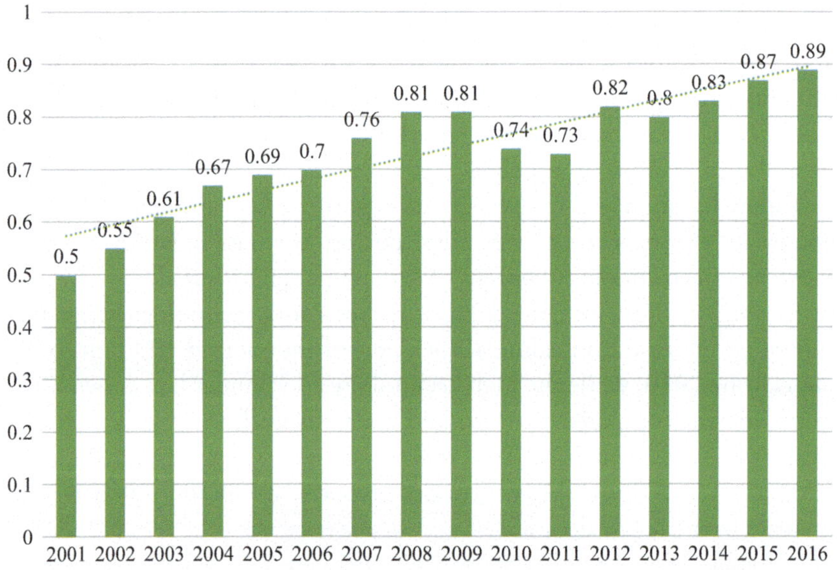

Fig. 2 World share of Turkey's exports (%) (2001–2016) (Source: TradeMap (via TIM))

cent in 2001 down to 21.9 per cent by 2016. In the meantime, the share of commodity exports of just GDP remains steady at around 17.5 per cent (both in 2001 and 2016), reaching a peak at 18.5 per cent in 2012. Combined with the value added by exporting sectors in the Turkish manufacturing sector, these data show that Turkey has somewhat of a comparative advantage in producing and exporting in some commodities, while in others, such as agricultural products like hazelnuts or tobacco, it should utilize factor endowments or take advantage of terms of trade differences. Table 6 shows little change in the share of capital goods from Turkey's exports, an insignificant decline in intermediate goods, and a significant rise in consumption goods. These data alone signal stagnation in industrial growth in terms of export content.

Foreign trade policies thus focus on increasing the share of Turkish exports worldwide, horizontally and vertically integrated sectors to yield efficiency in production chains, a hike in value added through technology and innovation, better coordination among parties including lobbying groups, and increased public awareness for competitiveness.

4 Collective Action in Governing the Commons: Reindustrialization and Trade

Industrialization is the key to sustainable economic growth, as suggested by European history as well as late-industrialized countries such as Japan. As Rowthorn and Wells (1987: 75) underline, the importance of industrialization, regardless of a country's trade structures or whether it specializes in non-manufacturing or manufacturing, is such that successful industrialization enables a country to reconcile two important objectives: higher per-capita domestic demand for manufactures and maintaining external balances.

Theoretically, there are vast differences between industrialized and developed countries' experiences with economic planning in a wide range of highly centralized and controlled to strategically guided models in the

Table 6 Turkey's annual exports by BEC (2011–2016)

Category	2011	2012	2013	2014	2015	2016	USD in Millions % Change
Capital goods	**14,192**	**13,734**	**15,592**	**16,107**	**15,392**	**15,891**	**3.2**
Capital goods - (except transport equipment)	7,745	8,125	8,939	9,229	8,499	8,186	–3.7
Transport equipment, industrial	6,447	5,608	6,653	6,878	6,893	7,706	11.8
Intermediate goods	**67,942**	**82,656**	**74,817**	**75,171**	**68,433**	**66,890**	**–2.3**
Food and beverages, primary, mainly for industry	4,031	4,204	5,058	4,719	3,761	3,665	–2.5
Food and beverages, processed, mainly for industry	45,718	59,141	49,773	50,214	47,347	46,449	–1.9
Fuels and lubricants, primary	132	237	252	235	182	139	–23.5
Parts and accessories of capital goods	4,432	4,508	5,028	5,253	4,535	4,299	–5.2
Parts and accessories of transport equipment	7,988	8,164	9,009	9,288	8,595	8,927	3.9
Other, primary, mainly for industry	209	289	352	294	239	384	60.5
Other, processed, mainly for industry	1,832	1,831	1,891	1,696	1,618	1,791	10.6

(*continued*)

Table 6 (continued)

Category	2011	2012	2013	2014	2015	2016	USD in Millions % Change
Fuels and lubricants, processed	3,601	4,282	3,454	3,473	2,155	1,236	−42.7
Consumption goods	**52,219**	**55,556**	**60,732**	**65,088**	**59,146**	**58,877**	**−0.5**
Passenger motor cars	6,485	6,069	6,856	7,255	6,899	8,355	21.1
Durable	10,465	12,460	13,318	14,984	13,130	12,807	−2.5
Semi-durable	13,069	13,434	14,775	15,946	14,626	14,650	0.2
Non-durable consumption goods	7,878	8,406	9,344	9,998	8,694	8,564	−1.5
Food and beverages, primary	5,512	5,390	5,784	6,297	6,185	5,690	−8.0
Food and beverages, processed	5,893	6,486	7,501	8,125	7,407	6,925	−6.5
Gasoline	2,616	3,026	2,837	2,300	2,058	1,721	−16.4
Non-industrial transport equipment	301	284	317	183	147	166	13.1
Other	**555**	**516**	**661**	**1,243**	**869**	**871**	**0.3**
Total	**134,907**	**152,462**	**151,803**	**157,610**	**143,839**	**142,530**	**−0.9**

Source: TurkStat

Broad Economic Categories is among the World Trade Organization's (WTO) classification of goods

post-Second World War period. Following the long nineteenth century of rapid industrialization, Britain, for instance, witnessed a period of deindustrialization during the 1950s. Though referring to this experience 'negative deindustrialization', Rowthorn and Wells (1987: 248) conclude that even if it happened to be a 'positive' event, deindustrialization would be inevitable.

Industrial policy aimed at changing the industrial structure and inducing employment towards industry is a medium- to long-term effort by its very nature and thus involves planning (Yülek 2015: 21). The dilemma that governments face regarding their strategic orientation towards industrial policy resembles that of planning decisions and the extent of market interventions, Yülek (2015: 21) also points out. At the crossroads for upgrading its industrial base and joining the club of 'high-income' countries, Turkey has a lot to learn from previous experiences that developed countries faced in the 1980s and 1990s.

The underlying argument in the cases of most developed countries is that, whether they are highly centralized as in France or strategically guided as in Japan and Sweden or shaped by market-oriented planning as in the US and UK, they become 'mature' after a long period of industrialization. Rowthorn and Wells (1987: 245–46) give three potential explanations for the decline in the UK's manufacturing employment: the *net failure effect*, the *maturity effect*, and the *specialization effect*. The first refers to poor economic performance of the manufacturing industry in terms of creating jobs, whereas the second effect relates to unavoidable job losses due to the economy's relative level of maturity, and the third is related to the structural change in foreign trade and its impact on manufacturing employment.

As Krugman (1988: 2) points out, the massive capital inflows to the USA in the 1980s had as their counterpart a substantial reallocation of resources out of US tradeable sectors, with employment and capacity falling sharply in many export- and import-competing industries. This 'deindustrialization' in the USA had as its counterpart a corresponding growth of capacity abroad.

In popular discussions of the failure of US trade to turn around more quickly, a common theme is that uncertainty has inhibited the adjustment process – that both US and foreign firms have been reluctant to shift resources, both because they have viewed the strong dollar as likely to return and because in an uncertain environment they have adopted a general 'wait-and-see' attitude (Krugman 1988: 2). There is now widespread concern that the sluggish response of trade flows to the exchange rate, brought about in part by past exchange rate volatility, will lead to further future volatility because the declining dollar will now have to 'overshoot' its long-run level in order to persuade US firms to invest in the 'reindustrialization' that is now needed.

On the one hand, the reindustrialization issue is about trade policy owing to its significant and direct impact on resource allocation, real effective exchange rates, and relative wages in an economy. It is, however, like heads or tails with the institutional setting and industrial policy design. The proponents of 'reindustrialization' in the USA, for instance, called upon central bodies to formulate new policies via new institutions to revive the country's industrial base, as was the case with Reconstruction Finance Corporation (RFC) during the New Deal or the Japanese Ministry of International Trade and Industry (MITI). Bailing out traditional or old industries as well as cities, for instance, was long discussed among the proponents of reindustrialization in order to reverse the economy's growing tendency towards service sectors. This call for partial planning or policy coordination oriented towards the reindustrialization of the country with 'a second industrial revolution', however, also failed (Babacan 2015: 53).

'Industrial policy, often referred to as "reindustrialization" or "revitalization", should aim at transferring resources from declining industries into growing industries", replied Adlai Stevenson, former chairman of the Subcommittee on Industrial Policy and Productivity for the Senate Democratic Task Force on the American Economy, in an interview to the question on the definition of industrial policy. All in all, the main idea put forward by Stevenson and Bartel (1981: 41–42) is that an industrial policy should focus on adjustment financing, not bailouts; distinguish cyclically unemployed from structurally unemployed and favour the latter; and could have a better chance at working at the regional level, not national. Last but not least, Stevenson and Bartel (1981: 43) proposed an independent institution to provide funds/other needs for industrial development and begin with a radical restructuring of basic or essential industries.

A voice critical of the proposals surrounding a central administrative body to plan or design a national industrial policy during the 1980s was that of Miller (then chairman of the Federal Trade Commission) et al. (1984: 37), who called it ineffective and a cure worse than the perceived disease, owing to the overall design of the political system in the USA. The remedy, accordingly, is economic and political liberalism. Eizenstat (1984: 49–50) in his reply to Miller's article proposed a council on industrial competitiveness that would be designed as a forum composed of representatives from business, government, labour, and the general public. Better coordination of microeconomic policies among different government bodies as well as the alignment of policy choices between social groups via such a formal mechanism was expected to eliminate any source of information asymmetry as well.

Citing Etzioni's three distinct possible policy options on reindustrialization in the US economy during the 1980s, Norton (1986: 33) stated that the Reagan administration's choice had insufficiently targeted supply-side economics that in turn yielded more consumption, not investment. This policy option was then followed by semi-targeted reindustrialization with an idea of releasing resources to the private sector but channelling them to infrastructure and capital sectors.

Specialization in intermediate goods production that are widely tradable could then lead to better utilization of industrial capacity at home while creating an economy that was competitive worldwide. Public procurement could assist countries in acquiring capabilities in key industrial sectors, as argued by Yülek (2015: 22), and in turn could increase the international competitiveness of firms and, hence, the economy (Yülek 2015: 22).

Aysan and Hacıhasanoğlu (2007) find that manufacturing exports are negatively related to unit labour costs. Decomposing the unit labour cost into its two components also shows that an improvement in productivity increases exports, while an increase in nominal wages decreases it. The results also imply that the nominal wage is an important factor in declining sectors, while productivity is a stimulus in rising sectors.

Focusing on exchange rate volatility and its impact on resource allocation and relative earnings, Krugman (1988: 21) claims that the range of real exchange variation is wider in an uncertain world and that a large exchange rate movement that leads to deindustrialization must be offset by a subsequent overshooting in the opposite direction. Corresponding to the identification of the uncertainty problem put forward by Krugman (1988), yet differing in its recipe for the case of Turkey, Ünal (2016: 87) suggests that Turkey target the exchange rate under a new institutional setting, while on the fiscal side it should keep the nominal wage growth rate under the productivity growth rate in non-tradable goods.

Lin (2012: 115–6) calls for rethinking of structural economics in a new framework, which he recommends organizing around four ideas. The first is the economy's factor endowments and their structure (relative abundance of natural resources, labour, and human and physical capital), where they are subject to change over time. At different phases of economic development, the optimal structure of the economy should be different as well, according to Lin. Second, the industrial structure in an economy should be taken as endogenous and refer to a point on a spectrum of development from an agrarian economy to a high-income industrialized economy. Thus, Lin (2012: 116) states that industrial upgrading and infrastructure improvement in a developing country should not necessarily refer to those in high-income countries. Third, the market remains the fundamental mechanism for effective resource allocation, and industrial diversification, upgrading, and corresponding improvements in soft and hard infrastructure are essential to produce a dynamic process of economic development. Fourth, Lin argues that agglomeration and clustering are crucial in terms of reducing transaction costs in any given industry, making it globally competitive, owing to the increased level of specialization in production.

With regard to Lin's (2012) arguments, one structural issue closely linked to the labour market in Turkey is education, particularly vocational education. Though the Turkish educational system has come a long way in the last 15 years in terms of infrastructure, the transformation of the fixed capital investment into high educational quality as a critical component for going above and beyond the middle-income economy, is expected to take some time. Returns on education, productivity issues, teacher and instructor quality, and wage standards are all parts of this discussion. Higher education (i.e. universities) is yet another component of the larger issue of human capital. A stunning piece on the importance of vocational education in the reindustrialization of the US economy by Etzioni (1981: 9) states that (a) vocational education is not best served when it is run in institutions dominated by general educators, especially if those educators are not supportive of job education, (b) more interaction is needed between those generating jobs and those who provide vocational education, and (c) it does not follow that places of employment should provide more vocational education; they might tend to be too focused on job training rather than a well-rounded education. This concept of switching the responsibility of training from schools to places of employment has a particularly negative implication for small businesses that cannot afford to offer training or whose employees must have a variety of skills instead of training limited to one specific area. Turkey should take bold steps to reassess its education policy in a comprehensive way that embraces labour market components.

5 Conclusion

Over the last quarter century, many countries have witnessed what is called deindustrialization, which mainly manifests itself as a declining share of manufacturing employment in the total employment picture. Despite the heterogeneity in its underlying causes, such as changes in productivity levels over time, deindustrialization is still a common phenomenon across countries. As Tregenna (2011: 19) puts it rightly, reindustrialization after deindustrialization requires greater effort compared to what is required for earlier industrialization. Decisive and effective industrial policy is crucial for successful reindustrialization, and ties to foreign trade policies should predominate in its institutional design as well as implementation. This chapter represents an attempt to provide insight into the structural relationship between foreign trade and industrialization efforts in the case of Turkey.

Turkey was among the best-performing developed and developing economies in terms of exports in the 2000s. The country witnessed improvements both in number of competitive products and in the share of such products in its gross exports. With an increase in middle- and high-technology components in its exports, Turkey should now introduce new products to world markets through R&D activities and innovation-led growth strategies that further enhance industrial upgrades to expand into various sectors.

Aydın et al. (2007: 49) conclude that none of shocks in 1994, 1998, and 2001 had a path-breaking impact, though the shock in 2001 did have a level-shifting impact on the import elasticity of export supply. As a result, it seems the import elasticity of exports increased by about 50 per cent from 1987 to 2006. Some sectors have been successful at integrating into world markets, especially following the Turkey–EU customs union agreement, which enables them to expand their export market share by producing for the external market during turbulent periods. High import dependence and low real effective exchange rate elasticity shield them from the detrimental effects of real appreciation of the Turkish lira (Aydın et al. 2007: 49).

Another argument regarding the importance of reindustrialization based on efficiency-led and technology-driven production is from the perspective of a middle-income trap. As Yağcı (2017: 97–98) asserts, industrial activity and manufacturing constitute a major challenge in avoiding the middle-income trap and achieving sustainable economic and social development in Turkey.

A broad array of factors cause countries to enter and become stuck in an alleged middle-income trap. Engel and Taglioni (2017: 124) discuss these factors, which include macroeconomic and microeconomic factors related to industrial structure, trade profile, demographics, income distribution, macroeconomic management, and the quality of institutions.

For East Asian countries, an empirical study that focused on the middle-income trap and presented a vast literature review on the middle-income trap was conducted by Kumagai (2015: 18), who suggests that it is necessary to develop an industry on the backbone of labour-intensive primary goods production that enables an upgrade to capital goods production. While this is essential and true of most middle-income countries, certainly it is not enough for overcoming this so-called trap. An international trade perspective that enhances the network and, thus, spillovers between countries that are relatively equivalent in level of industrialization would yield positive results, as stated by Kumagai (2015: 18), who concluded that the industrial upgrading process through the backward linkage from consumption goods to capital goods, parts, and components is more successful in non-trapped higher-income countries. For trapped countries, he argues, there is a tendency to depend on the export of primary commodities, and industrialization would appear to be driven by forward linkages to processed goods. This narrow industrial base is thus a possible cause of the middle-income trap (Kumagai 2015: 18).

Yağcı (2017: 106) stresses that Turkey must prioritize industrialization as a key policy option in order to achieve the status of developing state, and he proposes traversing the middle-income trap via reindustrialization. The findings of a research paper by Meçik and Afşar (2015: 106) on deindustrialization processes in OECD countries indicate that industrial employment is positively correlated with per-capita income levels, fixed capital, and FDI inflows.

Engel and Taglioni (2017: 125) provide several recommendations borrowed from country experiences with avoiding the middle-income trap primarily have to do with structural, industrial, and trade policies as well as social policy. Macroprudential policies for avoiding sudden stops as well as regulating private-sector activities play a significant role. Measures taken for regional integration and developing knowledge network externalities are also important for spillovers on both the individual and institutional level. Labour markets should be flexible enough to enable skilled workers to move up within the value chain from low-value-added sectors to higher-value-added ones. Differentiation between state-owned companies and private ones as well as product and factor markets in order to achieve higher levels of technology for industrial upgrade through newly developed industries is also essential.

Gür et al. (2017: 151) propose a comprehensive approach to industrial transformation that would increase Turkey's competitiveness in the world. Their approach incorporates education, technology, and industry perspectives. The complementary element in such an approach would be efficient coordination among state institutions. In that regard, Yeldan and Yıldırım (2015: 84) stress that development is not only specialization in the same set of products but innovating and developing new products while defining the role of the state as an active entrepreneur not a sole Walrasian middleman or an invisible arbitrator. Therefore, the design of investment incentives for the purpose of attracting FDI as well as domestic entrepreneurs is critical to avoid the middle-income trap.

Turkey must do more to attract greater foreign capital in high-technology-factor-intensive and high-skilled-labour-intensive strategic sectors such as health, finance, education, and manufacturing. To accomplish that, it should create a strategic roadmap for upgrading its industrial and financial ecosystems. Dynamic and international scale economies and their sources are also crucial to understand in order to improve Turkey's capacity to create a national ecosystem of industry composed of tradable intermediate goods where external economies involve the diffusion of knowledge, as stated by Helpman and Krugman (1986: 38). Such external economies stemming from a diffusion of knowledge, technology and innovation, or learning by doing (i.e. experience) are usually the result of economies of scale in intermediate goods production.

To sum up, in the case of Turkey, Lin's (2012: 215) arguments on the middle-income trap could be useful. He defines such a trap as a country's inability to continue on the path of industrial upgrading, which then results in stagnation of per-capita income compared to world leaders. Lin (2012: 220) further argues that income stagnation in low- and middle-income countries reflects a failure in designing and implementing strategies for dynamic structural transformation. Turkey is at a crossroads in finding the optimal level of state intervention and guidance in industrial transformation for maximizing benefits from trade spillovers. As stated so well by Kutlay (2011: 85), the limits of a functionalist political economy in Turkey could concisely be referred to as industrial capacity in terms of competitiveness, state–business and business-to-business interactions, and social coherence in terms of the design of policy, both domestic and foreign.

References

Ahn, JaeBin, Dabla-Norris, Era, Duval, Romain, Hu, Bingjie and Njie, Lamin. 2016. *Reassessing the Productivity Gains from Trade Liberalization*, IMF Working Paper, WP/16/77.

Alaya, Marouane and Mezghani, Imed. 2013. *The Growth of Turkey in World Trade: Opportunity or Threat for MENA Countries?* The Economic Research Forum (ERF) Working Paper, No. 763.

Aydın, Faruk, Saygılı, Hülya and Saygılı, Mesut. 2007. *Empirical Analysis of Structural Change in Turkish Exports*, The Central Bank of the Republic of Turkey (CBRT) Working Paper, No. 07/08.

Aysan, A.F., and Y.S. Hacıhasanoğlu. 2007. Investigation into the Determinants of Turkish Export-Boom in 2000s, *The. Journal of International Trade and Diplomacy* 1 (2): 159–202.

Babacan, Mehmet. 2011. Whither Axis Shift: A Perspective from Turkey's Foreign Trade. *Insight Turkey* 13 (1): 129–157.

———. 2015. Change and Continuity in Economic Planning: A Methodological Survey. In *Economic Planning and Industrial Policy in the Globalizing Economy*, ed. Murat Yülek, 43–58. Switzerland: Springer.

Baysan, Tercan, and Charles Blitzer. 1991. Turkey. In *Liberalizing Foreign Trade: The Experience of New Zealand, Spain and Turkey*, The IBRD/World Bank Project, ed. D. Papageorgiou, M. Michaely, and A.M. Choksi. Cambridge, MA: Basil Blackwell Inc.

Bhagwati, Jagdish. 1978. *Foreign Trade Regimes and Economic Development: Anatomy and Consequences of Exchange Control Regimes*, NBER Conference Series. Cambridge, MA: Ballinger Publishing Company.

Chenery, Hollis B. 1961. Comparative Advantage and Development Policy. *The American Economic Review* 51 (1): 18–51.

Civan et al. 2013. The Effect of New Turkish Foreign Policy on International Trade. *Insight Turkey* 15 (3): 107–122.

Eizenstat, Stuart E. 1984. Reindustrialization Through Coordination or Chaos? *Yale Journal on Regulation* 2 (1): 39–51.

Engel, Jakob and Taglioni, Daria. 2017. The Middle-Income Trap and Upgrading Along Global Value Chains. In *Global Value Chain Development Report 2017*, 119–139. World Bank Group, Washington, DC: USA.

Etzioni, Amitai. 1981. *Reindustrialization and Vocational Education*, The Ohio State University The National Center for Research in Vocational Education Occasional Paper No. 76, pp. 1–12.

Gür, N., S. Ünay, and Ş. Dilek. 2017. *Sanayiyi Yeniden Düşünmek: Küresel Teknolojik Dönüşümün Dünya ve Türkiye Ekonomisine Yansımaları*. İstanbul: SETA Kitapları.

Helpman, Elhanan, and Paul R. Krugman. 1986. *Market Structure and Foreign Trade*. 2nd ed. Cambridge, MA: The MIT Press.

Isard, Walter. 1954. Location Theory and Trade Theory: Short-Run Analysis. *The Quarterly Journal of Economics* 68 (2): 305–320.

Johnson, Robert C., and Noguera, Guillermo. 2016. *A Portrait of Trade in Value Added Over Four Decades*, NBER Working Series, No. 22974. Cambridge, MA.

Krueger, Anne. 1974. *Foreign Trade Regimes and Economic Development: Turkey*, NBER Conference Series. New York City: Columbia University Press.

Krugman, Paul R. 1988. *Deindustrialization, Reindustrialization and the Real Exchange Rate*, NBER Working Paper Series, No. 2586. Cambridge, MA.

Kumagai, Satoru. 2015. The Middle-Income Trap from the Viewpoint of Trade Structures: Are the Geese Trapped or Still Flying? *Journal of International Commerce, Economics and Policy* 6 (3): 1–23.

Kutlay, Mustafa. 2011. Economy as the 'Practical Hand' of 'New Turkish Foreign Policy': A Political Economy Explanation. *Insight Turkey* 13 (1): 67–88.

Lin, Justin Y. 2012. *The Quest for Prosperity: How Developing Economies Can Take Off.* Princeton: *Princeton University Press.*

Meçik, O., and M. Afşar. 2015. Ekonomide Sanayisizleşme ve OECD Ülkelerine Etkileri. *Hacettepe University Journal of Economics and Administrative Sciences* 33 (2): 85–111.

Mevel, S., J. Moll de Alba, and N. Oulmane. 2016. Optimal Trade- Integration Schemes in North Africa: Toward a Pro-Industrialization Policy. *Journal of Economic Integration* 31 (3): 569–608.

Miller, J.C., T.F. Walton, W.E. Kovacic, and J.A. Rabkin. 1984. *Yale Journal on Regulation* 2 (1): 1–37.

Norton, R.D. 1986. Industrial Policy and American Renewal. *Journal of Economic Literature* 24 (1): 1–40.

Porter, Michael E. 2009. *The Competitive Advantage of Nations, States and Regions.* Harvard Business School Advanced Management Program Presentation, pp. 1–27.

Rodrik, Dani. 1992. The Limits of Trade Policy Reform in Developing Countries. *The Journal of Economic Perspectives* 6 (1): 87–105.

Rosenfeld, Stuart A. 1997. Bringing Business Clusters into the Mainstream of Economic Development. *European Planning Studies* 5 (1): 3–23.

Rowthorn, R.E., and J.R. Wells. 1987. *De-Industrialization and Foreign Trade.* Cambridge: Cambridge University Press.

Stevenson, Adlai E., and Richard D. Bartel. 1981. Reindustrialization: Politics and Economics. *Challenge* 23 (6): 39–43.

Turkish Exporters Assembly (TIM) Report on Development of Exports, 2001–2016 Report. http://www.tim.org.tr/files/downloads/%C4%B0hracat%C4%B1n%20Geli%C5%9Fim%202001-2016.pdf. Accessed 11 Aug 2017.

Tregenna, Fiona. 2011. *Manufacturing Productivity, Deindustrialization and Reindustrialization*, United Nations University- WIDER Working Paper, No. 2011/57.

Ünal, Emre. 2016. A Comparative Analysis of Export Growth in Turkey and China through Macroeconomic and Institutional Factors. *Evolutionary and Institutional Economic Review* 13 (1): 57–91.

Yağcı, Mustafa. 2017. The Political Economy of AK Party Rule in Turkey: From a Regulatory State to a 1 Developmental State? *Insight Turkey* 19 (2): 89–113.

Yeldan, E., and Yıldırım, D. 2015. *Küreselleşme ve Sanayisizleşme Bağlamında Türkiye'de ve Dünyada Demokrasi Açığı* (Democracy Deficit in Turkey and the World in the Context of Globalization and De-Industrialization). *Çalışma ve Toplum* 2: 65–88.

Yülek, Murat. 2015. Revisiting National Economic Planning and Industrial Policy: Concepts, Experiences and the Ecosystem. In *Economic Planning and Industrial Policy in the Globalizing Economy*, ed. Murat Yülek, 3–27. Switzerland: Springer.

Challenges of Turkish Family Businesses Related to Effective Management Strategies

Huseyin Cirpan and Nihat Alayoglu

1 Introduction

Family businesses are generally regarded as the backbone of an economy – they create wealth and provide jobs. In 2014, small and medium-sized enterprises (SMEs) constituted 99.8 per cent of all entrepreneurships in Turkey, providing 73.5 per cent of all jobs and more than half of all wages. They also created 53.5 per cent of added value and made 55 per cent of all investments (TUIK 2016). Almost all of these companies are owned and managed by families. Big companies owned by families are not included in these statistics. However, despite their many positive aspects and cultural advantages – specifically in speed of decision-making, unity of purpose, efficiency of communications, loyalty, and the commitment of employees (Nicholson 2008) – there is also a negative side. Family conflicts, incompetent members of the next generation,

H. Cirpan (✉) • N. Alayoglu
School of Business, Istanbul Medipol University, Istanbul, Turkey

A. F. Aysan et al. (eds.), *Turkish Economy*,
https://doi.org/10.1007/978-3-319-70380-0_17

extravagant lifestyles, and nepotism are just some of the more frequent criticisms about family businesses (Kets de Vries 1996).

Given the relative importance of family businesses in the Turkish economy, scholars have been showing increasing interest in them in the hope of identifying what makes a family business sustainable. There is contentious debate surrounding the question of whether the involvement of family members in a business is a blessing or curse. At the outset, it is important to be clear about what makes a business a family business and to establish the main features that are idiosyncratic to family businesses. A commonly accepted criterion of a family business relates to who owns the business and thus has the power to make the critical and strategic decisions.

A family business involves two separate and conflicting entities, family and business. It is widely accepted that the working dynamics of these two entities are almost opposite to one another. While the family system is an arena for the emotional concerns and conflicting needs of family members, the business system is all about performance, growth, and change (Carlock and Ward 2001). The goals of these systems are also very much at odds with each other. The family's purpose is mainly about social and emotional support and cohesion among family members. However, the business is about survival, growth, profitability, and sustainability. The attitude towards these systems varies for individuals. It can be grossly generalized that one would expect to have one's needs around belonging and love fulfilled within a family and one's survival, career, and status needs fulfilled in business (Kets de Vries 1996).

There has also been a huge debate about what comes first, family or business, in times of critical challenges that an entrepreneur will inevitably face. While an entrepreneur's choice of what comes first, family or business, basically depends upon his (the male form is used for simplicity) personal life values, the meaning he ascribes to family and business, and his expectations in life in general and with respect to family and business in particular, it can be argued that an entrepreneur does not have to take an either/or approach but that can take a both/and approach by attending to the peculiar needs of family and business and making these two systems feed off one another as part of a reciprocal feedback loop (Leach and Bogod 1999). In this chapter, we take the both/and approach and suggest ways of reconciling family issues and business requirements to achieve the right alignment and balance between them in order to attain happiness and fulfilment in family and wild success in business. Many issues examined in the family business literature arise from the enmeshed relationships of family and business, from not setting boundaries between these two different systems. The business founder occupies an in-between position, and the main responsibility to align these systems lies with him. Therefore, in this chapter, we focus on the founder-entrepreneur in general, his mindset with respect to business and family, the psychological make-up that drives his behaviour and his relationships with his siblings, other family members, and non-family members in particular.

As mentioned earlier, positive effects can come from a family business when the right approach is followed. Specific issues or dynamics make family businesses different from non-family firms. Every specific dynamic, depending on how it is approached, can be a blessing or a curse for the welfare of the family and the business. Using the Pareto principle, we will choose and concentrate on fundamental issues that are especially relevant to Turkish family businesses and Turkish culture. For every issue or dynamic, we will outline the basic findings in international family research and will then explore the issue in question with special reference to the Turkish case and the effect of this characteristic on business performance. We will then move on to explain how to reconcile the intricacies of that family issue and the requirements of sustainable business management and suggest some systems and strategies for the effective management of business and family.

2 Dynamics of Family Businesses

Sustaining a business is a formidable challenge, given the amount of competition all businesses face. Family businesses feel extra pressure surrounding the issues of management and sustainability. It is an almost unquestioned truth that only around 30 per cent of family businesses make it to the second generation and only 7–10 per cent to the third. As the family grows, with children growing and being employed in the company, management issues become increasingly complicated. Before launching into a discussion of family-related issues, we will very briefly consider the main requirements for keeping a business healthy and sustainable over time.

Cadbury (2000) summed up the organizational requirements for a family business to manage effectively the consequences of growth under three headings: (1) recruit and retain the best people for the business; (2) develop a culture of trust and transparency; and (3) define logical and efficient organizational structures. These headings are related to human resources, culture, and management systems, which are equally relevant to non-family businesses. Here we will concentrate on what hinders the founder-entrepreneur achieving and sustaining these requirements. In light of the statistics cited earlier about transitions to the next generations, it would not be an exaggeration to claim that the subject of succession is the most commonly studied area in family business. The essential question is: what are the determinants of a successful business transition?

Research results indicate that there are three basic determinants of successful transitions in family businesses. Family business transitions occur more smoothly (1) when heirs are better prepared, (2) when relationships among family members are more trust-based and affable, and (3) when family businesses engage in more planning for taxation and wealth-transfer purposes. Of these factors, relationships within the family have the single greatest impact on successful transitions (Morris et al. 1997, 398). As with organizational requirements, these areas are also related to human resources, culture, and systems. The difference is that they are specific to family businesses. It is unnecessary to emphasize the role of the founder in these areas. In the process of meeting these requirements, an entrepreneur will have to overcome some hindrances, especially ones related to the idiosyncratic nature of family-specific relationships.

2.1 Issues Related to Founder-Entrepreneur

It can be postulated that all issues are in one way or another related to the founder-entrepreneur. However, under this heading, we will be looking closely into the inner psychic dynamics of the entrepreneur: why does he behave the way he does? What deep fears affect his approach to the business, non-family members, and especially his children as successors in the business?

Fear of Losing Control: One-Man Control

A family business is set up by an entrepreneur, and if all goes all right, it flourishes and grows. There comes a time when the founder needs resources outside of the company. Although there is a need for external resources, the founder's insistence on having singular control over the firm retards the firm's development by limiting management capacity (Rutherford et al. 2006).

This insistence on the part of the founder to have such total control stems from the fact that the founder approaches business in a way similar to how parents see their children. Research has shown that when parents hold their newborn babies in their hands just after birth, the primary feeling that pops up is one of fear and anxiety for the baby's future. As they raise their child, all their behaviours in relation to the child are shaped by this fear and anxiety. They watch out and are alert for any threats coming from the outside world (Yazgan 2008). The founder of a business regards it as his baby, so he behaves in the same way that parents do. He will try to protect his business by exerting almost total control and taking a hands-on management style, not allowing it to grow as a separate entity. Consequently, the founder identifies with his business, which would not be the case after a certain growth stage of a non-family business – just as parents should let go of their children to allow them to forge their own identity apart from that of the parents and be able to stand confident on their own.

Many founder-entrepreneurs have experienced hardships, such as poverty, dislocation, or illness, in their childhood, and these experiences have a powerful effect on shaping how they view the world and other people. As a result, entrepreneurs sense a feeling of needing to be in control (Kets de Vries 1996). This need has an effect on how they run their business. As the business grows, it is expected that the entrepreneur will employ managers to delegate tasks to which he himself cannot give attention. The need for control hampers this process, and as a result, the business suffers since talented non-family members leave the company owing to the micro-management by the entrepreneur.

In a study conducted through in-depth interviews with company founders and their siblings who are in management in Konya, a Central Anatolian city, the following statement – made by one founder – reflects founders' general feelings and mood about their business:

> *I, as a founder, manage this company with the understanding of 'Gate – Scale – Company Safe'. Where I sit, I can see the door and the scale; the company safe is under my table. Actually, I don't have any operational position in the company; I only have meetings with my sons and managers in the morning.* (StrategyCo. 2015, 4)

This approach may be understandable at the start-up phase, but at later stages it becomes an ever-increasing burden on the firm. Eventually, the company is left with mediocre managers who would not be able to leave the business because of their own incompetency. Another aspect of a micro-managing or domineering style of leadership is that it tends to 'attract "yes-men", people having the characteristics of a dependent personality who are hardly the kind of people to move the company forward' (Kets de Vries 1993, 67).

This strong need for control may stem from the founder's psychological make-up. He may believe that 'my business is me or a reflection of who I am'. During the present authors' consultancy, one entrepreneur said 'My main prayer is to die while working at [the] office'. This is very much related to the ego development of the founder (for more, see Kegan 1982). The intervention to overcome this need for control is essentially a psychodynamic process through which the founder separates his identity from his company and achievements and starts his individuation process (Kaye 1996).

The Question of Succession

As mentioned earlier, almost all work and research on family business is related to transferring leadership to the next generation. It seems that succession is the holy grail of family business research. The purpose of this interest is to determine what factors enable certain family firms to succeed while others fail. Overemphasis on the succession issue may cause the founder-entrepreneur to develop a counterproductive perspective about who will succeed him. There are a few different approaches among entrepreneurs.

As stated earlier, when heirs are well prepared for the handover, the generational transition goes smoothly. This is easier said than done. One of the main themes that arose during our field experience regarding the preparation of heirs is that the founder wanted to compensate for his weaknesses in the business with his heirs, regardless of their aptitude or the possible needs of the organization when the heirs take over. In other words, the founder sees his heirs as being extensions of himself rather than individuals who will be taking over leadership of the company on their own. An example of this is one founder who wanted his son to become a certified accountant rather than an entrepreneur who could sustain the business and make it grow.

Quite a few complexities arise in such a situation. First of all, if there are several potential successors, the first question is: who will take the leadership position? If there is more than one candidate, sibling rivalry is likely to arise (Grote 2003). Secondly, the founder-entrepreneur assumes that all his children are very much interested in becoming involved in his business, which may not be the case. One way or another, the success of the business is generally measured by the transfer of leadership to the second generation (Kaye 1996). As a result, the heirs are forced to acquire their education in areas related to business or to the founder's wishes. This lack of interest, or being forced to take any position, raises the issue of lack of motivation and commitment on the heirs' part, and as a result, performance suffers and becomes mediocre.

A third complexity results from the ego development of the parents, not allowing their children to go through a healthy individuation process. When the ego development of parents is high, they will allow and encourage their children to follow the individuation process, becoming separate, self-confident adults (Kets de Vries and Carlock 2010). If parents' ego development level is low, the children's individuation and ego development stay low, and eventually these children become dependent on their parents and reliant on the family business for survival. These children turn out to be 'prisoners' or 'addicts' of the family business who stay in the business, even though they are neither happy nor successful (Kaye 1996). This addiction creates a vicious circle and has a negative impact on the children's self-esteem. These children will not be seen as talented or confident by the founder, which serves as a strong confirmation of his belief that he should always be in control.

There is a completely different side to the question of succession. Earlier it was stated that a smooth transition to the next generation is possible if the heirs are well prepared. A founder-entrepreneur will undoubtedly have gone through some very hard times and faces many challenges to make his business successful, and he may seem obsessed with his business. By being so preoccupied, he neglects his family. Eventually, this neglect leads to feelings of quilt. To overcome these feelings, he starts bribing his family to compensate for his not having been available for them by providing them with goods and spending lavishly on them. This behaviour turns out to be a so-called Faustian bargain (Kets de Vries 1993). Aside from these feelings, he came from nothing in terms of wealth. Early pioneers among Turkish entrepreneurs experienced very severe poverty, deprived of the good things in life, and by following this line of thought – to say, for example, 'we have not lived our lives, in the end we are earning for him' – the entrepreneur will allow his family and children to have extraordinary luxuries, spending out of proportion. This lifestyle distorts his children's perspective on life and business, and they will never make an effort to prepare themselves for taking over the business.

Erdoğmuş (2004) argued that potential successors to the founder-entrepreneurs of SMEs in Turkey were not seen as ready and qualified to take over and move the firms forward. As a result, the founders do not identify a successor and make a management transfer plan (Ateş 2005).

Lack of Trust for Professionals

Along with the need for control, suspicion of other people is very common among most founder-entrepreneurs. This proclivity among entrepreneurs might have evolved out of childhood experiences of hardship and victimization (Kets de Vries 1996). Entrepreneurs are always on the look-out so as not to lose what they have worked so hard to build. Some degree of suspicion can work in a constructive way by making the entrepreneur vigilant to the competitive environment and developments that may influence the performance of the business. When this distrust takes over or becomes unhealthy, an entrepreneur starts scanning the environment for something to confirm his suspicions.

Lack of trust in others is a very common phenomenon among Turkish entrepreneurs. Actually, distrust of others seems endemic among Turkish people in general. Research shows that the trust level among people is as low as 8 per cent. The cost of this distrust is very high in terms of efficiency and transaction costs and raises the question of agency (Gur and Alayoglu 2017).

The consequences of this distrust for business are serious: Turkish family businesses employ people whom they can trust, especially within the family circle or with references. This is especially true of some positions like finance, purchasing, and warehouse positions, regardless of the individuals' competence for those positions. This approach is actually counterproductive in some ways. Firstly, less qualified people for a position can fulfil the requirements of the job and cause business performance to fall behind and hamper the efficient work of other parts of the organization since they do not work in isolation. Secondly, this employment of family members or implied 'trusted' privileged employees may indirectly cause other family members to lose their faith in the company, resulting in a deterioration of their commitment to the company and causing the affected individuals to look for work elsewhere. In the long run, these companies suffer from bad reputations, and such companies find it quite hard to attract bright and talented employees. Among many people, family firms are seen as rather unappealing places to work, so they are regarded as the last option for work (Gur and Bjørnskov 2017).

2.2 Issues Related to Family Culture

Effect of Socioemotional Wealth

In recent years, in search of a model that explains the idiosyncratic nature of family firms or what makes them different from non-family-controlled businesses, some researchers have proposed a so-called socioemotional wealth (SEW) approach (Gomez-Mejia et al. 2007). Gomez-Mejia et al. (2007) conceptualized socio-emotional endowments as affective endowments that a family acquires by controlling a firm, including having the family's name on the firm, the appointment of family members to important posts, exercising unrestricted personal authority, and having family influence over the firm.

Berrone et al. (2010, 87) say that 'the value of socioemotional wealth to the family is more intrinsic, its preservation becomes an end in itself, and it is anchored at a deep psychological level among family owners whose identity is inextricably tied to the organisation'. SEW suggests that families do almost anything to protect their socioemotional endowment, even when this has a financial cost. Research shows that families are willing to incur a significant risk to protect their socioemotional wealth (Gomez-Mejia et al. 2007).

Role Confusion in Relationships

In a family business, some conflicting roles are occupied by the same people. For example, the founder-entrepreneur may experience the most severe role confusion. On the one hand, he wears a founder's hat and an owner's hat, and, on the other, he puts in long days at work, and he still occupies the position of father and figurehead of his family. This confusion is multiplied as his son/daughter or brother/sister or some relatives start joining the business. How is he going to behave towards his son – as a son or an employee? There is even the question of how they will address each other: as dad or Mr X? How does he manage to switch roles, or does he even have to? He has a blood relationship with his son or daughter and easily gets emotional, so it can be difficult to keep him/her accountable, as one could with a non-family member.

In a sibling partnership company, partners may confuse their roles, too: are they siblings or partners? Actually, they are both. They cannot deny the fact that they are siblings, and again, past emotional charges, both positive and negative, will rear their head. A partnership has very different dynamics than a blood relationship. In Turkish culture, an older elder brother will feel entitled to have the upper hand in terms of leading and making decisions based not on merit but on just being an older brother, although all siblings have equal shares in the business. They are siblings in life but partners in business. The problem becomes aggravated when younger brothers don't communicate and suppress their feelings because of the cultural pressure of being respectful. It seems that many ignore this fact and continue to behave as only siblings, which harms the quality of the relationship.

One solution to this kind of role confusion is to design the relationship out of which a charter is crafted. This kind of relationship design clearly sets the boundaries and clearly establishes everyone's roles and responsibilities and how to keep everyone accountable. A typical constitution covers expectations, desires, and relationship design and provides all sides with guidance on how to handle some emotional issues such as personal style, values, money, and power. Potential sources of conflict are identified and suggested resolutions discussed. One of the main advantages of a partnership charter is that it provides a structure for siblings to address issues that will make or break their partnership. Within that structure, the needs, priorities, personalities, and circumstances of the siblings dictate what aspects will be emphasized (Gage 2004).

Gender Issue in Succession and Employment

Although researchers often give little attention to the effects of 'gender and ethnicity' when studying family companies (Velasco et al. 2013), it is of particular importance to consider the gender issue in Turkish culture. There are publicly well-known women successors in some big companies whose business performances are very high in terms of growth and sustainability. According to the field experience of this chapter's authors, this seems to be an exception in the Turkish case rather than an ordinary process experienced around the country. In many parts of the country, sons are seen as the necessary heirs of a company and family legacy. This unquestioned tradition of succession of sons may hold the company back and prevent the family taking advantage of latent talent and cause some resentment among female family members and friction in family circles, since girls are no longer complacent and compliant to this tradition, though they do not have enough courage and power to change it.

Since this issue is related to culture and how girls are perceived, it is hardly possible to create a system wherein families pay attention to this sensible and culturally specific matter. It is only a matter of time before the culture will change, as companies become international and founder-entrepreneurs interact with other cultures and see the benefits of giving all children equal opportunities in family businesses.

The Question of Nepotism

The most fundamental problem that crops up again and again in family businesses is to favour family members over non-family members, regardless of merit. Family logic often overrules business rationale. Founders of firms tend to overlook the weaknesses of their beloved sons or daughters. The appointment of an incompetent family member can trigger a couple of problems in company operations (Kets de Vries 1996). Firstly, this kind of appointment undermines the trust level of non-family members because of an imbalance between contributions and rewards. Secondly, as a result, this lack of trust negatively affects job satisfaction, motivation, and job performance, causing highly qualified non-family members to leave the company.

Appointing family members to positions for which they are not qualified complicates the process of performance measurement and compensation. A very common mistake that family businesses make is that family members, especially children, are paid not according to the normal compensation range of the position but according to their perceived lifestyle and needs. This policy of emotional compensation is not aligned with business logic and irritates non-family members. It is strongly advised that children be paid on the basis of their position in the company. From an emotional perspective, the family may like to support those children whose compensation is not enough to cover their lifestyle expenses. This support should be given by clearly stating that this is not for the work they do but it is of family support.

Overlooking Family Conflicts

It is only natural for conflict to arise among family members. For example, personal differences among family members in terms of values, motivations, and needs can lead to conflict in the family in general and in the business in particular. On an individual level, the strong identification of family members with the firm itself, and the intensity of emotions among family members because of what the business means to each one of them, may be additional causes of interpersonal conflict.

Traditionally, conflict used to be regarded as a characteristic that negatively affected the performance and survival of family firms. Recent research has shown that not all conflict is inherently detrimental to firm performance. On the contrary, some moderate conflict may serve to improve a firm's effectiveness. In the literature, two kinds of conflict are outlined: task conflict and relationship conflict (Kellermanns and Eddleston 2006).

It is widely accepted that 'relationship conflict is associated with resentment, animosity, anger, frustration and hostile behaviors' (Kellermanns and Eddleston 2006, 358). These kinds of highly charged emotions resulting from this kind of conflict may have a catastrophic impact on both family and business. Quarrels and infighting within a family firm can result in insufficient attention being focused upon business needs and performance (Kets de Vries 1993). Kellermanns and Eddleston (2004) also argue that the potential benefits of task conflict can be reduced or even lost when relationship conflict is present in family firms.

One can ask what is optimal in terms of conflict. Kellermanns and Eddleston (2006, 360) state that 'low levels of relationship conflict and moderated levels of task conflict will lead to superior performance in family firms'. It is not easy to achieve this optimum level given the complexities related to business and family issues. It is beyond the scope of this chapter to explain all approaches to conflict management. Suffice it to mention that four basic conflict management approaches are studied in the research: avoidance, contending, compromising, and collaborating (for more information see De Dreu and Van Vianen 2001).

What is unhealthy is if family members overlook a conflict rather than confront it and engage in crucial conversation to resolve it and move forward. Although there is no research regarding how Turkish families approach conflicts, as an observation of the authors, it can be argued that Turkish businesses tend to use an avoidance strategy when a conflict arises. Because of the overlapping of the family and the business, and the continual interactions of family members, the strategy of avoiding conflict might allow family members to focus on the tasks at hand, but the overarching problems that created the negative emotions will linger and fester (Kellermanns and Eddleston 2006). A high use of avoidance in family firms has been associated with low satisfaction with family life, high sibling rivalry, and low mutual trust (Kaye and McCarthy 1996).

The overlooking of relationship conflict in a family cannot be sustained and will have a devastating effect on business performance in the long run. Therefore, it is recommended that family members learn how to collaborate and talk over problems and integrate all members' views into the decision-making process.

2.3 Issues Related to Business Management

As mentioned earlier, there are three main requirements for family businesses to effectively manage growth and sustainability, namely, to work with the very best people for the business, to create a culture of trust and transparency, and to put in place rational and efficient business structures (Cadbury 2000). In this part of the chapter, we will focus on topics and issues that may have a negative impact on these three basic requirements.

Consciousness of Life Cycle of Firm

Much research has been done on the various life cycle stages of enterprises, within which various features and issues are faced (e.g. Adizes 1988). It is clear that organizational challenges and managerial approaches vary as the enterprise evolves. As both the family and the business grow, challenges become increasingly difficult to handle. Given the peculiar nature of family businesses, it is of paramount importance to be attentive and become mindful of the stage in which the business finds itself at a particular moment and what kind of management style is needed to survive and be competitive, and to adjust the business strategy, organizational structure, and even the leadership and management team accordingly.

Research shows that the most common factor in successful and sustainable family businesses – indeed, valid for all types of business – is the ability to adapt to both external and internal challenges. External challenges come from the market and the macro environment of the global and national economy, politics, technology, and so forth; internal challenges originate from the family and the firm.

We have outlined the main traits of the founder-entrepreneur, i.e. having freedom and autonomy, not bound to structures, and being innovative. These wonderful qualities may serve the business at the start-up and growing stages but may become a curse in a later stage of stabilization and creating structures for management of the firm. At the very least, the main traits of the founder-entrepreneur may not be compatible with the requirements of the firm for creating rational structures. The founder might get stuck in the old patterns that made him successful in the first place and might resist adapting to the present realities of the firm and the market. The mismatch of the senior executive's leadership style with the company's development stage can have a devastating effect on strategy and growth.

There is another life cycle adjustment that is required for the success of a family business. This adjustment is about the founder-entrepreneur's life cycle, related to how he behaves over the years (Schwass 2005). This perspective includes the life cycle of a founder-entrepreneur over one generation of the family business, and suggests differentiating the life cycle into three separate phases, which differ in features and requirements: 'do', 'lead to do', and finally 'let do' (Schwass 2005). The 'do' phase is about building up the business, setting the groundwork, and being actively engaged with the day-to-day operations of the firm. The main focus of the entrepreneur at this stage is to penetrate into the market and obtain the cash flow the firm needs. The second phase, the 'lead to do', starts with the promotion of the successor to the leadership role with clearly defined authority and responsibilities. Lastly, the 'let do' stage is about the founder's retirement, leaving the business altogether to the successor's 'do' stage of his cycle.

Ateş (2005) established that founder-entrepreneurs in Turkey are very reluctant to identify their successors when they are still alive out of fear that there will be conflicts among potential successors. This hinders the preparation of the successor to take on all responsibilities in the business. It is also very common for succession to be determined by family-culture-based criteria of age or gender rather than rational and justifiable reasons.

Separation of Ownership and Management

A firm needs to grow in order to be able satisfy the needs of a growing family. To this end, it is important to create a 'meritocratic' culture where a rigorous selection process for the successor is applied and professional preparation of family members for managerial positions are in place (Chrisman et al. 1998). However, it is unreasonable for a family to assume that it will continue to produce the best management competencies within the family or that it can always match the requirements of the external market in terms of competence. The dynamic and complex nature of business aggravates the problem that business requirements are always changing. To be able to ensure that the management requirements of a business will be met and the challenges of the complex business world will be tackled, management of the business should be professionalized and made separate from ownership (Chittoor and Das 2007).

Based on their consulting experience and anecdotal evidence from three case studies of family businesses, Chittoor and Das (2007, 73) argue that management succession to a non-family professional manager has a positive impact on succession performance. They also suggest some mechanisms that smooth the inclusion of non-family managers in leadership positions: (1) creating some exit mechanisms for family members who may pursue their own entrepreneurial ambitions or other careers of interest; (2) selecting a successor with some experience within the business rather than an outsider; and (3) including key professional managers on the firm's board of directors.

Findings from a field survey among the members of the Aegean Automotive Association show that Turkish founder-managers have a generally negative approach to transferring business management to non-family members (Peksaygılı and Tutan 2015). Kula (2005) researched the impact of the roles, structure, and process of boards on the performance of Turkish firms and argued that the separation of the chairman and top manager positions has a significant, positive impact on subsequent business performance.

Corporate Governance Structure

Corporate governance is accepted as one of the key determining factors in the health of a system and its ability to survive economic shocks (Iwasaki 2014, 207). Corporate governance is defined as 'a guidance and management structure aligning and organising ownership management and business management. Corporate governance comprises three different elements: the stockholders' assembly, the board of directors and the top management team' (Brenes et al. 2011, 280).

Based on their field survey in Ghana, Sarbah and Xiao (2015, 52) argue that 'good governance is a must for every business, but for family businesses, corporate governance is a crucial paradigm shift, so significant that it determines the continuity or growth of every family business. The main goal of good corporate governance is to give direction for families in the business as they move on to the next stage of development of their businesses, and its consequences on the family and the business as a whole'.

In a research survey conducted among SMEs based in the south-eastern region of Turkey, Demir and Sezgin (2014) found that SMEs are for the most part aware of the necessity of establishing some sort of managerial structure for the sake of firm survival, and the first generation is quite cautious regarding the delegating of managerial responsibilities to even the younger generation working in the firm.

It seems that, although some basic institutionalization applications, like having an organization chart and job descriptions and preparing strategic plans, are accepted and implemented quickly in family businesses where the first and second generations work together in Turkey, many firms fall short of implementing so-called later-phase policies in connection with governance structures, like those related to identifying a successor, preparing a succession plan, and effectively applying a family charter. As a result, many family firms do not make it to future generations (Erdoğmuş 2004; Ateş 2005; Peksaygılı and Tutan 2015).

One study done on the İstanbul Stock Exchange (ISE)-listed companies in Turkey found that Turkish companies, whether high-performance companies (HPCs) (57.90 per cent) or lower-performing ordinary companies (ORDs) (50.68 per cent), generally score only moderately well in terms of measures for corporate governance. However, HPCs in Turkey scored higher on norms of good corporate governance than comparable, but lower performing Ordinary companies (ORDs) (Needles et al. 2012).

Board of Directors: Processes and Composition

The sound application of corporate governance is very much related to the board of directors. The questions surrounding how board members are selected, how the board functions, and the responsibilities of the board ultimately affect the operations of the management team.

It seems that founder-managers of businesses hardly need a board of directors. Over the generations, task conflict increases among family members, and consequently, advice and arbitration for resolving conflicts require the intervention of a board (Bammens et al. 2008). In particular, the third generation of sibling partnerships requires 'the installation of formal governance mechanisms to control employed siblings, and this can be considered even more important for the cousin consortium generational stage' (p. 167) due to the decreased level of intentional trust.

How a board functions is of critical importance to the performance of the firm. Based on their research on Turkish family firms, Kula and Tatoglu (2006, 630) found four general processes related to the business performance: (1) access to information: useful exchange of ideas at board meetings, with members provided with detailed financial information about the company, effective information gathering, enough outside information gathering, and sufficient briefing by top management; (2) effectiveness of board: effective board meetings, where the board is more effective than top management, and the existence of plans for critical issues in future; (3) fiduciary responsibility: accountability to shareholders; and (4) performance evaluation: use of formal procedures to evaluate the board.

Research shows that the attributes of the board that are related to lowering bankruptcy risk are the size of the board, the age and experience of directors, gender diversity, director (co)location, and networks (multiple directorships). Associated with a higher bankruptcy risk are board instability, previous failure experiences, and, albeit weakly, the number of independent directors (Wilson et al. 2013, 1383).

Effective Management of Non-family Members

One of the biggest challenges faced by family businesses is the attraction and effective management of non-family employees. Attracting qualified non-family employees and fostering value-creating attitudes and behaviours among them can be major factors in the success or failure of family firms (Velasco et al. 2013).

The main obstacle to achieving this effective management is the lack of proper human resource management practices and the widespread application of nepotism, mentioned earlier. Removing this obstacle requires putting in place effective corporate governance structures and the application of human resource management practices. Cetin et al. (2016) found that the inability of family businesses to implement human resource systems has its roots in nepotism in recruitment and in the compensation and promotion of employees.

3 Suggestions and Comments

It seems obvious that keeping a family business together and enabling it to grow and flourish is beneficial, particularly for all family members, but also for the wider economy. The business must develop in order to fulfil the needs of a growing family, and so structures and strategies must be built and implemented in such a way that the diverse and conflicting needs of all stakeholders are addressed effectively. However, these needs must be aligned in a way that considers the 'egalitarian culture' of the family on the one hand and the 'meritocratic culture' of the business on the other (Schwass 2005).

Many scholars and family business advisors look for best practices to inspire and guide families in business to achieve success, long-term continuity, and effective succession. Kets de Vries (2017) suggests four main areas to focus on for the continuity of a family business. Under these headings, the main challenges facing Turkish businesses related to the sustainability of both family and business are written as a priority checklist to which owners should pay special attention. The most important ones are shown in bold:

1. *Focus on the Future* – for continuity and sustainability:

    - **Succession planning,**
    - **Proactive next-generation development activities to produce successful leaders,**
    - Fostering intergenerational entrepreneurship and entrepreneurial growth,
    - Ongoing family-in-business education and development programmes and processes.

2. *Focus on Fairness* – to create trust among all stakeholders:

    - **Giving everyone a voice, creating the perception that everyone can make a difference;**

- **Employment, promotion, and compensation of family members based on competence and merit;**
- Communication, including regular family meetings, and conflict resolution processes;
- Emphasis on family unity, culture, and values; avoidance of factional politics;
- Judicious management of family/business interactions and consistency in practice.

3. *Write a Constitution* – to guide family and business interactions:

- **Governance structures and processes including independent boards, family council, or code of conduct;**
- **Clear roles, responsibilities, and boundaries for all employed family members;**
- Establishment of family-in-business policies before the need for conflict resolution arises;
- Creating a unifying purpose for the family and family philanthropy.

4. *Build a Strong Board* – for effective management of business:

- **Hiring and retaining professional non-family executives;**
- **Having respect for the role of management and for managers; avoiding meddling;**
- Timely use of outside resources and assistance (e.g. advisory boards and professional advisers).

Each family business is unique and has its own set of individual idiosyncrasies, inimitable experiences, and resources resulting from the interactions of family members (its 'familiness'), which influence its business and which can be leveraged to create a competitive advantage (Dana and Smyrnios 2010). Given the uniqueness of each family and the business founder (entrepreneur), it is therefore reasonable to challenge the assumption that the success and sustainability of a business can be improved by the application of a set of best practices, learned from the studies of so-called best-performing family businesses. We tend to ignore special features and peculiar conditions that might result in a powerful impact on the success of the best-performing family businesses. Therefore, any reported success from the use of best practices is unlikely to be replicable unless the conditions (e.g. personalities, family size, family background, business features, or environmental factors) that made those practices successful are also emulated.

In their book *Unconventional Wisdom*, Lief and Denison state that, in relation to any particular family business:

> Once a competitor succeeds in opening the cultural treasure trove, he finds little to emulate. No patterns, no blueprints – only what is. The firm's culture is as intangible as one's personality – it can be described but not copied. This quirky uniqueness may hold the key to family enterprise success. (2005, 66)

Dana and Smyrnios (2010) argue that it is not possible to produce the requisite changes in habits and behaviours of family members unless some kind of therapeutic intervention takes place. Because every entrepreneur is unique and every family is different, each business must find its own way to overtake the competition in order to become successful. As a first step, the entrepreneur needs to look inward to check his intentions and mindset regarding his dream and the impact he hopes to create. He then needs to identify any discrepancy between his own intentions and reality and then start changing his assumptions and beliefs about himself, his family, and his business. Otherwise, nothing will change.

References

Adizes, Ichak. 1988. *Corporate Lifecycles: How and Why Corporations Grow and Die and What to Do About It*. Englewood Cliffs: Prentice Hall.

Ateş, Özgür. 2005. *Aile Şirketleri:Değişim Ve Süreklilik*. Ankara: ASO Yayınları.

Bammens, Yannick, Wim Voordeckers, and Anita Van Gils. 2008. Boards of Directors in Family Firms: A Generational Perspective. *Small Business Economics* 31 (2): 163–180.

Benavides-Velasco, Carlos A., Christina Quintana-García, and Vanesa F. Guzmân-Parra. 2013. Trends in Family Business Research. *Small Business Economics* 40 (1): 41–57.

Berrone, Pascual, Cristina Cruz, Luis R. Gomez-Mejia, and Martin Larraza-Kintana. 2010. Socioemotional Wealth and Corporate Responses to Institutional Pressures: Do Family-Controlled Firms Pollute Less? *Administrative Science Quarterly* 55 (1): 82–113.

Brenes, Esteban R., Kryssia Madrigal, and Bernardo Requena. 2011. Corporate Governance and Family Business Performance. *Journal of Business Research* 64 (3): 280–285.

Cadbury, Sir Adrian. 2000. *Family Firms and Their Governance: Creating Tomorrow's Company from Today's*. London: Egon Zehnder International.

Carlock, Randel S., and John L. Ward. 2001. *Strategic Planning for the Family Business: Parallel Planning to Unify the Family and Business*. London: Palgrave.

Cetin, Sefa, Yadigarjon Gayipov, and Tahir Akgemci. 2016. Problems and Solutions in Human Resources Management of Family Business: A Research in Konya City. *Postmodern Openings* 7 (1): 79–105.

Chittoor, Raveendra, and Ranjan Das. 2007. Professionalization of Management and Succession Performance – A Vital Linkage. *Family Business Review* 20 (1): 65–79.

Chrisman, James J., Jess H. Chua, and Pramodita Sharma. 1998. Important Attributes of Successors in Family Businesses: An Exploratory Study. *Family Business Review* 11 (1): 19–34.

Dana, Lucio E., and Kosmas X. Smyrnios. 2010. Family Business Best Practices: Where from and Where to? *Journal of Family Business Strategy* 1 (1): 40–53.

De Dreu, Carsten K.W., and Annelies E.M. Van Vianen. 2001. Managing Relationship Conflict and the Effectiveness of Organizational Teams. *Journal of Organizational Behavior* 22: 309–328.

Demir, Özcan, and Eray Ekin Sezgin. 2014. Aile İşletmelerinde Kurumsallaşma ve Sürdürülebilirlik: TRB1 Bölgesinde Yapılan Bir Araştırma. *Turkish Studies* 9 (5): 707–725.

Erdoğmuş, Nihat. 2004. *Aile İşletmeleri: İkinci Kuşağın Yetiştirilmesi*. İstanbul: İGİAD Yayınları.

Gage, David. 2004. *The Partnership Charter: How to Start Out Right with Your New Business Partnership (or Fix the One You're In)*. New York: Basic Books (AZ).

Gomez-Mejia, Luis R., Katalin Takacs Haynes, Manuel Nuñez-Nickel, J. L. Jacobson Kathyrn, and José Moyano-Fuentes. 2007. Socio-Emotional Wealth and Business Risks in Family-Controlled Firms: Evidence from Spanish Olive Oil Mills. *Administrative Science Quarterly* 52: 106–137.

Grote, Jim. 2003. Conflicting Generations: A New Theory of Family Business Rivalry. *Family Business Review* 16 (2): 113–124.

Gur, Nurullah, and Nihat Alayoğlu. 2017. The Importance of Trust for Partnership and Collaboration in Volatile Economic Conditions. In *Global Business Strategies in Crisis*, ed. Ü. Hacioğlu, H. Dinçer, and N. Alayoğlu, 139–150. Cham: Springer International Publishing.

Gur, Nurullah, and Christian Bjørnskov. 2017. Trust and Delegation: Theory and Evidence. *Journal of Comparative Economics* 45 (3): 644–657.

Iwasaki, Ichiro. 2014. Global Financial Crisis, Corporate Governance, and Firm Survival: The Russian Experience. *Journal of Comparative Economics* 42 (1): 178–211.

Kaye, Kenneth. 1996. When the Family Business Is a Sickness. *Family Business Review* 9 (4): 347–368.

Kaye, Kenneth, and Catherine McCarthy. 1996. Healthy Disagreements. *Family Business*, Autumn, 71–72.

Kegan, Robert. 1982. *The Evolving Self.* Cambridge: Harvard University Press.

Kellermanns, Franz W., and Kimberly A. Eddleston. 2004. Feuding Families: When Conflict Does a Family Firm Good. *Entrepreneurship Theory and Practice* 28 (3): 209–228.

———. 2006. Feuding Families: The Management of Conflict in Family Firms. In *Handbook of Research on Family Business*, ed. Panikkos Zata Poutziouris, Kosmas X. Smyrnios, and Sabine B. Klein, 358–368. Cheltenham/Northampton: Edward Elgar.

Kets De Vries, Manfred F.R. 1993. The Dynamics of Family Controlled Firms: The Good and the Bad News. *Organizational Dynamics* 21 (3): 59–71.

———. 1996. *Family Business: Human Dilemmas in the Family Firm.* London: International Thomson Business Press.

———. 2017. Saving a Family Business from Emotional Dysfunction. *Harvard Business Review*, February. https://hbr.org/2017/02/saving-a-family-business-from-emotional-dysfunction. Accessed 16 July 2017.

Kets De Vries, Manfred F.R., and Randel S. Carlock. 2010. *Family Business on the Couch: A Psychological Perspective.* New York: John Wiley & Sons.

Kula, Veysel. 2005. The Impact of the Roles, Structure and Process of Boards on Firm Performance: Evidence from Turkey. *Corporate Governance* 13 (2): 265–276.

Kula, Veysel, and Ekrem Tatoglu. 2006. Board Process Attributes and Company Performance of Family-Owned Businesses in Turkey. *Corporate Governance: The International Journal of Business in Society* 6 (5): 624–634.

Leach, Peter, and Tony Bogod. 1999. *Guide to the Family Business*. London: Kogan Page Publishers.

Lief, Colleen, and Daniel Denison. 2005. How Family Business Culture Is Different. In *Unconventional Wisdom: Counterintuitive Insights for Family Business Success*, ed. John Ward, 57–76. West Sussex: John Wiley & Sons.

Morris, Michael H., Roy O. Williams, Jeffrey A. Allen, and Ramon A. Avila. 1997. Correlates of Success in Family Business Transitions. *Journal of Business Venturing* 12 (5): 385–401.

Needles, Belverd E., Ahmet Turel, Dilek Sengur, and Aslı Turel. 2012. Corporate Governance in Turkey: Issues and Practices of High-Performance Companies. *Accounting and Management Information Systems* 11 (4): 510–531.

Nicholson, Nigel. 2008. Evolutionary Psychology and Family Business: A New Synthesis for Theory, Research, and Practice. *Family Business Review* 21 (1): 103–118.

Peksaygılı, Mutlu, and Mehmet Ufuk Tutan. 2015. Aile İşletmelerinde Yönetim Devri ve Temel Kurumsallaşma Uygulamaları: Ege Otomotiv Derneği Üyeleri Çalışması. *Journal of Yaşar University* 10 (37): 6432–6441.

Rutherford, Matthew W., Lori A. Muse, and Sharon L. Oswald. 2006. A New Perspective on the Developmental Model for Family Business. *Family Business Review* 19 (4): 317–333.

Sarbah, Alfred, and Wen Xiao. 2015. Good Corporate Governance Structures: A Must for Family Businesses. *Open Journal of Business and Management* 3: 40–57. https://doi.org/10.4236/ojbm.2015.31005.

Schwass, Joachim. 2005. *Wise Growth Strategies in Leading Family Businesses*. New York: Palgrave Macmillan.

Strategi Co. 2015. *Konya Kurumsal Yönetim Algı Araştırması Raporu*. İstanbul: Türkiye Kurumsal Yönetişim Derneği.

TUIK. 2016. *Statistics*. http://www.tuik.gov.tr/PreHaberBultenleri.do?id=21540. Accessed 16 July 2017.

Wilson, Nick, Mike Wright, and Louise Scholes. 2013. Family Business Survival and the Role of Boards. *Entrepreneurship Theory and Practice* 37 (6): 1369–1389.

Yazgan, Yankı. 2008. *Aile Kalmak, Şirket Olmak*. İstanbul: Türkiye Kurumsal Yönetişim Derneği.

Index[1]

[1] Note: Page numbers followed by 'n' refer to notes.

A. F. Aysan et al. (eds.), *Turkish Economy*,
https://doi.org/10.1007/978-3-319-70380-0

The manufacturer's authorised representative in the EU is Springer
Nature Customer Service Centre GmbH, Europaplatz 3, 69115 Heidelberg,
Germany. If you have any concerns regarding our products, please
contact ProductSafety@springernature.com

Printed and bound by CPI Group (UK) Ltd, Croydon, CR0 4YY
30/09/2026
02225654-0005